MW01617139

PIETER BRUEGEL AND THE ART OF LAUGHTER

PIETER BRUEGEL AND
THE ART OF LAUGHTER

WALTER S. GIBSON

UNIVERSITY OF CALIFORNIA PRESS
BERKELEY LOS ANGELES LONDON

University of California Press
Berkeley and Los Angeles, California

University of California Press, Ltd.
London, England

© 2006 by The Regents of the University of California

Library of Congress Cataloging-in-Publication Data

Gibson, Walter S.
Pieter Bruegel and the art of laughter / Walter S. Gibson.
p.   cm.
Includes bibliographical references and index.
ISBN 0-520-24521-0 (cloth : alk. paper)
1. Bruegel, Pieter, ca. 1525–1569—Criticism and interpretation.
2. Peasants in art.   3. Wit and humor in art.
4. Laughter—Netherlands—History—16th century.
I. Bruegel, Pieter, ca. 1525–1569.   II. Title.
ND673.B73G474   2006
759.9492—dc22   2005043050

15   14   13   12   11   10   09   08   07   06
10   9   8   7   6   5   4   3   2   1

TO THE MEMORY OF MY WIFE

Good friends who come to read this book,
Strip yourselves first of affectation;
Do not assume a pained, shocked look,
For it contains no foul infection,
Yet teaches no great perfection,
But lessons in the mirthful art,
The only subject for my heart.
When I see grief consume and rot
You, mirth's my theme and tears are not,
For laughter is man's proper lot.

FRANÇOIS RABELAIS

CONTENTS

LIST OF ILLUSTRATIONS

*Only dates inscribed on the works themselves
are given in the list that follows and in the
captions. More approximate dates are given
in the text where the work is discussed.*

ACKNOWLEDGMENTS

In the fourth chapter of my book *Pleasant Places*, published in 2000, I discussed laughter in the general context of recreation and its role in the thought and society chiefly of seventeenth-century Holland. In the present study, I examine the subject of laughter more closely, shifting the purview to the Southern Netherlands of the sixteenth century and focusing on Pieter Bruegel the Elder and the Antwerp of his day. In doing so, I return to several subjects treated in more summary form in some of my earlier publications. My ideas concerning Bruegel's peasant revels were first adumbrated in a small book of 1977 and further developed in a volume of the Franklin D. Murphy Lectures, published in 1991 by the University of Kansas, while the chapter on Bruegel's *Dulle Griet* expands a short paper presented at a Bruegel symposium in Berlin in 1975 and published several years later, in 1979. Representing my second thoughts on these two topics, their treatment here continues the discourse of those earlier efforts and in the case of the *Dulle Griet* may be said to supersede it. If "second thoughts are ever wiser," I can only hope this old saying may continue to hold true.

During the final stages of preparing this book, in November 2003, I had the great privilege of presenting some of its major themes in the Twelfth Gerson Lecture, sponsored by the University of Groningen, which published it as *The Art of Laughter in the Age of Bosch and Bruegel*. I would like to thank the Gerson Foundation for the opportunity to speak before an interested and informed audience, and my thanks go also to the many other institutions that allowed me to present my ideas in a public forum, among them the Metropolitan Museum of Art, Austin Peay State University in Nashville, the University of Virginia, the Memphis Brooks Museum of Art, Colby College in Waterville, Maine, and the Museum Boijmans Van Beuningen, which held a Bruegel Symposium in 2001. I also presented some of my ideas on two occasions at Williams College, a faculty colloquium and that most challenging of audiences, perhaps, an undergraduate class; for the latter opportunity, I am indebted to Zirka Filipczak. I also thank the two readers of the manuscript, John Oliver Hand and Alison Stewart, for their valuable comments and suggestions. Stewart's superb knowledge of peasant imagery in sixteenth-century German prints was particularly helpful. Many colleagues generously responded to my queries and helped in myriad other ways: Adolph Monballieu, whose well-informed studies remain indispensable to any Bruegel scholar, as well as Nadine Orenstein, Charity Cannnon Willard, Philips Salman, Yoko Mori, Eduard Buijsen, E. P. Kwaadgras, Elaine Block, and Katharine Fremantle. They have my warmest thanks, as do Eddy de Jongh, who secured an important article for me, and Johan Verberckmoes and Lyckle de Vries, who sent offprints of their articles that proved highly relevant.

I had the good fortune to serve as an outside reader for Claudia Goldstein's doctoral dissertation, completed in 2003 for Columbia University. Dr. Goldstein has generously allowed me to cite material from her work, but my frequent references to it in the following pages can only hint at the wealth of information she presents. Now under revision, it will constitute when published a major contribution to our understanding of the material culture of later-sixteenth-century Antwerp, including the artistic production of Bruegel and his colleagues.

This book could never have been undertaken, much less completed, without the library staff, past and present, of the Sterling and Francine Clark Art Institute in Williamstown, Massachusetts. Nancy Spiegel, Bonghee Lis, and Karen Bucky worked efficiently to secure needed books and articles on interlibrary loan. Robert Volz, Keeper of the Chapin Library of Rare Books, Williams College, helped me locate relevant material in his collection. As so often in the past, I have been assisted by Gerbrand Kotting and the staff of the Rijksbureau voor Kunsthistorische Documentatie, The Hague; and the staff of the Rijksprentenkabinet, Amsterdam. They all have my heartfelt thanks, as do the many individuals who helped me obtain some crucial photographs, especially Alexander Babin, Liza Abramova, Vladimir Matveyev, Alexander Wied, Ron Spronk, William Robinson, Meg Grasselli, and Jennifer Jones. My final thanks go to Fronia W. Simpson, who edited the text with her usual care and intelligence. They also go to Stephanie Fay, Fine Arts Editor at the University of California Press, whose counsel early on enabled me to shape this book, and who was extremely helpful at every stage of its preparation.

WALTER S. GIBSON

Pownal, Vermont

September 2004

DECIPHERING BRUEGEL

But do you faithfully believe that Homer,
in writing his *Iliad* and *Odyssey*, ever had in mind
the allegories squeezed out of him by Plutarch,
Heraclides, Ponticus, and Phornutus, and which Politian
afterwards stole from them in his turn? If you do, you are
not within a hand's or a foot's length of my opinion.

RABELAIS

In his *Schilder-boeck,* first published in 1604, the artist and writer Karel van
Mander eloquently characterized Pieter Bruegel the Elder as a supremely
comic artist. There are few of Bruegel's works, he insisted, that the observer "can contemplate seriously and without laughing, and however
straightfaced and stately *[stuer wijnbrouwigh en statigh]* he may be, he has at
least to twitch his mouth or smile."[1] But for much of the past century we
have generally approached Bruegel's art as anything but a laughing matter.[2] Attention has been focused, instead, on the serious-minded, didactic Bruegel, whose paintings and drawings, like the allegorical dramas so
popular in his lifetime, are assumed to be "vol scoone moralisacien" (full
of lovely moralizations).[3] For us, Bruegel is the painter-philosopher, the
pictor doctus, or learned painter (as he has been recently called),[4] who com-
mented variously on humanity's sin and folly and on its proper relationship to God and the natural world, moral lessons that he often con-

cealed, moreover, so that they were accessible only to the more astute viewer able to penetrate the surface realism of his art.

This view of Bruegel has been influenced to a great extent by a persistent misreading of a Latin epitaph on the artist that the Antwerp cartographer Abraham Ortelius added to his *Album amicorum* (friendship album). Long unknown, it was discovered by A. E. Popham, who published it, in part, in 1931. Ortelius, apparently composing his text in several stages beginning in 1574, some five years after Bruegel's death, claimed that the artist had "depicted many things that cannot be painted, ... in all his works he often gives something beneath what he paints."[5] As some scholars have cogently pointed out in recent years, Ortelius specifically relates this remark to Apelles and Timanthes, two Greek artists of antiquity discussed by Pliny the Elder.[6] Pliny praised Apelles because "he painted the unpaintable, thunder, for example, lightning and thunderbolts,"[7] and acclaimed Timanthes for his ingenuity, citing several examples. One is the painting of the Sacrifice of Iphigeneia: having depicted the bystanders in various attitudes of grief, Timanthes conveyed the greatest grief of all, that of Iphigeneia's father, by veiling his face.[8] In another painting, Timanthes evoked the enormous size of a sleeping Cyclops by showing some satyrs measuring his thumb with a staff.[9]

Ortelius thus was celebrating, not Bruegel's "hidden" meanings, but his realism and his remarkable inventiveness. In fact, to compare these particular artists from antiquity with Bruegel was very perceptive on his part. Popham himself suggested that Ortelius, with the phrase "Bruegel here painted many things that cannot be painted," may well have had in mind a painting by Bruegel in his own possession, the *Death of the Virgin* (Fig. 1).[10] Indeed, with its crowd of mourners, some veiling their faces, it brings to mind Timanthes' *Sacrifice of Iphigeneia*. Similarly, Bruegel's two versions of the *Tower of Babel* (Fig. 2) rival, even surpass, Timanthes' depiction of the sleeping Cyclops measured by satyrs. In Bruegel's works, the multitude of antlike figures swarming over the surface of the tower and the vast and minutely detailed landscape that sprawls in its shadow convey its monstrous dimensions.[11] Finally, Bruegel, in the *Gloomy Day* in

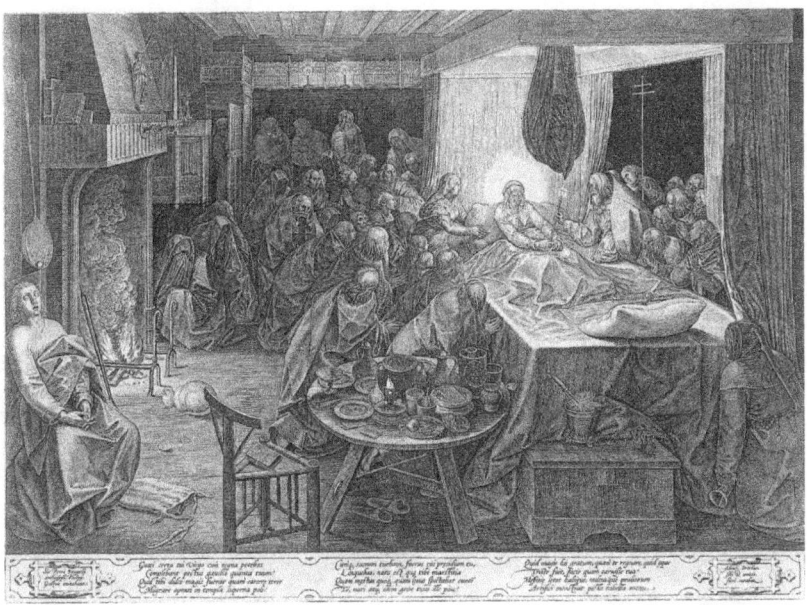

FIGURE 1. Philips Galle, after Pieter Bruegel the Elder, *Death of the Virgin*, 1574, engraving and etching. Amsterdam, Rijksmuseum.

his *Labors of the Months* series (Fig. 3), brings to mind Apelles' ability to paint lightning and thunder.

As it happens, this modern misreading of Pliny on Timanthes has a precedent in Karel van Mander's *Lives of the Artists*. Van Mander was familiar with Pliny's description of Timanthes' *Iphigeneia*, for he included it, most appropriately, in his poetic treatise on painting, *Den grondt der edel vry schilder-const*, in the chapter on the depiction of emotions.[12] Nevertheless, he appealed to this very same passage elsewhere in claiming that all of Timanthes' work contained "hidden meanings [*heymelijcke verstanden*]."[13] Van Mander also tells us that the Dutch artist Cornelis Ketel, "like the ancient Timanthes, brought about many *heymlijcke verstanden* in his works."[14] Significantly, however, Van Mander never mentions Bruegel in this misconstrued context, although later writers have been all too eager to do so.

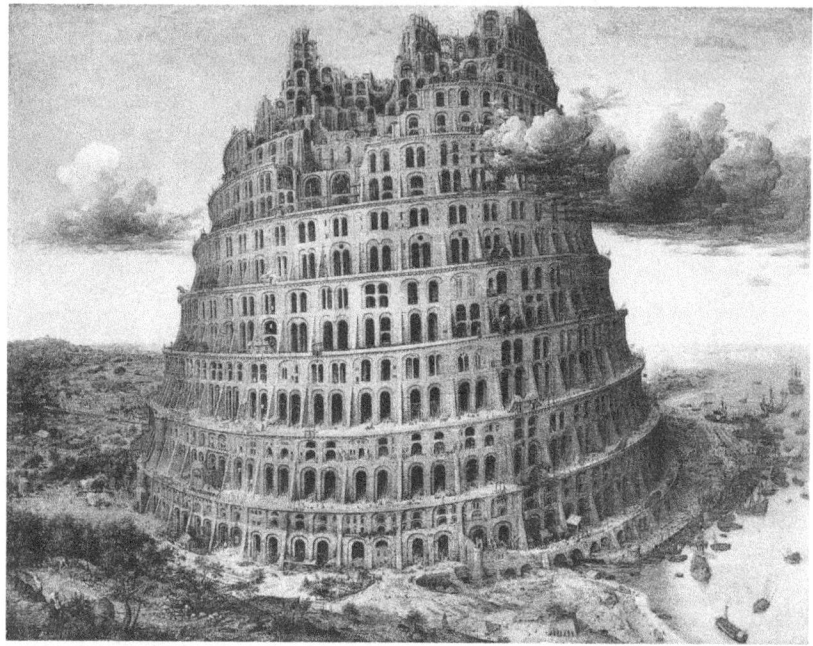

FIGURE 2.   Pieter Bruegel the Elder, *Tower of Babel.* Rotterdam, Museum Boijmans Van Beuningen.

Charles de Tolnay, in his monograph on Bruegel's paintings, published in 1935, soon after Popham's article of 1931, reprinted Ortelius's epitaph in its entirety as proof that "to the eyes of his contemporaries, Bruegel's art was esoteric."[15] Few later scholars have seriously disputed this claim, and many have sought to interpret Bruegel's imagery through a painstaking iconographic analysis of its details, an approach that owes much to the seductive influence of Erwin Panofsky's "principle" of disguised symbolism, first elaborated in his *Early Netherlandish Painting* of 1952. Panofsky claimed that the Flemish painters of the fifteenth century attempted "to reconcile the new naturalism" of their art "with a thousand years of Christian tradition" by developing a system of "concealed or disguised symbolism" that "was applied to each and every object, man-made or natural."[16] Panofsky's "principle" of disguised symbolism has been enthusi-

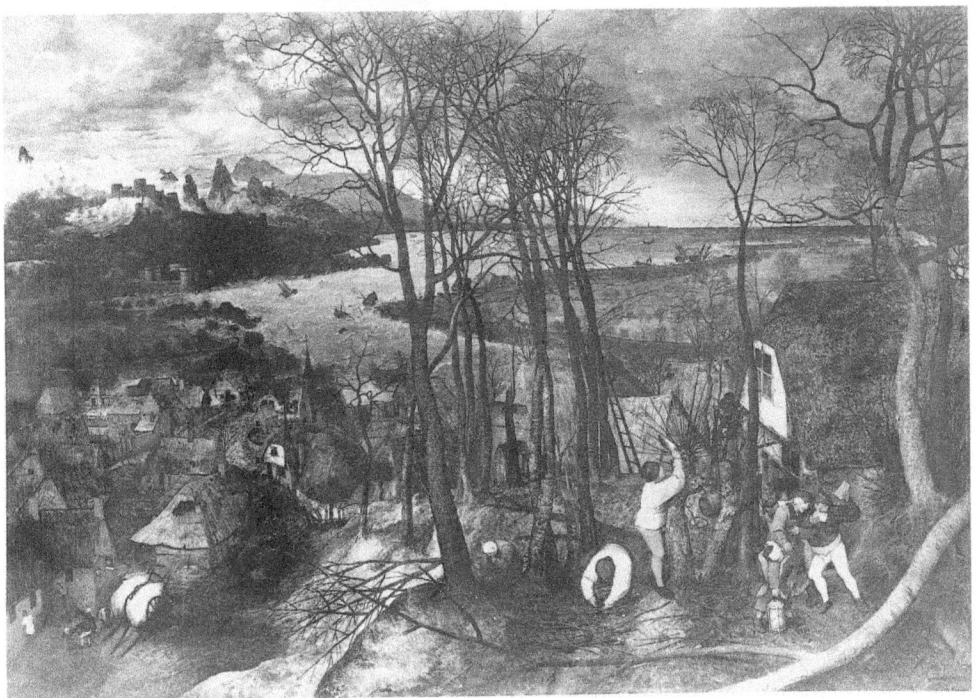

FIGURE 3. Pieter Bruegel the Elder, *Gloomy Day*, 1565. Vienna, Kunsthistorisches Museum.

astically embraced by many later scholars, chiefly, I believe, because it allows them to demonstrate that Netherlandish paintings possessed an intellectual and spiritual content of considerable complexity, in effect rescuing its practitioners—from Van Eyck to Vermeer and beyond, and certainly including Bruegel—from the old and often-repeated charge that their meticulous reproduction of the visible world was trivial and without meaning. In an article of 1933, for example, the eminent Austrian scholar Otto Pächt could speak of fifteenth-century Netherlandish painting as displaying "an almost embarrassingly objective reportage."[17] Even earlier, in 1927, the English critic Roger Fry had characterized Flemish painting as concerned with the "immediate, actual reality in an uncritical spirit," in contrast to the Italian "passion for abstract truth and for law."[18] Indeed, Fry saw Jan van Eyck as merely a reporter, capable of nothing more than "impassive objectivity," and he stigmatized Pieter Bruegel as "essentially an illustrator rather than an artist. He is the counterpart in his day of a great cartoonist."[19] It is perhaps understandable, then, that much modern scholarship has treated Bruegel's own realism, which his contemporary Ortelius had praised (in his epitaph on the artist) as vying with nature herself, as a mere veil obscuring the artist's "real" subject matter.

Numerous writers, impelled both by Panofsky's "principle" of disguised symbolism and by their own misunderstanding of Ortelius's epitaph, have expended considerable effort and ingenuity on "deciphering" Bruegel (to paraphrase the title of a book on Bosch by Dirk Bax).[20] A few illustrations, I think, will demonstrate this point. Bruegel's *Peasant and the Nest Robber* (Vienna, Kunsthistorisches Museum) is traditionally seen as illustrating the proverb "He who knows where the nest is, knows it; he who has the nest, has it," which alludes to the futility of knowledge unaccompanied by action. In a recent article, however, Pierre Vinken and Lucy Schlüter maintain that the peasant youth in the foreground personifies Everyman about to tumble into the abyss of death, a reading developed through a minute analysis of the picture, including various plants and the peasant's staff and discarded hat.[21] Peter Dreyer elucidates what he discerns as the *sensus mysticus*, or mystical sense, of Bruegel's *Alchemist* (see Figs. 20, 21) as an allegory of the fall and salvation of mankind, contrasting the two alchemies, material and spiritual.[22] Finally, Kenneth Lindsay, reading Bruegel's *Netherlandish Proverbs* (see Fig. 19), assures us that the artist "injected [sixteenth]-century proverb usage with the power of Medieval theological symbolism."[23]

Some scholars subsume a large number of Bruegel's works in a single system of religious or philosophical thought. Jürgen Müller locates the wellspring of Bruegel's art in Sebastian Franck's *Paradoxia*, a mystical work first published in 1534.[24] For Herbert Stein-Schneider, Bruegel expresses the teachings of Hendrick Niclaes, founder of the Family of Love, a religious sect active in Antwerp during Bruegel's lifetime.[25] Stein-Schneider claims that even Bruegel's *Labors of the Months* (a series one might have assumed devoid of esoteric content) was inspired by the allegorical landscapes described in Niclaes's *Terra pacis* (Land of Peace), a forerunner of Paul Bunyan's *Pilgrim's Progress*.[26] Since Stein-Schneider believes that Niclaes revived the medieval Catharist heresy—an accomplishment, incidentally, that has apparently escaped the notice of scholars of the Reformation[27]—he triumphantly concludes that Bruegel was a "peintre hérétique," whose works were accessible only to Niclaes's neo-Catharist circle.[28]

This last endeavor may represent an extreme example, but even the more thoughtful examples of such all-encompassing readings, including Müller's detailed study, seem to take for granted that in his art, Bruegel sought to articulate and develop a consistent philosophy, whether his own or that of another. While such an assumption may be valid for artists who worked for religious institutions or a princely court, it does violence to our understanding of the way artists earned their living in the competitive commercial world of Bruegel's time and long afterward. Indeed, the *schilderspand*, the galleries where painters and other artists offered their wares, occupied the second story of the new bourse, or stock exchange, officially opened in 1532, and the Four Winds, the shop of the famous print publisher Hieronymus Cock, was not far away, the two locations demonstrating the close ties between art and commerce in sixteenth-century Antwerp.[29] Hence Bruegel, in designing the prints issued by Cock, surely had to consider his publisher's sense of the marketplace, its tastes and interests,[30] and in painting, probably largely to fulfill commissions, he had to respond to the demands and expectations of his patrons.

Bruegel exegetes have found particularly happy hunting grounds in three of his paintings—the Detroit *Peasant Wedding Dance* and the two rustic scenes in Vienna, *Peasant Kermis* and *Peasant Wedding Feast*—that will occupy us in later chapters. The *Wedding Dance* (see Fig. 41), for instance, has been described as a "dance of death"; the two Vienna panels have been thought to embody the deadly sins, generally Lust and Gluttony.[31] The *Wedding Feast* (see Fig. 43) has attracted the most attention: it has been identified as an allegory of the church (personified by the bride) aban-

doned by Christ, as an allegory of misused generosity (in this case the
bride personifying Generosity herself), and as an image of the Last Judgment, in which the two bagpipers evoke the angels sounding the trump
of doom.[32] ("Hoe geleerde, hoe verkeerde," as a current Netherlandish
proverb has it; that is, The more learned, the more wrong!)[33] No wonder David Freedberg was moved to exclaim, with reference to the
influence exerted by Ortelius's epitaph: "What havoc the adoption of this
viewpoint has wrought amongst the interpreters of Bruegel's art! It is as
if it has provided the license for those critics who always insist on finding more in Bruegel's painting than even Ortelius can have dreamed."[34]
Indeed, those who have sought to "penetrate the secret thought of the
artist," as De Tolnay put it,[35] have often done so with a zeal unchecked
by common sense or historical plausibility, sustained chiefly by the con-
viction that Bruegel's profundity matched their own and that he addressed
an audience sufficiently erudite, not to say patient, to decipher his pictorial conundrums.[36]

I would not deny that multiple layers of often complex meaning can
legitimately be discerned in Bruegel's imagery. An outstanding example
is his *Elck*, or *Everyman*, a drawing of 1558, published shortly thereafter as
a print by Hieronymus Cock (see Fig. 18), but even in this case, the message was not hermetic, accessible only to an elite circle. Bruegel's contemporaries would have been familiar with its various details, and anyone who
examined it closely could easily fathom its ultimate meaning.[37] Moreover,
Bruegel had no need to juggle the various details in his *Peasant and the Nest
Robber* to create a visual sermon whose contortions of meaning would have
defeated the most perceptive contemporary viewer: the artist had access,
after all, to a visual tradition that presented death and earthly transience
much more effectively, a tradition, in fact, that he had drawn on some
years earlier in his *Triumph of Death* (Madrid, Museo del Prado).[38] As the
Belgian scholar R. H. Marijnissen wisely cautions us, "Before inventing
scholarly explanations of subjects which today suggest a rebus or code
message, we should ask whether the solution is not actually much sim-
pler than we think."[39]

Thus Bruegel was no erudite philosopher creating finespun allegorical fantasies in the isolation of his studio. The positive results that attempts to decipher his imagery have yielded lie precisely in the valuable insights we have gained into the manifold relationships between his art and the world in which he lived and worked.[40] His *Seven Virtues* drawings of 1559–60 for the most part illustrate the homely, everyday aspects of each virtue that would have appealed to anyone purchasing the prints that Cock published after them.[41] As for his *Elck* (see Fig. 18), we can now appreciate it as a witty condemnation of the greed and self-seeking that Bruegel must have seen all too often in the mercantile Antwerp of his time. Similarly, his *Blind Leading the Blind* (see Fig. 37), painted in 1568, may well comment on the religious and political struggles that darkened the last years of his life and ultimately erupted into the Eighty Years' War between the Netherlands and Spain.[42]

We have also come to appreciate the many connections between Bruegel and the Netherlandish rhetoricians of his time, and since they help us to understand his imagery, we would do well to know them better. Briefly, the chambers of rhetoric, or *rederijker kamers*, were literary societies that sponsored private and public performances of drama and poetry; they also participated in various civic occasions, often organizing the allegorical floats that appeared in the annual religious processions of the period.[43] Almost every town in the Netherlands had at least one *rederijker kamer*; Antwerp, because of its size and wealth, boasted three, of which the most famous was the Violieren (Gillyflower). The *rederijkers* practiced a range of dramatic forms, from *sinnespelen* (now spelled *zinnespelen*), or allegorical plays, descended from medieval morality plays, to *kluchten*, or farces, of which more later. What is probably a *zinnespel* figures in Bruegel's *Allegory of Temperance* (Fig. 4); it shows a makeshift stage on which stand two personifications, one clearly labeled *Hope*, both observed by a fool from behind the curtain. Bruegel's familiarity with *rederijker* drama should come as no surprise: He belonged to Antwerp's Guild of St. Luke, the artists' guild with which the Violieren had been closely associated since the late fifteenth century, and his friend Hans Franckaert seems to have been active in the Violieren.[44] In 1561, several years before Bruegel moved to Brussels, the Violieren played host to a great *landjuweel*, or literary and dramatic competition, attended by most of the *rederijker kamers* of Brabant.[45] It was inaugurated by a magnificent public procession comprising some 23 allegorical floats, almost 1,400 *rederijkers* on horseback, and still more riding in 200 wagons, all brilliantly costumed. Prizes were awarded for the best poems, plays, and pageants, and even the best costumes. Bruegel must have been among the crowds that watched the proceedings; we can speculate on his participation in creating some of the floats for the Violieren. Conversely, Bruegel's *Elck* print of about 1558 may well have inspired a series of floats that appeared in a procession celebrating the Feast of the Assumption in August 1563. The floats castigated the self-seeking and other shortcomings of Everyman, and one tableau showed an operation for the stone of folly whose details recall Bruegel's design on the same theme, called the *Witch of Mallegem,* published as a print in 1559.[46]

Thus, in the years since Ortelius's epitaph was first published, we have come to know much more about Bruegel and his times. But in the reevaluation of the artist resulting from these efforts, no less than in the industrious search for his hidden messages, Van Mander's "humorous" Bruegel has generally been ignored or even dismissed out of hand as the rhetorical effort of a writer removed from the artist by almost a generation and thus lacking a true understanding of his art.[47] Van Mander, however, may not have been so very wrong after all. He records an incident in Bruegel's lifetime in which viewers responded to Bruegel's art much as he describes. This incident appears in Van Mander's account of Hans Vredeman de Vries, the famous architectural scene designer of Bruegel's day. Vredeman once painted for a wealthy patron (the Brussels government official Aert Molckeman) a mural showing a summerhouse in perspective, perhaps resembling one of the elaborate open-air pavilions that Vredeman included in several of his drawings of idealized Renaissance palaces, later issued as engravings by Hieronymus Cock (Fig. 5).[48] More to the point, we are told that Bruegel, as a joke, added to the mural the

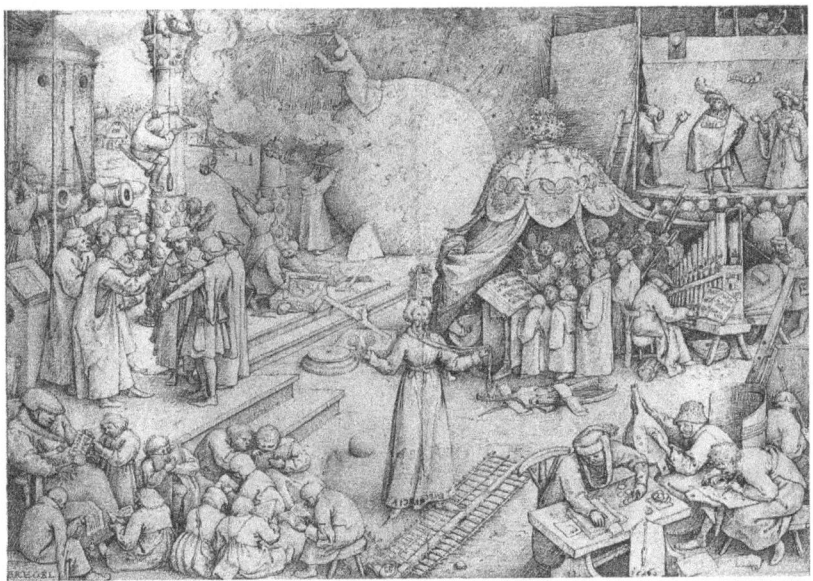

FIGURE 4. Pieter Bruegel the Elder, *Allegory of Temperance*, drawing, 1560. Rotterdam, Museum Boijmans Van Beuningen.

figure of "a peasant in a befouled shirt occupied with a peasant woman."[49] This embellishment of Vredeman de Vries's presumably elegant wall painting with rutting peasants caused much laughter, and Molckeman was so enchanted with it that he refused to have it painted out.[50] Van Mander places this episode sometime in the 1570s, and because this was after Bruegel's death (1569), the veracity of his account has been doubted. Yet Van Mander most likely knew Vredeman de Vries personally and may have heard the story from him when Vredeman visited Amsterdam in 1603. Adolph Monballieu has plausibly suggested that Vredeman de Vries painted the mural for Molckeman sometime in the 1560s when Bruegel was living in Brussels, where Vredeman de Vries, although based in Antwerp, had many artistic contacts.[51] This brief anecdote suggests that Bruegel's contemporaries reacted to at least some of his art with amusement and outright laughter.[52]

In fact, we can understand a significant part of Bruegel's art and his

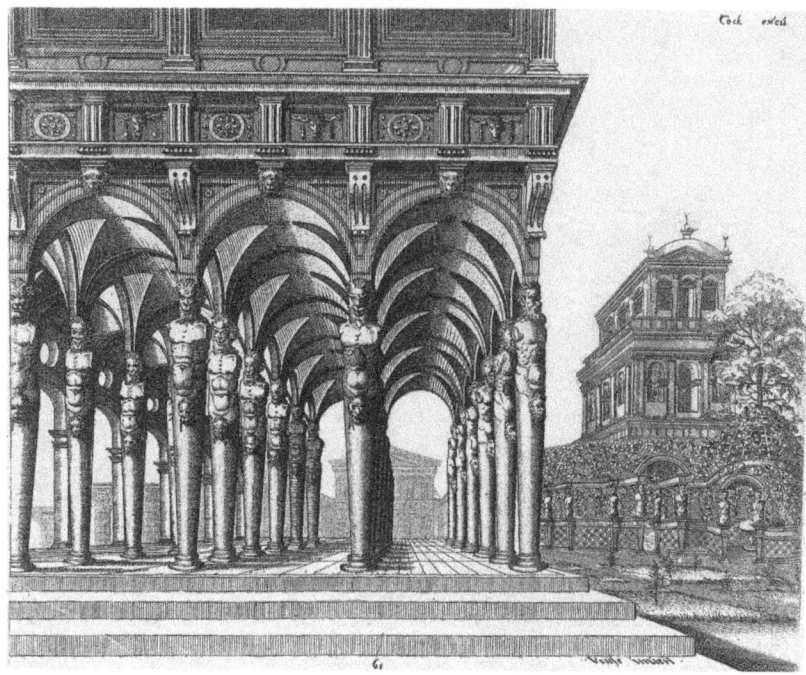

FIGURE 5. Jan or Lucas van Doetecum after Hans Vredeman de Vries, *Palace and Pavilion,* 1560, engraving. Berlin, Staatliche Museen, Preussischer Kulturbesitz, Kupferstichkabinett.

treatment of it in the context of the humor that evoked laughter in his time. In his overtly moralizing images, Bruegel employed laughter to convey his meaning more effectively—I shall examine his brilliantly conceived *Elck* more closely, but some of his other works seem to have been designed to amuse the viewer, much like the literary productions of the Flemish *rederijkers.* Chapter 1 explores the commodity of laughter in the sixteenth century. Meaning both "something useful" and "anything bought and sold," *commodity* well defines laughter as Bruegel's contemporaries understood it. Not only was it desirable and necessary to one's physical well-being, but it was also an important staple in the marketplace. Chapter 2 examines its production, particularly in Bruegel's paintings and prints,

with special attention to his remarkable ability to depict the human physiognomy, a gift that culminates in his three paintings of festive peasants
now preserved in Detroit and Vienna. Far from being the "dark conceits"
favored by the emblem makers of the period and by allegorists of all centuries, including our own, these magnificent works represent prime examples of Bruegel's art of laughter. For these three paintings, we turn to
an auction held at Antwerp in 1572, the subject of Chapter 3, that strongly
suggests the source of commissions for Bruegel's peasant scenes—not the
circle of intelligentsia around Ortelius and the publisher Christophe
Plantin, as has been claimed, but wealthy magnates and government
officials. Chapter 4 explores the role of real peasants, and of rustic existence in general, in the life and thought of these wealthy patrons and
others of their social class, and Chapter 5 considers the social situations
in which these paintings might have been viewed and enjoyed. Chapter 6
turns to the *Dulle Griet*, Bruegel's most ambitious evocation of Hieronymus Bosch, in which the younger artist manipulated traditional comic
material to create an image of Hell whose poor devils are bedeviled in a
manner never dreamed of by the older master. The epilogue returns us
to the broader context of laughter in Bruegel's time, and Bruegel's own
place in that context as one of the most original artists of the sixteenth
century.

CHAPTER ONE

THE COMMODITY OF LAUGHTER IN THE SIXTEENTH CENTURY

In memory of Hilde Junkermann, who knew,
perhaps better than most, the value of laughter.

If there is a mistake worse than believing that the present and the past are the same, it is thinking that they are completely different. There may be worlds of difference between yesterday and today, but the past is not a different world. We are continuous. The past draws us to itself and we learn from it precisely because we discover ourselves there under altered conditions.

STEVEN OZMENT

The specific forms of the thought of an epoch should not only be studied as they reveal themselves in theological and philosophical speculations, or in the conceptions of creeds, but also as they appear in practical wisdom and everyday life. We may even say that the true character of the spirit of an age is better revealed in its mode of regarding and expressing trivial and common-place things than in the high manifestations of philosophy and science.

JOHAN HUIZINGA

How much people of the sixteenth century laughed, in what manner, and at what: on these topics there is very little agreement. The Dutch scholar Hessel Miedema once insisted that persons of refinement and erudition in this period seldom laughed at all, but, to quote Miedema, "contented themselves by smiling with the mouth closed. The harder someone laughed, the closer he was to the object of that laughter: the aggressive scoffer, the doltish peasant."[1] By this token, we must conclude that Aert Molckeman and his friends did not comport themselves like gentlefolk, but I am not so sure.[2] As it happens, Miedema gives no source for his statement, but he may have been referring to what has been described as the upper classes' gradual withdrawal from participation in popular culture, including the traditional festive culture of the marketplace and countryside, as unworthy of their higher status, as well as their increasing internalization of the ethos of self-control. This is a social phenomenon that many scholars have studied: Peter Burke, Robert Muchembled, and above all Norbert Elias.[3] But as Elias himself is at pains to emphasize, in the sixteenth century, this "civilizing process," as he calls it, was only in its earliest stages,[4] and a wide gulf still existed between the ideals of proper behavior and the everyday comportment of actual people. Nowhere, perhaps, is this more evident than in the case of laughter.

Aristotle first proposed that laughter is a uniquely human characteristic. Although some writers have denied this claim (among them Desiderius Erasmus, who insisted that dogs and monkeys also laugh), it became a commonplace in the Renaissance.[5] Juan Luis Vives, a Spanish humanist scholar residing in the Netherlands, explained that other creatures cannot laugh because they do not have a face like ours.[6] As the German poet-satirist Johann Fischart later summed it up in his version of Rabelais's *Gargantua*, "full-throated laughter / Is the true distinguishing characteristic of Man."[7] But laughter had also long been condemned by serious minds as frivolous and even sinful, and these critics supported this opinion with references to the Sermon on the Mount, in which Christ said, "Woe to you that now laugh: for you shall mourn and weep" (Luke 6:25); in fact, it was often claimed that Christ himself had never laughed.[8]

This was the opinion, for example, of the early church father John Chrysostom,[9] who traced the dreadful consequences of laughter: it leads often to foul speech, and from foul speech to foul actions, and so on to murder.[10] Writing much later, in the twelfth century, the German nun and visionary Hildegard of Bingen expressed a similar idea when she described the faculty of laughter as one of the unfortunate results of original sin.[11]

The English writer Richard Rolle, however, was able to speak of good laughter, calling it "mirth in the love of God," which "exists only in the righteous,"[12] and a compatriot, the mystic Margery Kempe, found cause for laughter in the trials she suffered for Christ.[13] Similarly, in Bruegel's century, Queen Marguerite of Navarre, sister of Francis I of France, wrote of the "divine mirth" that rose within her[14] and named laughter an attribute of the followers of the evangelical faith that sustained them even in the face of torture and death.[15] Nevertheless, majority opinion held that there was little enough for good Christians to laugh about, especially when they contemplated eternity. This is the gist of a story long popular in the Middle Ages. When a king who never laughed was questioned about his solemnity, he replied that he was threatened by four swords: the memory of Christ's death on the cross, uncertainty about the hour of his death and the fate of his soul, and fear of the Last Judgment.[16]

Bruegel's century too decried laughter, at least in its more extreme manifestations. In a volume on physiognomy first published at Antwerp in 1554 and reprinted there ten years later, Jan Roelants insisted that much laughter was the sign of a foolish, unstable, and gullible nature (and also, he added, the sign of a great lover).[17] Writing somewhat earlier, Juan Luis Vives did not argue against laughter as such but condemned hearty laughter as "excessive outbursts that shake the whole body," and as "convulsions of the ignorant, the peasants, children, and women."[18] Such opinions anticipate by two centuries Lord Chesterfield's dictum that "frequent and loud laughter is the characteristic of folly and ill manners; . . . There is nothing so illiberal, and so ill-bred, as audible laughter."[19] Vives counseled young maidens never to respond with laughter in public when a man laughed, lest they be thought an easy catch.[20] In like fashion, widows were advised by several Italian writers to avoid hearty laughter and even broad smiles.[21] For his part, Erasmus insisted that "loud laughter and the immoderate mirth that shakes the whole body . . . are unbecoming to any age but much more so to youth. . . . And the person who opens his mouth wide in a rictus, with wrinkled cheeks and exposed teeth, is also impolite. This is a canine habit. . . . The face should express mirth in such a way that it neither distorts the appearance of the mouth nor evinces a dissolute mind." Erasmus offered this prescription for the right kind of laughter in his immensely popular *De civilitate morum puerilium*, a little book on manners for children.[22] First published in 1530, this work went through more than a dozen editions in that year, was soon translated into several vernacular languages, including a Netherlandish edition of 1559, and inspired many later treatises on social conduct and proper behavior.[23] But while the flood of conduct books published from the sixteenth century on is truly impressive, it would nonetheless be hazardous to write a history of humor based exclusively on these manuals of etiquette. As one Dutch scholar has sensibly remarked, while such handbooks were certainly read, it may be asked to what extent their contents were taken to heart by the middle and upper classes.[24]

In any case, I know of no one who has made a careful study of how the upper classes of the sixteenth century laughed and to what extent this laughter might have differed, if at all, from that of the *'tgemeyn volck* (the common folk).[25] Perhaps no such study is possible. But we can approach this subject obliquely through a famous treatise on refined behavior, Baldesar Castiglione's *Book of the Courtier*, a dialogue composed when the author was at the court of the duke of Urbino and first published in 1528. In the second part of his book, Castiglione devotes considerable attention to the subject of laughter. Laughter, we are told by Cardinal Bibbiena, one of the speakers, "is something so peculiarly ours, that, to define man, we are wont to say that he is a risible animal. . . . But what laughter is," he continues, "where it abides, and how it sometimes takes possession of our veins, our eyes, our mouth, and our sides, and seems apt to make us burst, so that no matter what we do we are unable to repress it—this I will leave to Democritus [the laughing philosopher of antiquity] to tell, who would be unable to do so, even if he should promise as much."[26] But Bibbiena does discuss the various types of humor that evoke laughter. These range from witty remarks and anecdotes to practical jokes.[27] As an example of the latter, he tells how on one occasion two fine ladies, having been tricked into believing that an uncouth but elegantly dressed peasant was really a polished dancing master, tried to converse with him as a near social equal. This took place in the presence of other members of the court, who were in on the deception and, in Castiglione's words, "everyone's sides ached from laughing."[28] Significantly, Castiglione apparently did not condemn this hearty laughter as a breach of polite manners.

The Book of the Courtier was still widely read in the later sixteenth century in various translations, including French, English, and German. An Italian edition was in the library of Cardinal Granvelle, one of Bruegel's patrons, while a French edition was acquired sometime before 1568 by the Protestant Huijsch van Alkemade, a resident of Leiden.[29] Although a Dutch translation appeared only in the following century, two Spanish editions were published at Antwerp during Bruegel's lifetime.[30] It was also familiar to Bonaventure Des Périers, a secretary of Queen Marguerite of Navarre and the author of a number of books, including a moral treatise and translations from the classics. In his Nouvelles récréations et joyeux devis, first published in 1558, some years after his death, we may discern echoes of Castiglione (as well as Rabelais) in his claim that "the noblest lesson for life is Live well and rejoice. . . . Odds boddikins! Let's laugh! And with what? With our mouths, noses, chins, throats, and all our five natural senses. But that's not enough if we don't laugh with our hearts."[31] And if these words do not constitute a recommendation for hearty laughter, then we may turn to an anecdote told of the famous English buffoon Richard Tarleton: once when he performed before Queen Elizabeth I, she "bade them take away the knave for making her laugh so excessively."[32]

More to the point, however, many people saw laughter as a positive virtue. Whatever moves us to laughter, Cardinal Bibbiena tells us in The

Courtier, "restores the spirit, gives pleasure, and for the moment keeps one from remembering those vexing troubles of which our life is full."[33] Laughter is the sweetest gift of nature, as the Flemish scholar Erycius Puteanus put it sometime in the following century.[34] The nature of laughter, its sources, and the objects and situations that excite it had been discussed by the ancient writers, among them Quintilian, whose chapter on laughter in the *De institutio oratoria* Folly herself described in Erasmus's *Praise of Folly* as "longer than the whole Iliad."[35] Cicero too devoted an extensive section to laughter in his *De oratore*, the very text that inspired Castiglione's characterization of laughter quoted above.[36] It was probably also due in large part to Cicero and Quintilian that laughter occupied many other writers in the sixteenth century, with a particular emphasis on its effects on the body and the mind.[37] In 1579 the French physician Laurent Joubert published a treatise devoted exclusively to laughter, *Traité de ris*. Joubert, a professor of medicine at the University of Montpellier (where, appropriately enough, François Rabelais had been a student), informed the reader that "God has ordained, among man's enjoyments, laughter for his recreation in order to conveniently loosen the reins of his mind."[38] This was true even for the clergy. As the Catholic schoolteacher and poet Anna Bijns pointed out in a *referein*, or poem, first published in 1528, if priests sometimes laugh and sing and make merry, so what? They are people, too, and need to unwind; he who is never merry is a beast.[39] Indeed, many people in Bruegel's day would have agreed with the Dutch diplomat Jacob van der Burgh, who wrote in the next century to a compatriot, the statesman and poet Constantijn Huygens: "I would not wish a wise man never to laugh and deprive himself of a faculty that is proper to him and not given to the rest of [God's] creatures."[40]

Laughter was especially prescribed as an antidote to what Thomas Nashe, about 1593, called "foggy-brained melancholy," the terrible affliction of the spirit that some centuries earlier Hildegard of Bingen had insisted was, like laughter, another of Adam's punishments for original sin.[41] There were two kinds of melancholy. "Natural" melancholy was one of the four temperaments, and those who possessed it tended to be intellectual. The "pathological" strain of melancholy, however—what is now diagnosed as clinical depression—was a disabling condition caused by a superfluity of black bile that made the body excessively cold (or hot) and dry; its victims tended to be fearful, incapable of positive thought or action. Both types of melancholia, especially the pathological sort, could be alleviated by means of medicine, diet, and pleasant diversions, but above all by laughter. Among the warm, moist passions believed to counteract the adverse effects of the cold, dry passions, laughter was the one that best expanded the heart and stimulated the production of new blood.[42] The *Homeric Hymns to Demeter* offers perhaps the earliest recorded use of "laugh therapy" for melancholy: Demeter plunged in grief for the loss of her daughter, Kore, who had been kidnapped by Hades, was roused to laughter by the jokes and mockery of the servant woman Iambe.[43]

Thus, whatever incited laughter was good for the body and soul, especially those of the melancholic. The sixteenth-century Italian physician Giovanni Marinello, for example, advised pregnant women to avoid fear and melancholy by laughing heartily (although another writer cautioned that a belly laugh at some ribald story might abort the baby).[44] That is also why the jokes and antics of Richard Tarleton, we are told, cured Queen Elizabeth's melancholy "better than all her physicians."[45] Thanks to the pioneering work of Herman Pleij, and a number of younger Dutch and Belgian scholars, we now know that an abundance of literature was published from the later fifteenth century whose function, often expressly stated, was to recreate weary and melancholic spirits by inciting laughter.[46] The most famous is *Gargantua and Pantagruel*, whose often salacious episodes François Rabelais justified on the grounds, according to the introduction to his fourth book, that he wanted to "give such little relief as I could to the sick and unhappy."[47] The publisher of a sixteenth-century Netherlandish translation of the German *Til Eulenspiegel* informed prospective readers that he hoped this account of Eulenspiegel's tasteless, often quite vulgar pranks would not offend, but lighten and renew the spirit.[48] Similar claims were made for the often risqué stories in *De pastoor van Kalenberg,* a collection of German origin first published in a Netherlandish edition in the earlier sixteenth century.[49]

But it was above all the jest books, called *cluchtboeken* (now spelled *kluchtboeken*) in the Netherlands—that is, collections of anecdotes—that often stressed the recreational function of their contents. Barbara Bowen gives an excellent introduction to these jest books in her *One Hundred Renaissance Jokes,* published in 1988, containing comic stories from no fewer than twenty-seven collections written and published between 1343 and 1559.[50] One of the earliest was a collection of anecdotes in Latin compiled by the Italian humanist Poggio Bracciolini in the early fifteenth century; it was often republished in the sixteenth century throughout Europe, including the Netherlands, and influenced later jest books.[51] Among these was the *Facetiae,* or *Facetious Stories,* by Heinrich Bebel, professor at the University of Tübingen, the three books of which appeared between 1508 and 1512. Another was *Schimpff und Ernst* (Jest and Seriousness) by the Franciscan preacher Johannes Pauli, first published in 1522, in which the humorous stories outweighed the serious ones two to one. The Netherlandish collection circulating in Bruegel's time was *Een nyeuwe clucht boeck,* or *A New Book of Anecdotes,* published at Antwerp by Jan Wijnrijcx in 1554. A truly portable volume, scarcely two by four inches, it nonetheless contained 253 anecdotes, a few taken from Bebel, but the vast majority of them derived from Pauli.[52] Some were serious anecdotes, but about half of them conform to the definition of *clucht* or *boerd* offered by a Netherlandish-French dictionary of 1572: "something that is said in sport and not for imparting knowledge."[53] A revised edition of the *Nyeuwe clucht boeck* appeared at Antwerp in 1576, advertising itself on the title page as a "*Clucht Boeck* containing many recreative stories and jokes."[54] Travelers could easily have carried little volumes like these to while away the long hours at sea or on the road; indeed, a similar collection published in 1555 by the German poet–book dealer Georg Wickram bears the title *Rollwagenbüchlein,* meaning in effect "a little book for reading while traveling in a *rollwagen,* or carriage."[55]

Joubert lists among the causes of laughter pratfalls and the acciden-

tal display of the buttocks and genitalia, apparently without condemning them.[56] Similarly, the stories in the *kluchtboeken* are occasionally bawdy,
and many show no qualities we might call socially redeeming. What kind
of stories are they? The *Nyeuwe clucht boeck* of 1554 prefaced its anecdotes
with the assertion that they included "all social ranks and professions of
the world,"[57] a promise amply realized in the succeeding pages. We encounter a throng of knaves and swindlers, court jesters, prostitutes,
erring wives and their lovers, priests, students, merchants and tavern keepers, and various ancient rulers, including Vespasian, Titus, and Charlemagne. We also read tales of murder almost as suspenseful as modern
detective dramas and the tragedy of Rosimunde, daughter of the Lombard prince Alkinus, which is as lurid as any Jacobean tragedy. Among
the more lighthearted stories is the one about two dumb Hollanders who
travel to Antwerp and go hungry on the road because they are served no
butter with their eggs, contrary to the custom at home. When they arrive in Valenciennes, because they cannot speak French, one fellow tries
to pantomime his wish to have something to eat but has a tooth pulled
instead.[58] As it happens, this tale is most likely an ethnic joke, for the Netherlanders to the south traditionally viewed Hollanders as dull-witted.[59]
Another anecdote concerns the artist who made paintings of beautiful
children. Asked why his own children were so ugly, he explained that he
made the former in the daytime and the latter at night—a tale that goes
back at least to the fifth century A.D., when it was told by Macrobius,
and reappears later in various forms in collections of anecdotes, including one compiled by Petrarch.[60]

The final story in the *Nyeuwe clucht boeck* of 1554 involves a bride on her
wedding night, two kitchen assistants, and a bowl of *witmoes*, or wheat porridge, that was administered to a most unsuitable part of the anatomy.[61]
A number of these anecdotes, among them some of the bawdiest (though
not, as it happens, the tale of the bride and the kitchen assistants), have
moral lessons attached to them, but we may suspect that these embellishments were prompted chiefly by a desire to make such stories respectable.[62] It may be asked if people did not regularly neglect the "les

son" of such *kluchten* in favor of their salacious details, much like the young man in a twelfth-century collection of exemplary stories, the *Disciplina clericalis*, whose avid interest in tales of unfaithful wives has little to do with the moral instruction they supposedly provide.[63] Moreover, like the *kluchtboecken*, published collections of popular songs and *refereinen* of the period, even some from the pen of Anna Bijns, have scatological and obscene subjects.[64]

More to the point, the libraries of members of the upper classes contained such collections of comic stories. A collection of late medieval *fabliaux*, the *Cent nouvelle nouvelles* (Paris: Antoine Vérard, ca. 1495), was in the library of Margaret of Austria, regent of the Netherlands, where it kept company with historical works, moralizing treatises (including Thomas à Kempis's *Imitatio Christi*), and other edifying literature.[65] Similar volumes of comic tales were owned by the lord of Vianen Hendrik van Brederode, the fervent Protestant writer Philips van Marnix van St. Aldegonde (who also owned two copies of Boccaccio's *Decameron*), and Jan van Brouchoven, burgomaster of Leiden and *rentmeester*, or bailiff, in the Rhineland.[66] In Italy, Saint Filippo Neri's favorite reading, we are told, was a book of *facetiae*, his maxim being that "a light spirit acquires perfection more easily than a melancholy one."[67] It is very likely that when such gentlefolk read one of these stories, whether silently to themselves or aloud to friends, they permitted themselves a chuckle or even a guffaw.[68] The French buffoon Tabarin performed before Marie de Médicis, queen of France, in 1619, and the dedication of a published collection of his jokes indicates that these anecdotes were intended for everybody, including the court and other members of the upper classes.[69] A number of anecdotes, in fact, were attributed to some of the famous court fools of the sixteenth century, such as Kunz von der Rosen, a court fool of Emperor Maximilian I, and Klaus Narr (Claus Fool), who served the elector Friedrich of Hanover in a similar capacity.[70] Narr had already figured as "Claeus Nar" in three anecdotes in the *Nyeuwe clucht boeck* of 1554, one of them scatological,[71] and his name was attached to a collection of 627 anecdotes published toward the end of the sixteenth century, and a volume of jests purportedly by Richard Tarleton appeared about 1600.[72]

Laughter was also an important commodity offered by the Netherlandish *rederijkers*. The *rederijkers* are most often consulted today for their *scoone moralisacien*, the morality plays that were characterized in the religious drama *Mariken van Nijmeghen* (Antwerp, 1518) as being better than a sermon,[73] intended, according to one document of the period, "for the teaching and edification of all people."[74] But the *rederijkers* also provided much entertainment of a more lighthearted kind. The foundation charter of the Fonteine chamber of Ghent, established in 1448, stated specifically that its most important task was to provide pleasant and good recreation against "melancholy, the greatest enemy of humanity."[75] As the Belgian scholar Dirk Coigneau has observed, a substantial portion of *rederijker* literary and dramatic production was comic in nature.[76] It included *refereinen in 't sotte*, that is, "in a foolish mode," with each stanza ending in a single-line refrain (the other two types being *in 't wijs* and *in 't amoreuze*, or in the wise and amorous modes),[77] as well as a variety of plays: *esbattements, tafelspelen,* and *kluchten*. While many of the *esbattements* and *tafelspelen*, or banquet plays (of which more later),[78] sought to instruct their audience in good Christian virtues, other *rederijker* plays were intended as pure entertainment: they are clearly *recreaties*, a term with something of the meaning of the English *recreations* and employed in the sixteenth century to designate an amusing or entertaining play.[79] In a *tafelspel* for a Twelfth Night celebration, the character called Prologue says that he serves to create joy and drive away "alle zware gheesten" (all heavy spirits).[80]

Some of these plays dealt with social satire, on the venerable principle of *ridendo dicere verum* (to tell the truth with laughter).[81] By this means, as Erasmus explained, "what is sinful in individuals is brought out not by a reprimand but by the enticement of a joke,"[82] supremely exemplified by his own *Praise of Folly*. But while, as one recent scholar has wisely remarked, "the relationship between humor and satire is not an easy one,"[83] other *rederijker* plays seem to have been nothing more than *recreaties* pure

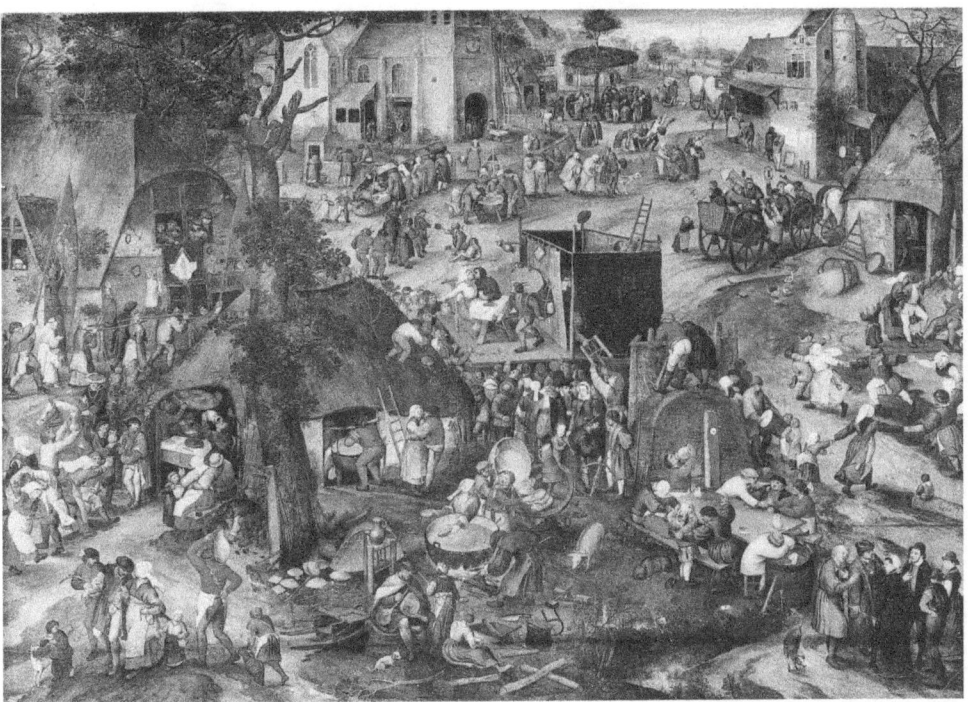

FIGURE 6. Peeter Baltens, *Peasant Kermis with the "Clucht van plaijerwater."*
Amsterdam, Rijksmuseum.

and simple, especially the *kluchten*.[84] These were farces,[85] often involving
peasants—husbands and wives, wives and their lovers, and the like—in
comic situations. One of these was the so-called *Clucht van plaijerwater*,
probably written for the Violieren chamber of Antwerp at the beginning
of the sixteenth century.[86] It seems to have enjoyed considerable popularity in Bruegel's time, for its performance was often included in depictions of village kermises. A good example can be seen in a painting by
Peeter Baltens, made probably sometime after 1550 (Figs. 6, 7).[87] Its plot
can be briefly summarized. A wife feigns a severe illness and sends her
husband on a wild-goose chase for *plaijerwater* (phony water), whose supposedly miraculous powers will cure her—all this so that in her husband's
absence she can enjoy her priest-lover. Her plot is foiled, however, when

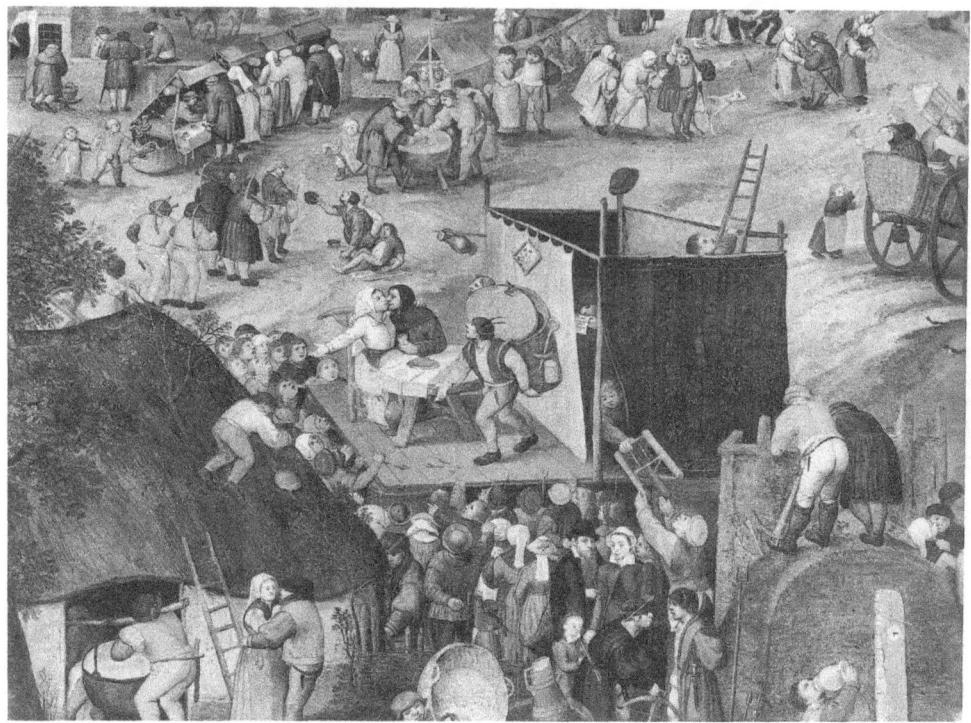

FIGURE 7.   Detail of Fig. 6.

the husband encounters a poultry seller who informs him of the deception and smuggles him back into his house concealed in a large basket,
where, as we can see in Baltens's painting, he catches the guilty pair.[88]

Plays like this must have provided a welcome relief to the didactic *spelen van sinne.*[89] At the beginning of her oration, Erasmus's Folly says of her
audience, "as soon as I came out to speak to this numerous gathering, the
faces of all of you immediately brightened up with a strange new expression of joy. You all suddenly perked up and greeted me with congenial
laughter."[90] We may imagine that a similar crowd greeted the actors in
a *klucht*, when they first appeared onstage. *Kluchten* could be performed on
many occasions. During the triumphal entry into Brussels of Prince Philip
of Spain, later Philip II, in April 1549, two *kluchten* were performed in

the evening on a stage erected in front of the city hall. In attendance was a German observer, Dr. Franz Kram, who later described the plays in fair detail. Both resembled *Plaijerwater*, in that their plots involved wives who deceive their dim-witted husbands to be with their lovers, and this entertainment, it seems, was well received by the crowd of viewers. Everyone in the audience laughed, Dr. Kram remarks rather disapprovingly, not only the men (and none more heartily than Aert Molckeman and his friends, we may suspect, if they were present) but even the women and young maidens.[91] Although the Violieren chamber of Antwerp condemned such comic plays as *ijdel dichtinge* (vain rhymes) from which nothing good comes, this opinion would probably have been shared by few in the audience.[92]

Like the courts and wealthy households everywhere in sixteenth-century Europe, each *rederijker* chamber had at least one fool who figured prominently in its dramatic activities, including the great *landjuweel* held in Antwerp in 1561.[93] These fools also conducted their own festival in Brussels in July 1551, presided over by a "king." All participants on this occasion, audience as well as fools, had to swear loyalty to this mock king and to protect wayward nuns and monks, wastrels, vagabonds, the ne'er-do-well of all kinds: whoever asks these people to work for their living will be exiled from the Kingdom of Fools.[94] The groups targeted here, of course, had long been denounced by preachers and moralists of all stripes; however, we may doubt the people present on this occasion were very much edified, if only because they were asked to seal their oaths with a particularly obscene gesture.[95] The balance between moral instruction and pure entertainment, always a delicate one, tipped on this occasion decisively toward the latter. And there can be little doubt that Bruegel's contemporaries spared neither effort nor expense to make sure that they had appropriate opportunities for laughter.

CHAPTER TWO

BRUEGEL'S ART OF LAUGHTER

The ridiculous may be defined as a mistake or deformity
not productive of pain or harm to others; the mask,
for instance, that excites laughter, is something ugly and
distorted without causing pain.

ARISTOTLE

Up to now we have deduced and by several means shown the object
of laughter to be, if not an indecent, [then] an ugly and ridiculous
thing excluding any pain, danger, or discomfort, which
would move us to pity.

JOUBERT

In view of the spate of books, plays, and songs in Bruegel's time that were
written to elicit amusement and laughter, we may ask if some works of
art might have been created for the same purpose. Indeed, some years
ago Paul Barolsky plausibly argued that many Italian Renaissance paintings, among them some that Panofsky and other scholars have interpreted
as profound Neoplatonic allegories, were intended primarily to amuse
those who beheld them.[1] In northern Europe, such works surely would
have included many of the pastiches after Bosch that were produced in
great numbers in Antwerp in the sixteenth century (Figs. 8, 9). Their
creators seem less concerned to warn us of the punishments awaiting sin-
ners in the hereafter than to entertain us in the here and now; their frol-

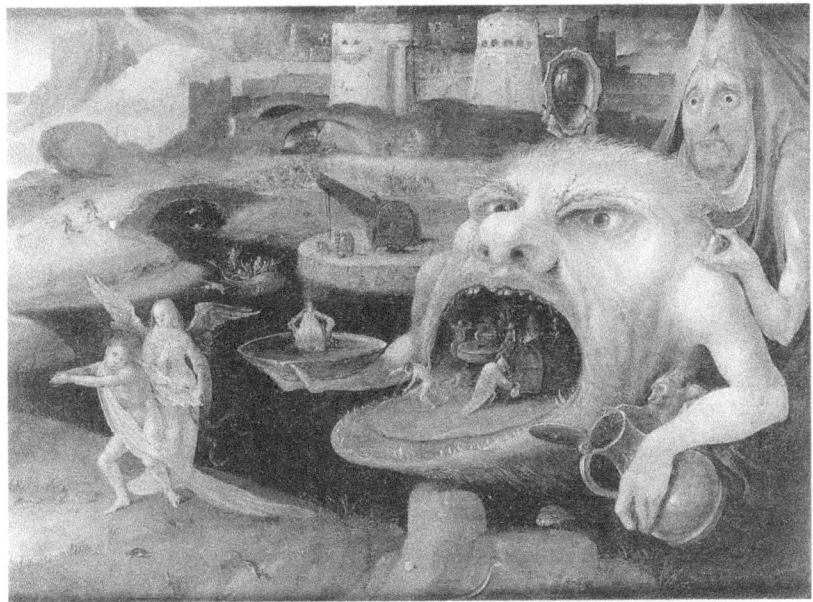

FIGURE 8. Attributed to Jan de Cock, *Vision of Tundale*. New York, Sotheby's,
11 January 1990, lot 37.

icking devils are hardly more threatening than the "bogey men and fantasies" that swarmed around Aeneas in Erasmus's description of the underworld.[2] In fact, they are hardly more serious than what we find in one
of Bosch's own likely visual sources, the fantastic creatures that had long
disported themselves in the margins of medieval manuscripts. It is frequently asserted, and I think correctly, that such decorative embellishments were added chiefly for the amusement of readers.[3]

I am encouraged in these speculations by a book of woodcuts published in Paris in 1565 that contains a whole army of Boschian monsters—
no fewer than 120 of them (Figs. 10–12). The title page (Fig. 10) informs
us that they are the *Songes drolatiques de Pantagruel*, or the Droll Dreams of
Pantagruel, intended "for the recreation of witty minds." In his preface
to this volume, the publisher Richard Breton assures us that he will leave
the deeper meanings of these images to others to decipher; for his part,

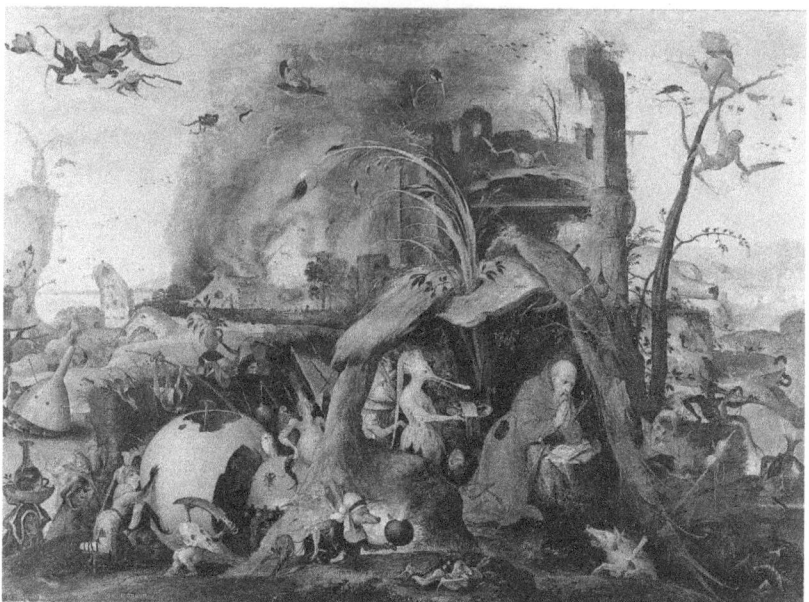

FIGURE 9. Jan Mandijn, *Temptation of St. Anthony.* Haarlem, Frans Hals Museum.

he offers them simply as objects of laughter, as an antidote for melancholy, and as a pastime for the young.[4] Indeed, in their incongruous conjunctions of human and animal parts with everyday objects made by men, these figures recall the kind of art described by Horace in his *Ars poetica*: "If a painter chose to join a human head to the neck of a horse, . . . so that what at the top is a lovely woman ends up below as a black and ugly fish, could you my friends, keep from laughing?"[5] Such hybrid forms had been common in ancient Roman decoration, vigorously condemned by Vitruvius, and rediscovered toward the end of the fifteenth century, when they were known as *grotteschi*, or grotesques.[6] While some writers of the sixteenth century, especially Pirro Ligorio, believed that the forms of ancient grotesque decoration were as fraught with significance as the *Hieroglyphics* of Horapollo,[7] there were many others who

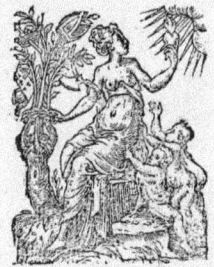

LES
SONGES DROLA-
TIQVES DE PANTAGRVEL,
ou font contenues plufieurs figures
de l'inuention de maiftre François Rabelais : & dernie-
re œuure d'iceluy,
pour la recreation
des bons
efprits.

A PARIS,

Par Richard Breton, Rue S. Iaques,
à l'Efcreuiffe d'argent.

M. D. LXV.

FIGURE 10. *Les Songes drolatiques de Pantagruel,* Paris: Richard Breton, 1565, title page. Cambridge, Mass., Harvard College Library, Houghton Library, Department of Printing and Graphic Arts, Typ. 515.65.802.

saw them as meaningless. Daniele de Barbaro, for example, in his Italian translation of Vitruvius published in 1556, characterized grotesques as the dream fantasies that "represent confusedly the images of things."[8] For his part, Rabelais speaks of grotesques as "devices . . . lightheartedly invented for the purpose of mirth."[9] Early in the next century, Randle

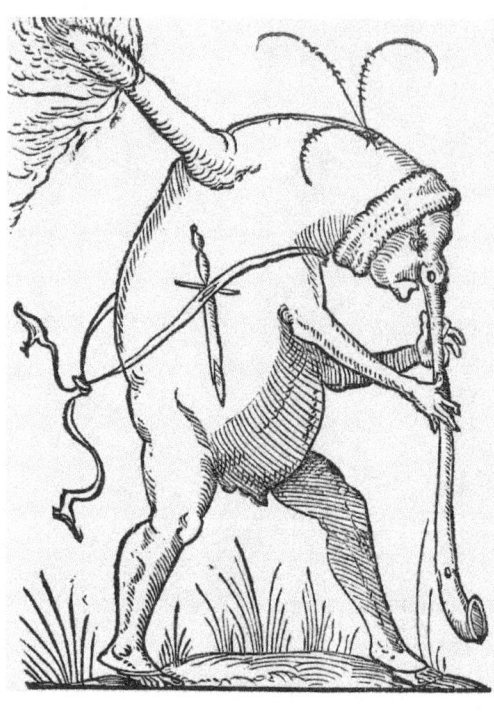

FIGURE II.
Les Songes drolatiques de Pantagruel,
Paris: Richard
Breton, 1565, fol.
37v. Cambridge,
Mass., Harvard
College Library,
Houghton Library, Department
of Printing and
Graphic Arts,
Typ. 515.65.802.

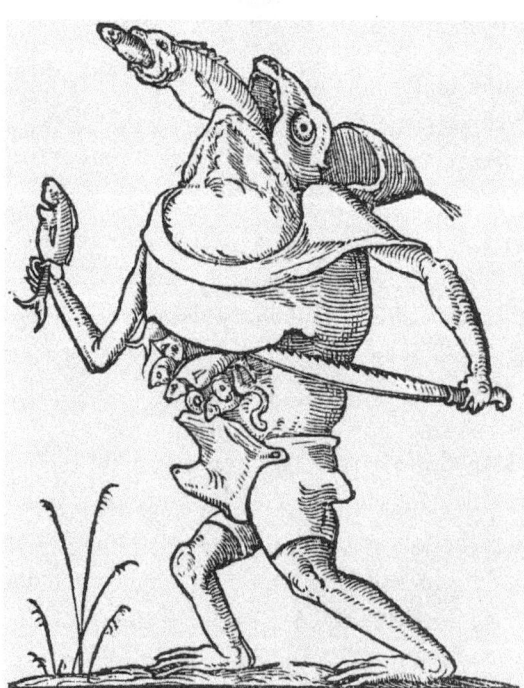

FIGURE 12.
Les Songes drolatiques de Pantagruel,
Paris: Richard
Breton, 1565, fol.
47r. Cambridge,
Mass., Harvard
College Library,
Houghton Library, Department
of Printing and
Graphic Arts,
Typ. 515.65.802.

Cotgrave defined grotesques as "pictures wherein . . . odde things are represented without anie particular sense, or meaning, but onlie to feed the eye."[10] Not only the grotesque but incongruity in general, it should be added, was often adduced as a major source of laughter by various Renaissance writers, Joubert among them,[11] and we may assume that it was the incongruity of the rutting peasants in Vredeman de Vries's mural of a fashionable summerhouse that roused Molckeman and his friends to such hearty laughter.

Breton's *Songes drolatiques* are considerably less elegant than ancient and Renaissance grotesques, but they belong to the same genre. Although he attributed the invention of these deformed little figures to "Master François Rabelais," they of course have nothing to do with Rabelais. The publisher was most likely exploiting a name well known to the reading public. Indeed, it has been suggested that some of the figures may have been inspired by the prints after Pieter Bruegel in circulation at that time.[12] However this may be, the *Songes drolatiques de Pantagruel* alerts us to an important aspect of the audience response to Bruegel's overtly didactic prints that has all too often been overlooked. Prime examples occur in his *Seven Vices* series of 1558, the details of each vice unfolded in its own "mythical country," as De Tolnay aptly put it,[13] which were issued as prints by Hieronymus Cock. In the *Allegory of Sloth* (Fig. 13), for example, Queen Sloth, as we may call her, reposes against a reclining mule, her head and one shoulder nestled on the Devil's *oorkussen*, or pillow, a proverbial attribute of Sloth.[14] She and her followers are sunk in sleep, oblivious to the warnings of the bell ringer and the whimsical clock from which a human arm reaches to point at the ominous hour of eleven: time is running out. The indolence pervading Sloth's kingdom is well suggested by the snails and slugs crawling around her, as well as by the oversize oaf in the middle ground, too lethargic, it seems, to empty his bowels without prodding from the little men in the boat.

It is significant that when Christophe Plantin sent a batch of prints to a print seller in Paris, he identified Bruegel's *Seven Vices* as the "seven sins, droleries [*7 pechez droleries*]."[15] Plantin also uses the word *drolerie* to

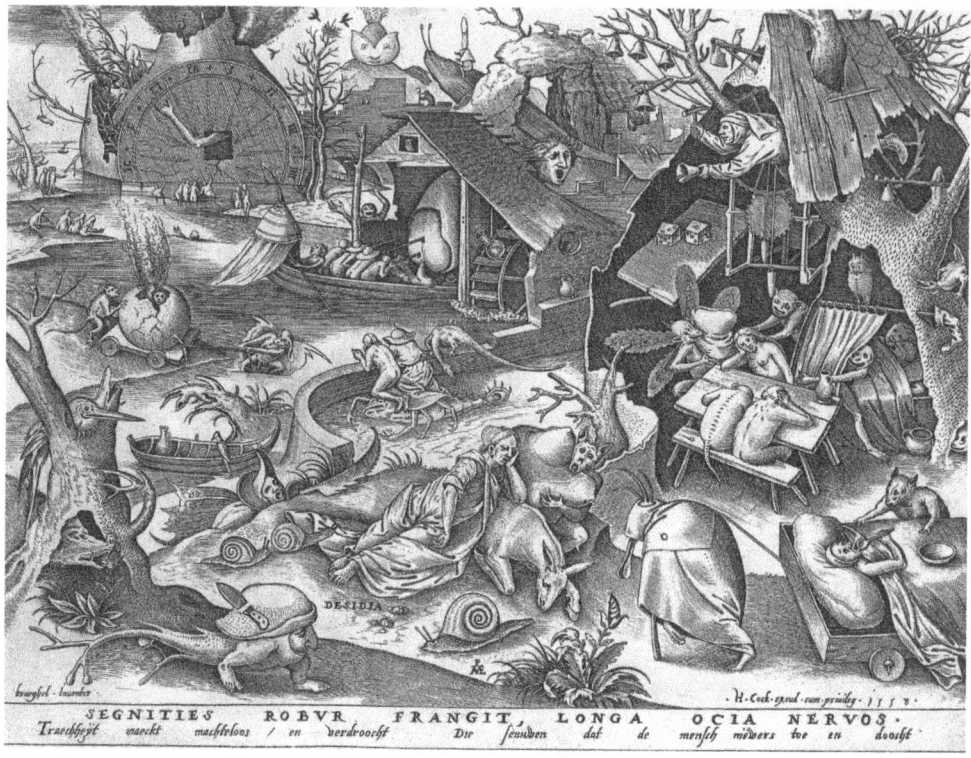

FIGURE 13.   Pieter van der Heyden after Pieter Bruegel the Elder, *Allegory of Sloth,* engraving and etching, 1558. Washington D.C., National Gallery of Art, Rosenwald Collection.

identify several other prints after Bruegel, the *Temptation of St. Anthony* (*Sainct Anthonie drolerie*) and the *Patience* (*Pacience drolerie*).[16] While the word *drolerie* in earlier centuries had the sense of the demonic or evil, by Bruegel's time it had acquired strong overtones of the humorous.[17] In the case of Bruegel's "droll sins," it is surely the humor that dominates, as it did, for example, for Giorgio Vasari, who described Bruegel's *Seven Vices* series as showing "demons of various forms, which was a fantastic and laughable work *[che furono cosa fantastica e da ridere]*."[18] For Dominicus Lampsonius, in his verses accompanying the *Effigies,* a collection of artists' por-

traits published by Hieronymus Cock's widow in 1572, Bosch was essentially serious in meaning, but Bruegel's evocations of Bosch were "certainly worthy of laughter."[19] A generation later, Karel van Mander would
tell us that it was because of Bruegel's many "spectres and burlesques
[spoockerijen en drollen]" in the style of Hieronymus Bosch that he was known
as "Pier den Drol," or Piet the Droll, and it is evident that Van Mander
included such drollen among those of Bruegel's works that, so he claimed,
incite laughter.[20]

This humor is equally evident in Bruegel's Allegory of Pride (Fig. 14).
Pride herself flaunts her sumptuous and very fashionable gown in the
middle foreground,[21] her haughty demeanor mocked by the frog-faced
Devil grinning at us from behind her skirt. She gazes fondly at her reflection in her hand mirror, a traditional attribute of Pride that is humor-
ously repeated at lower left, where one monster admires his posterior in
a looking glass, and another, with a ring piercing his lips, regards himself
in a second mirror. The feathers of Pride's emblematic peacock recur in
unlikely contexts throughout the foreground, protruding from the tails
of several other monsters, including the hybrid creature at lower left (a
figure perhaps inspired by Horace's fish-woman?). At the right is a barber-
cum-beauty-shop. A nude man on the roof defecates into a bowl suspi-
ciously close to the mortar and pestle resting on a lower level. It may well
be the source of the liquid with which two attendants wash the hair of
the woman below. Pride's love of vain display is further manifested in
the ornate cupola rising from the roof of the beauty parlor and in the
elaborate structures in the left background, while pride of rank dominates the boatlike structure suspended in a tree, in which a group of naked
people kneel in homage to a figure clad only in an oversize helmet. Just
below and to the right, an owl-headed monster wears a crown whose four
stages surpass the tripartite design of the papal tiara.

The same comic fantasy can be discerned in other prints from this
series. A few details must suffice. In Gluttony, the legs and lower torso of a
nude man protrude from a hole smashed into the side of a wine or beer
barrel; that he is in imminent danger of drowning is suggested by his

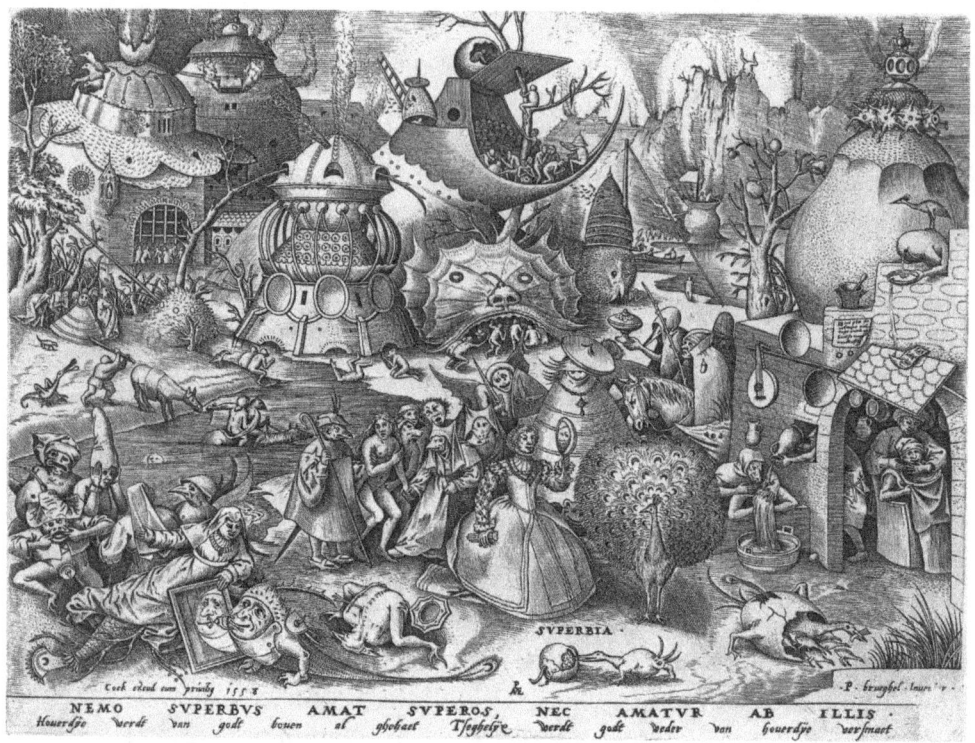

FIGURE 14. Pieter van der Heyden, after Pieter Bruegel the Elder, *Allegory of Pride*, engraving and etching, 1558. Washington, D.C., National Gallery of Art, Rosenwald Collection.

equally nude companion who frantically addresses his prayers to heaven. A barrel also figures at the lower right in *Avarice*: this time, a demon rolls a man in a cask filled with coins and fitted with sharp spikes; the man snatches at more coins scattered on the ground, apparently oblivious both to his pain and to the coins trickling away through a bunghole. In *Lust* (again at lower right), one hooded devil nonchalantly slices off his *membrum virile* with a large carving knife. The viewer will find similarly absurd details in these prints. But with all their antic humor, these images treat serious subjects whose content is indicated in the inscriptions below. Sloth, we are warned, "takes away all strength and dries out the nerves until man is good for nothing," while "Pride is hated by God above all, at the same time, Pride scorns God." This coupling of *nut en vermaeck* (or "profit and pleasure"), as Van Mander would later put it,[22] was a venerable practice, and not only among the *rederijkers*. Preachers had long employed exempla, or little exemplary stories, some of them comic, not only to illustrate a point but also to keep their listeners awake.[23] Indeed, Boccaccio could justify the often ribald tales in his *Decameron* on the grounds that since "the sermons our good friars preach nowadays . . . are full of jests, jibes and jokes, I thought these trifles would not have been inappropriate in my stories, written as they were to relieve women of melancholy."[24] Some people, however, took a dimmer view of this custom. One was Margaret of Austria, who in 1525 instructed abbots and priors of cloisters to forbid preachers to corrupt *'t gemeyn volk* (common folk) with indecent stories.[25] Despite such concerns, however, many late medieval biblical and morality plays are interlarded with comic scenes to attract audiences,[26] and in the allegorical plays of the *rederijkers*, the very *sinnekens* (allegorical personifications) engaged in seducing humanity into sin and eternal damnation frequently engage in farcical interludes that are often extremely funny even to the modern reader.[27]

Nevertheless, it is difficult to imagine that Bruegel's contemporaries bought prints of the *Vices* chiefly to learn about the dangers of sin; they surely had imbibed this lesson from more edifying sources from childhood on.[28] Just as people attended performances of the *kluchten* to be entertained, it is equally likely that they acquired Bruegel's *Seven Vices* to admire and laugh at his ingenuity in transforming the old moral lessons into magnificently comic images. But Bruegel was not the only artist who put moralizing images to comic use. The German artist Hans Weiditz did the same in his many single-leaf woodcuts. A good example is his print of about 1521 (Fig. 15), featuring a grotesque peasant couple, the woman balancing an outsize glass drinking vessel on her head. According to the German verses inscribed above the image, she wiggles her bottom as she dances and her nose is well adjusted to the tankard; hence the vessel on her head alludes to her propensity to drink, just as, the same verses in-

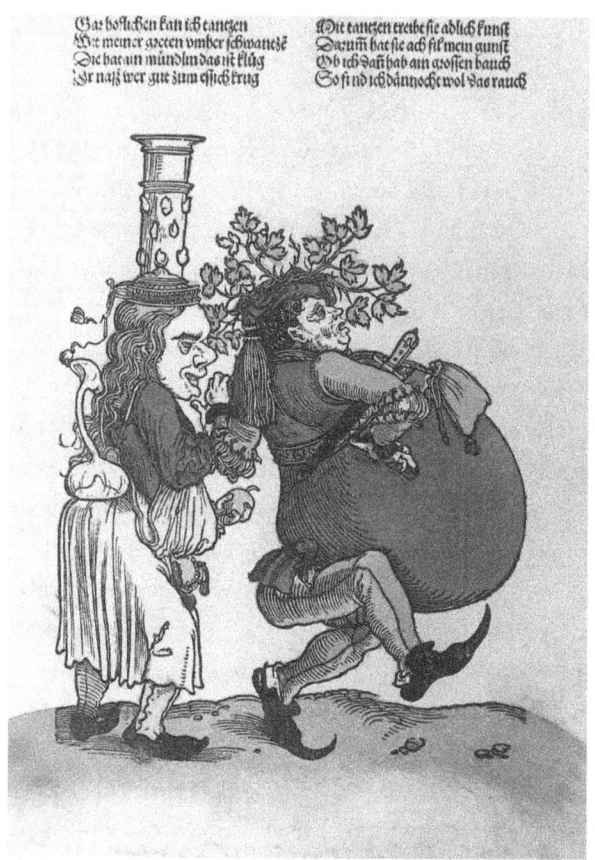

FIGURE 15. Hans Weiditz, *Grotesque Couple,* hand-
colored woodcut. Gotha, Stiftung Schloss Friedenstein,
Schlossmuseum.

form us, the grossly distended paunch of her partner testifies to his gluttony. Weiditz's woodcut probably pokes fun at the peasants and warns
against drunkenness and gluttony, but as Alison Stewart observes about
this and similar woodcut subjects by the artist, it must have been intended
primarily to evoke laughter.[29]

In a similar manner, the curious wedding feasts painted in tempera
on linen produced by the Verbeeck family at Mechelen during the mid–

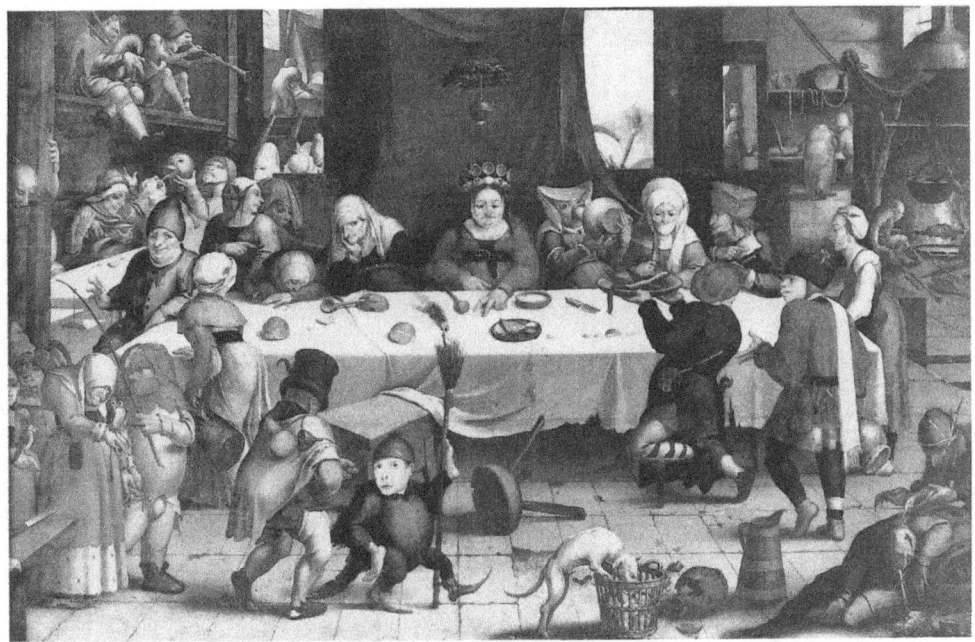

FIGURE 16. Attributed to Jan Verbeeck, *Grotesque Banquet*. Bilbao, Museo de Bellas Artes.

sixteenth century most likely had a moralizing significance (Fig. 16). They show a crowned bridal figure at a banquet table presiding over a curiously motley company, and, as I have suggested elsewhere, these scenes may well have been inspired by the saying "to sit by the bride," referring to those who suffer the consequences of their own folly.[30] Nevertheless, even as beholders pondered this lesson, they must also have chuckled over the grotesque, often semidemonic creatures capering through these pictures. The same can be said, I suspect, of a great many works of the period that we now study with such learned solemnity, including Sebastian Brant's *Narrenschiff*. This book was reprinted so many times and translated into Latin, Netherlandish, and other languages not only for its moral messages but for the very medium in which these messages were delivered, filled with what a twentieth-century translator of the work called

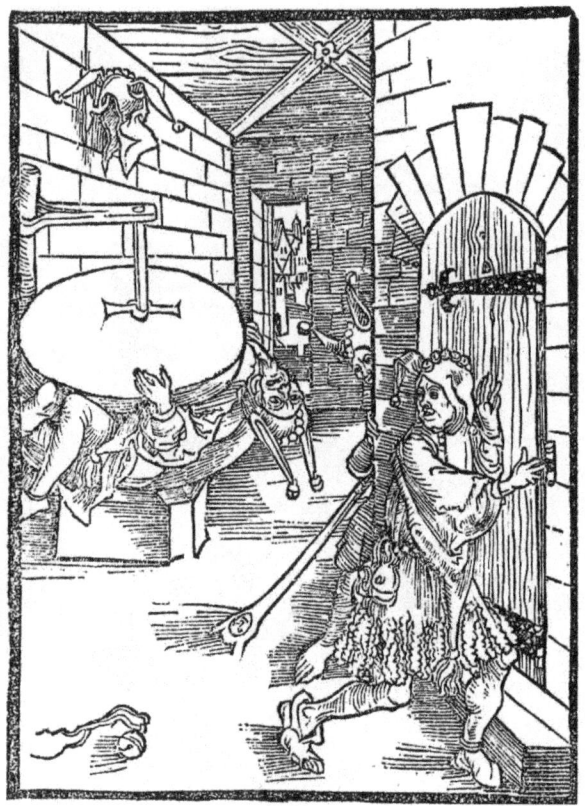

FIGURE 17. *Fool between Two Millstones,* woodcut in
Sebastian Brant, *Stultifera navis,* Basel, 1497. Williams-
town, Mass., Chapin Library of Rare Books, Williams
College.

its "ribald, teasing humor,"[31] and for its wealth of diverting illustrations.
Among them are the title page depicting a boatload of carefree fools em-
barking for Narragonia, the land of fools, and the woodcut showing a fool
squeezed between two millstones (Fig. 17), illustrating a proverbial expression that comments on how people who cause discord often get
crushed by the very forces they set loose.[32]

As several of these images show, the literal depiction of proverbs con-

stituted an important source of wit in this period, both in the written
and spoken word and in art. Several scholars have suggested that the published collections of vernacular proverbs so popular in Bruegel's day were
meant as much for amusement as for moral reflection on their often wry
commentaries on the human condition.[33] A good instance occurs in the
Nyeuwe clucht boeck, concerning a widow whose law case remained unset-
tled in court for some years. Her friends advised her to grease the judge's
palm, which she did literally (with butter), shaming the judge into bringing her case to a conclusion.[34] The *rederijkers*, especially, employed proverbs
and proverbial expressions for didactic purposes,[35] and about 1550 a cit-
izen of Amsterdam, Reyer Gheurtz, assembled a collection of some two
thousand proverbs, presumably for the use of a local *rederijker* chamber,
De Eglentier, of which he was a member.[36] But the *rederijkers* also exploited
proverbs purely for their humorous potential. Some striking examples occur in the procession inaugurating the Antwerp *landjuweel* of 1561. The
fool of the Mechelen (Malines) chamber asked bystanders: "Waer kyckt
den zot?" (Where does the fool look?), to which he provided his own
answer: "Wtter mouwe" (literally, From out of the sleeve), that is, to play
the fool.[37] Jeurken, the chief fool of the Violieren, rode in state on horseback, escorted by two attendant fools on foot, one of them playing a vi-
olin, the other trying to coax music from the jawbone of a large animal.[38]
The latter musician personifies the *kaakspeler*, or jawbone player: to play
on the jawbone was to acquire ill-gotten gains.[39] Jeurken himself displayed
a motto boasting "I am so handsome I do not know myself,"[40] an inver-
sion of the proverbial Socratic injunction "Know thyself."

Bruegel shared this interest in proverbs, as we can see from some of
the drawings he made for Cock's printmakers. Among them is *Big Fish Eat
the Small* (1557), in which the basic proverb is reversed by fish disgorging
their prey, not only the large whalelike creature that is being disembow-
eled but the smaller fish as well. Another is the *Ass in School* (1556), inspired by the old adage "You can send an ass to school, but he will return still an ass."[41] And in his *Elck* of 1558 (Fig. 18), Bruegel introduced
a number of visual jokes. The central proverb, "Each seeks his own ad-

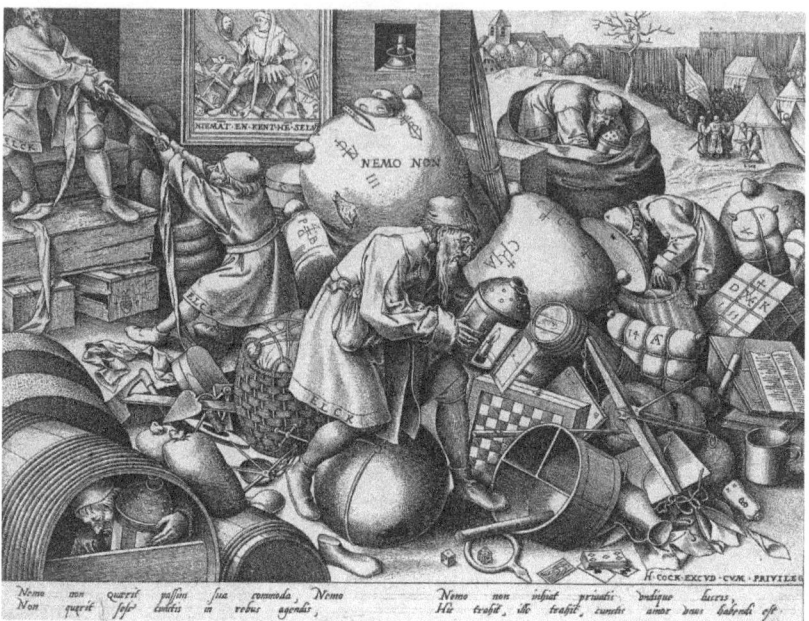

FIGURE 18.   Attributed to Pieter van der Heyden, after Pieter Bruegel the Elder, *Elck,* engraving and etching, ca. 1558. Oxford, Ashmolean Museum.

vantage," is personified by the bespectacled old man, Elck, that is, Every-man, who in his tireless search of *eigenbaet* (*eigenbaat* in modern Nether-landish), or self-interest, repeatedly rummages through a pile of bales and barrels, a game board, and other objects symbolizing the material goods of this life. As some scholars have suggested, the lantern he carries may allude ironically to Diogenes, the ancient philosopher who carried a lighted lamp in broad daylight in his quest for an honest man and who spurned the very things for which Elck so avidly searches.[42] The tug-of-war engaged in by the two men at upper left informs us that "each tugs for the longer end," while the picture-within-a-picture on the back wall comments on this sorry spectacle: dressed as a fool and seated amid a lit-ter of broken household objects, Nemo, or Nobody, contemplates his im-age in a mirror. His significance is explained by an inscription below: "No-body knows himself." Punning on the name Nemo, this phrase also, of

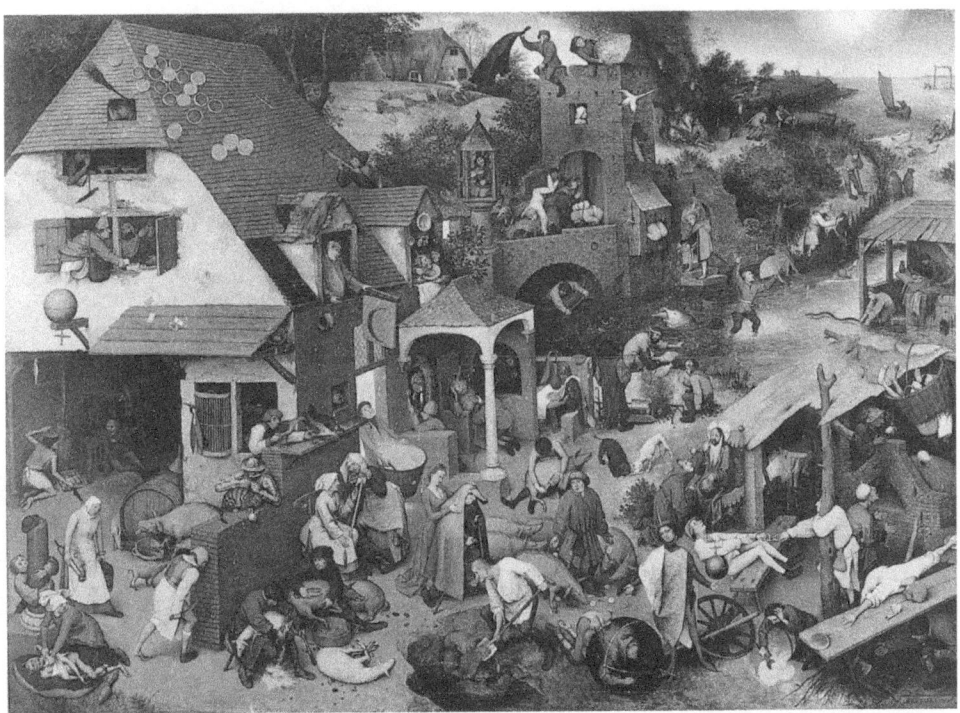

FIGURE 19. Pieter Bruegel the Elder, *Netherlandish Proverbs*, 1559. Berlin, Staatliche Museen, Preussischer Kulturbesitz, Gemäldegalerie.

course, alludes to the famous "Know thyself."[43] The didactic lesson of *Elck* is thus conveyed through a witty manipulation of proverbial material that must have provoked viewers to laughter even as they reflected on its ultimately serious message.[44]

The same can be said for Bruegel's *Dulle Griet*, as we shall see, and the *Netherlandish Proverbs* in Berlin (Fig. 19), his most extensive treatment of proverb images. This last painting contains between 85 and 126 proverbs (scholars differ as to the actual number), including the figure of the *kaakspeler* (perched in a little tower just above the center of the composition), acted out in a setting of village and countryside.[45] This teeming landscape may indeed show *des weerelts abuisen* (deceptions of this world), as

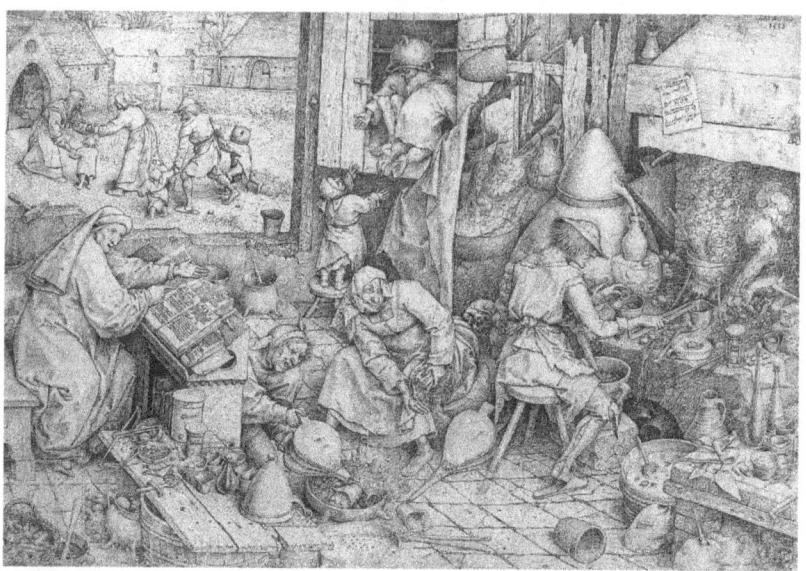

FIGURE 20.   Pieter Bruegel the Elder, *Alchemist,* ca. 1558, drawing. Berlin, Staatliche Museen, Preussischer Kulturbesitz, Kupferstichkabinett.

Frans Hogenberg proclaimed on the print that most likely inspired Bruegel, but it is also an antic vision of a universal madhouse, whose denizens have been released for a summer frolic.[46]

   This penchant for verbal wit is also evident in Bruegel's *Alchemist* (Fig. 20), a drawing done about 1558 and certainly one of his funniest inventions. Here we are confronted with a dilapidated makeshift laboratory littered with vials, retorts, and other alchemical equipment. At the right, a man sits at a hearth, involved, we assume, in the usual attempt to transmute base metals into gold. This operation of "the vayne & disceytfull craft of alkemy," as one sixteenth-century writer called it,[47] is apparently directed by the man clad in the long gown of a scholar, probably the chief alchemist, sitting at the reading desk. He is the type of impostor who appears in two of Erasmus's colloquies, gulling his victims with fair words and with such tricks as pretending to create precious metals out of lead by throwing into the alchemic fire a hollowed-out coal filled with a bit

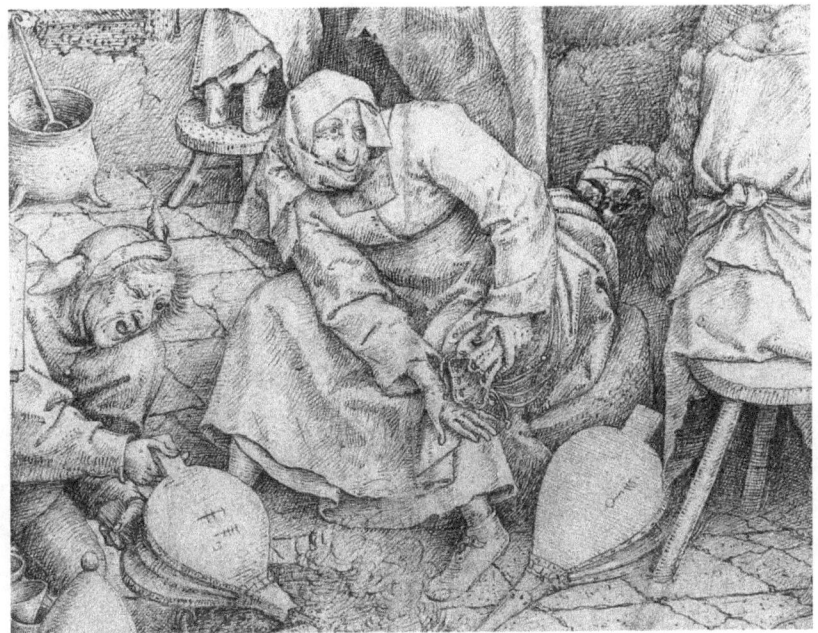

FIGURE 21. Detail of Fig. 20.

of silver.[48] In Bruegel's drawing, the utter futility of this endeavor is indicated by the open book in which the master alchemist points to the words *Alge-mist*, a pun on the words *alchemist* and *al-gemist*, Netherlandish for both "all is lost" and "all is dung," that is, "nothing."[49] The destitution of this household is evident in the tattered clothing of the man at the fireplace who is, as Vasari described it, "distilling away his brains,"[50] and by the empty purse that the wife displays to the viewer (Fig. 21). One of the children wears a cooking pot on its head, and why not? There is probably nothing in the larder to fill the pot, and the destiny of this hapless family is revealed through the window at the back, where we see it being received into the poorhouse.[51] The long-robed alchemist is not among them, having departed, presumably, to find another victim.[52]

But if the *Alchemist* is one of the finest examples of Bruegel's art of laughter, it is also one of the earliest manifestations of his remarkable

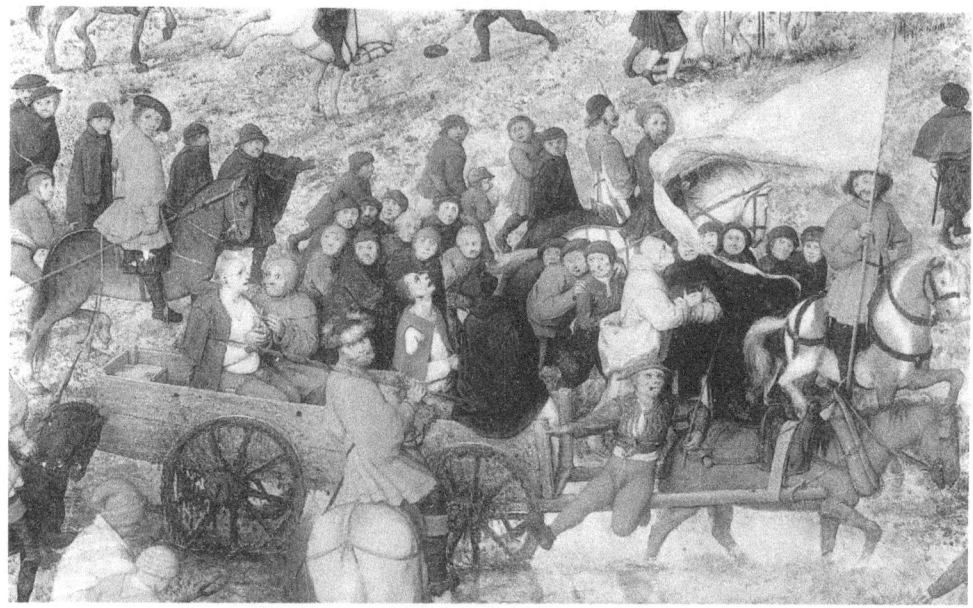

FIGURE 22.   Detail of Fig. 35.

eye for human physiognomy, especially apparent in the old wife with her
witless grin and the face of the fool screwed up with exertion as he pumps
frantically with the bellows (see Fig. 21).[53] This aspect of Bruegel's art is
frequently overlooked. It is true that his faces, especially of secondary
figures, such as the onlookers who gape at the unfortunate thieves in his
Christ Carrying the Cross of 1564 (Fig. 22), often appear as if they had been
formed with the same cookie cutter, with eyes and mouths resembling
raisins pressed into dough. It may have been such figures that led Otto
Benesch, for example, to describe Bruegel's faces as masks and to claim
that the artist understands humanity "as an anonymous mass, subservient
to the great laws that govern the earth," and prompted Robert Delevoy to
assert that Bruegel lacked the talent to "render a smile or the psychologi-
cal content of a gaze."[54] But these observations hardly do justice to Bruegel's
remarkable ability to depict the human countenance in its various ex-

pressions. This was, in fact, a very important part of his art of laughter and must have appealed greatly to his contemporaries.

Several centuries after Bruegel, Joshua Reynolds would insist that an artist should never express the human passions, "all of which produce distortion and deformity, more or less, in the most beautiful faces."[55] How widely this opinion was shared by earlier artists I do not know, but it is my impression that until the sixteenth century, the prevailing subject matter in Netherlandish painting offered only limited opportunities for representing the human face in its more animated moments. Scenes of Christ's Passion often contain expressive figures, especially those of the tortured Savior or the grieving Mary and her companions, their "tears streaming and yet maintaining [their] dignity," to paraphrase what a fifteenth-century Italian writer said of a painting by Rogier van der Weyden.[56] Generally, the heroes and heroines of sacred history, and often even its villains, adopt attitudes of noble restraint appropriate to their station. This treatment of history subjects persisted long after 1500. A striking example occurs in a *Judgment of Solomon* by Frans Floris, done about 1547 (Fig. 23); the participants, including the two mothers, contemplate the prospect of judicial infanticide with stoic indifference.[57] It must be noted in passing, however, that this expressive restraint in depictions of sacred and secular histories did not detract from their effectiveness. Viewers had long projected into such images the emotions that they expected the depicted figures to experience, based on their familiarity with the stories.[58] When Ortelius, for example, commissioned from Philips Galle an engraved copy of Bruegel's *Death of the Virgin* (see Fig. 1), he appended to the print a poem, perhaps of his own composition, describing this picture "that shows the happy bearing of sadness on the faces of the just," as the apostles and other mourners both grieve for the Virgin's passing and rejoice at her future glorification in Heaven. And yet, the small-scale, generalized faces in Bruegel's picture show little of grief or joy;[59] nonetheless, we may assume that Ortelius's response was conditioned by his knowledge of the event as recounted in various literary sources and

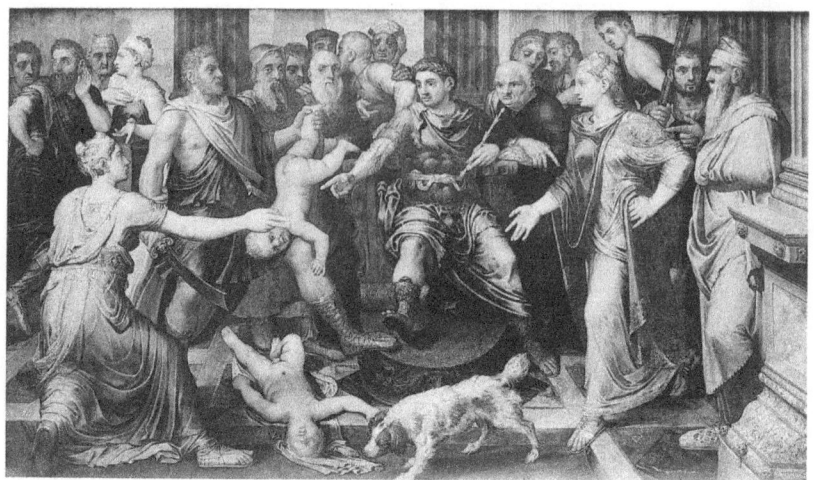

FIGURE 23. Frans Floris, *Judgment of Solomon.* Antwerp, Koninklijk Museum voor Schone Kunsten.

perhaps, too, by the profound pious meditations that generations of writers had developed around the Virgin's death.[60]

Indeed, the expression of emotions in the visual arts, except sadness or mourning, or an occasional exchange of tender glances between the Madonna and her Child,[61] was generally restricted to the lower classes, including those who had supporting roles in scenes of sacred history, especially the torturers of Christ. The contrast between the calm and dignified Savior and his voracious, beastlike tormentors had been exploited by fifteenth-century northern artists, Bosch among them,[62] and was further developed in various Passion scenes by Quentin Massys, Maerten van Heemskerck, and Jan Sanders van Hemessen (Fig. 24).[63] It is at this time that we also see the emergence of physiognomy as a "science" that purported to determine a person's character from his or her facial appearance. Although Leonardo da Vinci had dismissed "physiognomics" as a chimera, lacking "all scientific foundation,"[64] his was a minority opinion, for a number of physiognomical manuals appeared in the sixteenth century, among them Bartholomeaus Cocles's *Chyromantia,*

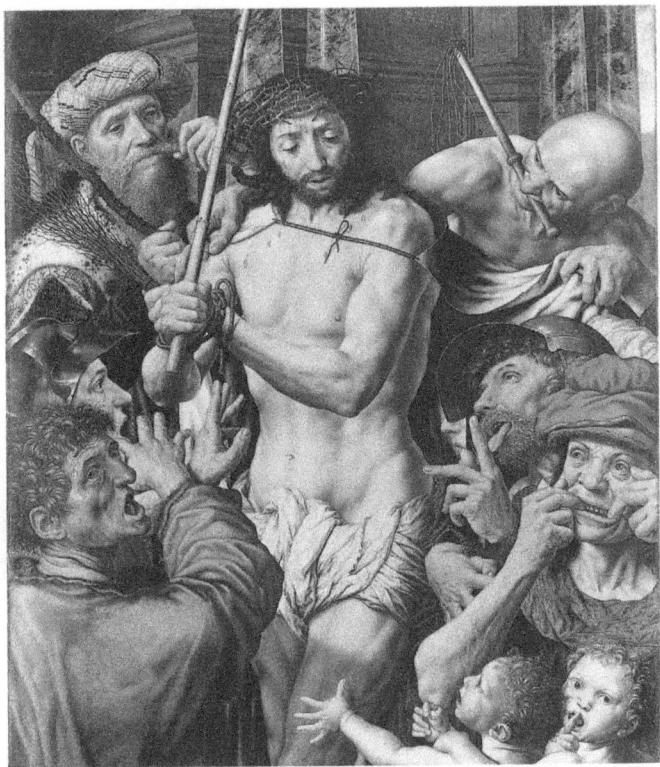

FIGURE 24. Jan Sanders van Hemessen, *Mocking of Christ*, 1544. Munich, Bayerische Staatsgemäldesammlungen, Alte Pinakothek.

whose first edition appeared in 1523, and Johannes Indagine's *Chiromantia*, first published in Latin in 1522, and in a number of later translations. A Netherlandish edition of the *Chiromantia* was published at Antwerp in 1554 by Jan Roelants, who treated the same subject more briefly in the first chapter of his *Nieu complexie boeck*, an astrological booklet first issued in the same year.[65] With their often copious woodcut illustrations, such books offered a gallery of different human faces, but to what extent artists availed themselves of such sources remains to be determined.[66] Nevertheless, in their very existence, the physiognomy manuals bear witness

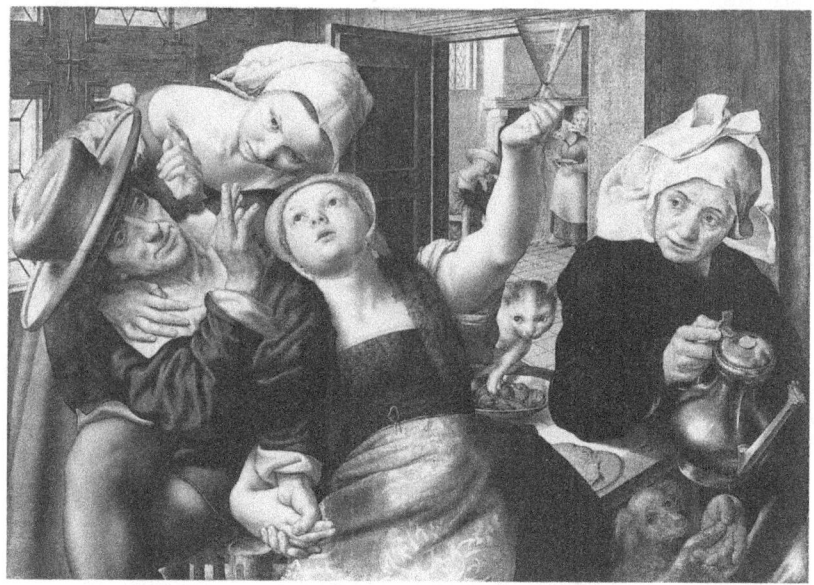

FIGURE 25. Jan Sanders van Hemessen, *Tavern Scene,* 1543. Hartford, Conn., Wadsworth Atheneum Museum of Art, The Ella Gallup Sumner and Mary Catlin Sumner Collection Fund.

to a rising interest in the human face both as an index of character and as a locus of emotional expression, particularly in response to a particular situation. In the dedication of his *Traité du ris* to Marguerite de Navarre, Joubert, for instance, awarded primacy over the human body to the face, because it makes "manifest and put[s] into evidence all the passions and internal movements, a condition truly human and praiseworthy," since, as he explained, man is a social and civil animal.[67]

As it happens, artists were slow to explore the possibilities of animated human faces offered by the secular "lowlife" subjects that were then coming into fashion. In many tavern interiors and rustic celebrations before Bruegel, the actors conduct themselves with much the same decorum that we often encounter in history paintings of the period. Van Hemessen's *Tavern Scene* (Fig. 25), for example, is often called a "Merry Company," although there is actually not very much merry about it. The middle-aged

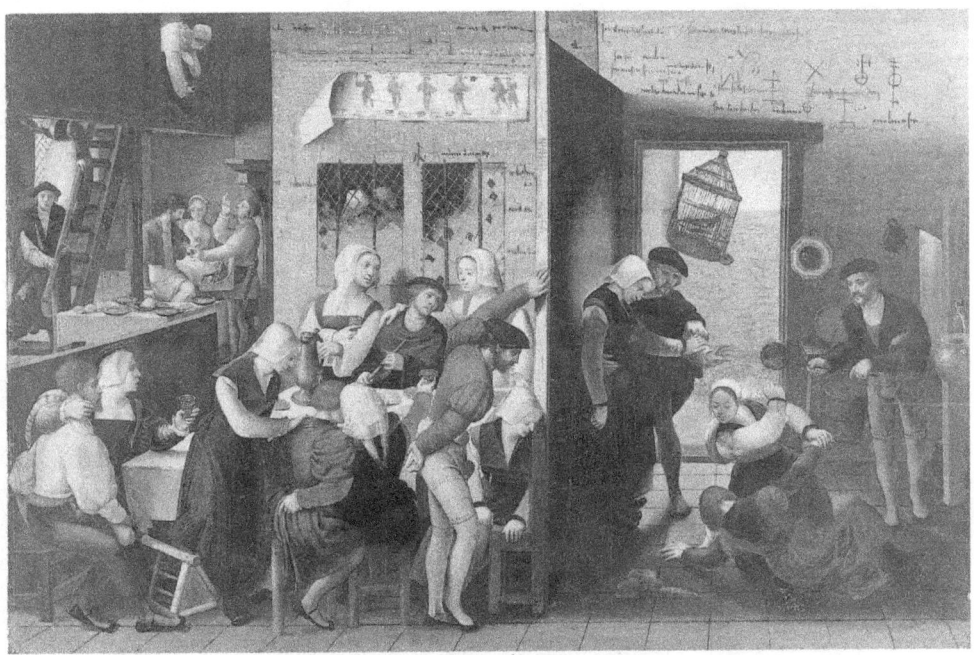

FIGURE 26. Jan van Amstel, *Bar-Room Brawl*. Berlin, Staatliche Museen, Preussischer Kulturbesitz, Gemäldegalerie.

man at the table receives the attentions of the young women with the same gravity with which they bestow them. And this from an artist who could endow the torturers of Christ with faces contorted in animal fe-rocity (see Fig. 24). A similar physiognomical restraint pervades the tavern interiors of the artist variously known as Jan van Amstel and the Brunswick Monogrammist (Fig. 26); his lively, well-posed figures show that he had looked long and intelligently at the art of Raphael and Michelangelo,[68] but their faces seldom betray their feelings, even when they are in the midst of a barroom brawl. In Pieter Aertsen's pictures of celebrating rustics, such as the *Peasant Festival* of 1550 (see Fig. 48), the sober, even stilted behavior of the participants belies the presumably fes-tive occasion. An important exception to this tendency, however, can be found in a number of close-up compositions showing only a few figures

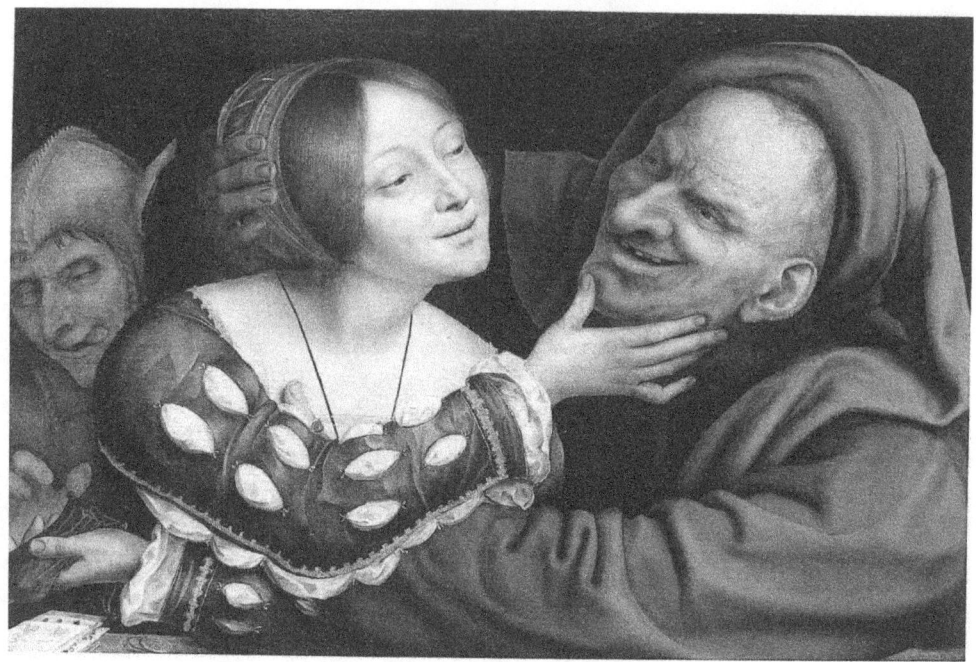

FIGURE 27. Quentin Massys, *Ill-Matched Lovers*. Washington, D.C., National Gallery of Art, Ailsa Mellon Bruce Fund, 1971.

in either bust- or half-length, thus allowing the artist to concentrate on the heads. An outstanding and probably early example is the *Ill-Matched Lovers* (Fig. 27), done about 1520–25 by Quentin Massys, one of the most gifted painters of the human countenance before Bruegel.[69] The unsuitable pairing of age and youth for lust or money was a popular artistic theme in northern Europe at this time,[70] but no artist ever treated it with greater humor. In Massys's painting, the feelings of the three bust-length players—the leering old man, the smiling courtesan who has extracted his purse, and the fool who receives it from her with a look of greedy anticipation—are deftly but vividly portrayed in their faces.[71] As with much Renaissance satire, the moral lesson conveyed by this work must have been eclipsed by the laughter it aroused.

Equally funny is a painting, perhaps a copy of a lost work by Massys

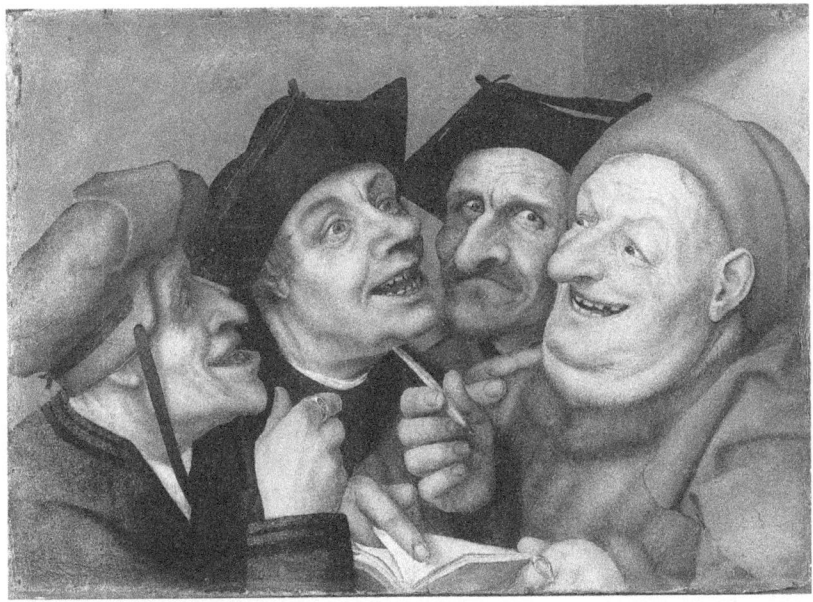

FIGURE 28. Follower of Quentin Massys, *The Contract*. Berlin, Staatliche Museen, Preussischer Kulturbesitz, Gemäldegalerie.

(Fig. 28), in which we can easily imagine the dialogue between the grinning corpulent burgher, all too eager to sign a document, and the three smooth-talking confidence men clustered around him.[72] Quentin's son Jan produced similar bust- or half-length compositions, although seldom with his father's finesse, depicting not only unequal lovers but also tavern companies, roistering peasants, and one scene of tax collectors confronting reluctant peasants.[73] This last subject was also treated in a more caricatural fashion in several paintings by Marinus van Reymerswaele.[74] We also have a number of small paintings of peasants drinking, making music, and the like, in which the merrymaking has been captured with varying skill.[75] One such painting, a *tafereel van dronkersse* (a painting of drunkards), was owned by the Antwerp banker Coenraerd Schetz; it may have resembled a panel executed in 1564 by Jan Massys (Fig. 29).[76]

The relation between comic subjects and the more intense moments

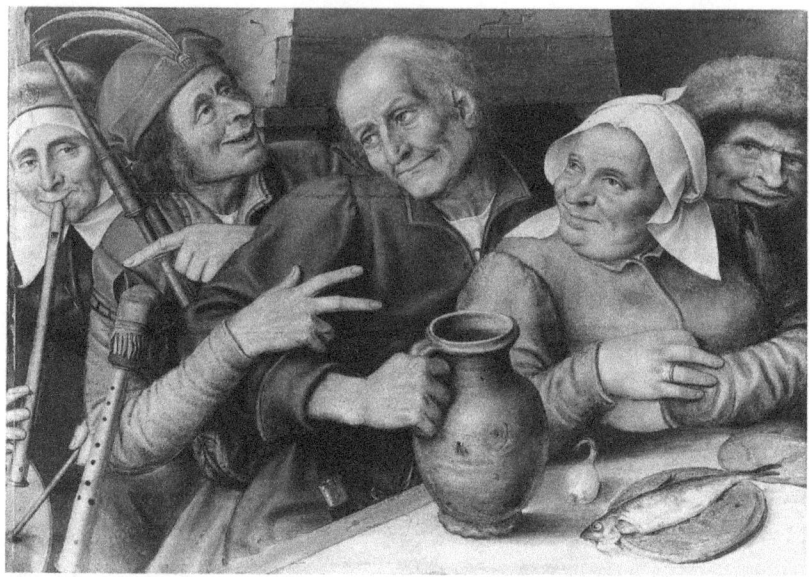

FIGURE 29. Jan Massys, *Peasants in a Tavern,* 1564. Vienna, Kunsthistorisches Museum.

of human passion was articulated much later, in the early eighteenth century, by the Dutch writer Arnold Houbraken, when he said, "it is the mark
of true comedy that one knows how to depict and imitate everything
equally naturally, both sadness and joy, composure and rage—in a word
all the bodily movements and facial expressions that spring from the many
impulses of the spirit."[77] This was hardly a novel opinion: the fourth-
century Latin grammarian Donatus, for example, cites Cicero as his authority when he tells us that comedy is an imitation of life, a mirror of
daily events, and an image of truth: "imitatio vitae, speculum consuetu-
denis, imago veritas."[78] In Houbraken's case, he was talking about a great
Dutch comic painter of the seventeenth century, Jan Steen (Fig. 30), and
in an echo of Van Mander's praise of Bruegel, Houbraken concluded by
observing that if people could see onstage a performance of Steen's life
(which he believed was as comic as Steen's art), they would be forced to

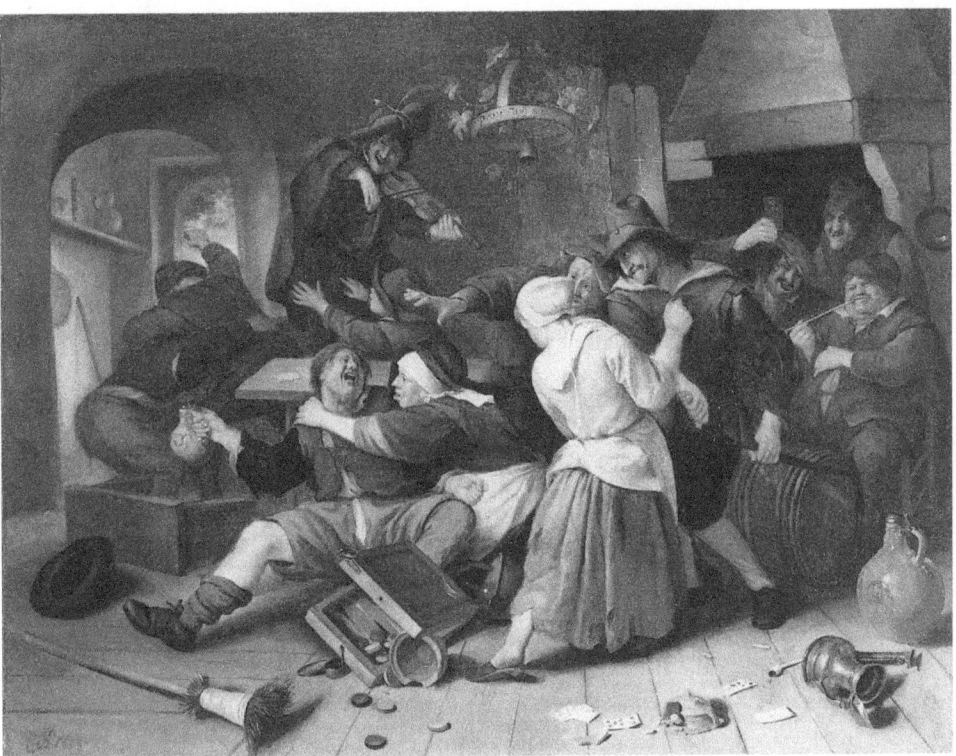

FIGURE 30.   Jan Havicksz. Steen, *Gamblers Quarreling*, ca. 1665. The Detroit
Institute of Arts, Gift of James E. Scripps.

"unfrown their faces."[79] However this may be, Houbraken offers us an
insight into the popularity of such paintings.

    Steen and many other artists, among them Jan Miense Molenaer, Adri-
aen Brouwer, and Adriaen van Ostade, painted humorous scenes of peasant brawls, smoke-filled tavern interiors, and the like. Why did people
buy such subjects? The answer often given is that these images showed
viewers precisely the sort of undesirable behavior they should avoid,[80]
much as the Spartans, Plutarch tells us, had their drunken slaves put on
a show at banquets, not to enjoy their foolish behavior, but to show their

young men by example how base it is to be seen drunk.[81] That one must
learn to recognize vice in order to avoid it and strive after virtue was an
idea circulated among the ancient authors, including Aristotle and Cato,
and was repeated by St. Jerome, the Venerable Bede, and scores of writers thereafter.[82] Both Coluccio Salutati and Jacob Landsberger insisted
that the salacious stories found in the pagan poets, and even in the Bible,
would repel Christian readers and encourage them to live virtuously.[83]
Similarly, plays featuring morally reprehensible characters and actions
were condoned on the same basis. Sixteenth-century editors of Terence's
comedies routinely stressed their didactic value: in a prologue to Stephanus
Riccius's edition of Terence (1566), for example, we read that "comedy
is . . . a mirror of life. Just as we may discern in a mirror the beauty of a
face and also its blemishes, so may we likewise perceive in comedy what
ought to be imitated, what ought to be shunned, what is appropriate to
an honorable life."[84] But if the low-life scenes of Brouwer, Adriaen van
Ostade, Steen, and others were intended by their makers to function
chiefly as "mirrors of morals," then the very numbers in which they were
produced and acquired might suggest to more literal minds that the
Dutch people were in perennial need of reminders of proper conduct.
While this is possible, I cannot help thinking that such pictures were
widely collected, and cherished by successive generations, not so much
for their edifying messages as for the astonishing virtuosity displayed by
their creators in rendering the human form convincingly and vividly in
the throes of often violent emotion.[85]

The comic scenes of Brouwer, Steen, and their colleagues have their
roots ultimately in the art of their sixteenth-century predecessors, including Pieter Bruegel. Bruegel's abiding interest in human physiognomy is evident not only in *The Alchemist* but in such studies as the head of
a gaping peasant woman now in Munich (Fig. 31). We also have the superb little head of a man (Fig. 32) whose prodigious yawn would cause
any viewer to respond in kind: "If one yawns, so yawns the other," according to a proverb current in Bruegel's day.[86] This latter picture has
often been attributed to Bruegel himself, although, for reasons not evi-

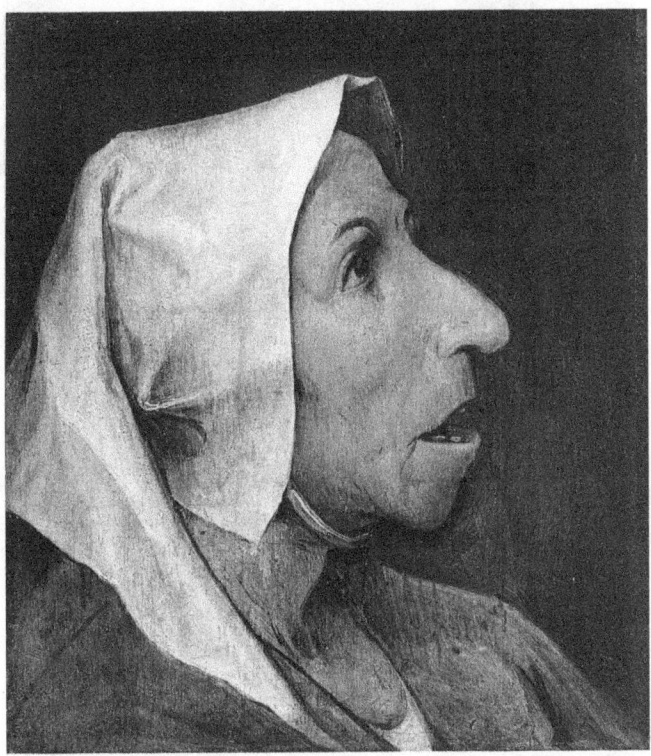

FIGURE 31. Pieter Bruegel the Elder, *Head of a Gaping Woman*. Munich, Bayerische Staatsgemäldesammlungen, Alte Pinakothek.

dent to me, recent authorities have considered it a copy after a lost original.[87] In any case, it is of much higher quality than several other paintings generally considered copies after Bruegel, a *Head of a Lansquenet* (Fig. 33), for example, and a *Head of an Old Man*.[88] It has been thought that these last two pictures, along with the *Yawning Man*, represent Anger, Envy, and Sloth, remnants of a series of the seven deadly sins, but that, I think, is to misconstrue their original function.[89] As Lyckle de Vries has pointed out, such studies were characterized in this period simply as *tronies*, meaning "head," "face," or "facial expression."[90] In fact, a couple of pictures

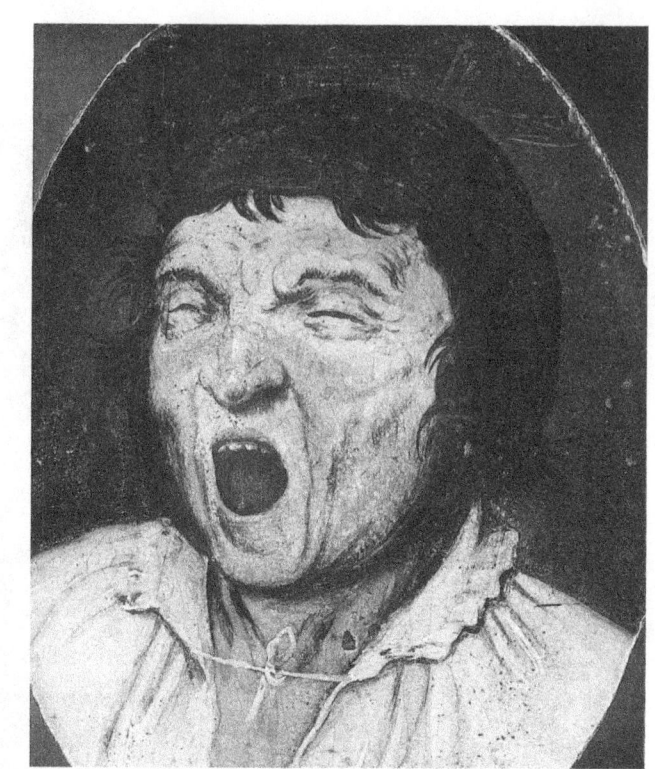

FIGURE 32.
Pieter
Bruegel
the Elder,
Yawning Man.
Brussels,
Musées
Royaux des
Beaux-Arts.

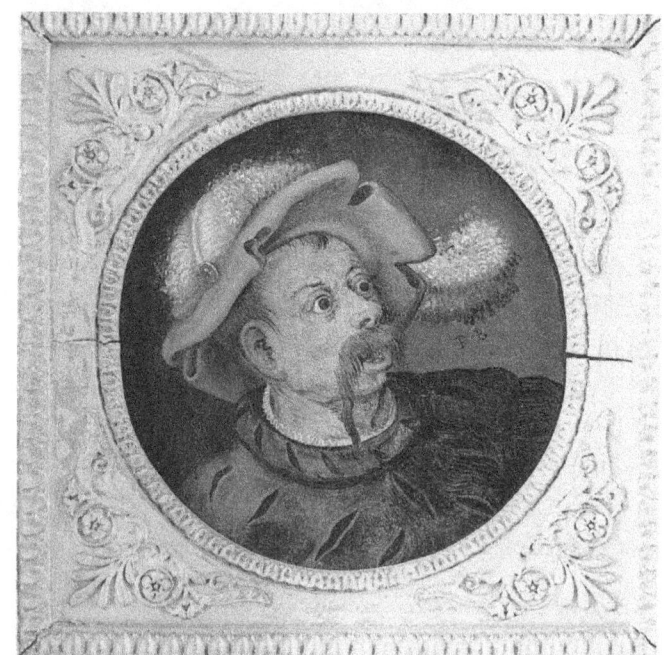

FIGURE 33.
After Pieter
Bruegel
the Elder, *Head
of a Lansquenet.*
Montpellier,
Musée Fabre.

by Bruegel on panel, designated simply as *klyne tronien,* or "little heads," were owned by Peter Paul Rubens; one of them may well have been the *Yawning Man.*[91] Studies of this kind were not unique to Bruegel. A number of small panels have come down to us from Frans Floris, the leading Italianate painter at Antwerp in Bruegel's day, depicting the single heads of men and women. They represent idealized types of youth and old age, although except for an occasional smile, they are considerably less animated in expression than the Brussels *Yawning Man,* and it has been plausibly suggested that Floris created them as models to be used by his workshop assistants.[92] Closer to Bruegel in spirit are such little panels as the *Old Woman Spinning* from the circle of Maerten van Cleve and the anonymous pair of pictures, *Smiling Peasant Couple,* all in private collections.[93]

If Bruegel made any *tronies,* as seems likely, they might have been intended as exercises for his own use, although he may have made them for collectors as well. Indeed, among the paintings owned by Michiel van der Heyden at Antwerp was a painting in tempera on linen of "a person with a big open mouth"; Claudia Goldstein has suggested that it depicted a yawning figure, somewhat like the *Yawning Man* attributed to Bruegel.[94] Moreover, an inventory made in 1589 of the estate of a deceased Antwerp resident, Maria le Martin, wife of Noel Boucq, lists "[e]en boermans ende drie boerinnen tronien" (one *tronie* of a peasant man and three of peasant women); no artist is given, so we can only speculate if they were by Bruegel.[95] In this connection may be noted two series of prints depicting heads of peasants. One contains a set of seventy-two heads on thirty-six sheets, generally thought to have been made by Jan and Lucas van Doetecum about 1564–65 and issued by an unknown Antwerp publisher (Fig. 34). The name of the designer is not given, but in the second and third states, issued respectively before 1652 by the Amsterdam print publisher Claes Jansz Visscher and in 1658 by one Alberts Elias of Weesp, Bruegel is credited as the "inventor."[96] Moreover, the second series, copies in reverse of a selection of twenty-four heads from the first set and first published in 1642, names not only Bruegel as the designer but none other than Adriaen Brouwer as the etcher.[97] The Doetecum

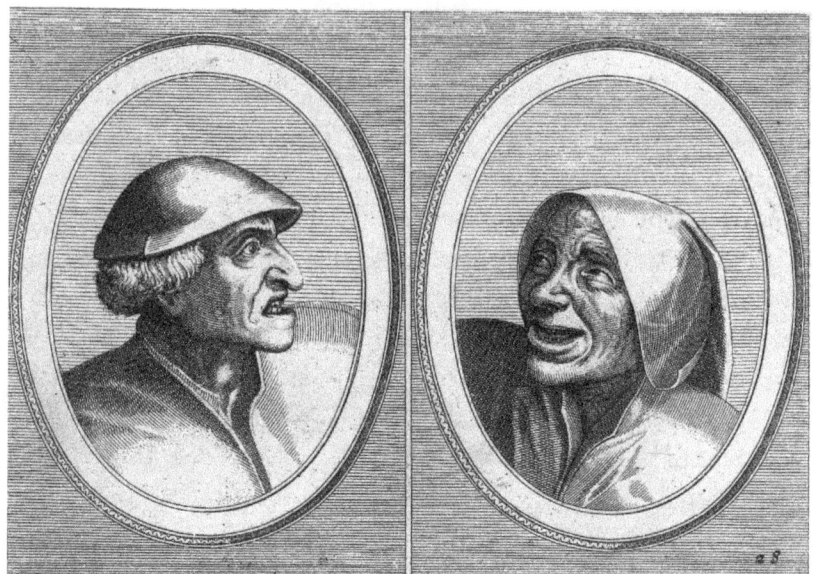

FIGURE 34. Jan or Lucas van Doetecum, *Peasant Man and Peasant Woman,* engraving, second state. Washington, D.C., National Gallery of Art, Andrew W. Mellon Fund.

series, moreover, may have been connected with Bruegel even earlier. A Leiden death inventory of 1588 lists "various peasant *tronies* done by Bruegel," probably prints, and in 1627 the art lover Arnoldus Buchelius noted in his journal that he had seen some old *tronies* in prints "which are ascribed to Bruegel."[98] Nevertheless, the heads in both series are difficult to relate to any of Bruegel's extant works, and if any of them actually go back to drawings from his hand is a matter of dispute.[99] But it is significant that such physiognomical studies were associated with Bruegel less than a generation after his death.

While the designer of the Doetecum prints remains a mystery, there is no doubt that Bruegel explored a wide range of expressive faces and gestures and, especially in his later work, often with considerably more subtlety than had his predecessors. Expressive figures can occur even on a small scale in his art. Van Mander singled out a *Massacre of the Innocents*

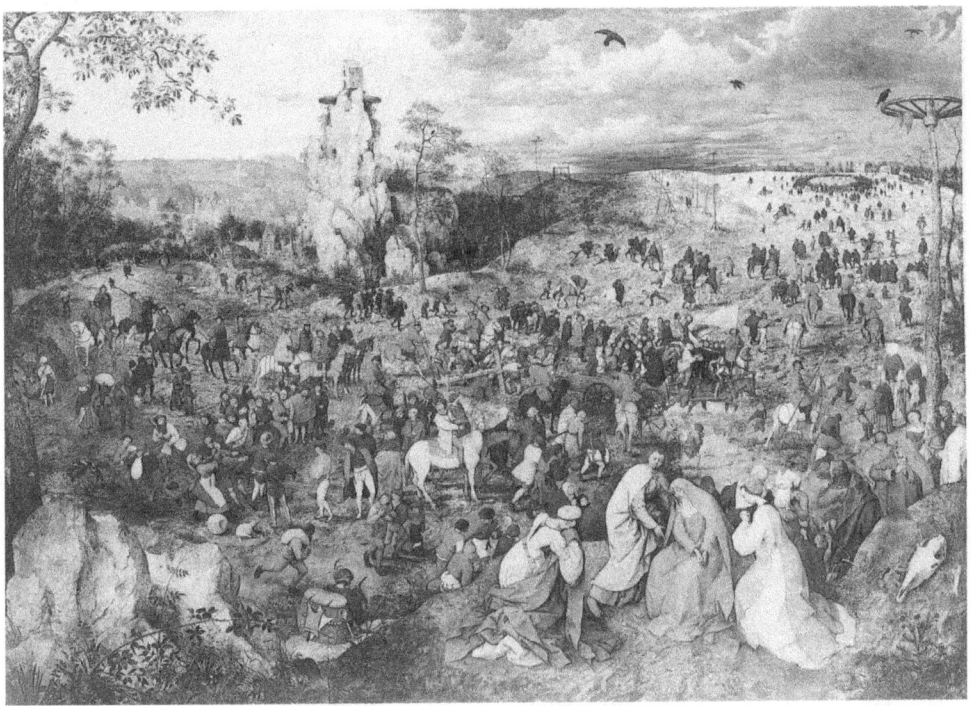

FIGURE 35.   Pieter Bruegel the Elder, *Christ Carrying the Cross,* 1564. Vienna, Kunsthistorisches Museum.

by Bruegel for its portrayal of human emotion, particularly the grief of a family begging one of the brutal soldiers to spare their child.[100] Van Mander most likely had in mind some version of that subject by Bruegel, of which the panel at Hampton Court, although damaged and disfigured with later overpainting, is usually thought the original.[101] Despite their diminutive scale, the villagers in this picture amply confirm Van Mander's judgment: they wring their hands and cry in despair or cluster around the royal herald in a futile plea for mercy. Among the crowd that streams after Christ in Bruegel's *Christ Carrying the Cross* of 1564 (Fig. 35), we encounter a whole gallery of faces expressing emotions ranging from simple curiosity to abject fear, the latter emotion vividly shown in the faces

of the two thieves (see Fig. 22), and, in case of the wife of Simon of
Cyrene, furious anger with the soldiers for pressing her husband into
service (Fig. 36). Such figures are in marked contrast to the group of
the holy women and St. John at lower right, who evoke the dignified
mourners of Rogier van der Weyden and other Netherlandish artists of
the fifteenth century.[102]

But Bruegel's most moving depiction of human emotions must surely
be his *Blind Leading the Blind* of 1568 (Fig. 37). What this image meant to
Bruegel's contemporaries is suggested by a New Year's poem by Anna
Bijns, published in a collection of her work in 1567, in which she appeals to
God to relieve the miserable condition of Holy Church and to enlighten
those who have been blinded and led astray from the true faith by false
prophets.[103] Bijns writes as a Catholic, of course, but Protestants would
have directed the same parable against Catholics and against other Protestant sects. Bruegel, however, transcends the requirements of a didactic parable not only, as we have been told, to distinguish among the various diseases of the eye afflicting these unfortunate creatures[104] but to
convey with great poignance their anguished, stumbling desperation. Indeed, if for modern viewers, these pathetic victims engage our sympathy
as real human beings, it is due to the artist's keen observation of reality.

But Bruegel also employed his physiognomical genius to achieve hap-
pier effects. A good example is the snoring peasant sprawled beneath a
tree in the *Wheat Harvest* (Figs. 38, 39); he is the perfect counterpart to
the *Yawning Man* in Brussels. Similarly, the leader of the rampaging housewives in Bruegel's *Dulle Griet* could well be the demented cousin of his
gaping woman in Munich (see Figs. 31, 71). Expressive heads also occur
in Bruegel's *Adoration of the Magi* in London (Fig. 40), dated 1564. This
subject had long been popular among the Antwerp painters, including
the Mannerist artist Jan van Doornicke and Doornicke's son-in-law,
Bruegel's own teacher Pieter Coecke van Aelst.[105] But while Coecke,
Doornicke, and other artists had usually endowed the three Magi and their
entourage with idealized features and the *statelyc*, or stately, demeanor appropriate to the occasion, Bruegel shows them as a rather disreputable

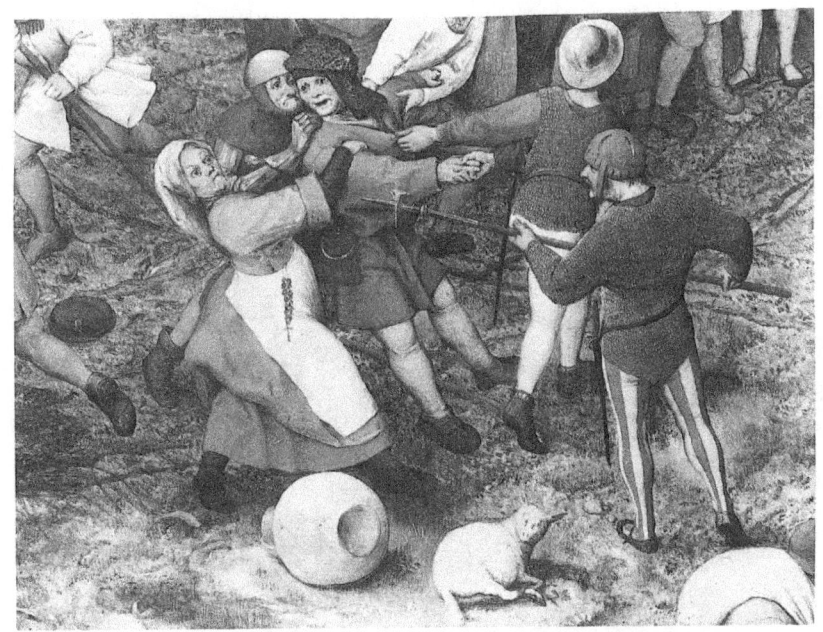

FIGURE 36. Detail of Fig. 35.

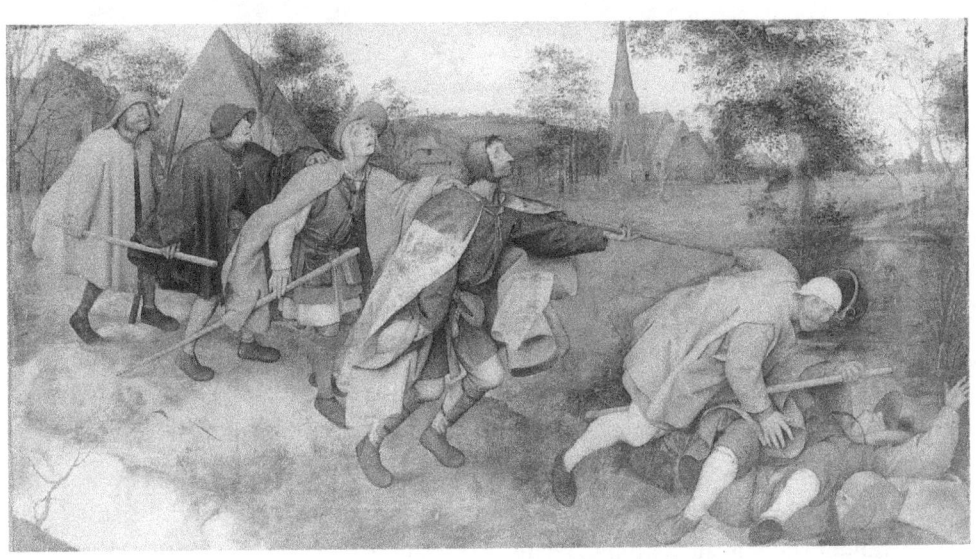

FIGURE 37. Pieter Bruegel the Elder, *The Blind Leading the Blind,* 1568. Naples, Museo di Capodimonte.

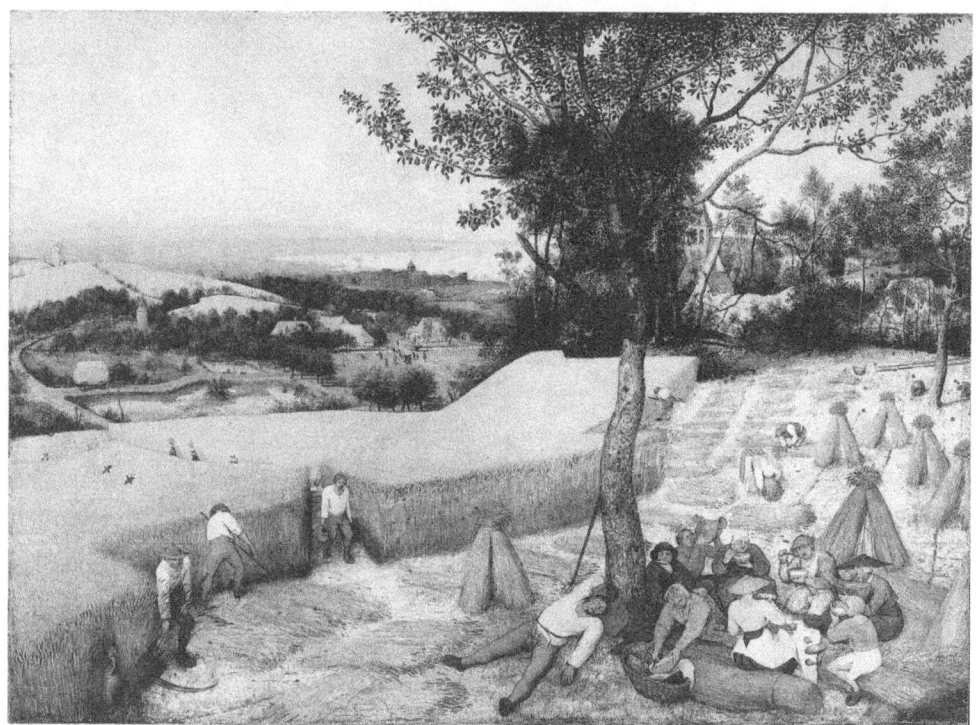

FIGURE 38. Pieter Bruegel the Elder, *Wheat Harvest*, 1568. New York, The Metropolitan Museum of Art, Rogers Fund, 1919 (19.164).

crew. One of the older kings, standing at the extreme left, submits his gift with an air of nose-lifted disdain; the soldier standing just behind the Virgin stares in pop-eyed wonder, awed perhaps not so much by the holy Infant as by the gifts he receives; while a bystander whispers urgently into Joseph's ear. Whatever motivated Bruegel to produce such an unorthodox version of a popular subject,[106] viewers likely would have been vastly amused by these comic figures and Bruegel's astonishing ability to render them in such lifelike terms.

This is not the place to explore in detail the development of Bruegel's physiognomical interests, but they culminate in the Detroit *Wedding Dance* (see Fig. 41) and above all in the two scenes of peasant revelry in

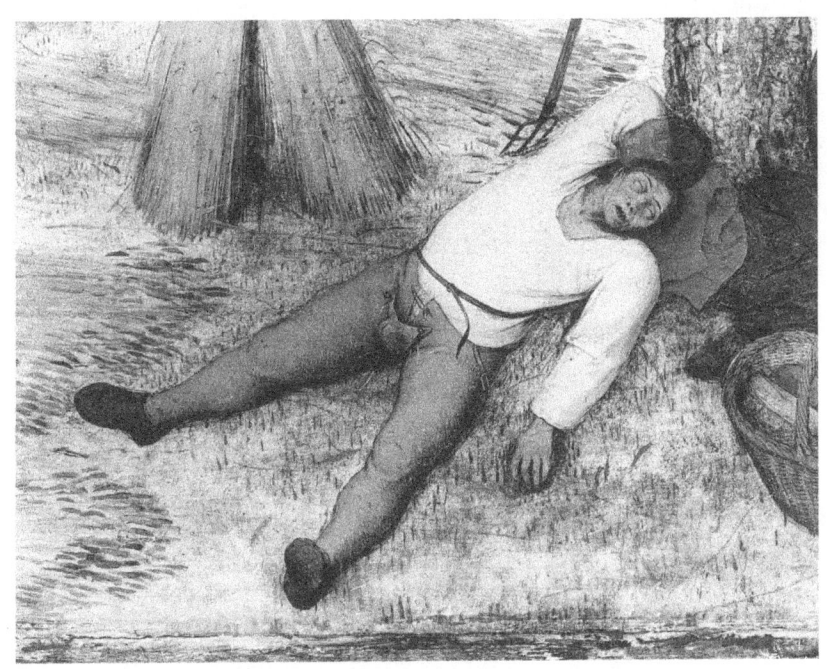

FIGURE 39. Detail of Fig. 38.

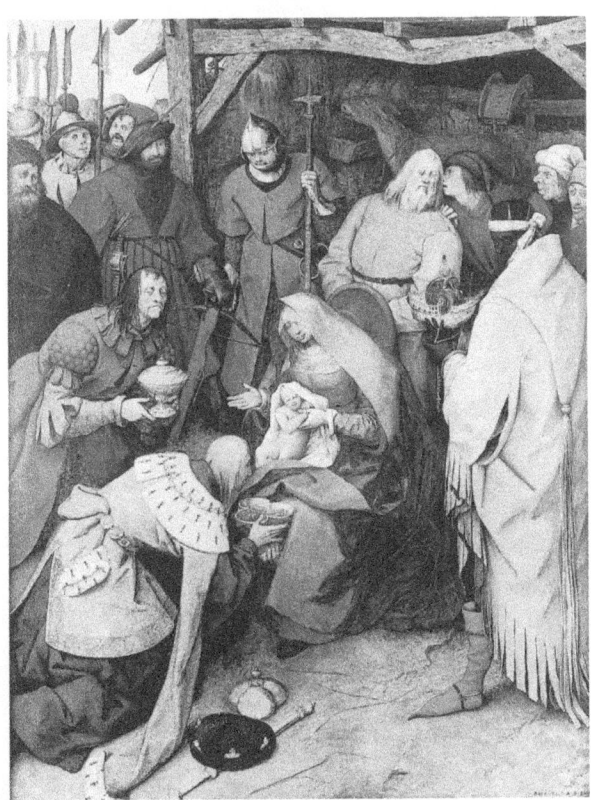

FIGURE 40.
Pieter Bruegel
the Elder,
*Adoration of the
Magi,* 1564.
London, The
National Gallery.

Vienna (see Figs. 42, 43). Unfortunately, scholars have mined these pictures so industriously for whatever nuggets of profundity they supposedly conceal beneath their vibrant surfaces that they have generally overlooked the marvels that Bruegel presents to the naked eye. This is indeed
a pity, for it is in these works that Bruegel shows the greatest diversity of
human types, ages, social interactions, and even personality, all realized
with an astonishing fidelity to nature. It is here that Bruegel's art of laughter finds its culmination. This will be evident, I think, when we consider
them in the original context in which they were most likely seen and enjoyed, a subject best approached through a forced auction that took place
in Antwerp just a few years after Bruegel's death.

CHAPTER THREE

A BANKRUPT AND HIS BRUEGELS

All is nought without money.

NETHERLANDISH PROVERB

He was . . . naturally subject to a malady that was called at that time "the lack
of money, pain incomparable."

RABELAIS

The forced auction that took place on 15 September 1572 involved the
household goods of a certain Jean Noirot, a former master of the mint
at Antwerp who had declared bankruptcy and thereafter had abandoned
his family. The documents related to this auction lay unnoticed in the
Antwerp archives until Luc Smolderen published them in 1995.[1] Probably due to the bad economic times caused by the escalating war between
the provinces of the Netherlands and their sovereign Philip II of Spain,
this auction yielded far less than had been expected, certainly not enough
to help Noirot's unfortunate wife and nine children. And it is doubtful
that Noirot's wife would have taken much comfort in the fact that the
two inventories made for the sale of her household effects constitute a
precious record of what must have been a major picture collection in
sixteenth-century Antwerp. Noirot owned about fifty paintings. This in
itself was not unusual: in a survey of 291 estate inventories made in Antwerp in the sixteenth century, Greet Stappaerts found twenty-five in-

ventories with more than thirty paintings, the largest containing sixty.[2] But although the estate inventories seldom identify the artists for the works listed, Noirot's includes the artists' names for a fair number of his pictures. He owned works by the leading Flemish painters of the day, among them five pictures by Pieter Bruegel the Elder: a winter landscape, two paintings of peasant weddings, and two peasant kermis scenes.[3] Four of Noirot's Bruegels, the winter landscape and three paintings of the peasant revels—the two wedding scenes and one of the kermis pictures—were hung in a room listed as *d'achter eetkamerken*, literally "the small back dining room,"[4] where they shared space on the walls with other paintings, among them portraits of Noirot and his family and a painting of the Virgin Mary.[5] Noirot's fifth Bruegel painting, a *Peasant Kermis*, was placed in an upper chamber, along with a *Peasant Wedding* attributed to Hieronymus Bosch. The attribution of this last picture to Bosch is uncertain, as he is not known to have painted any peasant scenes,[6] but there can be little doubt concerning the paintings ascribed to Bruegel. Bruegel had died in August 1569, only three years before this auction, so these were very likely genuine pictures from his own hand and not copies of the sort peddled by illegal art dealers, the subject of a city ordinance issued a few years later.[7] Moreover, one of the inventories of Noirot's household effects was taken in the presence of his wife and several close associates, who presumably would have known the circumstances under which these paintings were acquired.[8] And although we cannot with any certainty identify the peasant scenes with the *Wedding Dance* in Detroit or the two peasant scenes in Vienna (Figs. 41–43), they were most likely very similar.

Noirot seems to have had one of the largest collections of Bruegel's paintings at this time, and his choice of Bruegel subjects is especially interesting, since all but one of these paintings represented peasant revels. In addition to the four Bruegels and the "Bosch," he also apparently owned two other pictures of peasant weddings for which no artist is given.[9] This pronounced taste for rustic revels may be unique for the period: in the almost three hundred estate inventories in sixteenth-century Antwerp that scholars have examined, only twenty-five peasant

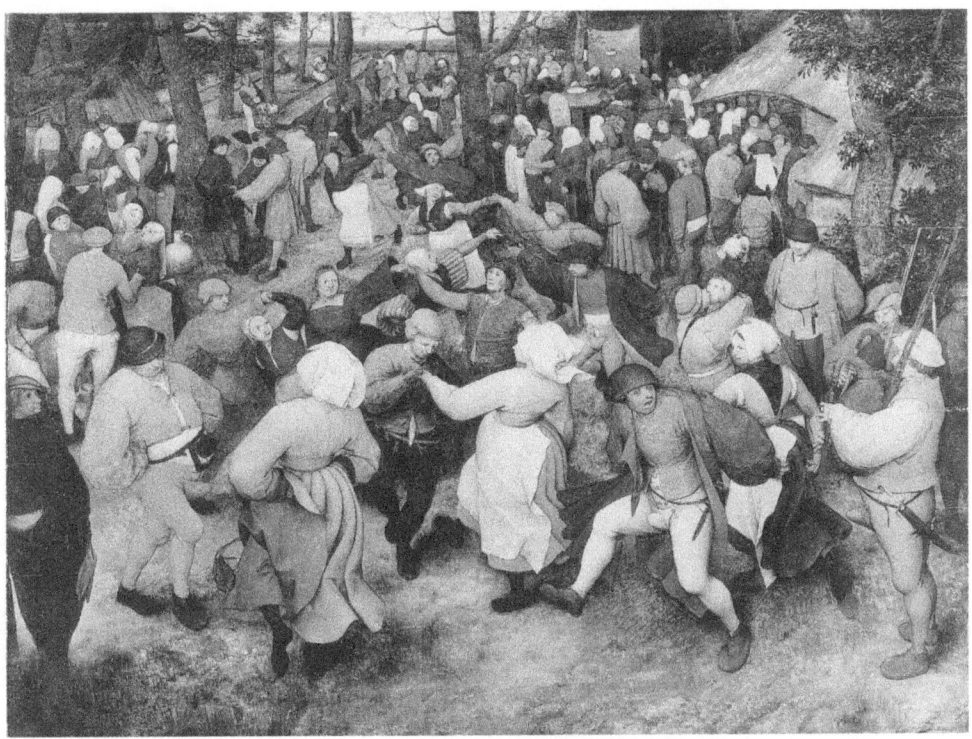

FIGURE 41. Pieter Bruegel the Elder, *Peasant Wedding Dance*, 1566. The Detroit Institute of Arts, City of Detroit Purchase.

scenes are recorded, among which are three "peasant dances," three "peasant kermises," and five "peasant weddings."[10] One of these pictures, a "peasant wedding on linen," was in the collection of Joris Veselaer, Noirot's colleague at the mint,[11] but even so, Noirot's taste for peasant subjects was unusual and thus raises some interesting issues that may be approached by asking this question: why did he hang three of his Bruegel peasant scenes in his dining room?

Margaret Sullivan, who published a monograph on Bruegel's two paintings in Vienna in 1994—a year, incidentally, before the publication of Noirot's auction records—offers one answer to this question.[12] She proposes that the Vienna panels were painted for a patron in the circle of

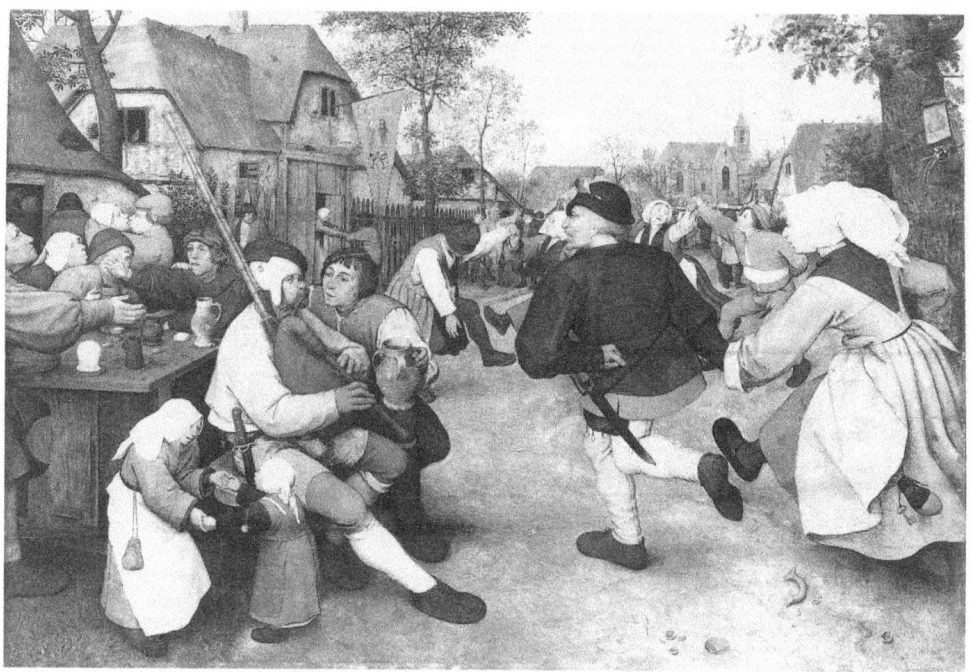

FIGURE 42. Pieter Bruegel the Elder, *Peasant Kermis.* Vienna, Kunsthistorisches Museum.

Christophe Plantin and Abraham Ortelius, which included many classical scholars engaged in editing the ancient Greek and Latin texts that
Plantin published. Members of this scholarly circle, sharing a philosophy
of life, aimed "to achieve serenity through reason and self-restraint,"as
Sullivan says, partly paraphrasing Ortelius, by "devoting themselves to
work, friendship, studying the 'whole of the Universe,' and meditating
on its Creator."[13] Their profound knowledge of classical literature, and
the literature of their own time that it inspired, Sullivan tells us, would
have led them to respond to Bruegel's rustic revels as allegories of human folly, in which figural poses, details of costumes, and the like were
interpreted according to various ancient texts. According to Ortelius,
Bruegel "depicted many things that cannot be painted" and "often gives
something beneath what he paints." Sullivan understands these words of

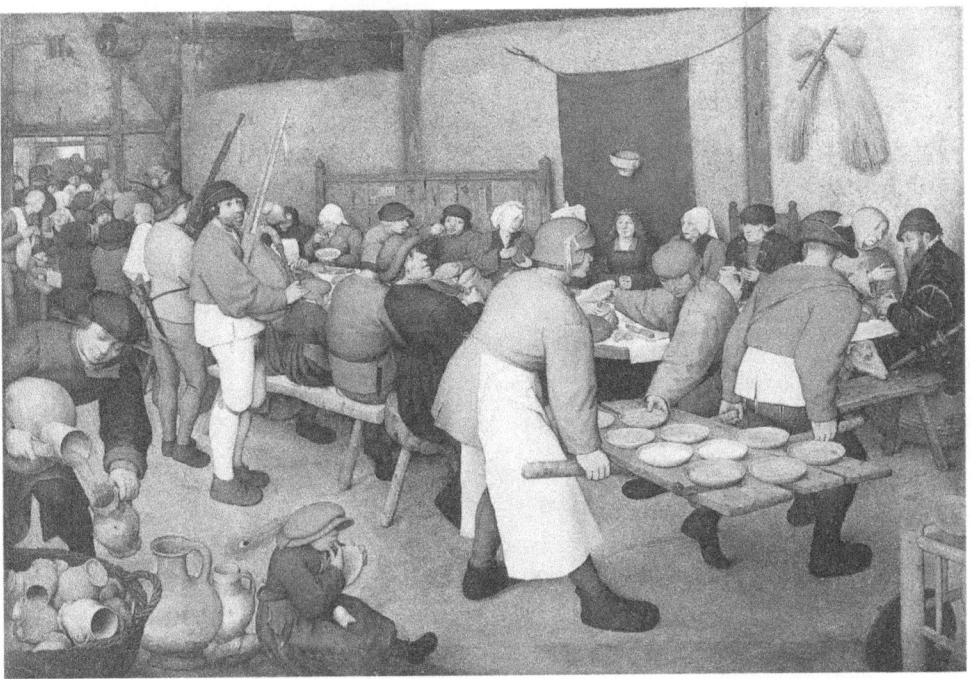

FIGURE 43. Pieter Bruegel the Elder, *Peasant Wedding Feast*. Vienna, Kunsthistorisches Museum.

Ortelius, not as tributes to Bruegel's realism and depiction of human expression, but as "a clear statement that Bruegel's friends and associates assumed there was a great deal of meaning inherent in the works [of the artist]."[14] That precise "meaning" for Sullivan can be conveyed by a few examples from her reading of the *Kermis* (Fig. 42). The male dancer entering from the right, wearing what Sullivan characterizes as unusually large shoes, would have recalled not only the appearance of contemporary peasants but also certain classical proverbs and quotations from Lucian and Horace that use the "large shoe" to signify the man who lives beyond his means; Bruegel's male peasant also resembles the blustering, bullying bailiff described by Ausonius in his *Espistles*. The peasant's black coat, the apparently contorted position of his legs, and the profile view of his face that allows us to see only one eye are among the details of this figure that mark him as a fool or worse.[15] His female companion, according to Sullivan, "resembles all the old libidinous women in ancient literature from Plautus and Menander to Horace . . . and Juvenal."[16] The lining of her skirt is yellow, the color that identified the prostitute in ancient drama and thus proclaims her questionable moral character.[17] Scarcely less sinful are the children and adolescents. Of the two girls dancing near the bagpiper (see Fig. 58), the elder child wears clothes that are too large for her: the skirt of her gown has been shortened (indicated by the visible hemline), and the sleeves are deeply folded back; her shoes and apron are equally oversize. These and other aspects of the figure lead Sullivan to conclude that she is "on the threshold of joining the elders in 'Folly's dance.'"[18] We may also deduce the developing moral character of her younger companion from the barely visible yellow lining of her under-skirt: it is "a pale echo of the bold yellow lining of the dress of the old fe-male dancer. . . . Will it become brighter and be displayed more promi-nently as she learns the grown-up dance?"[19] The humanists of the time were very much aware of "the importance of education and adult mod-els," Sullivan tells us, clinching her argument with quotations on the cor-ruption of children by the folly of their elders, taken from not only Se-bastian Brant and Erasmus but also Juvenal, Horace, and Varro.[20] Sullivan imagines Plantin and his colleagues present at a simple meal, looking at Bruegel's pictures,[21] and we in turn may imagine the host and his guests tossing out Greek and Latin proverbs and other quotations as they dili-gently examine each detail. As Sullivan assures us in another context, "When intelligent talk was essential for a dinner party worthy of the an-cients, a painting that could stimulate this kind of conversation was a valu-able asset for host and guests alike."[22] And if the members of this sober company were roused to laughter, it could thus only have been a heart-less, derisive laughter, as they contemplated Bruegel's peasant revels de-picting, we are told by Sullivan concerning the *Kermis*, "the careless, pa-gan life of people who are Christians in name only, the fools of the world about to be overtaken by death and time."[23] In particular, Ortelius and his friends would have appreciated Bruegel's rustic revels as commentaries on the shortcomings of their own countrymen.[24]

Sullivan gives us a valuable account of Antwerp's intelligentsia during Bruegel's lifetime,[25] and her deciphering of the details of Bruegel's two pictures is buttressed at every point by a wealth of texts and quite often with relevant images. But we are never quite certain if Sullivan understands this interpretation to have been deliberately contrived by the artist or if it existed only in the minds of his learned audience.[26] If the former, then Bruegel would presumably have been "a highbrow urban intellectual," as Herman Roodenburg puts it,[27] as well versed in classical literature as Ortelius and his colleagues. Conversely, he could have received detailed instructions from one of his patrons while he was executing these two paintings. Our confusion on this point is further complicated by Sullivan's suggestion that Bruegel infused the values of his learned associates even into paintings intended for patrons outside Ortelius's immediate circle, a suggestion that defies corroboration.[28] But Sullivan's thesis raises more serious problems. It fails to take into sufficient account not only what we know of Bruegel's actual patrons but also what we know of how people, including Ortelius, as we shall see, actually encountered the peasantry on festive occasions. Sullivan's picture of mealtime philosophizing, finally, is not the only, or perhaps not even the most common, way in which people conducted themselves on such occasions.

Let us begin with the question of patronage. Except for Ortelius, we do not know if anyone in Antwerp's scholarly circles actually owned any of Bruegel's paintings. This is true even of Hieronymus Cock, who published so many of his drawings, and Hans Franckaert, merchant and member of the Antwerp Violieren, who, according to Van Mander, was Bruegel's great friend. Franckaert seems to have been a merchant, possibly a dealer in small German wares, but we otherwise know little about him.[29] Bruegel's known patrons, on the contrary, seem to have been wealthy men who were prominent in public life. They included Cardinal Granvelle, archbishop of Malines and first councillor of Margaret of Parma, regent and half sister of Philip II. Granvelle possessed the *Flight into Egypt* now in London and several other pictures by Bruegel, most likely purchased before he was forced to leave the Netherlands in 1564.[30] Another patron was Niclaes Jonghelinck, a very well-to-do Antwerp businessman and receiver of the maritime tolls for the province of Zeeland. Jonghelinck owned one of the largest painting collections of the period.[31] Among them were perhaps as many as sixteen paintings that Jonghelinck installed in his suburban house, including the *Labors of the Months* of 1565, a *Tower of Babel*, and most likely the *Christ Carrying the Cross* of 1564, the artist's largest surviving picture.[32] To these patrons we may now add Jean Noirot, who in more prosperous days had acquired the five paintings by Bruegel.

As men of wealth, moreover, Granvelle, Jonghelinck, Noirot, and others of their class could easily have afforded Bruegel's most elaborate, sumptuous productions.[33] We have little evidence, of course, as to the prices that Bruegel's pictures commanded in his lifetime. Nevertheless, it must be kept in mind that Bruegel was no Herri Bles, a painter of the previous generation, whose workshop churned out scores of landscapes that copied or varied a few stock compositions (with figures occasionally added by more capable artists) and executed in an often slapdash fashion that facilitated their quick production and allowed them to be sold cheaply at home and abroad.[34] Such paintings were *dosijn werck*, roughly "works by the dozen," a contemporary term that seems to have been applied to cheaply and quickly produced pictures.[35] In contrast, Bruegel seems not to have had much of a workshop, if any; only a few surviving replicas of his paintings, the *Fall of Icarus, Massacre of the Innocents*, and *Sermon of St. John the Baptist*, may have originated in his lifetime.[36] And quite unlike the bulk of Bles's production, Bruegel's paintings were generally what we would now call "labor intensive," carefully executed in great detail. This is true even of such comparatively small panels as the *Suicide of Saul* of 1562, as well as of the more broadly painted *Labors of the Months*, which were apparently completed in the space of one year.[37]

That Bruegel's paintings commanded comparatively high prices is suggested by the valuations that were assigned to the pictures in Noirot's house. The most expensive picture, probably a *Diana and Acteon*—the artist is not given but Frans Floris is a likely candidate[38]—was valued at 151 guilders, followed by two paintings by Bruegel, a *Peasant Wedding* valued at 80 guilders and a *Peasant Kermis* at 42 guilders. The wording of these two Bruegel entries indicates that both pictures were painted in oils, one *op doeck*, that is, on cloth, probably linen, and the other support not designated, but possibly a wooden panel since it was given the higher value. The three other Bruegel paintings are described as simply *op doeck*, and since oil is not specified, the medium was most probably a water-based tempera, traditionally a cheaper medium. The majority of the peasant scenes that Stappaerts found in the Antwerp estate inventories were said to be painted on cloth, but whether in oil or tempera is generally unclear.[39] In Bruegel's case, his three other paintings on linen were evaluated at much lower prices, about 27–28 guilders each. Thus, two of Noirot's Bruegels were among his more costly pictures (did their purchase contribute to his impoverishment?) and might well have been as large and as sumptuous as the pictures now in Vienna and Detroit. The Vienna and Detroit paintings may be compared with the only extant picture that we know was owned by a personal friend of Bruegel: the *Death of the Virgin* in the possession of Abraham Ortelius, who, as we have seen, had it copied in an engraving (see Fig. 1).[40] Beautifully painted in grisaille on panel, it is fairly small (about 14½ by 22 inches), considerably more modest than Bruegel's three peasant scenes. Ortelius was an eminently successful cartographer, but his finances remained on a precarious footing until after the publication of his famous atlas, the *Theatrum orbis terrarum* of 1570.[41] It is possible, of course, that the *Death of the Virgin* was not commissioned but received as a gift from the artist.[42]

   In any case, the audience for Bruegel's paintings of rustic revels must be sought, not so much among the scholars and cartographers who may well have been Bruegel's friends, but among the artist's known patrons and their colleagues, merchants and government officials. Of these three men, Cardinal Granvelle was perhaps the most cultivated, a humanist well versed in ancient literature who also defended the work of Erasmus against the theologians of the University of Louvain.[43] Jonghelinck and Noirot were probably familiar with the classics, since their collections included mythological paintings.[44] Indeed, as Ethan Matt Kavaler has demonstrated, the contacts between Antwerp's artistic and intellectual circles and the merchants and government officials of the period were frequent and often close.[45] Cock dedicated several prints and print series to Granvelle and published a set of prints after the *Labors of Hercules* series that Frans Floris had painted for Jonghelinck.[46] Plantin, for his part, sold books to Granvelle, who in turn, after he had left the Netherlands, financially supported some of Plantin's enterprises and helped him publish the Polyglot Bible.[47] Plantin's scholars sometimes dedicated their editions of the classics to one or another Antwerp magnate or government official, while the wealthy and cultured Antwerp merchant Gillis Hooftman substantially underwrote the publication of Ortelius's *Theatrum orbis terrarum* in 1570.[48]

But as well educated as Granvelle, Jonghelinck, Noirot, and their colleagues may have been, it is doubtful that they possessed the profound knowledge of Greek and Roman literature that Sullivan ascribes, and probably correctly, to the circle of scholars around Plantin and Ortelius. As men of the world, Bruegel's known patrons were undoubtedly less concerned with the sort of philosophic life associated by Sullivan with Ortelius and his humanist circle than with the luxurious display of their wealth and social standing, in which the artist's paintings would have played an important role.[49] Thus it is the attitudes of this latter group toward the peasants and toward country life in general that we must now examine.

CHAPTER FOUR

RUSTIC REVELS

Nothing divides burgher and peasant other than the [city] wall.

JOHANNES AGRICOLA, 1529

How would Jean Noirot, Niclaes Jonghelinck, Cardinal Granvelle, and their peers have responded to Bruegel's peasant revels? Did they view them as visual sermons, as it were, on human folly? We cannot exclude such a possibility, since the peasants had traditionally been mocked in literature and drama for their loutish, uncouth ways, and their antics formed the plot of many a *rederijker* farce.[1] The peasant couple Bruegel contributed to Aert Molckeman's mural was equally uncouth, as we have seen.[2] Peasant festivities were also often criticized in real life for their drunkenness and violence; as a speaker in Erasmus's *Colloquies* says of an upcoming kermis: "Tomorrow this entire village will ring with carousings, dances, games, quarrels, and fights."[3]

The citizens of Antwerp, however, had long encountered peasants and their celebrations on what were essentially positive occasions.[4] We know that the city folk made excursions into the surrounding countryside on Sundays and holidays; indeed, one illustration in a costume book first published at Antwerp in 1577 shows the appropriate dress for a "Mulier Antwerpiana extra muros prodeambulans" (lady of Antwerp walking outside the walls of the city).[5] Once in the country, city people strolled, refreshed themselves with beer at the country inns—the tax on beer was

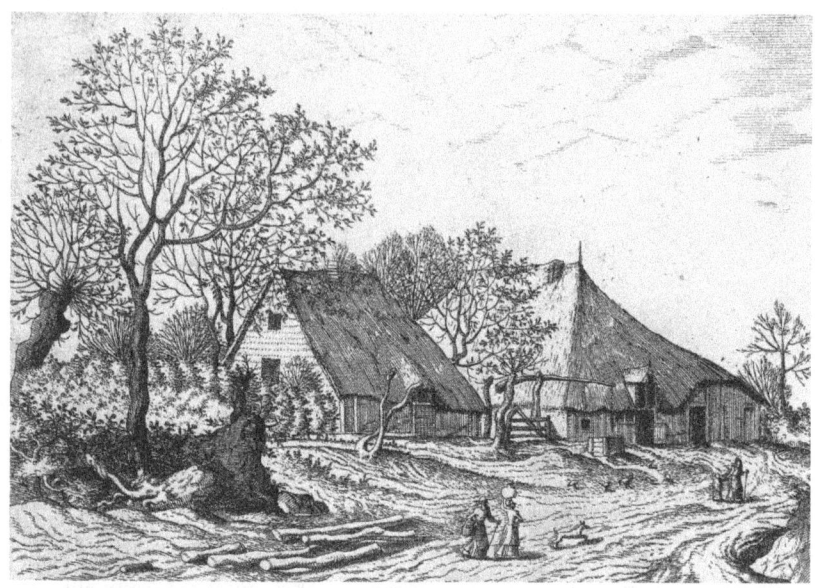

FIGURE 44.   Jan or Lucas van Doetecum, after Joos van Liere(?), Landscape, from the *Small Landscapes,* first series, 1559, engraving and etching. Amsterdam, Rijksmuseum.

lower there than in the city—and attended village festivals.[6] This world of bucolic peace and holiday leisure is superbly evoked in the two sets of the so-called *Small Landscapes* issued by Hieronymus Cock in 1559 and 1561 respectively (Figs. 44, 45), in which the hardworking farmers of real life have for the most part been replaced by people who walk or loiter along the country lanes or pause for a bit of gossip.[7]

The more affluent citizens of Antwerp themselves had country places, where they often spent holidays or the summer months.[8] They included Cornelis de Schott, member of a prominent Antwerp family, and the English factor Richard Clough.[9] The Antwerp government official Michiel van der Heyden enjoyed the rustic life at Crauwels, his sumptuous estate not far from Antwerp. Entrepreneurs soon exploited this desire for country places.[10] One of them, Gilbert van Schoonbeke, in 1547 bought the Goede ter Beke, a great tract of land just south of Antwerp, which

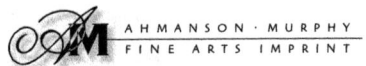

AHMANSON · MURPHY
FINE ARTS IMPRINT

THE AHMANSON FOUNDATION
has endowed this imprint
to honor the memory of
FRANKLIN D. MURPHY
who for half a century
served arts and letters,
beauty and learning, in
equal measure by shaping
with a brilliant devotion
those institutions upon
which they rely.

The publisher gratefully acknowledges the generous
contributions to this book provided by the Samuel H. Kress
Foundation and by the Art Endowment Fund of the
University of California Press Foundation, which is supported
by a major gift from the Ahmanson Foundation.

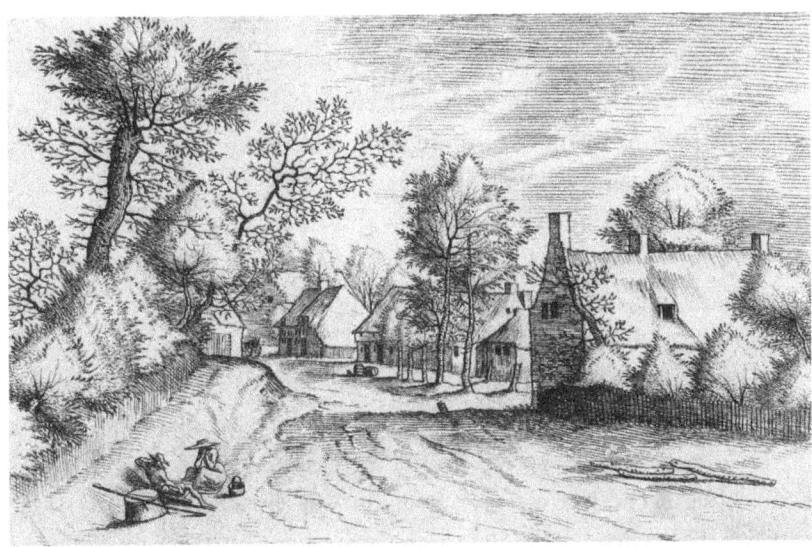

FIGURE 45.   Jan or Lucas van Doetecum, after Joos van Liere(?), Landscape, from the *Small Landscapes,* second series, 1561, engraving and etching. Washington, D.C., National Gallery of Art, Rosenwald Collection.

he subdivided into smaller but still sizable plots for country estates. Purchasers of these plots had to maintain the rural character of the area, for example, by planting a row of trees along the road before their houses.[11] Niclaes Jonghelinck purchased one plot here for his suburban villa, which he called the Jonghelinckshof.[12] And while Cardinal Granvelle kept his chief residence in Brussels, he not only owned La Fontaine, an imposing edifice with towers and a moat in the nearby village of Sint-Joost-ten-Node, but also built a mansion at Cantecroix in the vicinity of Antwerp.[13] It has been estimated that between 1540 and 1600 at least 250 country residences existed within a twenty-kilometer radius of Antwerp.[14] As it happens, Jean Noirot did not own a country house, but he and his family very likely enjoyed the country amenities as guests of people who did, among them, perhaps, Joris Veselaer, his colleague at the mint, and Niclaes Jonghelinck, whose brother Thomas was a master of the mint.[15]

The designations of these country places in contemporary records as *hof van plaisance* ("pleasure house" or "pleasure garden") and *speelhuys* (literally, "playhouse") suggest that they were indeed retreats, providing escape for their owners from the workaday world of Antwerp.[16] But the possession of one or more of these villas also demonstrated the wealth and prestige of their owners.[17] Some of the wealthiest citizens of Antwerp even acquired feudal seigneuries and titles with their country estates.[18] One was Antoon van Straelen, who for many years filled various high offices in the Antwerp city government, including that of burgomaster, and as "prince" of the prestigious Violieren of Antwerp, organized the famous *landjuweel* of 1561. He also became *heer*, or lord, of the seigneuries of Merksem and Dambrugge when he purchased these two "lovely villages near Antwerp," as they are described by a contemporary, Lodovico Guicciardini; an inscription on Van Straelen's portrait medal by Jacques Jonghelinck reads "Antoni A Straleus de Mercxem et Dambrugge."[19] We do not know how much Van Straelen involved himself in the daily operation of his estates, but it may be significant that when Plantin published his Netherlandish translation of Charles Estienne's famous manual on farming, *L'agriculture et maison rustique* (Agriculture and the country house), two years after its initial publication in Paris in 1564, he dedicated it to Van Straelen, "Lord of Mercsem, etc., Knight."[20]

Another titled landowner was Hendrik van Berchem, who purchased the seigneury of Berchem in 1555; in 1566 he subdivided a section of it, some pastureland traditionally known as the Papenmoer (Priests' Moor), into lots on which wealthy Antwerpeners, including the gentleman-painter Cornelis van Dalem, could build their country houses.[21] Jacob van Hencxthoven, a master of the mint and one of the evaluators of Noirot's picture collection, was *heer* of Hemiksem, a village not far south of Antwerp.[22] It may well have been this fashion for buying up manorial properties, incidentally, that inspired the Dutch theologian and writer Dirck Volckertsz Coornhert to comment rather acidly about rich commoners who strive to emulate the nobility, avid for titles and inventing their own coats of arms.[23] The three Schetz brothers, Melchior, Balthazar, and Caspar (or Gaspar), scions of a well-to-do Antwerp merchant family, were especially zealous in acquiring seigneuries and the titles that came with them. The eldest, Gaspar, elevated in 1564 to treasurer general of the Netherlands, was *heer* of Grobbendonck (or Grobbendoncq), a seigneury he inherited from his father, who had purchased it in 1545. Through purchases of his own, Caspar was also the *heer* of Meghen, Heyst, and the village of Hingene, in Flanders.²⁴ As for Melchior, Guicciardini describes him as "Seigneur of Rumpst, of Willebroeck, & other adjoining villages."²⁵

Of particular interest is the village of Hoboken, situated just outside the gates of Antwerp and famous for its three annual festivals. One of them is depicted in the *Hoboken Kermis*, a print published in 1559 (Fig. 46) after a drawing by Bruegel; the inscription below tells us in part that "the peasants rejoice in such feasts, to dance and jump and to drink themselves as drunk as beasts."²⁶ Fluttering above the inn at lower right is a banner inscribed "Dit is de Gulde van hoboken" (This is the Guild of Hoboken); its crossed arrows identify the guild as that of the Handbow Archers, which celebrated its feast on the day after Pentecost, generally in May.²⁷ In the middle distance a procession enters the village church, while the rest of the picture is given over to the festivities that follow, including games, dancing, and drinking, as well as a performance in progress, perhaps by the local *rederijker* chamber, on an open-air stage in the background. A fool strolls by in the foreground, holding two children by the hand.²⁸ The other two festivals commemorated the Birth of the Virgin (3 May), patron of the parish church, and the Discovery of the True Cross (8 September).²⁹

As it happens, Bruegel's *Hoboken Kermis* was issued by Bartholomeus de Mompere, who was manager of the *schilderspand* in these years and must have had a good notion of what would appeal to the public.³⁰ In this case he chose well, for Hoboken seems to have been a favorite spot for visitors from Antwerp, and not only for its three festivals. This is suggested by the mock "prognostications," pamphlets of social satire in the form of astrological New Year's predictions, that have survived from the years 1560–62. They assure their readers that in the spring the roads to Hobo-

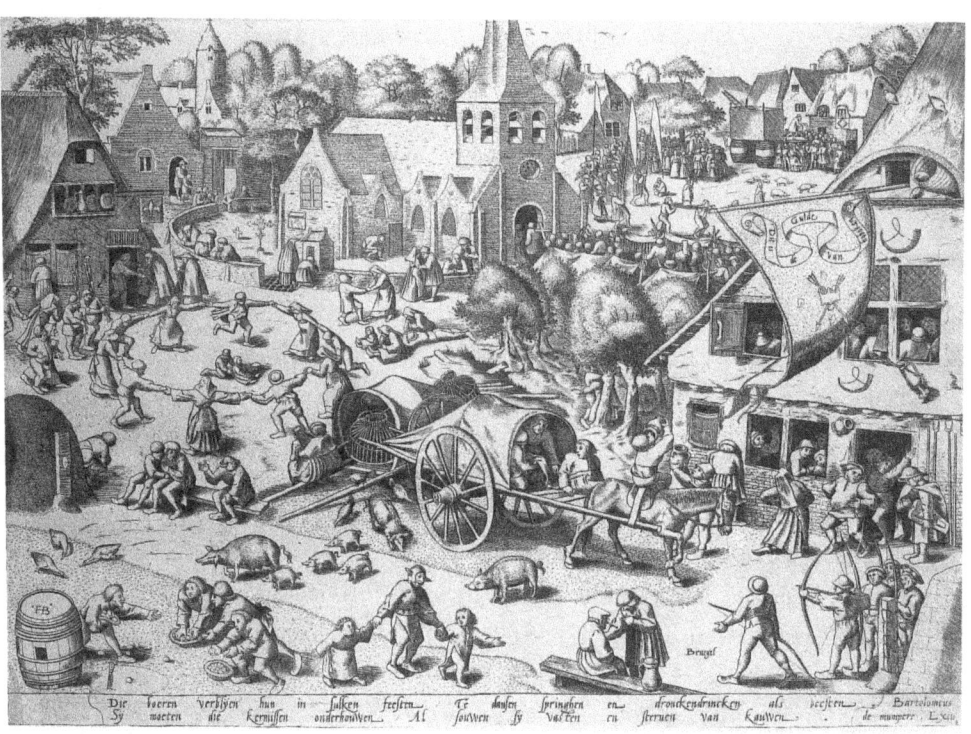

FIGURE 46. Frans Hogenberg, after Pieter Bruegel the Elder, *Hoboken Kermis,* 1559, engraving. Washington, D.C., National Gallery of Art, Rosenwald Collection.

ken will be crowded with lovers and ladies of easy virtue, and that in May many babies will be made.[31] But in spite of Hoboken's rather dubious reputation, it seems to have been a popular place for the country retreats of the upper classes as well; these included the Kasteel van Broydenborg, founded in the early sixteenth century, and Zorgvliet (literally, Flee care), established by the merchant Jean Plaquet in 1560.[32] Another country house in Hoboken was owned by the Florentine businessman and writer Lodovico Guicciardini, whose *Description de tout de le Païs-Bas* (Description of all the Low Lands), first published by Christophe Plantin in 1567, gives us a vivid picture of the Netherlands on the eve of the Eighty Years' War.[33]

Hendrik van Berchem had owned a *hof* nearby before he acquired the seigneury of Berchem.[34] The manor of Hoboken had originally belonged to William of Nassau (later known as William the Silent), but along with Rumpst, Willebroeck, and several other manors, was purchased by Melchior Schetz in 1559; in the following year Melchior transferred Hoboken to his brother Balthazar.[35]

As with the other manors in the Netherlands, the acquisition of Hoboken conferred responsibilities as well as honors. Thus, Balthazar took possession of Hoboken in a solemn "inauguration" in which he swore to uphold the privileges and rights of the villagers and to administer justice impartially, "So help me God and all his saints." In turn, the villagers promised that they would serve their lord with the same loyalty and obedience with which they had served his predecessors.[36] Balthazar may well have commissioned a painting to commemorate this occasion; at least Van Mander describes a picture by Gillis Mostaert, now unfortunately lost, that showed the Schetz brothers being "received very ceremoniously by the peasants of Hoboken."[37] How common such ceremonies were would be difficult to say, but the Antwerp panel maker Godevaert van Haecht records in his journal that when Antoon van Straelen was formally installed as lord of Merksem and Dambrugge on 22 September 1565, the occasion was dignified by a procession on horseback to these manors; it comprised many guilds, archers' companies, and "nations" (associations of foreign merchants), including almost all the Germans, to honor him as "prince" of the Violieren, whose members were also in attendance; all this occurred, Van Haecht adds, in foul weather.[38]

Hoboken, of course, was the very village whose inhabitants had been stigmatized in Bruegel's *Hoboken Kermis* as getting "as drunk as beasts." Is it possible that Bruegel's contemporaries did not take this judgment as seriously as modern scholars do? In any event, Balthazar Schetz was certainly not ashamed to proclaim his association with his newly acquired manor. In his portrait etched by Lambert Sauvius in 1561, the inscription proudly identifies Balthazar as "Lord of Hoboken," the very title by which he is identified by Guicciardini.[39] Schetz also augmented Hoboken's territories by acquiring adjacent properties; among them was the Kasteel van Berchem, the estate formerly owned by Hendrik van Berchem, whose castle Schetz expanded.[40] Like most of his fellow *heren*, Balthazar probably governed Hoboken through his deputies,[41] but he and Melchior apparently took their seigneurial responsibilities very seriously. In 1562 they made over the local beer and wine taxes to the village, and in the following year the local brewers received the right to pay only one-half of the taxes that were levied in Antwerp, while citizens of Antwerp were allowed to come to Hoboken to drink any time they wished.[42] The new lords of Hoboken also patronized the local kermises; in 1565, for example, Balthazar Schetz invited seventy guests from Antwerp to spend three days in the village on the occasion of a festival.[43]

The Schetz brothers were not alone in their paternalistic treatment of their manor. The clearest evidence comes from the journal of the Sire de Gouberville, a Norman squire living in this period, who describes in detail how closely he associated with the peasants on his estate, helping them when they were sick or in debt and attending their weddings and baptisms.[44] It is true that Gouberville resided permanently on his land, while the Netherlandish *heren* spent only certain holidays and perhaps the summer months on their manors. Nevertheless, other Netherlandish landlords subsidized the local guilds and *rederijker* chambers, and at least one family, the lords of Beaufoorde, belonged to the local archers' guild of their manor, endowing it with numerous gifts and serving as its honorary head or "king."[45] A wealthy Antwerp merchant of the next generation, Martin della Faille, contributed money to the parish church of Vichte, a village that he owned.[46]

We can imagine Balthazar and Melchior presiding over one of their rustic celebrations very much as we see in a picture painted by Jacob Grimmer in 1583, with figures by Gillis Mostaert (Fig. 47).[47] Whether or not depicting an actual place, it vividly represents an event that must have occurred frequently, even after 1566, when Antwerp and its environs were caught up in the beginnings of the Eighty Years' War. According to Godevaert van Haecht, as early as 1567 the villages around Antwerp were affected

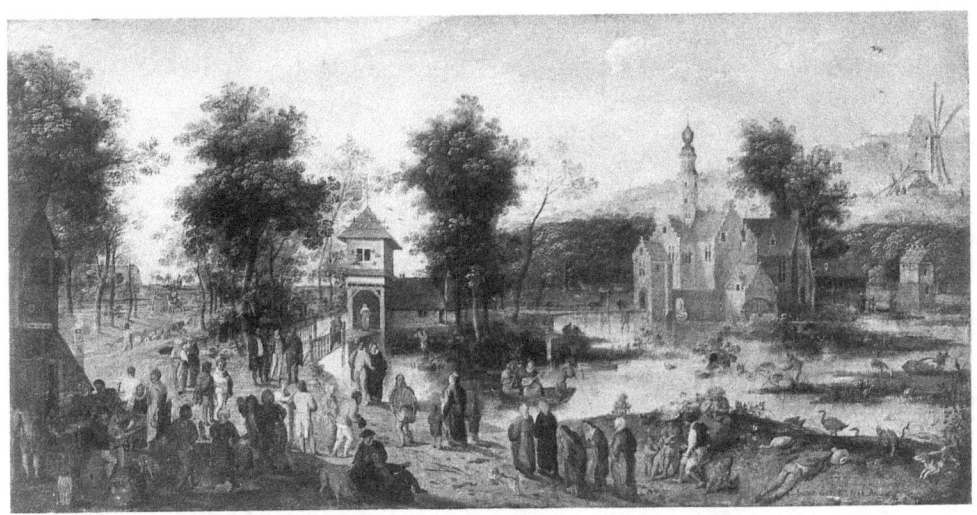

FIGURE 47. Jacob Grimmer and Gillis Mostaert, *Castle with a Country Festival,* 1583. Vienna, Kunsthistorisches Museum.

by the turmoil, Berchem being almost deserted by the fleeing Calvinists.[48] Nevertheless, the traffic between town and country did not cease completely in the following decades. Indeed, in his *Lofsang van Braband* (Hymn to Brabant), published in 1580, the Antwerp poet Jan van der Noot reports that during this time, while some people went into exile, others escaped the war by retiring to the country (presumably to their estates), where they "took their pleasure in agriculture, growing and planting, sowing and reaping."[49] Grimmer's picture, however, shows not rustic labors but rustic leisure: in the center, an elegantly dressed couple, most likely the lord and lady of the manor, watch a rather noisy celebration in progress before the village tavern. "I wish further," Estienne counsels the reader in an English translation published in 1600 of his *L'agriculture et la maison rustique,* "that he [the landowner] carrie himselfe pleasant and courteous unto his folke, not commaunding them anything in his cholor.... Let him speake familiarly with them, let him laugh and jest with them sometimes, and also either give them occasion, or else suffer them to laugh and be merrie ..., but I wish him not to be too familiar with them for the avoiding of con-

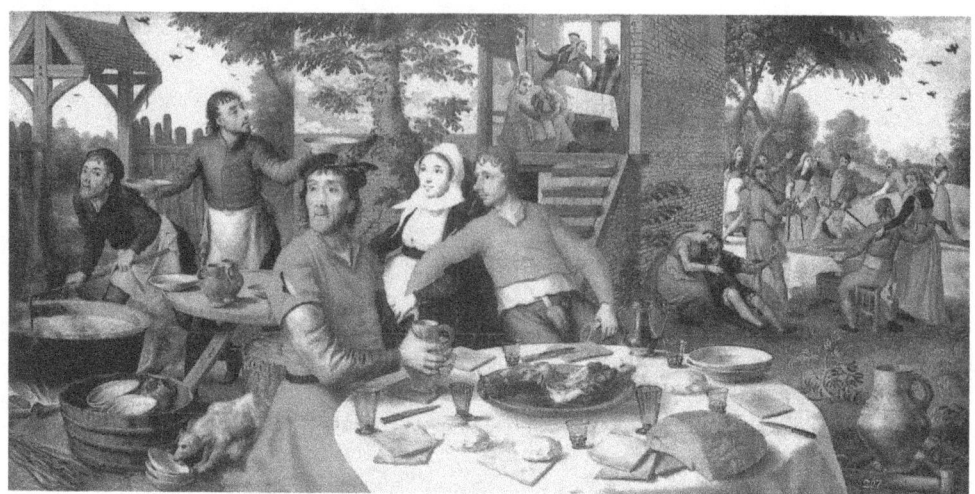

FIGURE 48. Pieter Aertsen, *Peasant Festival,* 1550. Vienna, Kunsthistorisches Museum.

tempt. . . ."⁵⁰ It is in this friendly but dignified fashion, one suspects, that the Schetz brothers comported themselves with the peasants of Hoboken, just as the seigneur and his wife seem to do in Grimmer's painting. Behind this couple is the manor house, whose importance is signaled by its imposing tower and moat. In the middle ground, not far to the right of the gatehouse, some of the castle inhabitants amuse themselves in a more decorous manner, singing and playing the lute.

In his *Den Spiegel der deucht, The Mirror of Virtue,* a treatise on deportment published in 1515 at Antwerp, Thomas van der Noot acknowledged the attraction of kermises for townspeople and told his readers that they could attend them, so long as they conducted themselves discreetly.⁵¹ Writing a generation or so later, Guicciardini tells us that the Netherlanders would travel twenty-five or thirty leagues (roughly fifty to sixty miles) to attend not only a wedding of family or friends but also those "processions in the summer, which they call kermises."⁵² And this was in the face of the attempts of both Charles V and Philip II to limit kermises or ban them altogether.⁵³ Given the numerous occasions in real life when the

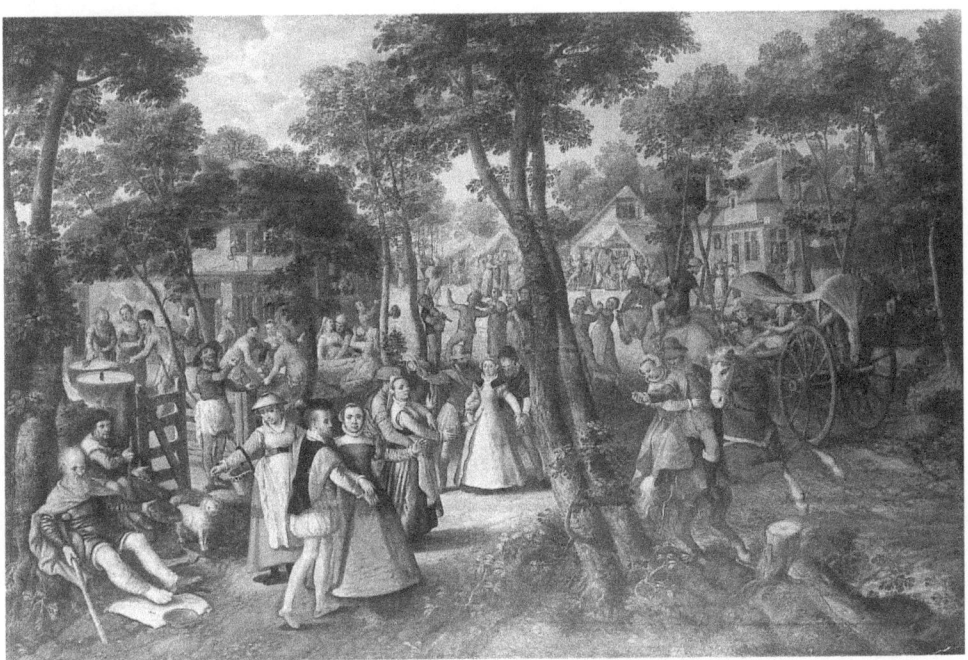

FIGURE 49. Joachim Beuckelaer, *Village Kermis,* 1563. St. Petersburg, The State Hermitage Museum.

inhabitants of city and country mingled, it is not surprising that fashionably dressed urbanites appear in many Flemish paintings of rustic festivities produced during the second half of the sixteenth century. Already in Pieter Aertsen's *Peasant Festival* of 1550 (Fig. 48), the earliest Flemish painting of such a subject known to us, a distinguished bearded gentleman sits at the table within the little building, possibly a tavern, in the middle ground, while in the right middle distance one city man joins a country dance, while another one, seated against the wall, dallies with a village girl.[54] Similar amorous exchanges between courtly gallants and shepherd lasses had occasionally appeared in earlier Flemish tapestries,[55] but in the peasant scenes by Aertsen's successors, the city folk generally conduct themselves with greater propriety.[56]

In Joachim Beuckelaer's *Village Kermis* of 1563 (Fig. 49), several fashionably dressed couples promenade through a village kermis. In the left middle ground, two large kettles simmer over open-air fires. A man stirs one of the kettles; from the other a second man ladles some of its yellow contents into a bowl held by a woman. If we accept a suggestion once made by Jan Grauls (in connection with Bruegel's *Peasant Wedding Feast*),[57] it is possible that the kettles contain a *pottagie van rijs* (now called *rijstpap* or *rijstepap*), a delicacy that can be roughly described as a sort of rice pudding, which formed the culinary highlight of many a festive occasion.[58] A *pottagie van rijs* was served, for example, at the annual feast of the Antwerp schoolmasters' guild in 1542; the guild accounts list the ingredients purchased for it: twenty-five pounds of rice, eighty-one pots of milk, and eight and a half pounds of sugar, as well as lesser quantities of butter, ginger, cinnamon, and saffron. Saffron was employed, we are informed in an Antwerp recipe book of about 1514, to give it a yellow color.[59] The truly gargantuan quantities of ingredients required suggest that the *pottagie van rijs* for the schoolmasters' feast was prepared in a large kettle much like the two depicted in Beuckelaer's painting.

City folk appear in other scenes of rustic celebrations. Maerten van Cleve's *Peasant Wedding Feast*, done about 1570 and known today only in several copies (Fig. 50), features a lively round dance in the foreground while other guests carry gifts to the bride enthroned before an open-air canopy. Isolated at the far left are a seated well-dressed man and woman who, to judge from the way the man holds his partner's hand, take advantage of the festivities to engage in a courtship of their own.[60] Conspicuous by their fine clothing, urbanites attend another country festival in a riverside village in a painting by Gillis Mostaert, dated 1583 (Fig. 51). Several dances are in progress, one in the foreground led by a bagpiper; other holiday makers have arrived by boat at lower left and climb the steep bank to join the fun. Once again we see several open-air kettles, as in Beuckelaer's picture of 1563, but it is not clear if they contain a *pottagie van rijs*. The circumstantial detail in which the artist has rendered the various buildings—manor house, cottages, church, and taverns—suggests that he may well have had a specific place in mind. Indeed, the picture has

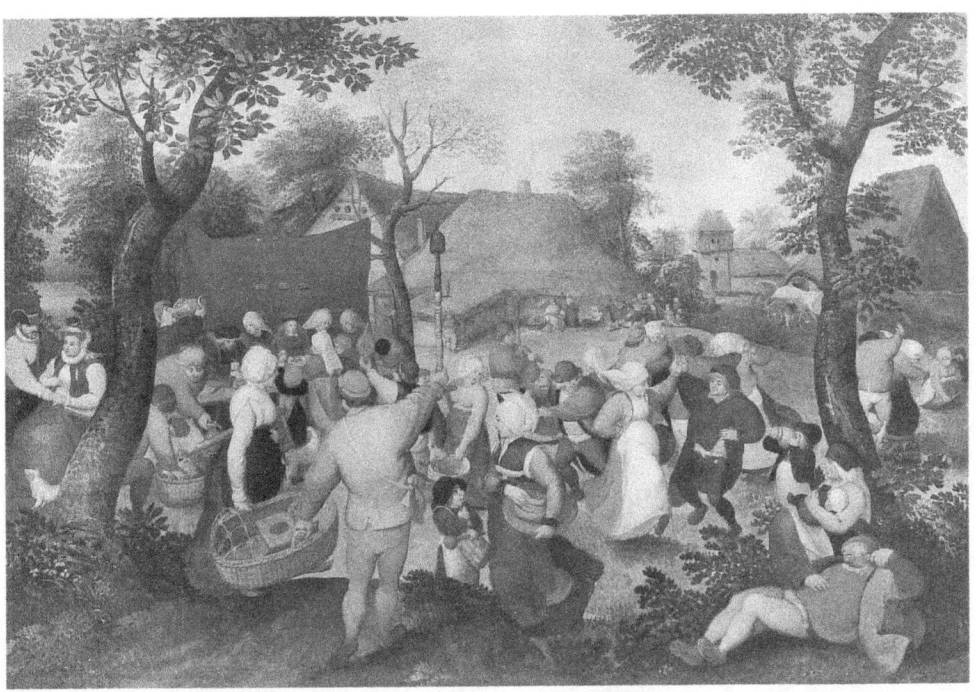

FIGURE 50. Maerten van Cleve, *Peasant Wedding Feast*, ca. 1570. Antwerp, Museum Mayer van den Bergh.

been identified as possibly a view of Hoboken,[61] although it might represent any village of Bruegel's day, perhaps Ste.-Anneken, which lay in Flanders across the Schelde River from Antwerp and, between 1559 and 1562, was owned by that city.[62] Even before this episode, Ste.-Anneken had long been a favorite resort, to judge from its prominence in various sixteenth-century views of Antwerp, including a woodcut of 1515.[63] In any case, "let the peasants have their kermis," inscribed on the banner above the tavern in a print of another peasant celebration after Bruegel, the *St. Joris Kermis*,[64] is a sentiment, one suspects, that would have been shared by many of Bruegel's contemporaries.

Generally the townspeople are content simply to observe the festivities, but occasionally they interact with the villagers, as we can see, for

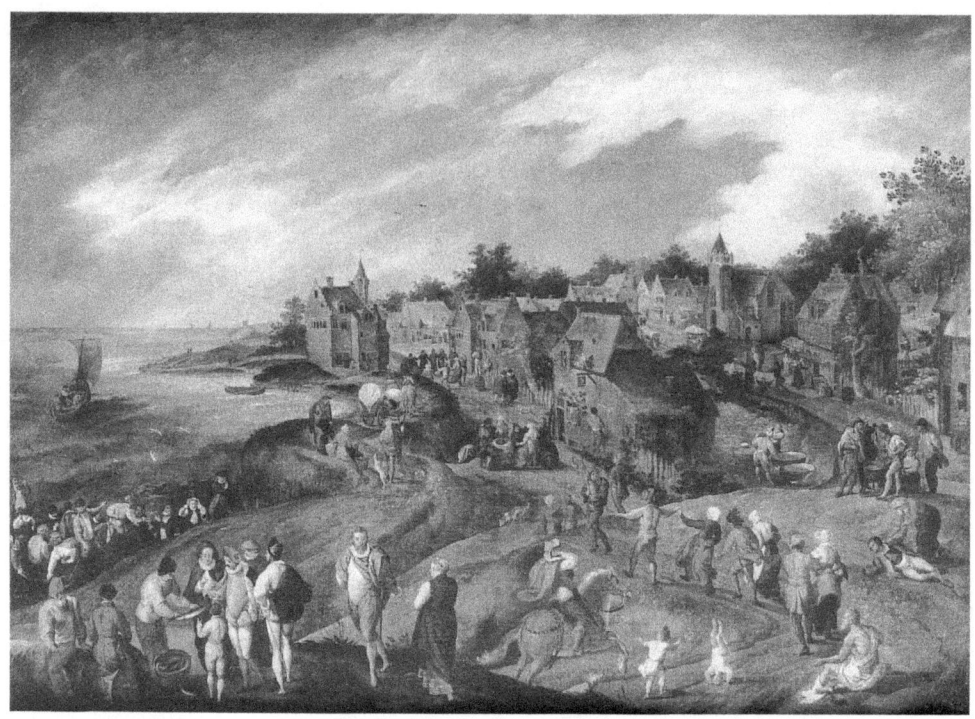

FIGURE 51. Gillis Mostaert, *Country Festival,* 1583. Present location unknown.

example, in Peeter Baltens's *Peasant Kermis with the "Clucht van plaijerwater"* (see Figs. 6, 7). Although one well-dressed couple and their little girl turn away from the crowd just beneath the makeshift stage,[65] another group of city people converses with a couple of villagers. Urbanites may also pursue their own amusements. In his *View of the Schelde near Antwerp* of 1587 (Fig. 52), Jacob Grimmer contrasts the country dance and its bagpipe accompaniment in the right middle distance with the elegant picnic on the grass in the left foreground, where several couples sing or dance to the sound of the more refined instruments favored by the upper classes, lutes and a viola da gamba. Stringed instruments—the harp, the viol, the lute, and others of their kind—had long been associated with upper-class entertainment. An English manuscript of the seventeenth

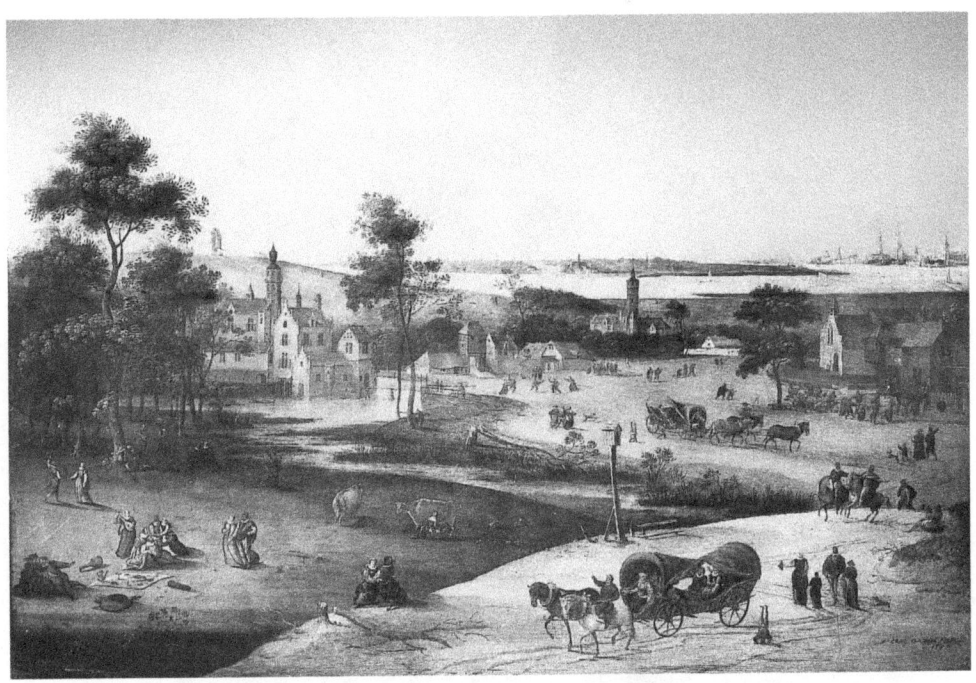

FIGURE 52.   Jacob Grimmer, *View of the Schelde near Antwerp*, 1587. Antwerp, Koninklijk Museum voor Schone Kunsten.

century (but most likely reflecting opinions long current) explains that "all the actions that one does in playing of the lute are handsome; the posture is modest, free and gallant, . . . and whereas other instruments constrain the body, the lute sets it in an advantageous posture."[66] The bagpipe, however, was the instrument of choice of the lower classes, especially the peasantry,[67] and, unlike the lute, hardly displays the performer at his best: the bapiper must distort his face, distending his cheeks with the effort of blowing, as we can see in Bruegel's drawing of a peasant musician that has been dated to the mid-1560s (Fig. 53).[68] But even worse, the bagpipe was a common symbol of human folly in general, not least, perhaps, because its shape appeared to more ribald viewers as resembling the male genitals.[69] In a chapter of his *Narrenschiff*, Sebastian Brant characterizes the bagpipes as the dunces' instrument; in the ac-

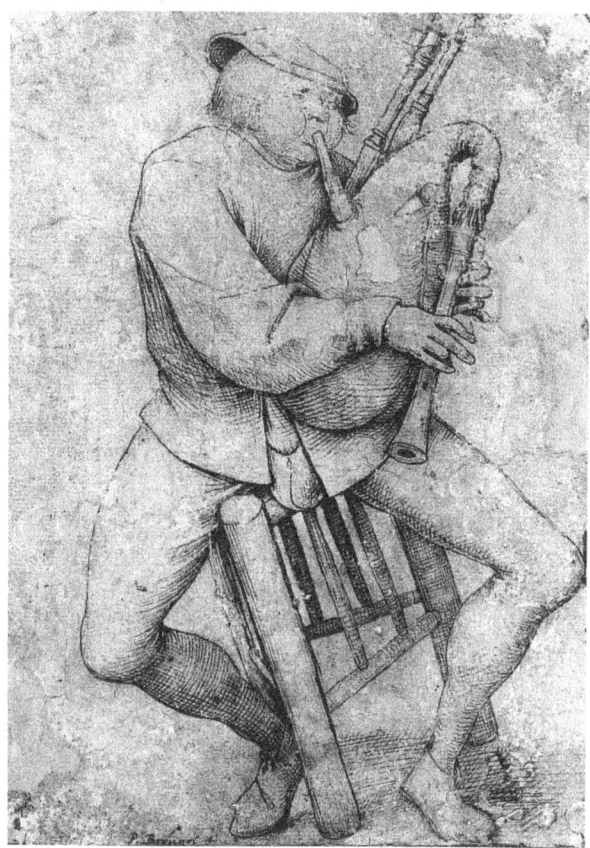

FIGURE 53. Pieter Bruegel the Elder, *The Bagpiper*,
drawing. Washington D.C., The Ian Woodner Collection, on deposit at the National Gallery of Art.

companying woodcut (Fig. 54) a fool puffs on a bagpipe, spurning the
more genteel harp and lute at his feet.[70]

But Brant's association of bagpipes and folly evidently did not reflect
a unanimous opinion on this subject. An emblematic illustration by
Theodore de Bry published toward the end of the century shows a group
of music makers, some rather rough-looking characters who may be peasants but who are certainly not members of the urban elite, performing

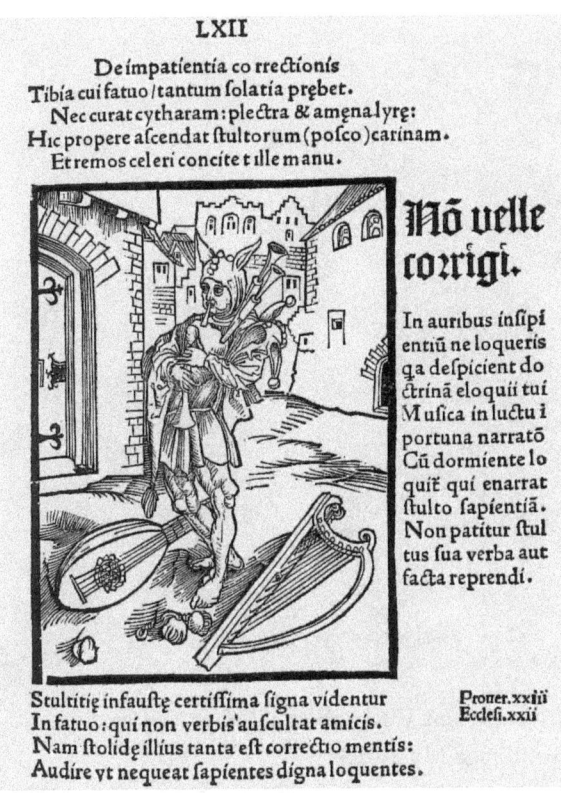

LXII

De impatientia co rrectionis
Tibia cui fatuo / tantum folatia prebet.
Nec curat cytharam : plectra & amena lyre :
Hic propere afcendat ftultorum (pofco)carinam.
Et remos cel eri concite t ille manu.

**Nō velle
corrigi.**

In auribus infipi
entiū ne loqueris
qa defpicient do
ctrinā eloquii tui
Mufica in luctu i
portuna narratō
Cū dormiente lo
quię qui enarrat
ftulto fapientiā.
Non patitur ftul
tus fua verba aut
facta reprendi.

Stultitie infaufte certiffima figna videntur
In fatuo : qui non verbis'aufcultat amicis.
Nam ftolide illius tanta eft correctio mentis :
Audire yt nequeat fapientes digna loquentes.

Prouer. xxiii
Ecclefi. xxii

FIGURE 54. *Fool Playing the Bagpipes,* woodcut in Sebastian Brant, *Stultifera navis,* Basel, 1497. Williamstown, Mass., Williams College, Chapin Library of Rare Books.

on a bagpipe and its equally humble companion the hurdy-gurdy; the Latin inscription below informs us merely that "Music entertains and adorns both mortals and gods."[71] A similar equivocation can be found in a *tafelspel* of about 1600, featuring a debate between the two brothers Bot Verstant and Cloucken Geest (roughly, Dense of Intellect and Stout-hearted Spirit), peasant and gentleman respectively. Among other things the two brothers argue about is whether the bagpipe or the lute makes the best music.[72] Neither instrument emerges clearly victorious, although at the end the gentleman turns to the audience and apologizes

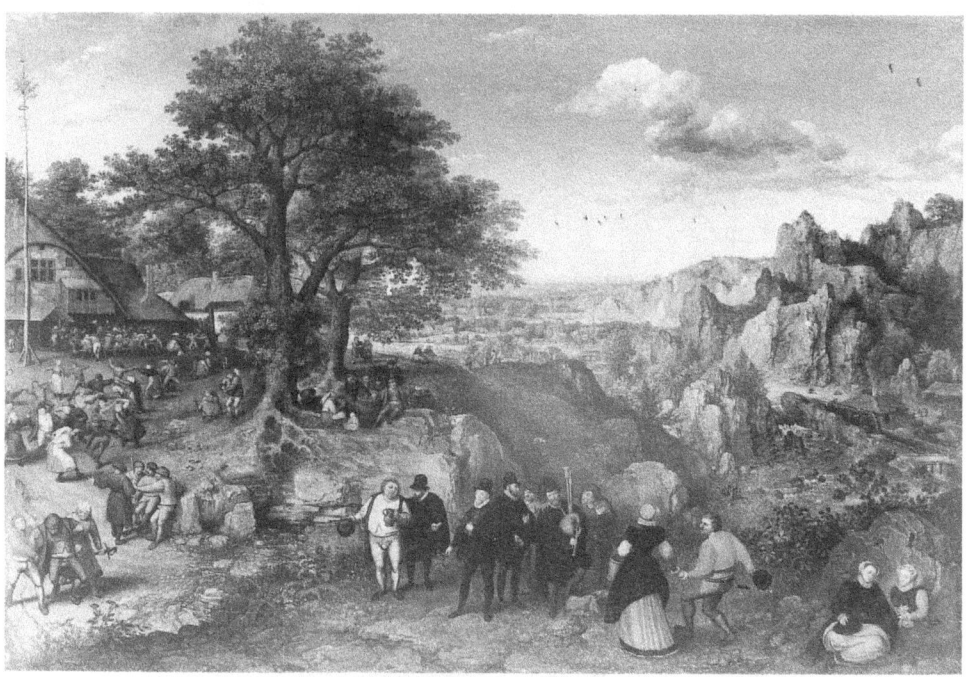

FIGURE 55. Lucas van Valckenborch, *Village Fair*, ca. 1577. St. Petersburg, The State Hermitage Museum.

for his boorish brother, explaining that "so must the wise pass their time with the dense."[73]

Toward the end of the play, Bot Verstant tells us that those present are his "nieces and nephews," presumably members of his refined audience who did not disdain the music of the lowly bagpipe.[74] This is also strikingly evident in Lucas van Valckenborch's *Village Fair* of 1577 (Fig. 55), in which a company of ladies and gentlemen attend a peasant festival. They have been joined in conversation by some peasants; one of the gentlemen holds a bagpipe, perhaps proffered by the countryman who puts a hand familiarly on his shoulder (Fig. 56). In the foreground a peasant clasps the hand of a well-dressed lady. Gentlemen may dally with country lasses, as we have seen in earlier tapestries and in Aert-

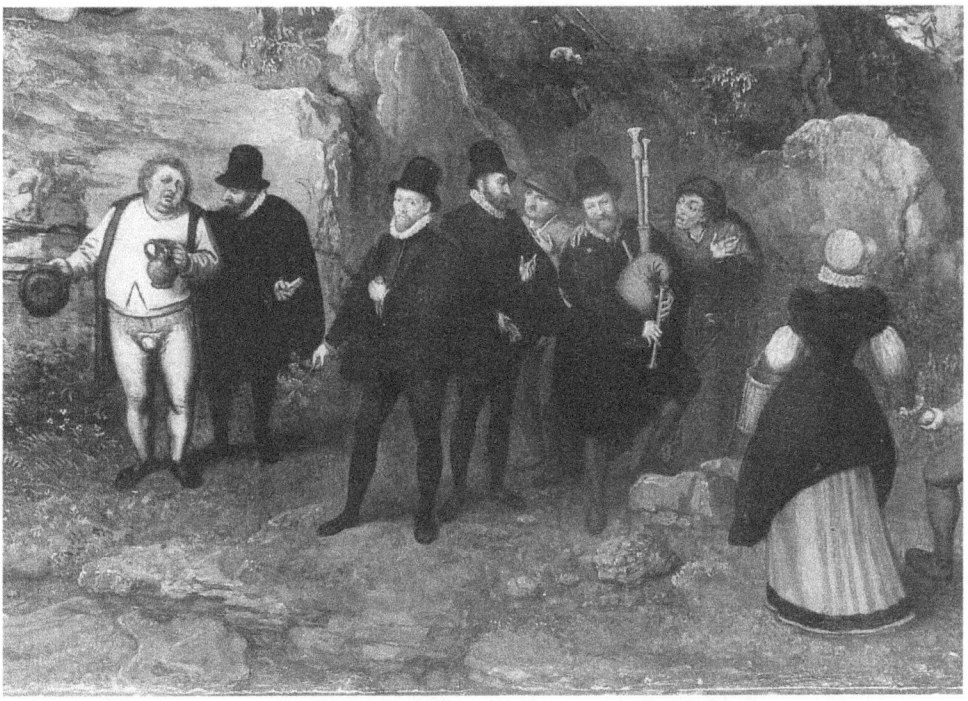

FIGURE 56.   Detail of Fig. 55.

sen's *Peasant Festival* of 1550 (see Fig. 48), but amorous encounters between countrymen and urban ladies are exceedingly rare. One example
occurs in a poem by Lucas D'Heere, published in 1565, in which a rustic lad woos a lovely city girl: he boasts of his fine new attire, including
a "jerkin of the latest cut," and vows to hack his rival to pieces if he pays
too much attention to the young lady.[75] It is doubtful that such loutish
courtship takes place in Valckenborch's painting; most likely the peasant simply assists his companion over the rough ground.[76] The reveling
villagers and the inn at the left are typically Netherlandish, even to such
details as the fight just to the left of the festive table in the background
and the drunken peasant at lower left, supported by two companions.
However, the imposing mountainous landscape at the right recalls not

Brabant and Flanders but the region of Liège, Namur, and Hainault, to the southeast.

In the seventeenth century a version of this picture was owned by Peeter Stevens, an Antwerp businessman and art collector. In his copy of Van Mander's *Schilder-boeck*, Stevens notes the date of the painting, 1577, and observes that the bagpiper is Valckenborch himself, with Abraham Ortelius standing just to his right.[77] The painting exists in three replicas; one is in the State Hermitage Museum, St. Petersburg, another in the Museo del Prado, Madrid. The third version, which was on the art market in 1996, bears Valckenborch's monogram and the date 1577 and may well have been the picture owned by Stevens.[78] The putative figure of Ortelius bears enough resemblance to known portraits of him to suggest that Stevens was repeating an authentic tradition. We also know that Ortelius was on a tour of the French-speaking Netherlands in 1577, visiting both Liège and Cologne in that year, and as Valckenborch was in nearby Aachen, a meeting between the two men is entirely possible.[79] It has also been suggested that the gentleman conversing with the heavy-set peasant at the left is the miniaturist Georg Hoefnagel.[80] We will probably never know if Valckenborch's picture depicts a specific place, if only because the general terrain, with a plateau on the left and a steep descent on the right toward an imposing mountainous vista, is a compositional type that he employed in a number of his landscapes.[81] Nor shall we ever know if this painting in some way commemorates an actual event. What seems evident, however, is that the artist and the cartographer were not averse to having themselves depicted in friendly conversation with representatives of a social class that Ortelius and his circle, according to some critics, supposedly saw as the very personifications of human folly when they encountered them in Bruegel's *Kermis* and *Wedding Banquet*.[82] But as B. A. M. Ramakers has cogently observed, even if Ortelius articulated an elevated ideal for the conduct of human life, this does not mean that he stood aside in disgust or contempt from the festive culture of his time.[83]

Ramakers's suggestion deserves further exploration, because it helps to explain why, for example, a peasant dance, the so-called Hoboken Dance, was included by Tilman Susato in his *Third Book of Music*, published in 1550 at Antwerp, although probably in a somewhat more elegant form than the original.[84] This was not uncommon: a *klompendans*, or clog dance (*bransle des sabots*), popular among the country people, appears in a Netherlandish collection of 1572, the *Liber levicum carminum* (Book of Light-hearted Songs), and similar dances can be found in the music and dance books of other countries in the sixteenth century.[85] And in the *Plaisir des champs* of 1583, a treatise on "hunting and all other virtuous and honest recreative exercises," the French cleric and royal chaplain Claude Gauchet devotes considerable attention to *le grand bransle* (the great branle) and other village dances.[86]

Indeed, Peter Burke asked some years ago if the upper classes gradually came to "associate popular culture with particular times and places of relaxation."[87] This is a pertinent question that deserves further study, but it can be answered, at least provisionally, in the affirmative.[88] Castiglione, for example, reports that the young noblemen of Lombardy attended peasant festivities, taking part in their dances and sports.[89] For his part, the French essayist Michel de Montaigne records in his travel journal for 7 May–21 June 1581, when he was in Italy, that after dinner he gave a dance for the peasant girls "and danced in it myself so as not to appear too reserved."[90] And it was in a similar festive context that Noël du Fail placed his *Propos rustiques*, or *Rustic Conversations*, first published in 1547 and reprinted in 1549 and 1573.[91] A lawyer, Du Fail was also lord of La Hérissy in Brittany and hence familiar with the people who lived and labored on his land, and in fact, his protagonists are the Breton peasantry. His book chiefly comprises a series of conversations, which the author supposedly records, of some elderly peasants who gather on a village holiday. They relax under a chestnut tree, drink wine, and reminisce about old times, including a memorable kermis at which even the presence of the village priest did not inhibit their merrymaking. Du Fail may give an idealized view of peasant life, but he takes an indulgent view of its coarser aspects and describes a Breton village of his time with enough realism that his *Propos rustiques* was consulted by Fernand Braudel for his great study of everyday life in early modern Europe.[92]

In the case of Antwerp, as Ramakers has convincingly suggested, Ortelius and his circle must have moved with similar ease between the learned culture of the humanists and the culture of the lower and middle classes, if only because the city had absorbed the folkways of the countryside into its own festive occasions.[93] This also explains why the Schetz brothers invited their friends and colleagues to attend the Hoboken festivals. We are coming to realize that there is not the gulf so commonly assumed between "high" and "low" culture, but a continuity between the urban elite and the lower classes, whether country peasant or city proletariat.[94] It is in this context, too, that we can best judge Van Mander's story about Bruegel and Hans Franckaert: the two friends, we are told, attended country weddings and kermises dressed as peasants and passed themselves off as relatives of the bride or groom.[95] It is not unlikely, of course, that the two men participated in rustic festivities, and even Van Mander's claim that they disguised themselves as peasants is not without historical precedent. Edicts promulgated in fifteenth-century Vienna and Strasbourg forbade townspeople to dress as peasants during carnival time.[96] Peasant costumes worn by city folk are recorded for the Nuremberg carnivals of the fifteenth and earlier sixteenth centuries.[97]

Just why urban revelers should favor peasant dress deserves further investigation, but I suspect that, like masquerades in general, such disguises temporarily freed their wearers on festive occasions from the usual social restraints: a fifteenth-century Nuremberg carnival play by Hans Folz, for example, refers to burghers dressed as peasants running into people's houses and catching women in the corners.[98] How long such practices survived is unclear, but in his Orchésographie, first published in 1589, Thoinot Arbeau characterizes the dance known as the "Branle of Haut Barrois": it is "danced by lackeys and serving wenches, and sometimes by young men and women of gentle birth in a masquerade, disguised as peasants and shepherds, or for a lark among themselves at some private gathering."[99] We do not know if Bruegel's countrymen shared this penchant for rustic disguises, but until we do, it would be hazardous to dismiss Van Mander's account as mere rhetorical embellishment.

In any case, Van Mander insists that Bruegel "knew how to attire these men and women peasants very characteristically in Kempish or other costumes."[100] (Kempen, or "Kempelandt," as it is spelled on at least one sixteenth-century map, was a large region extending from northeastern Flanders through much of Brabant.)[101] This is equally plausible: as Kavaler has noted, Bruegel's peasants display a much greater specificity of detail in their costumes than are usually seen in the rustic scenes of Aertsen, Baltens, or Maerten van Cleve.[102] This is not to say, of course, that Bruegel painted precisely what he saw; he filtered his experiences through conventions and compositions he had encountered in the art of his predecessors. For the most part, however, he rejected their stereotypes, particularly the loutish grins and other comic exaggerations that we find, for example, in Jan Massys's *Peasants in a Tavern* (see Fig. 29).[103]

Bruegel's effects are entirely more subtle. He also endows his peasants with a monumentality and vivacity that make the rustic celebrants of Pieter Aertsen (see Figs. 48, 67) seem spindly and unconvincing. In the *Wedding Dance* in Detroit, for example (see Fig. 41), the peasant dancers—the entire village, it seems, has turned out—present a kaleidoscope of shifting forms and colors. From the foolish look on the face of the male dancer at lower right, we may suspect that he is at least a little tipsy. Notable, too, is his distended codpiece, as well as those sported by a second man dancing in the foreground and the bagpiper at the right, details rescued from later overpainting only in the past century.[104] This article of dress might seem to confirm the view of many modern scholars that Bruegel's peasants were meant as embodiments of lust and other vices. However, we should not jump to conclusions, for the codpiece, first appearing about 1450, was part of male attire among all classes, from peasants and soldiers to kings and emperors. To judge from portraits of the period,[105] they were made conspicuous through the use of padding, a practice condemned by Montaigne as "that empty and useless model of a member that we cannot even decently mention by name, which however we show off and parade in public."[106] But none, I doubt, was as capacious as the codpiece sported by Panurge in Rabelais's *Gargantua and Pantagruel*,

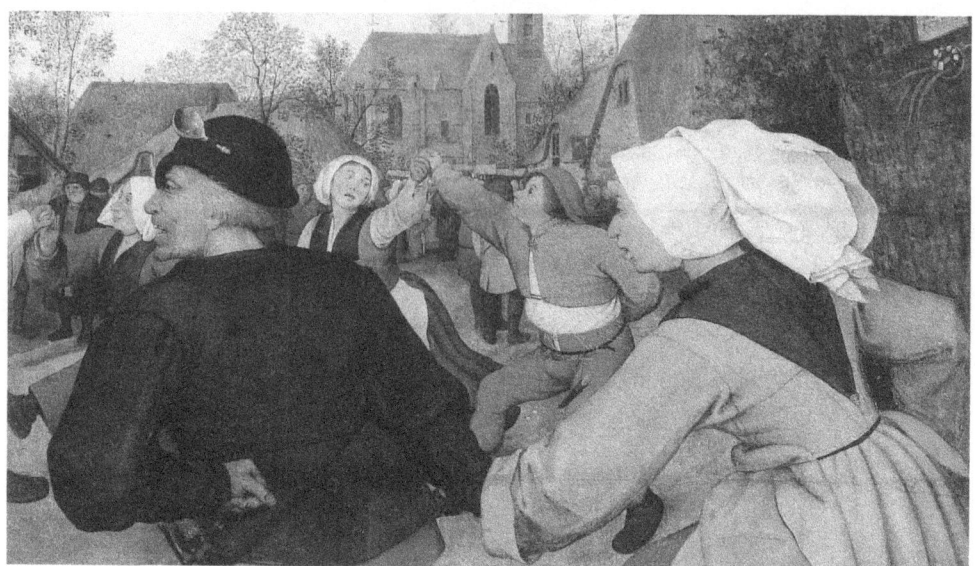

FIGURE 57. Detail of Fig. 42.

in which he concealed an orange and several other sizable objects.[107] Often
codpieces were elaborately decorated, a custom that Rabelais similarly
ridiculed in his description of the one made for the young Gargantua,
ornamented with embroidery, goldwork, and precious stones, an item of
haberdashery that, the author assures us, "was well furnished within . . .
having no resemblance to the fraudulent codpieces of so many young gentlemen which contain nothing but wind, to the great disappointment of
the female sex."[108] We can only speculate whether Bruegel's lusty countrymen will disappoint later on in the wedding festivities.

Similar expressive and often humorous figures throng the two peasant
scenes in Vienna (see Figs. 42, 43). In the *Kermis*, the couple hastening from
the right to join their reveling companions (Fig. 57) may well have been
inspired by an engraving in Sebald Beham's *Twelve Months* of 1546,[109] but
Bruegel takes advantage of the painting's larger scale to characterize
sharply the elderly male peasant and his younger partner. At lower left

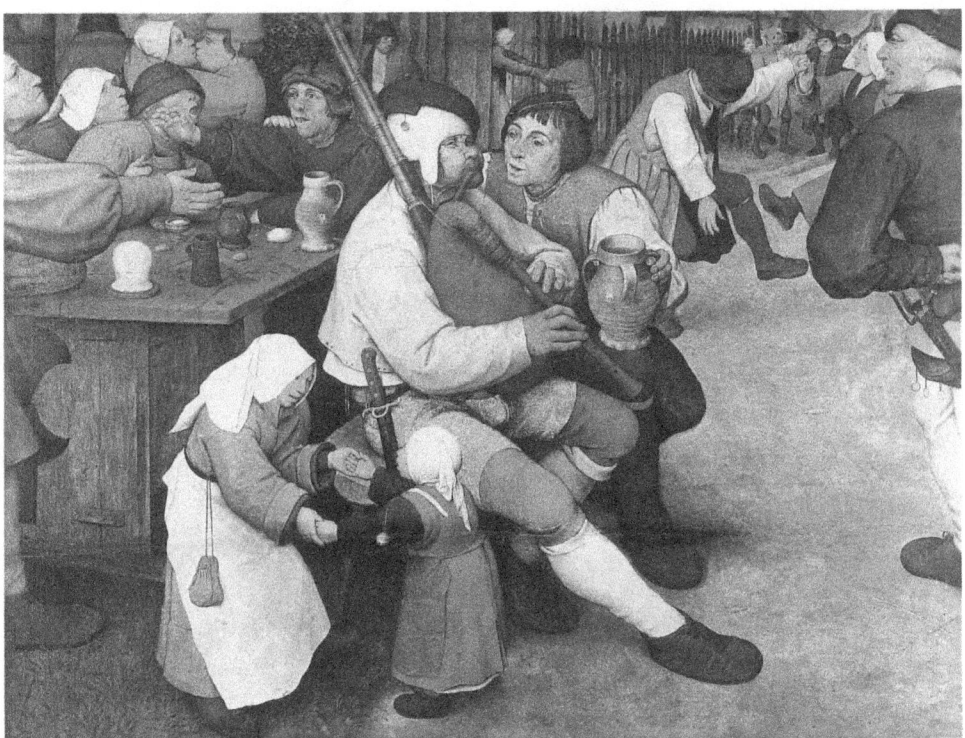

FIGURE 58. Detail of Fig. 42.

(Fig. 58), a young man chats with the grizzled old bagpiper,[110] while at the table behind them a violent argument has broken out among three men, obviously "in their cups,"as the old expression has it, which a housewife strives vainly to stop. This fracas is ignored by the slightly lumpish young couple farther back who embrace and kiss. Bruegel's attention to detail is especially evident in the larger of the two young girls dancing near the bagpiper and his companion in the Vienna *Kermis*. As we have seen, Sullivan has argued that the elder girl's outsize clothes signify that she is preparing to join the grown-ups' "dance of folly."[111] I wonder, however, if Bruegel's audience might more likely have assumed that she wears garments handed down from an older sister or some other relative, a practice, one suspects, common among all but the affluent until recently; if so, viewers would have marveled at his attention to this detail as well as many others.

If in the *Kermis*, Bruegel presents all the noisy release of social inhibitions common to a village fair, the *Wedding Feast* shows a more orderly gathering, but it is not without its moments of humor, from the boy seated at lower left, greedily licking his fingers, to the old man above him who pauses in his drinking to look expectantly at the food being carried in on a detached barn door by two stalwart youths, or the young man across the table who seems totally absorbed in putting food into his mouth. Like the peasant Bot Verstant in the banquet play *Bot Verstant en Cloucken Geest* described above, it is likely that many of the guests would rather die from overeating than from starvation.[112] They are entertained by two bagpipers at the left, their instruments decorated with festive tassels. One piper, however, has paused (see Fig. 66), his gaze fixed intently, it seems, on the makeshift tray; the shallow bowls distributed by the third youth are probably filled with *pottagie van rijs*, some of it colored yellow with saffron.[113] In contrast to the animated crowd is the bearded man in black who sits quietly conversing with the monk seated by his side. Any gentleman would easily have identified with this dignified personage (Fig. 59). A comparison of his physiognomy with Bruegel's portrait in Dominicus Lampsonius's *Effigies*, published in 1572, has led some scholars to suggest that this is a self-portrait, but the profile also somewhat resembles that of Bruegel's friend Hans Franckaert in the portrait medallion of him by Jacques Jonghelinck, although the latter has a curlier beard.[114] All this must remain conjecture, but the grave gentleman in the *Wedding Banquet* is clearly the lord of the manor, presiding graciously but with quiet detachment over a festive occasion of his dependents, much in the manner prescribed by Charles Estienne.

In all three of these scenes of rustic revels, Bruegel generally eschews the violence and drunken behavior that occur in the peasant celebrations depicted by the earlier Nuremberg printmakers and by such Flemish artists in Bruegel's time as Pieter van der Borcht and Hans Bol.[115] Indeed, Bruegel's country people conduct themselves with considerably more dis-

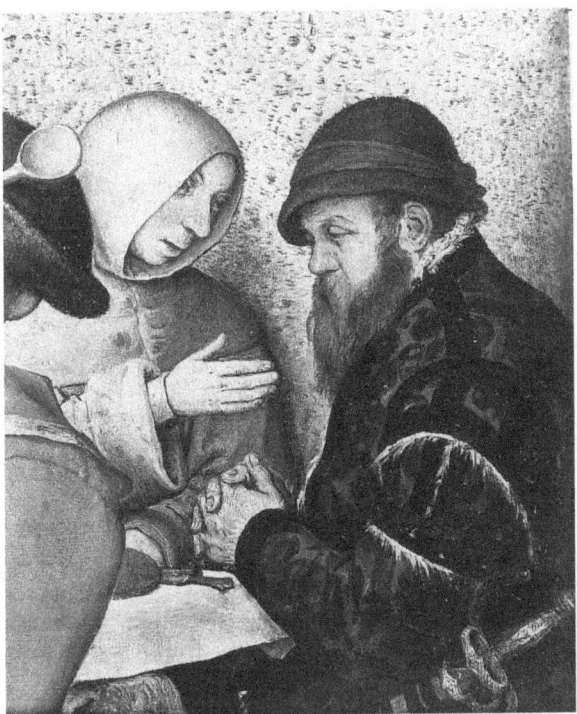

FIGURE 59. Detail of Fig. 43.

cretion than do the amorous immortals in the scenes of Olympian banquets that were being produced at this time by Frans Floris and his atelier (Fig. 60).[116] Especially on their good behavior are the peasants in the
Wedding Banquet; perhaps it is not too fanciful to suggest that Bruegel imag-
ined them as all too aware of the watchful eye of their landlord seated at
the head of the table.

In sum, when we look at these pictures for what they show, and not
for what many critics assume they conceal, we can understand why Ortelius said that Bruegel's works can hardly be described "as works of art,
but as works of Nature. Nor should I call him the best of painters, but
rather the very nature of painters."[117] If any of Bruegel's rustic revels hung
in the homes of the Schetz brothers, Antoon van Straelen, and other Ant-

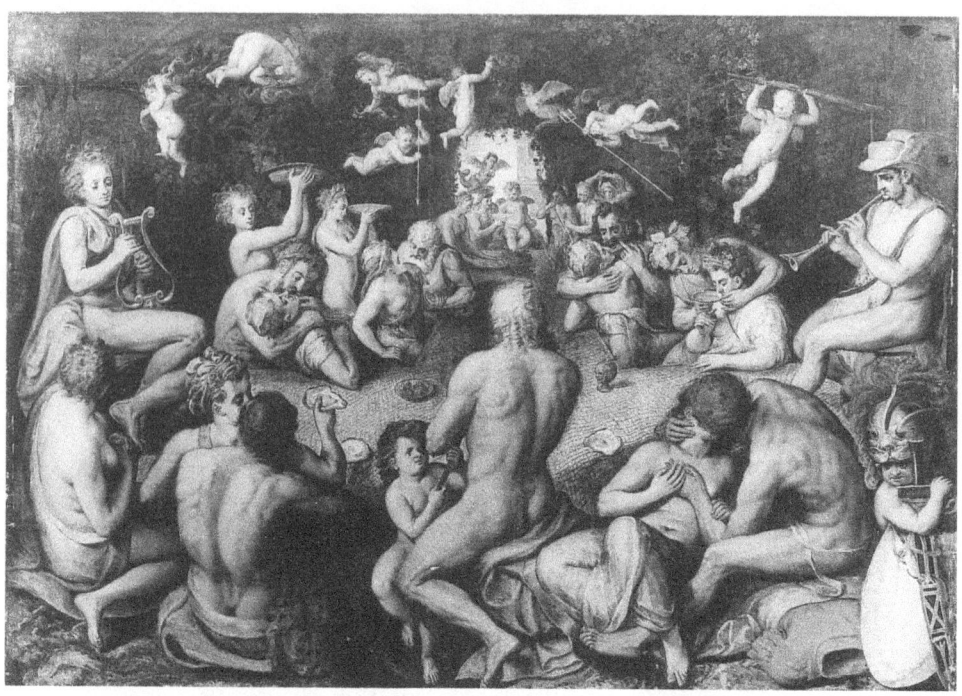

FIGURE 60. Frans Floris, *Banquet of the Gods*. Graz, Alte Galerie des Landes-
museums Joanneum.

werp magnates who gloried in the title of *heer* of some feudal manor, these
pictures would have proclaimed not only the wealth and prestige of their
owners but also the benign rule under which the villagers flourished and
celebrated their festivals undisturbed. And less fortunate urbanites would
have recalled with pleasure, surely, the many occasions when they had left
their city cares behind them to relax among the peasants at kermis time
or during extended holidays in the country in their own *speelhuysen* or as
guests of their wealthier associates.

    And even if the townsfolk regarded Bruegel's peasant antics with a
sense of their own social superiority—the superiority of the people of
the lute to those of the bagpipe—I suspect that their laughter would have
been indulgent. It would also have been a laughter not untinged, perhaps,

with the envy of the peace and freedom from care that townspeople of every age have attributed to the country folk, colored by Virgil's *Georgics* and *Eclogues*, by Horace's famous second epode ("Beatus ille": "Happy the man who far from business cares . . . works his ancestral acres"), and by the countless other poems and treatises before and after Virgil and Horace that exalted the rustic life over that at court or in the city. We will examine this subject at greater length in the epilogue, but we can appreciate a further dimension to this audience response only after we return to Jean Noirot and his dining room.

CHAPTER FIVE

MAKING GOOD CHEER

Eating and drinking hold soul and life together.

NETHERLANDISH PROVERB

If you look at the manners of everyday life, there is no race
more open to humanity or kindness [than the Netherlanders]
. . . and not prone to any serious vices, except that it is a
little given to pleasure, especially to feasting.

ERASMUS

As we have seen, Jean Noirot displayed three of Bruegel's rustic celebrations in his dining room, specifically his "small, back dining room."
To judge from contemporary records of work done on his residence, the
walls of this particular chamber had been marbleized in green, with black
baseboards and some wall paintings.[1] Against this presumably subdued
background, Noirot's Bruegels, if they were anything like the Detroit and
Vienna panels, must have glowed with life and color. At first sight, the
placement of these pictures was not so remarkable; because a family's social activity tended to center on the dining room, its decoration was often
more elaborate and costly than that of other rooms.[2] But more than their
decorative qualities may have prompted Noirot to embellish his dining
room with Bruegel's peasant scenes—if the hanging of pictures in a
sixteenth-century Antwerp house was not simply haphazard, dictated

chiefly by their order of acquisition or by the available wall space.[3] Although documentary proof is lacking, it has been plausibly suggested that Bruegel's *Labors of the Months* of 1565 were intended for the dining room of Jonghelinck's suburban villa, and that at least some of the market and kitchen scenes of Aertsen and Beuckelaer were destined for similar spaces.[4] The dining room would have been an appropriate space for scenes of agricultural labor and kitchen life, showing as they do the production and preparation of the food that ultimately reached urban tables.[5] We know of one Antwerp merchant, Aernout Pels, who displayed eleven pictures in his dining room; they included portraits and Old Testament subjects, but also two kitchen pieces.[6] While Bruegel's rustic revels show the peasants at their leisure, celebrating church holidays and weddings, and not at their labors, these pictures, too, would not have been out of place in a dining room.

To understand how Bruegel's rustic revels might have functioned in such a context, we may imagine Noirot, before he lost his fortune, or any wealthy Antwerp gentleman and his family, along with friends and colleagues, gathering in the dining room on festive or less formal occasions. They would have begun their meal with the *eerste tafel*, or first course, probably the customary salad or soup, followed by various meat and other dishes, finishing with the third course, consisting of fruit, cheese, nuts, and the like, *om die maghe te sluyten*, that is, "to settle the stomach," as we are informed by the *Nyeuwen coock boeck* of 1560.[7] As they lingered over each course, accompanied by French or German wines, or perhaps the more robust vintages from Spain and Portugal currently in fashion,[8] what did they talk about?

As we have seen, Sullivan imagines a philosophical banquet, much like those Erasmus describes in such colloquies as *The Godly Feast* and *The Poetic Feast*.[9] This represents a tradition going back to antiquity, including Plato's *Phaedo* and *Symposium*,[10] in which the banquet serves as the framework for an extended philosophical discussion, one of the conversations included in Cicero's term *sermo*.[11] A Renaissance example is Jean Bodin's *Colloquium of the Seven Secrets of the Sublime*, completed in 1588, which de-

scribes the six successive days when a small group of serious-minded gentlemen gather for dinner, listen to readings from Plato, modern tragedies,
and the like as they eat, and discourse endlessly on religion, Christian,
Jewish, and pagan.[12]

The philosophical banquet was thus very much a literary convention,
and it is not easy to determine how often such meals occurred in everyday life. Many writers recommended that meals combine food for the
body and the mind, with neither food too rich but always nourishing; indeed, Erasmus insisted that at dinner, it was best to "avoid foolish yarns
and enjoy profitable conversation."[13] This seems to have been the practice of Carolus Virulus, head of a gymnasium, or secondary school, in
Leuven (Louvain), who was "not as learned as he was good," as Vives characterizes him. Seeking to rectify this failing, he entertained the families
of his students and other guests at dinner and encouraged them to discuss their professions, so that "they would leave the table, the guest quite
happy, and the host wiser and better informed."[14] The Antwerp merchant
Gillis Hooftman, a Calvinist, may have had a similar desire for mealtime
edification when in 1568 he ordered, as decorations for his dining room,
five pictures of events in the life of St. Paul from Marten de Vos, who
had been recommended by Ortelius.[15]

As evidence of such temperate mealtime behavior, Sullivan also illus-
trates a painting by Frans Pourbus I, depicting a company of fashionably
dressed ladies and gentlemen, generally identified as the Hoefnagel
family, within an interior setting, perhaps a dining room (Fig. 61).[16] Iden-
tifying this scene as a wedding feast, Sullivan tells us that "[t]he expressions of the bride, groom, and the participants are serious, their costumes
simple and dark, food and drink receive minimal attention, and the behavior of these wedding celebrants is restrained, even solemn."[17] Sullivan has justly characterized the social atmosphere of this picture, but how
do we know that it is a wedding feast? Real-life weddings tended to be
more lively, to judge from some of the *tafelspelen* performed on such occasions (of which more later), as well as an epithalamium, or wedding
poem, by Jan van der Noot. Composed to celebrate the nuptials in 1563

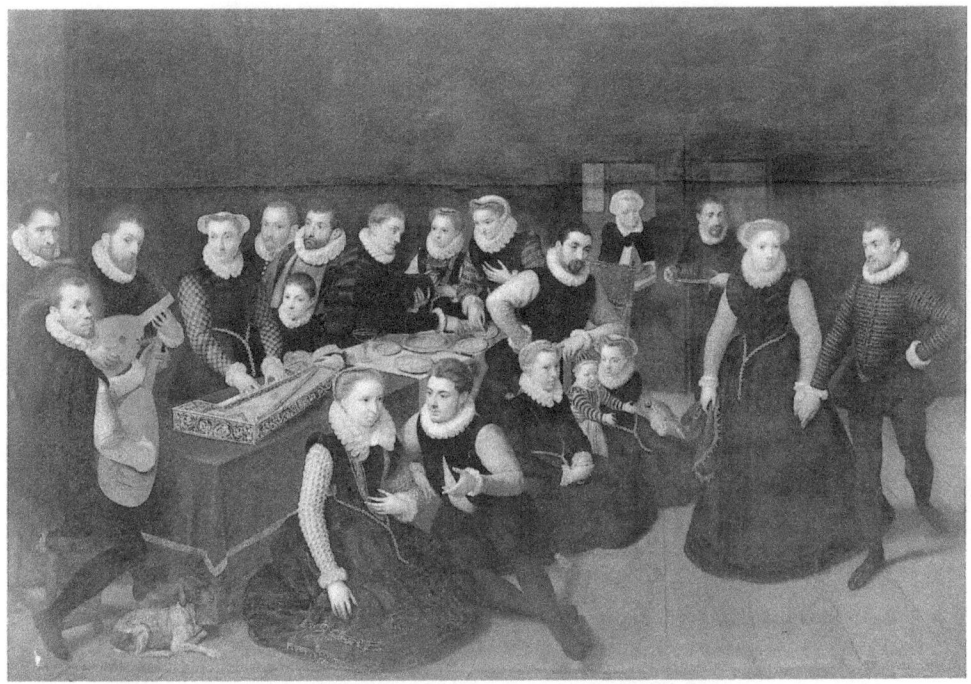

FIGURE 61. Frans Pourbus I, *The Hoefnagel Family.* Brussels, Musées Royaux des Beaux-Arts de Belgique.

of an Italian gentleman and a Brabantine lady, the poem describes the festivities following the marriage ceremony: they included a banquet and speeches, after which the guests danced until after midnight, only to indulge in more festivity the following day.[18] Even more to the point, can we assume that Pourbus's painting documents to any degree the actual behavior of people in this period? After all, it is most likely a family portrait, and however much ladies and gentlemen may have laughed in real life, and we have seen that they surely did, when it came to being recorded for posterity, they generally eschewed emotion of any kind. This restraint was probably an inheritance from the traditional devotional portraits that appear in the context of altarpieces and other religious images of the period, in which mortals comport themselves with proper, even anxious,

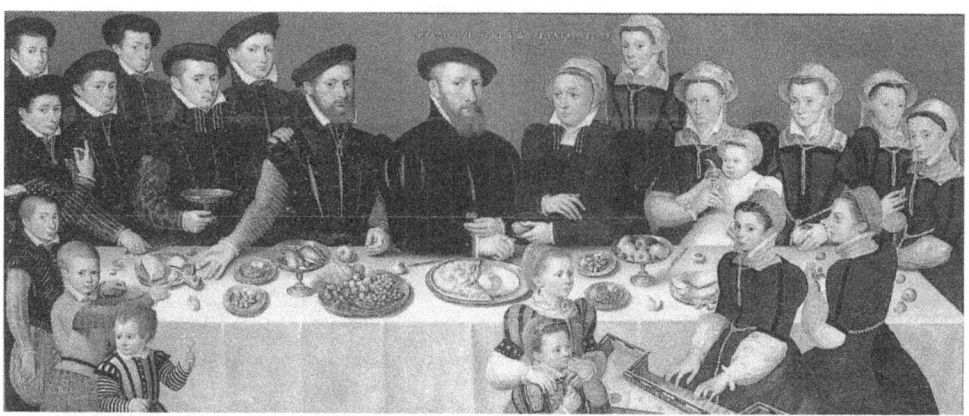

FIGURE 62. Attributed to Cornelis de Zeeuw, *Pierre de Moucheron and His Family*, 1563. Amsterdam, Rijksmuseum.

sobriety in the presence of the divine.[19] This tendency probably received strong reinforcement from the tradition of Roman portraiture, available to the sixteenth century in the form of marble busts and coins, as well as prints after both, which emphasized serious demeanor.

However that may be, the people of Bruegel's day preferred to have themselves depicted as straightfaced and stately ("stuer wijnbrouwigh en statigh," as Van Mander expressed it). *Statigh* and *statelyc* are old Netherlandish words that, like their English cognate *stately*, vividly convey such qualities as "distinguished," "aristocratic," "grave," "dignified."[20] It was precisely one of these words, *statigh*, we may remember, that Van Mander used to characterize the dignified man who is forced to smile in the presence of Bruegel's art.[21] And in his account of the lost painting by Frans Mostaert, the Schetz brothers are received by the citizens of Hoboken in a *seer statigh*, or "very solemn," manner.[22] A similar gravity dominates, for example, the portrait of the Antwerp merchant Pierre de Moucheron and his family (Fig. 62), dated 1563 and attributed to Cornelis de Zeeuw. Of French origin, De Moucheron was an ardent Calvinist, but this does not explain the unrelieved sobriety with which both parents and children regard the viewer.[23] In fact, had Miedema confined his dictum concerning laughter

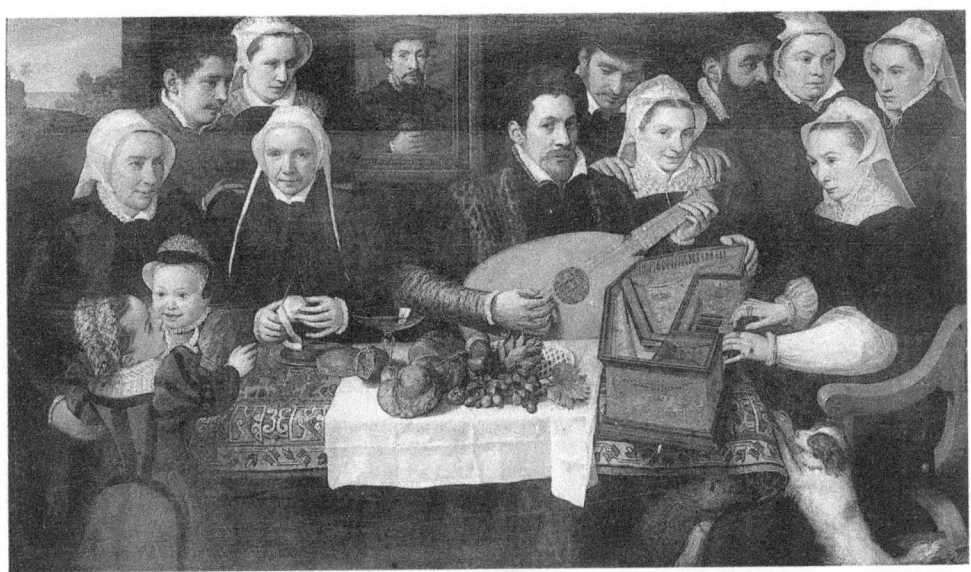

FIGURE 63. Frans Floris, *Family Portrait,* 1561. Lier, Museum Wuyts-van Campen-Caroly.

to portraits, he would have been right on the mark.[24] In the so-called Van Berchem group portrait that Frans Floris painted in 1561 (Fig. 63), the children at lower left interact with each other with slightly smiling faces, but the grown-ups conduct themselves with a gravity that belies the apparently convivial occasion in which they take part. But of course this family gathering does not so much commemorate an actual event as it serves as a compositional device.[25] Similarly, while the lute and clavichord, those eminently upper-class instruments, may in fact reflect the interests of those playing them, they also, and perhaps more cogently, symbolize love and family concord.[26] This is probably the case in Pourbus's "wedding" picture as well (see Fig. 61). Thus, it would be hazardous, to say the least, to accept such pictures as evidence of real-life behavior at the table.

Indeed, Erasmus's Folly quotes Horace to assure us, "dulce est desipere in loco," "it is delightful to be foolish at the proper time and place."[27] Folly may not be the most reliable authority on manners, even when invoking a revered ancient authority for support, but mealtime had long been seen as a preeminent occasion for relaxation, sociability, and laughter, both to recreate the spirit and to promote digestion.[28] This was the understanding, for instance, of the pilgrims who accompanied the English mystic Margery Kempe on her journey to the Holy Land in the early fifteenth century. Repelled by her spiritual groans and her unrelenting piety in general, they ejected her from their company at one point, readmitting her only on the promise (which she later broke) that she join their mealtime merrymaking and not speak of the Gospel in their hearing.[29] A late medieval treatise on table manners, the *Mensa philosophica*, among other things emphasizes the value of laughter at meals.[30] As Robert Burton would later recommend in his *Anatomy of Melancholy*, quoting the sixteenth-century medical writer Eobanus Hessus, the melancholy man should "feast often and use friends who are not still so sad / Whose jests and merriment may make thee glad."[31] It was a sentiment echoed in a Netherlandish proverb current in the seventeenth century and probably earlier: "A merry heart and sweet conversation serve well at the [dinner] table."[32] (We may note in passing that Geeraert Vorselman had a related end in view when he assured readers of his *Nyeuwen coock boeck* that his recipes would restore the appetites of those suffering from melancholy and excessive care.[33]) Erasmus's friend Sir Thomas More encouraged serious conversation and Bible reading at dinner, but thereafter, comic relief was provided by his fool, Henry Paterson.[34] For all their serious, scholarly endeavors, More and his humanist friends apparently enjoyed humor and comic stories; indeed, it is thought that More's brother-in-law John Rastell was responsible for *A Hundred Merry Tales*, a jest book first published in 1526.[35] In any case, More must have particularly esteemed Paterson for his levity, for he had him included in the group portrait of himself and his family that Hans Holbein painted about 1529.[36] Even Erasmus alludes to frivolous dinner entertainment in one of his colloquies: in *The Feast of Many Courses* (1527), a speaker recommends bringing in mimes and buffoons to "put on some comic pantomime," with actors to perform scenes from "everyday life" such as "a woman arguing with her husband over who's boss."[37] He could even tolerate speaking of ridiculous and squalid subjects as a means of relaxation (which would presumably have included mealtime conversations), but only so long, he cautioned, as the pleasure was mixed with profit.[38] Elsewhere, however, Erasmus was more circumspect. In his De civilitate morum puerilium, for example, he advises that at banquets "there should be joviality but no wantoness."[39] He probably would have counseled the same for less formal occasions; at least in several other colloquies, Erasmus has the speakers occasionally indulging in mild hilarity, albeit of a learned sort, at their meals.[40]

But if Erasmus advocated restraint and proper decorum at mealtimes, it is difficult to know how many people followed his advice. In fact, as Sullivan has observed,[41] it seems to have been a commonplace in Bruegel's day that the Netherlanders were inordinately fond of festivities: Guicciardini tells us that on birthdays, Twelfth Night, and other occasions, they give great banquets, inviting their friends and relatives, and enjoy themselves, "because they are naturally inclined to pleasures, feasts, [and] entertainments."[42] The Spanish biblical scholar Benito Arias Montano, sent by Philip II to Antwerp in 1568 to supervise the preparation of Plantin's Polyglot Bible, thought that the Netherlanders were excessive in their merrymaking.[43] It might be tempting to dismiss these comments as the ill-founded judgments of foreign observers, but much the same thing had already been said by Erasmus himself, who praised the manners of his countrymen: they possessed a gentle and straightforward nature, but still, they were given a little too much to pleasure, especially that of the table.[44] Sometime after Guicciardini and Montano, another native Netherlander, the Jesuit rector Carolus Scribanius, assures us that his countrymen have "a surplus of the sanguine humor in their constitution, the temperament most disposed to gaiety and laughter."[45] Thus it seems that Bruegel's fellow Netherlanders liked "to make good cheer," or, as they put it, "goede sier maken,"[46] which led to another excess, their tendency, as a current expression put it, "to celebrate the god Bacchus."[47] Guicciardini, for one, observes that the Netherlanders drink too much, night and day, to the great damage of their health and life, but perhaps they should be excused because the air of their country is extremely humid and melancholy.[48]

Such views of Bruegel's countrymen may well have been influenced by the Roman historian Tacitus, who in his *Germania* characterized the Germanic tribes as fond of entertainments and hospitality, and not particularly moderate in their drinking.[49] It was believed by Erasmus and others that the Netherlanders had descended from one of these tribes, the Batavians, and shared their proclivity to indulge.[50] Nevertheless, there must have been considerable truth in the observations of Erasmus and others; Goldstein, for example, describes the elaborate drinking vessels used in the Netherlandish drinking games of the period, including those so constructed that their contents had to be drained at a single draft.[51] In any case, the propensity of the Netherlanders "to make good cheer" can be seen above all in the *tafelspelen* that were performed at wedding banquets and on other special occasions. While some treat serious topics, much like the *spelen van sinne,* many are farces clearly in the spirit of the *kluchten,* intended to make the guests laugh and not much more, of which the farce *Bot Verstant en Cloucken Geest,* discussed above, is a prime example.[52] Fools, one or more in number, cavort through some plays; the titles of still others, such as *The Wine Can and the Piss Pot* and *The Man, the Wife, and a Herring,* indicate their equally lighthearted content.[53] Particularly bawdy is the wedding farce *St. Lasant,* published at Delft in 1597 but probably older, in which an old man makes a pilgrimage to a mock-saint to recover his virility.[54] We may doubt that the guests present at this play responded to its suggestive allusions with the solemn restraint shown by the company in the putative wedding feast by Frans Pourbus (see Fig. 61).

This is not to claim, of course, that serious subjects never dominated sixteenth-century dinners. Indeed, the opposite was true, if the Bible reading at Thomas More's table and Martin Luther's "table talk" are any evidence, and probably all the more so as the political and religious crises worsened in the Netherlands from the 1560s on. But there must have come a moment in even the most serious dinners when the assembled company sought respite in the antics of a fool like More's Henry Paterson or the jocularity of a farcical *tafelspel*. If the host and his guests exchanged stories, a practice recommended by Erasmus himself,[55] they most likely drew some of them from the published jest books and told others much in the same spirit. Such collections of anecdotes had long served to enliven the meal. Leon Battista Alberti, for example, gave his collection of stories (written before 1434) the title *Intercenales* (Dinner Pieces), to indicate that they were meant to be read over dinner; as with the *Nyeuwe clucht boeck*, its contents range from serious to amusing topics.[56] The *Mensa philosophica* offers a number of jokes deemed appropriate at mealtimes.[57] In the short preface to his third book of *Facetiae*, published in 1512, Heinrich Bebel tells us that some consider his stories "too lascivious and dirty," but he has heard them all told by "serious men at banquets," most of them in the presence of ladies (*apud matronas*).[58] The title page of the *Nyeuwe clucht boeck* of 1554 promises amusement for an honorable company (*eerlijc gheselscap*), although it does not specify the occasion; however, Georg Wickram dedicated his *Rollwagenbüchlein* of 1555 to an innkeeper famous for the stories with which he amused his guests at the table.[59] And while many of these stories would have failed the Erasmian test for proper dinner conversation, Erasmus gives us one colloquy, *The Fabulous Feast*, in which the guests amuse each other with frivolous anecdotes, some lifted from the old jest books, among them a story that would have been quite at home among the more scurrilous tales of *Een nyeuwe clucht boeck*.[60]

All this suggests that Bruegel's countrymen are likely to have agreed with the sentiments inscribed on a print by an artist working a generation later, *Evening* from Jan Saenredam's *Four Times of Day*, engraved sometime before 1599 after designs by Hendrick Goltzius (Fig. 64). It shows an elegant company eating and drinking around a table, including two lovers kissing, and its Latin verse tells us, "Evening drives sorrow and sadness far away, she lightens people's spirits and banishes care."[61] As Jan Jansz Starter asserts in his *Friesche Lust-Hof*, a collection of songs published at Amsterdam in 1621, on occasions of relaxation with food and drink, it is a good thing that sometimes one "de geck laet springen uyt de mouwen" (literally, lets the fool spring from the sleeves).[62] A distant echo of Ho-

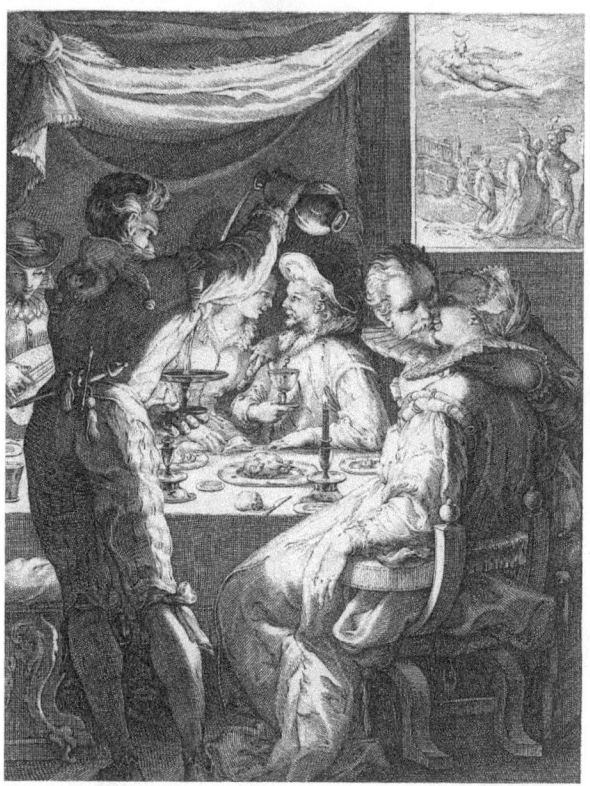

FIGURE 64.   Jan Saenredam, after Hendrick Goltzius,
The Four Times of Day: Evening, before 1599, engraving.
Amsterdam, Rijksmuseum.

race's famous "dulce est desipere in loco," this well-known expression was
exploited, as we have seen, by one of the fools in the Antwerp *landjuweel*
of 1561.[63] Starter also assures us that "everything has its time; it is praiseworthy that a man is wise in his calling and joyful in his drinking."[64] This
also sounds very much like an old proverb, and we may well ask if it, too,
was current in Bruegel's time.

     We shall never know if Jean Noirot's dinner parties were quite as un-
inhibited as the ones depicted in these two seventeenth-century prints,
nor if Noirot was more joyful in his drinking than he was wise in his call-

ing. But his dining room would have been a most appropriate place for pictures like Bruegel's two peasant scenes in Vienna or the Detroit *Wedding Dance*, not so much as models to avoid, or as moralities to contemplate, but as festive backdrops for mealtime sociability. Indeed, peasant revels seem to have had a fairly long association with urban dining rooms. Earlier in the century, Albrecht Dürer and other German artists were producing designs for table fountains, covered goblets, and the like, ornamented with egg wives, bagpipers, and other rustic figures.[65] As Goldstein has noted, stoneware drinking jugs of German and Netherlandish origins, often decorated with scenes of peasant dances and peasant weddings, were used in Antwerp households in the sixteenth century and later.[66] These designs were frequently taken from the prints of Sebald Beham, one of whose prints, as we have seen, inspired several figures in Bruegel's *Peasant Kermis*.[67] Finally, peasants figure in a number of *tafelspelen*, including those bearing such titles as "A Man and a Woman Dressed Like Peasants" and "A Drunken Peasant Who Goes Courting."[68]

Bruegel's rustic revels would thus have been appropriate decoration for a dining room. And if these pictures stimulated any conversation, as has been suggested, I suspect that the host and his guests would have been less likely to toss out Greek and Latin tags than the homegrown proverbs and old saws that came easily to the lips of most Netherlanders, regardless of class or education. If the dinner company had forgotten any of them, the numerous proverb collections in print could refresh their memories. Indeed, in 1568 Plantin himself published François Goedthals's *Proverbs anciens flamengs et françois*, a collection of homely expressions; Ortelius himself was happy to possess a copy of it, having obtained it from Plantin the same year.[69] This is not to claim, however, that the peasant scenes in Vienna and Detroit are "proverb pictures" in any sense of the word, but since proverbs comment on a great variety of everyday human experiences, the situations that Bruegel depicted would naturally have elicited common expressions and sayings. And why not? As the Protestant theologian and pedagogue Johannes Sturm tells us in his proverb collection, *Adagia classica* (Strasbourg, 1573), proverbs, among their other

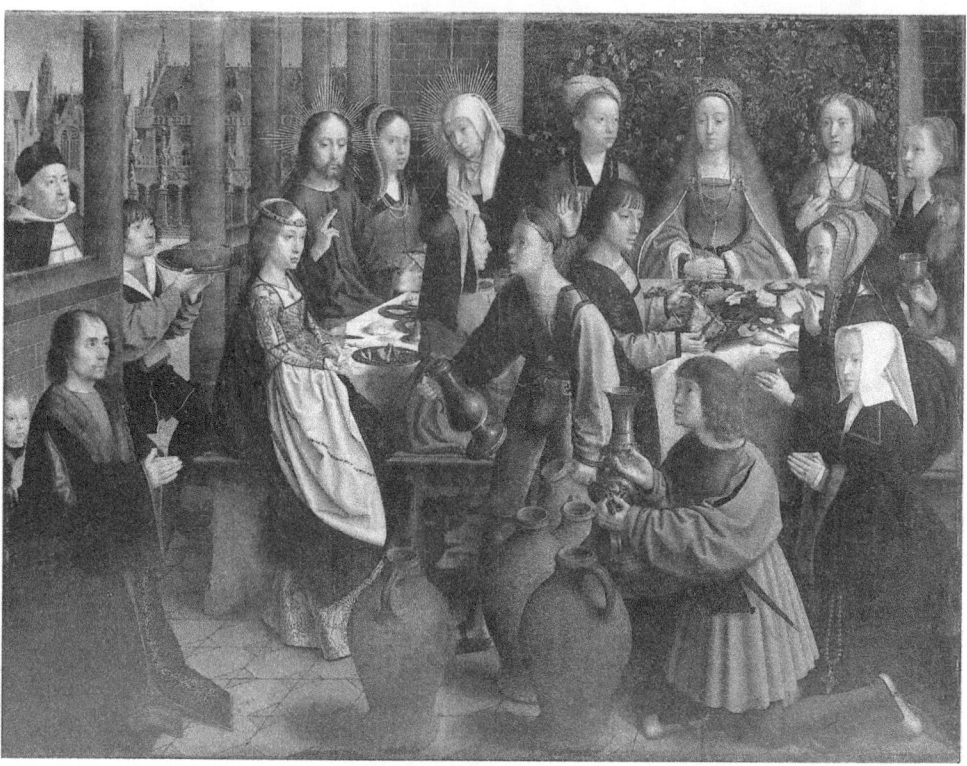

FIGURE 65. Gerard David, *Marriage Feast at Cana*. Paris, Musée du Louvre.

benefits, "increase our vocabulary, sharpen our understanding, and enliven the gatherings of family and friends."⁷⁰

Thus, when people contemplated Bruegel's *Kermis* (see Fig. 42), for example, they may have recalled the old adage that asserts, "It is a poor village (or church) that does not have at least one *kermis* a year."⁷¹ Conversely,
they might have remembered that "Het en is niet altyts kermisse" (It is
not always kermis time).⁷² Another proverb counsels us to "Let the nobility hunt, the peasants [have] their kermis, and the dogs mate, if you want
to stay out of a fight."⁷³ The *Wedding Feast* (see Fig. 43), in particular, would
have encouraged such homebred philosophizing. "In weddings and child-
birth," as another saying has it, "one maintains friendship."⁷⁴ Looking at

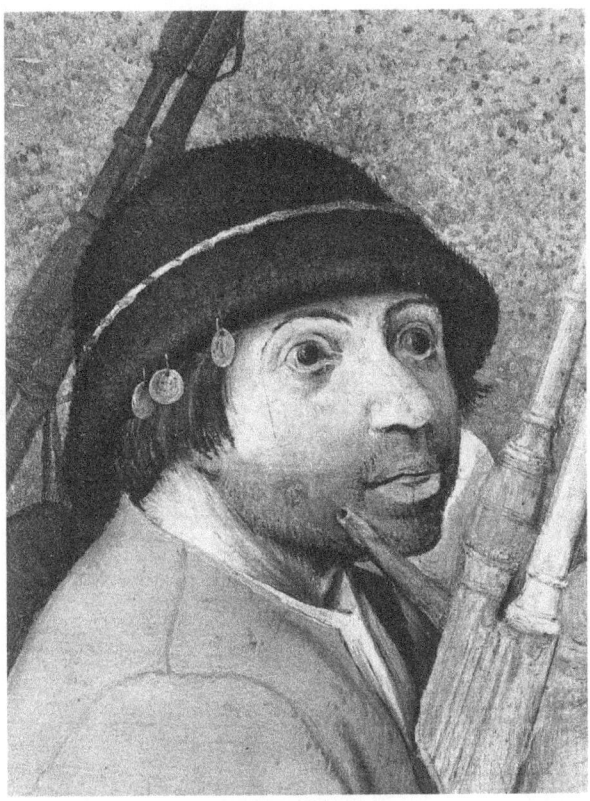

FIGURE 66. Detail of Fig. 43.

all this eating and drinking, viewers might have recalled the adage about guests who "sooner sit by the wine jug than by the bride."[75] And if the serving man and row of jugs at lower left were inspired by traditional depictions of the Marriage Feast at Cana, as we see in a painting of this subject by Gerard David (Fig. 65), and Bruegel was thereby slyly suggesting that only a similar miracle could satisfy all these thirsty guests, these details would only have added to the humor of his feast.[76] As for the bagpiper who has stopped playing to cast a yearning look at the *pottagie van rijs* being brought in by the two stalwart youths on a barn door serving as a makeshift tray (Fig. 66), he is a figure adapted from earlier

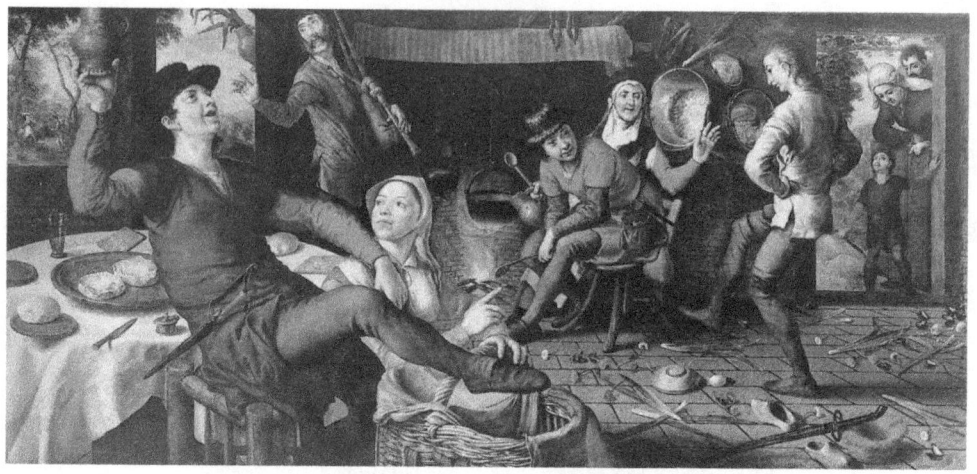

FIGURE 67.   Pieter Aertsen, *The Egg Dance,* 1557. Amsterdam, Rijksmuseum.

art, perhaps his counterpart in the left background of Aertsen's *Egg Dance* of 1557, now in Amsterdam (Fig. 67).[77] Bruegel's audience would surely have marveled how the artist painted him so that "Die honger ziet hem wt den ogen," that is, "hunger looks out of his eyes."[78] It could also be said of him as well as of his counterpart in the *Kermis* who is proffered, it seems, a jug of beer (see Fig. 58), "If the bagpipe is not full, it does not screech," or perhaps, "The sack must be full if you want the old geezer to play."[79] In both sayings, of course, the sack or bagpipe refers both to the rustic musical instrument and to the bagpiper's empty belly.

Another stock figure revitalized by Bruegel is the amply proportioned bride (Fig. 68). Although she sits enthroned in the middle ground, the whole composition focuses on her. Both her crown and her long flowing hair were traditional attributes of virginity;[80] equally traditional is the cloth of honor behind, although in this case, the crown seems constructed of paper and the simple, rustic cloth behind her is affixed by means of a rake to a great stack of hay. Customary, too, most likely, is her *statelyc* pose, hands folded and eyes demurely lowered, in contrast to the animated woman on her left. The bride was expected to show a reserved demeanor

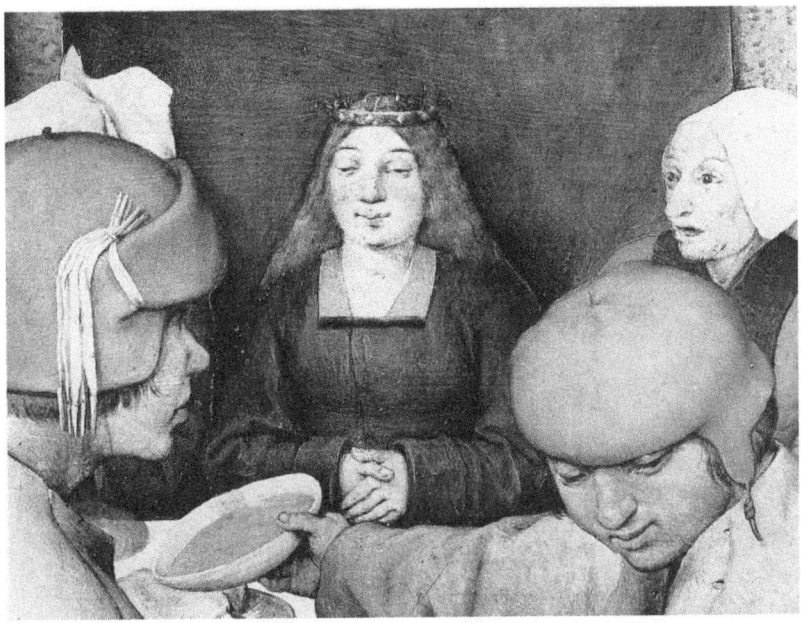

FIGURE 68. Detail of Fig. 43.

during the wedding festivities; she is almost always depicted as such, for example, when she presides at the Marriage Feast at Cana (see Fig. 65).[81] The old German expression "to sit there like a peasant bride" might have come to mind, as well as a Netherlandish variant, to be "as quiet as a bride."[82] But it is precisely here that Bruegel has fashioned one of his greatest comic figures. Perhaps it is not reading too much into this bride to suggest that her modesty seems assumed: is she a *vuile bruid*, as Bruegel's contemporaries termed a woman made pregnant before marriage?[83] "Not all are virgins who wear long hair," as Erasmus reminds us.[84] A *vuile bruid* figures in a *Peasant Wedding Dance* engraved by Pieter van der Heyden and bearing Bruegel's name as the inventor (Fig. 69).[85] As in the Detroit painting, it shows the bride seated at the table with her female companions; the accompanying verses describe how the girls wiggle their behinds and how the bride does well to sit, since she is full and sweet, that is, with child. The tone of these observations seems hardly censorious but jocu-

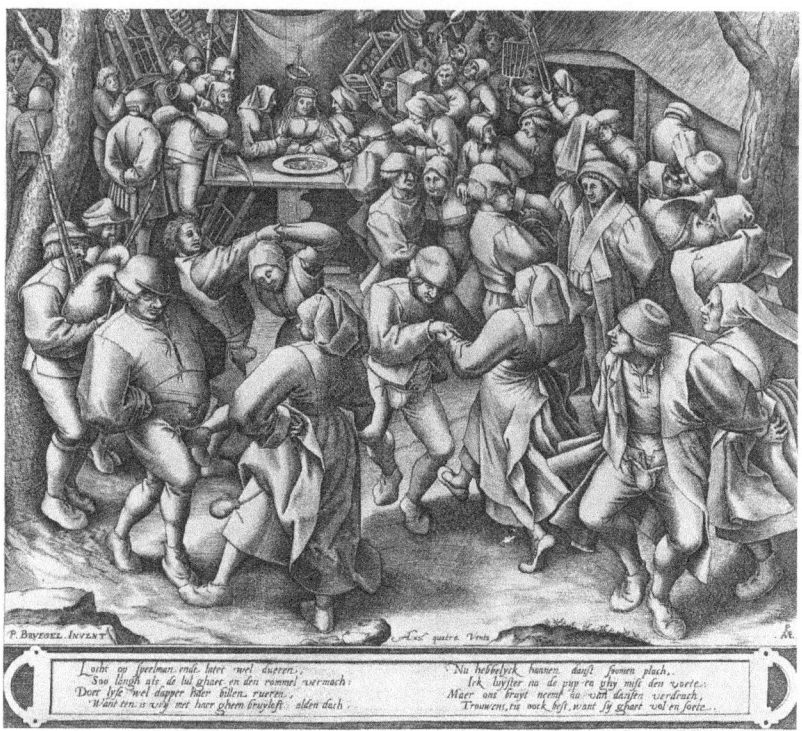

FIGURE 69. Pieter van der Heyden, after Pieter Bruegel the Elder(?), *Peasant Wedding Dance*, engraving, after 1570. New York, The Metropolitan Museum of Art, Harris Brisbane Dick Fund, 1933 (33.52.29).

lar and lighthearted, much in the spirit of the occasion. We may also wonder if the bride in the *Peasant Wedding Feast* is like the brides characterized by an English playwright of the next century, whose thoughts are "even acting of those hot and lustful sports / Are to ensue about midnight."[86] Whatever the case, it is not easy to define her slightly simpering expression. If any classically educated viewers of Bruegel's peasant scenes felt the urge to show off their knowledge of ancient literature, they may have quoted from Ovid's description of the feast of Anna Perenna, when the common folk gather near the banks of the Tiber; here they drink, sing, and "trip in dances lubberly, while the spruce sweetheart skips about with streaming hair." The last detail will undoubtedly call to mind the bride dancing in the Detroit *Wedding Dance* (see Fig. 41).[87]

In any event, to have inspired these or similar pleasantries would not have transformed Bruegel's peasant revels into allegories of sin, as we have been so often assured, but would only have enhanced the good-natured appeal of the rustic festivities that he so brilliantly portrayed. These paintings would surely have lightened the spirits of all who contemplated them, no matter how "straightfaced and *statigh*," as Van Mander would later put it, they might be on other occasions. Even Noirot must have responded to such images with laughter, or at least "twitched his lips in a smile," before he was overtaken by the events that ultimately drove him to bankruptcy, exile, and the loss of his prized Bruegels in the forced sale of 1572.

CHAPTER SIX

THE DEVIL'S NEMESIS:
GRIET AND HER SISTERS

And there is no anger above the anger of a woman. It will be more agreeable
to abide with a lion and a dragon, than to dwell with a wicked woman.

ECCLESIASTICUS 25:23

But honorable women should
Forgive me what I say, I would
Not wish to injure their good name.

SEBASTIAN BRANT

Taking proverbs literally was a favorite source of laughter in Bruegel's century, as we have seen, and Bruegel habitually exploited the visualization
of common expressions and sayings for humorous effect. Perhaps his most
bizarre effort occurs in a painting he executed some years before the two
scenes of peasant revels in Vienna. This is the *Dulle Griet* (Fig. 70), in which
an army of housewives (to judge from their bonnets and aprons) attack
and plunder devils in a fire-flickering infernal landscape. A wild-eyed
crone, considerably larger in scale than her followers, leads the ravaging
horde. She rushes across the center foreground, sword in hand, her
mouth open, apparently in a scream, and her thin, scraggly gray hair
streams from beneath her helmet (Fig. 71). With her left arm she clutches
an unlikely assortment of gold and silver vessels and common household

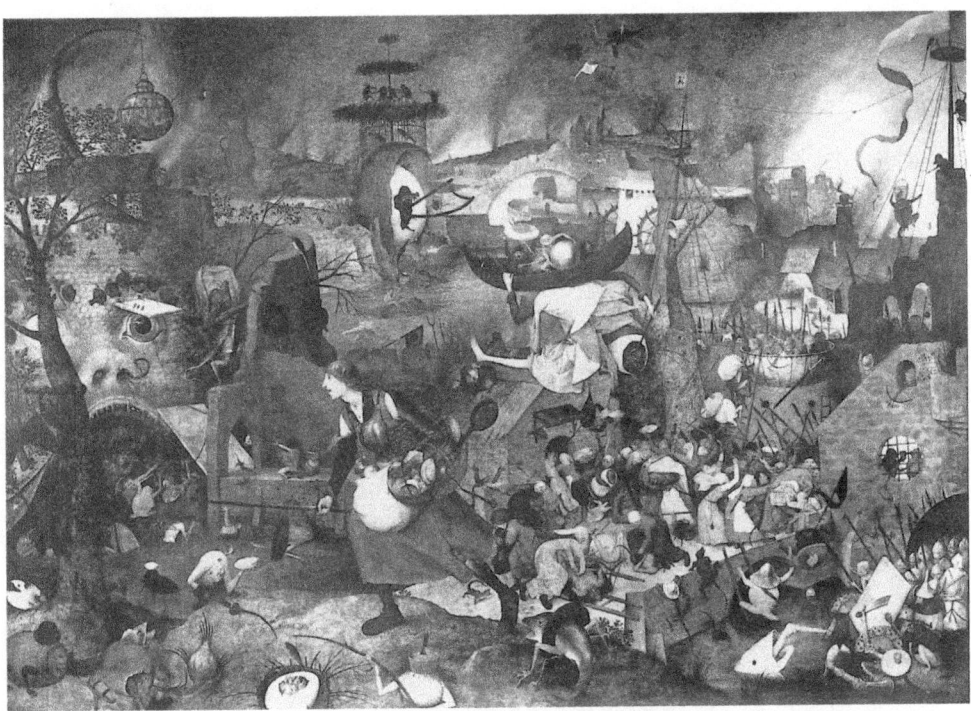

FIGURE 70. Pieter Bruegel the Elder, *Dulle Griet*. Antwerp, Museum Mayer van den Bergh.

objects. Before this onslaught the demons prance about impotently or cower within ruinous buildings; at the left, a giant grotesque head, much as the fish in Bruegel's *Big Fish Eat the Small*, regurgitates a slew of unclean creatures outside the walls of Hell. Even more than the *Vices* series, *Dulle Griet* evokes the shape-shifting, hallucinatory world of Bosch, and a recent examination of the picture by reflectography revealed the date, only partly legible to the naked eye, to be 1561,[1] close in time to Bruegel's other Boschian paintings, *Fall of the Rebel Angels* of 1562 and most likely the *Triumph of Death*. Within the hellish setting of the *Dulle Griet* Bruegel gave new expression to one of the stock characters of fifteenth- and sixteenth-century comedy and proverbial lore.

The painting in question was first described by Karel van Mander, who

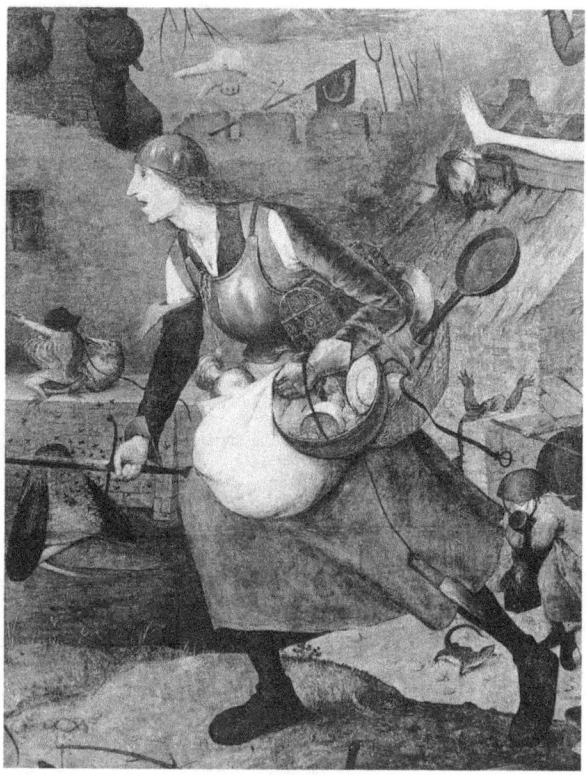

FIGURE 71. Detail of Fig. 70.

believed (evidently he was not sure) that it was one of the pictures in the palace of the emperor (that is, Rudolf II). The subject, Van Mander tells us, is "Dulle Griet die een roof voor de Helle doet" (Dulle Griet who loots in front of Hell).[2] His cryptic statement was carefully investigated in the past century by Jan Grauls, the eminent Belgian philologist and folklorist.[3] According to Grauls, the name Griet was by Bruegel's day a disparaging term for any ill-tempered, scolding woman, and he cites the saying "Where two Griets are in one house, no barking dog is needed."[4] Although Grauls could find no citation of this proverb earlier than the seventeenth century, it already occurs in Goedthals's proverb collection of 1568.[5] Griet also appears as a character in several Netherlandish *kluchten*, where she is called, among other things, Griet Sourmouth and Cross-eyed Griet, ladies evidently not very amiable in character.[6] Significantly, Griet was also a popular name for large cannons, probably as a tribute to their noisiness. In the fifteenth century, the great gun at Edinburgh Castle was called Mons Meg (because it had been cast at Mons, Flanders), as well as Muckle [Great] Meg and Roaring Meg, while Dulle Griet was precisely the name given to the giant cannon placed in the Friday Market at Ghent in 1578.[7] Grauls further observed that the word *dulle* should not be translated as "mad" or "crazy," as had been customary, but as "wrathful," "angry," or "hot-tempered." Finally, Van Mander's account of Dulle Griet's activity refers to an old Flemish proverb: "He could plunder in front of Hell and return unscathed." Grauls found variants of this expression in three proverb collections published in the Netherlands between 1549 and 1568, as well as in a political song of the period.[8] In fact, it seems to have been so common that Joos Lambrecht included it in his *Naembouck*, not a proverb collection this time, but a Flemish-French dictionary (unknown to Grauls) that was published in a second edition at Ghent in 1562.[9] Finally, as Grauls noted, the anonymous compiler of the Kampen proverb collection renders the expression as "*She* could plunder in front of Hell and return unscathed."[10]

Although there have since been many attempts to explain this picture,[11] Grauls's interpretation remains the most convincing chiefly because he situates its subject matter firmly within the popular culture of Bruegel's time. His identification of the main figure, moreover, is confirmed by a *factie* presented in the Antwerp *landjuweel* of 1561, in which one of the disreputable women summoned to the marketplace is none other than "Griet die den roof haelt voorde helle," that is, "Griet who robs in front of Hell."[12] Nevertheless, Grauls did not exhaust the full significance of the work, for we can clarify the folkloric themes to which Bruegel responded.

To begin with, a clue to the broader meaning of his painting can be found in the variant of the proverb "*She* could plunder in front of Hell and return unscathed." Although seldom noted, the context in which this expression occurs in the Kampen collection is significant, for it appears at the end of the group of proverbs concerning henpecked husbands: "Who would have peace in his home must do what the wife wants"; "Who would live in peace must let his wife have the upper hand"; "It is sad at home when the hen crows, but the rooster does not." And further down on the same page we encounter: "A blind man is a poor man, but poorer still is a man who cannot control his wife."[13] Its appearance among these other proverbs suggests that the expression "She could plunder in front of Hell and return unscathed," while describing any ill-tempered woman, could apply specifically to the quarrelsome and domineering wife, a favorite target of Renaissance satire. Sebastian Brant devoted a whole chapter in his *Ship of Fools* to the "odious, evil, poisonous wife, / Once she is married, prone to strife"; Jan van den Berghe included quarrelsome wives in his *Leenhof der ghilden* (that is, assembly of the guilds, or orders of fools), a poem of social satire published in 1564; and Thomas Nashe called her a "domesticall Furie to disquiet him [her husband] night and day."[14] Those "who always come home to find a shrew for a wife," we are informed in one fifteenth-century Netherlandish farce, "have suffering equal / To those in the abyss of Hell."[15] Indeed, the shrewish wife is frequently enountered in the literature and art of the fifteenth and sixteenth centuries.[16] We are assured by a verse in Goedthals's proverb collection that "an old wife without scolding" is one of the "five things one seldom sees."[17]

The shrew and her kind also figure prominently in an allegory of marital strife depicted in a Dutch print that, to judge from the style of the costume, was originally produced fairly early in the seventeenth century (Fig. 72).[18] The long rhyming inscription below informs us that the print shows Bigorne, a beast that feeds on suffering husbands who seek escape from their shrewish wives in his jaws;[19] his companion Scherminckel, whose head and forequarters appear in the left foreground, but repeated in full figure in the left distance, feeds only on good wives, an apparently meager diet that hardly sustains him. Scherminckel, also known as Chichevache (Pinchbelly, literally, "lean cow") and Chicheface ("lean muzzle"), is the elder of the two mythical beasts, first appearing, as far as we

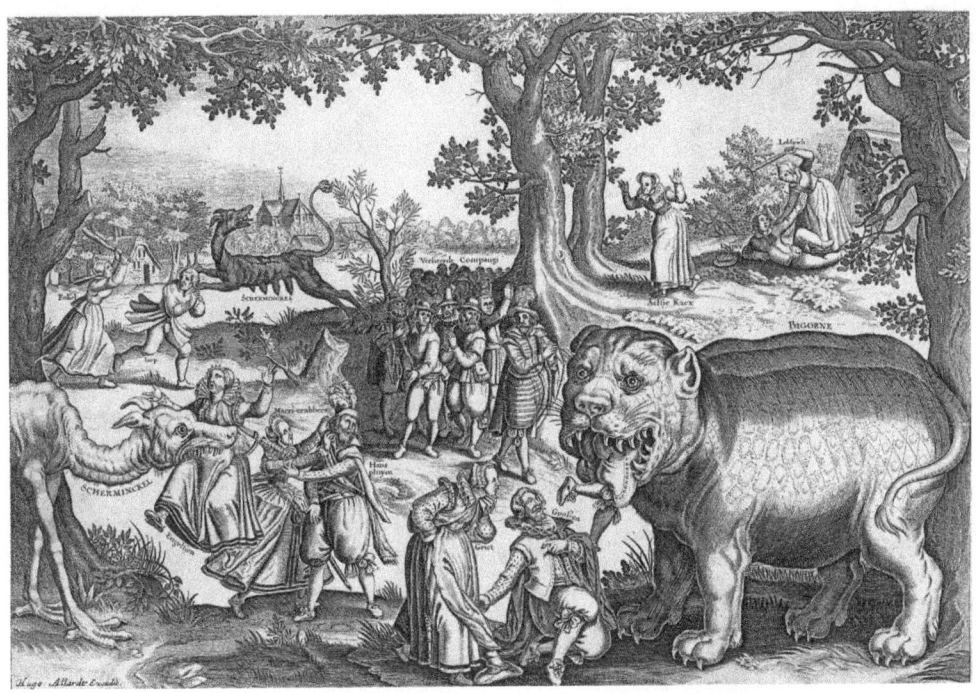

FIGURE 72. *Bigorne and Chichevache,* engraving, Netherlandish, early 17th century. Amsterdam, Rijksmuseum.

know, in a fourteenth-century French poem. It was familiar to Chaucer, who in the "Clerk's Tale" admonishes wives never to emulate the virtues of the Patient Griselda, "Lest Chichevache yow swelwe in hire entraille!" (that is, "swallow you in her entrails").[20] In a poem by John Lydgate, Chichevache was joined by Bycorne, (Bigorne), a name that one scholar derives from *bicornis,* meaning "two horned," alluding to the cuckolded husband.[21] Bigorne came to eclipse his emaciated companion, but only in the Netherlandish engraving under consideration is the irate woman from whom the long-suffering husband seeks salvation in Bigorne's maw most aptly labeled "Griet."

In Bruegel's picture, Dulle Griet's cohorts imitate her aggressive behavior: they plunder the hapless devils and attack them with sticks, clubs,

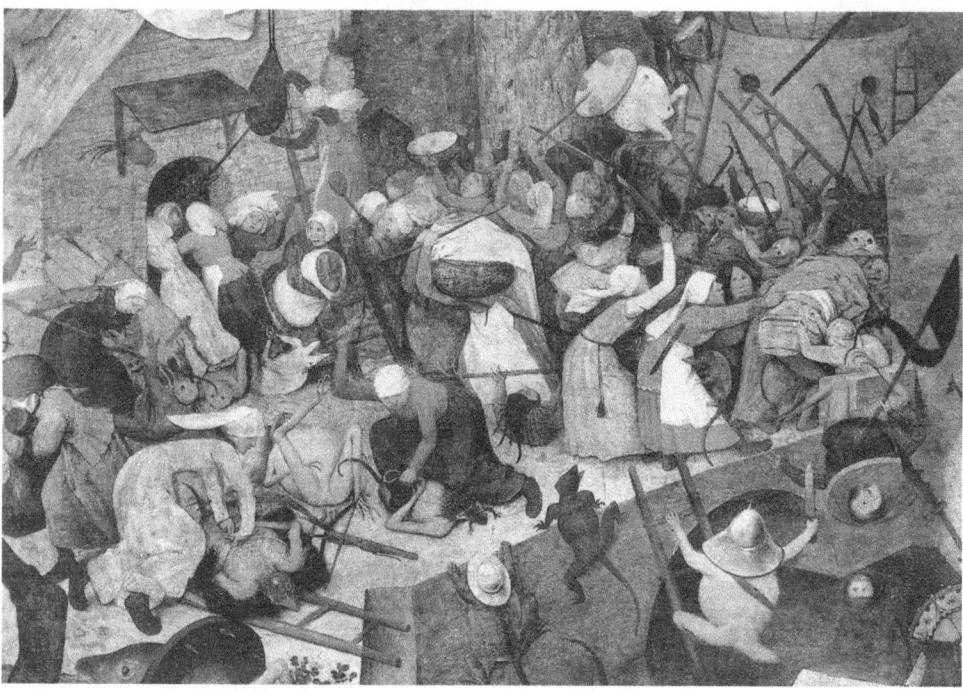

FIGURE 73.   Detail of Fig. 70.

and swords (Fig. 73). One dauntless housewife even humiliates her victim by tying him to a pillow. For this last detail, Bruegel once again turned
to a familiar expression. As Grauls has observed, in the famous play
Mariken van Nijmeghen, Mariken's ill-tempered aunt, raging at her niece,
says that she is so angry that she could tie up the Devil, "or bind him to
a cushion as if he were a babe."[22] In another Netherlandish play of the
period, a beleaguered husband complains that his quarrelsome wife must
have been one of the seven wives who bound the Devil to a pillow.[23] I
have yet to find this expression in any proverb collections of the period,
but it must have been long current. An Italian engraving of about 1460
shows a battle between women and devils, in which the latter are clearly
getting the worst of it (Fig. 74). One devil has been suspended from a
gallows, the despairing words "O bad company" issuing from his mouth.

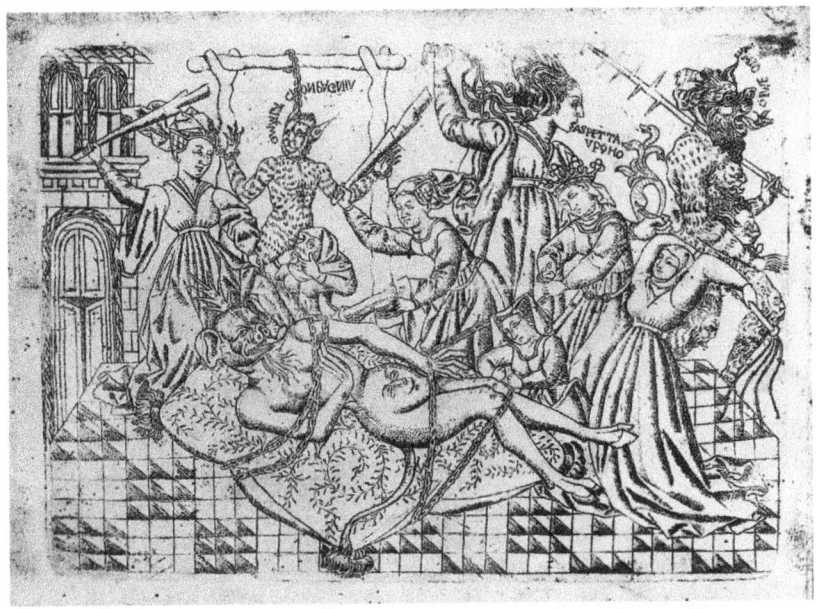

FIGURE 74. *Women Fighting Devils,* engraving, Italian School, 15th century.

A second devil departs in haste, crying, "Alas, alas!" chased by a whip-wielding woman who urges the demon to "Wait up a bit!" while several of her companions secure a third devil with chains to a large cushion.[24] A woman binding the Devil to a cushion occurs in a number of choir stall carvings, including those at Aershot and Dordrecht,[25] and Bruegel also depicted this motif in his *Netherlandish Proverbs,* painted in 1559 (Fig. 75).

Such scenes stand in marked contrast to the cordial relations that the Devil traditionally enjoyed with women. He had easily cajoled Eve into eating the forbidden fruit,[26] and in one English mystery play connives with Noah's wife to keep her husband from completing the ark.[27] He regularly collaborated with witches, both young and old. At least one preacher of the early fifteenth century insisted that witchcraft went all the way back to Eve, who wanted to be an enchantress.[28] Medieval folk-lore, moreover, credited him with a mother and a grandmother, the for-mer known as the Devil's dam, a personage whose name crops up several

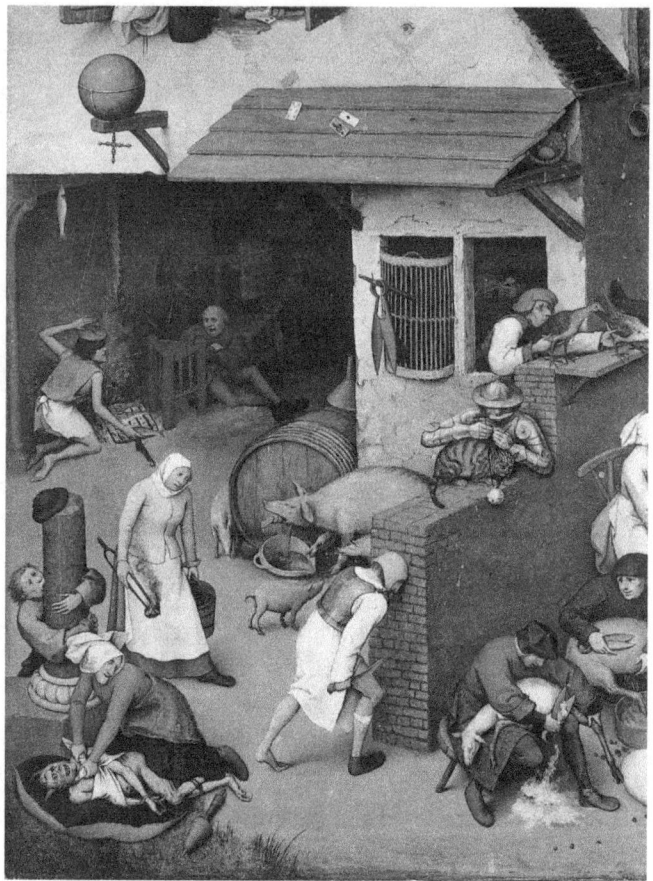

FIGURE 75. Detail of Fig. 19.

times in the plays of Shakespeare.[29] Several Netherlandish proverbs current in Bruegel's time mention the Devil's mother: "To outrun the Devil
and meet his mother" and "What the Devil cannot do, there he sends his
mother."[30] She appears, as it happens, in a print by Israhel van Meckenem, *The Virgin on Crescent Moon* of 1502.[31] At the bottom of the print,
angels attack devils, accompanied by an inscription that says, in part,
"Who defiled Adam besides me and my mother [*matrem meam*]?"[32] In this
case, the Devil's dam must be the voluptuous siren at bottom center,

immediately below the Virgin's feet; the apple she holds probably alludes to original sin.[33] But in addition to his mother, the Devil could also have a wife and children, as we shall see.

A major exception to these amicable relations between women and the Devil, however, was the virago. When she went on the rampage, she did not fear to attack even the denizens of Hell.[34] As we are told in Goedthals's proverb collection of 1568, "One woman makes a din . . . , two women a lot of trouble, three an annual market, four a quarrel, five an army, and against six . . . the Devil has no weapon."[35] But a single shrew was enough to send the Devil fleeing, the subject, in fact, of "Daz Jad von Wirtemberg," a German poem of the fourteenth or fifteenth century. An army of devils assembles on a wide field to battle a lone evil woman. The opponents fall upon each other and soon the devils are beaten, their leader killed, and the survivors chased back to the Underworld, where the Devil's mother, wife, and children find refuge in the towers of Hell. The poet concludes with the advice, "Who now would seek to plunder Hell, he should take along with him an evil wife and he will succeed."[36] A similar idea informs a broadsheet published at Augsburg about 1475 (Fig. 76). The woodcut shows a squad of devils attacked by a ferocious old woman armed with a large ladle; several devils lie wounded or dead, while some of their companions retreat from the battle. The woodcut does scant justice to the accompanying verses, which recount how the evil woman (übel weyb) vanquished more than a thousand devils, forcing the others to flee to the safety of Hell. The devils' fate is likened to that of a man married to a shrewish wife who opposes his every wish.[37] A variant of this perennial battle between women and the denizens of Hell occurs in a fifteenth-century carnival play in which three old women steal the Devil's cattle grazing outside the gate of Hell. In an attempt to protect his property, Lucifer and his companions attack the women but are driven back. One of the victors concludes the play by boasting of all the trouble old women cause in the world: not even the Devil can withstand them.[38] A novel twist to this topos occurs in a tale in *Een nyeuwe clucht boeck*, where we are told that many men have a devil lying beside them in bed, that is, their wives.[39]

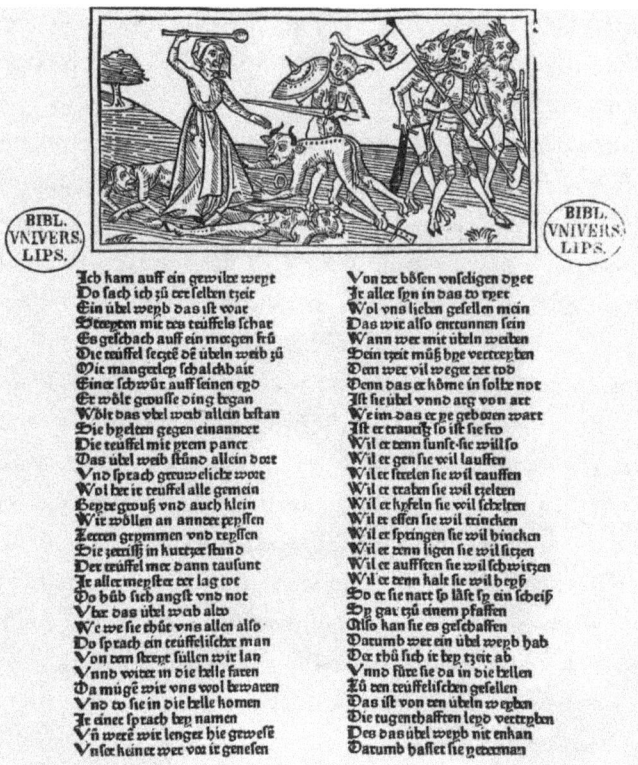

FIGURE 76. *Old Woman Confronting Devils*, ca. 1475, woodcut, Augsburg. Leipzig, Universitätsbibliothek der Universität Leipzig.

It was no wonder, then, that a virago was called a *helleveeg*, literally, a "damned [one] from Hell," a homely old Netherlandish word still in use.[40]

In the sixteenth century, the Nuremberg poet and playwright Hans Sachs exploited such ill-fated encounters between the Devil and old women for comic effect. In his poem "Der teuffel mit dem kaufman und den alten weibern," a poor merchant becomes rich by selling his soul to the Devil. When the time comes to keep his end of the bargain, he escapes by confronting the Devil with two old women who thrash him unmercifully.[41] In another poem, "Der teufel nam ein altes weib zu eh" (1557),

Sachs describes how the Devil comes up to the surface to seek a wife. He marries an old woman who is rich but ugly, and she beats him up so much at night that he finally runs away. On learning that his wife has gone to court to get him back, the Devil returns thankfully to Hell.[42] Sachs's carnival play *Der Teüffel mit dem alten Weyb*, written in 1545, tells how an old woman was engaged by the Devil to break up a marriage in exchange for a pair of shoes. With her lies, she creates dissension between a married couple with such disastrous effect (the husband kills his wife) that the horrified Devil gives her the shoes at the end of a staff, saying, "Your poisonous tongue makes my hair stand on end."[43] This last is a tale that apparently dates from at least the fifteenth century: frescoes of this period survive in some Scandinavian churches that show the Devil offering the woman a pair of shoes attached to the end of a long pole.[44] Martin Luther repeats this little tale in several of his writings as proof that the Devil hates happy marriages and does everything possible to break them up.[45]

Encounters between the Devil and his nemesis appear in German prints of the same period. A woodcut of about 1532 by Sachs's fellow Nuremberger, the artist Barthel Beham, shows Belzepock (variant of Beelzebub) being attacked by an old woman (Fig. 77). According to the verses above the image, the Devil craves feminine company. Seeing an old woman, he asks her the way to the Pfarrhof (or "rectory," a euphemism for a brothel), where he hopes to find a young woman or two. After a short exchange, she snatches up a stick and gives him a good walloping. The verses conclude with a warning to the reader to avoid such evil-tempered creatures: the man who possesses one suffers both Purgatory and Hell on earth.[46] In an engraving by Jacob Binck (Fig. 78), dated 1528, a woman clubs the Fiend over the head with her distaff.[47] Daniel Hopfer's etching, undated but done sometime before 1536, the year of his death (Fig. 79), depicts the Devil collapsing beneath the blows of three old women while other devils flutter helplessly about; around one arm of the fallen victim is wound a banderol inscribed "GIB . FRID," or "give peace," presumably his words of surrender.

In none of these tales and images is the old woman armed with any-

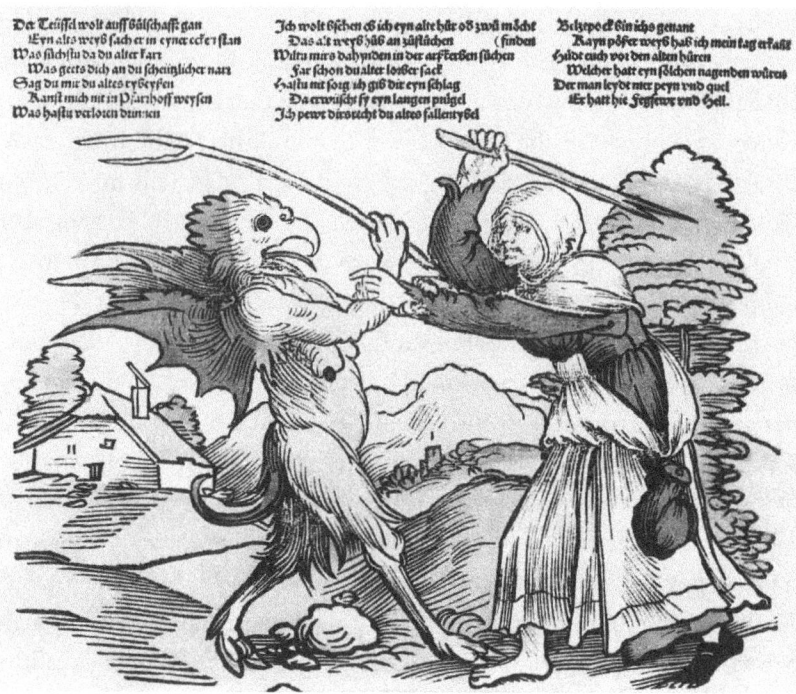

Der Teüffel wolt auff bülschafft gan
Eyn alts weyß sach er in eyner ecke stan
Was sichstu da du alter fart
Was geets dich an du scheintzlicher natz
Sag du mir du altes erbseysel
Kanst mich nit in Pfarrhoff weysen
Was hastu verloren drinnen

Ich wolt sschen ob ich eyn alte hůt od zwů möcht
Das alt weyß hůb an zůsuchen   (finden
Wiltu mirs dahynden in der arsskersten suchen
Far schon du alter lotter sack
Hastu mit sorg ich gib dir eyn schlag
Da erwischt sy eyn langen prügel
Ich peut dir ostecht du altes sallentybel

Belzebock bin ichs genant
Kayn pöser weyß haß ich mein tag erfast
Holdt euch vor den alten hůren
Welcher hatt eyn sölchen nagenden würtes
Der man leydt mer peyn vnd quel
Er hatt hie Fegfewr vnd Hell.

FIGURE 77. Barthel Beham, *Old Woman Thrashing a Devil*, ca. 1532, woodcut. Gotha, Stiftung Schloss Friedenstein, Schlossmuseum.

thing more than a club or distaff, or perhaps a rope, and she is never clad in armor. Bruegel's Dulle Griet, however, wears various odds and ends of military gear, including a breastplate, with a mailed glove and a kind of metal cap on her head; this martial costume is parodied by the little helmet-monster squatting on the wall behind her (in much the same way that the demons parody the attributes of Superbia in Bruegel's *Allegory of Pride* (see Fig. 14). Griet also brandishes a sword in her right hand, while a knife dangles from her belt. Such warlike costume was in Bruegel's day considered totally unfit for a woman, although there were exceptions, including, of course, the Amazons of antiquity. Similarly, in her *Treasure of the City of Ladies*, Christine de Pizan advised baronesses to show the spirit of a man and to know how to handle weapons in order to defend the ter-

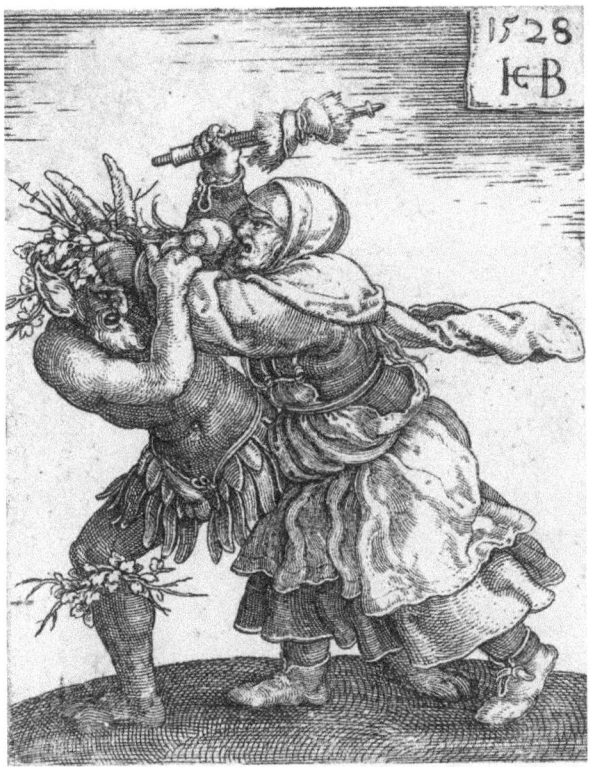

FIGURE 78.   Jacob Binck, *Old Woman Clubbing the Devil*,
1528, engraving. Vienna, Albertina.

ritories of their husbands in their absence.[48] A print published sometime
after Bruegel's death portrays Kenau Simonsdr. Hasselaer, a woman who
actively participated in the defense of Haarlem during the Spanish siege
of 1572–73 (Fig. 80). In full battle dress and bearing a spear, she displays
the severed head of "Dom Pero" (that is, Pedro), an enemy soldier she
has dispatched, and whose body lies on the ground behind her; Kenau's
pose and the composition in general recall many depictions of the period
of the Old Testament heroine Judith displaying the head of Holofernes.[49]

But Griet is neither a noble lady nor a heroine, ancient or modern,[50]
and Bruegel may have been partly inspired by the topos of the Fight for

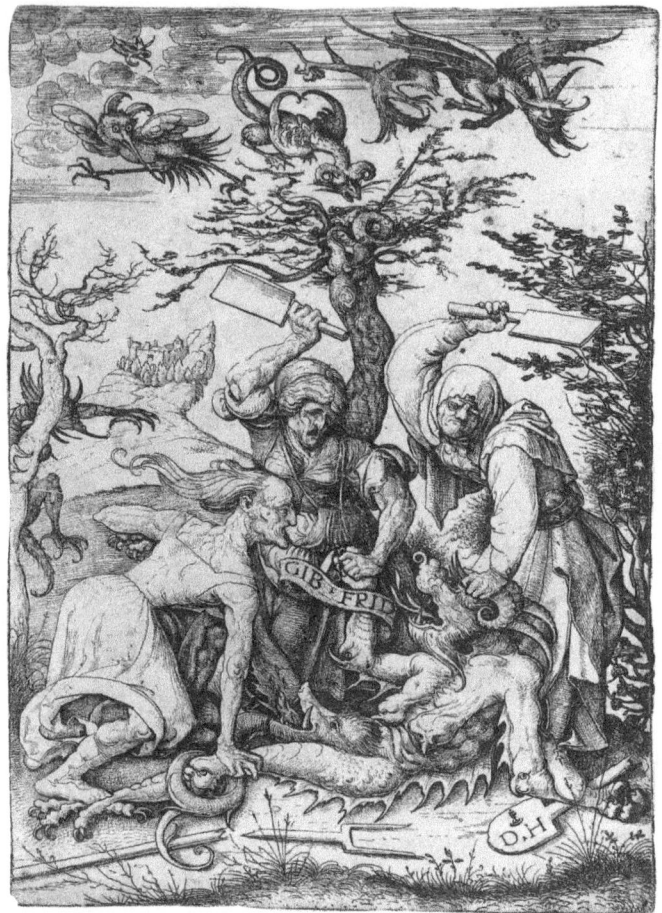

FIGURE 79. Daniel Hopfer, *Three Old Women Thrashing the Devil*, etching. Amsterdam, Rijksmuseum.

the Breeches, in which the wife often clinches her victory over her husband by appropriating his breeches and occasionally his wallet and knife as well.[51] This subject inspired an engraving by the Monogrammist MT, a German artist active in the early 1540s (Fig. 81), in which the wife has already pulled on her husband's hose and breeches, its distended codpiece a sly comment on her aggressive virility in contrast to the impotence of her cringing husband. The struggle for the breeches also inspired a car-

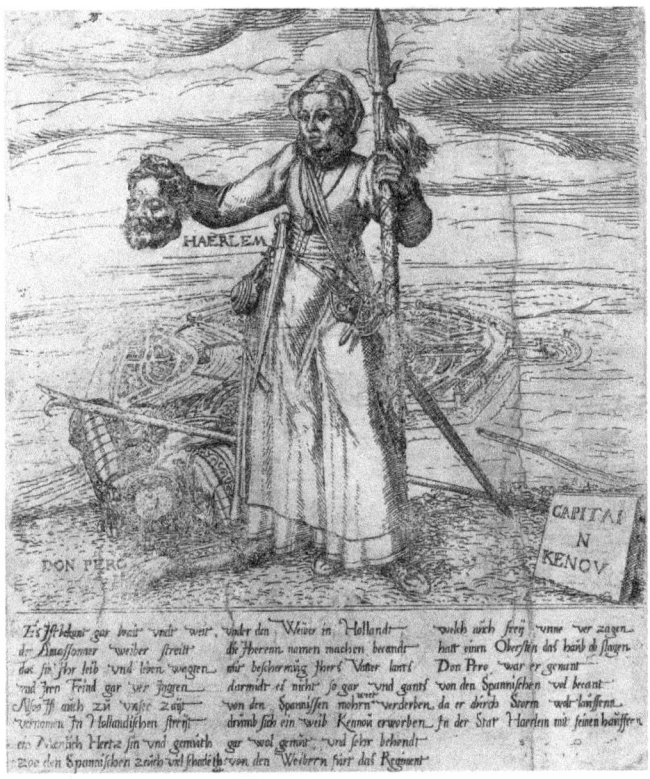

FIGURE 80. *Kenau Simonsdr. Hasselaer,* etching. Amsterdam,
Rijksmuseum.

nival play of 1553 by Hans Sachs.[52] Erasmus may well have witnessed similar performances, for in *The Feast of Many Courses,* as we recall, he has one
of the speakers recommend that mimes and buffoons be engaged to
present such commonplace subjects as "a woman arguing with her husband over who's boss."[53] But Griet's sword may allude more specifically
to yet another proverbial saying. In both Joos Lambrecht's dictionary of
1562 and Goedthals's volume of 1568, the Netherlandish proverb "To rob
in front of Hell and return unscathed" is followed by its French equivalent: "He could go to Hell with sword in hand."[54] As for the booty that
she has snatched from the infernal regions, including jewelry and odds

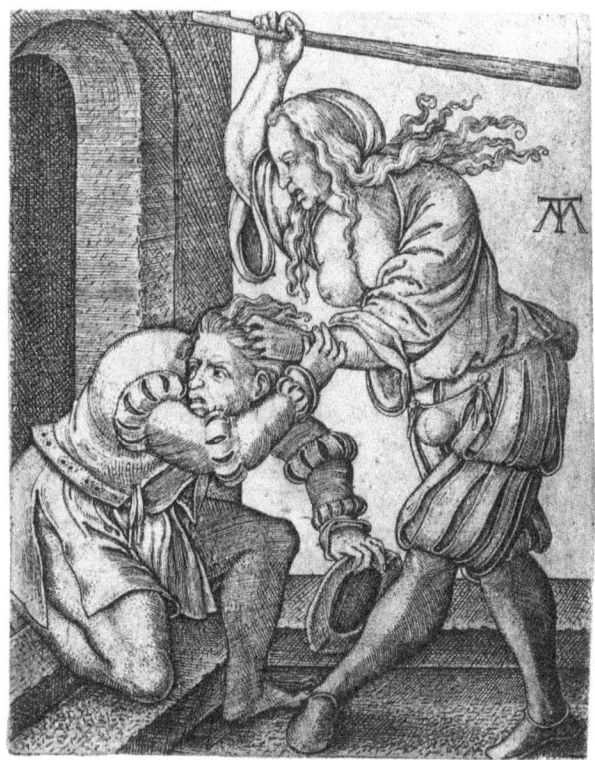

FIGURE 81. Monogrammist MT, *The Fight for the Breeches*, ca. 1540–43, engraving. London, British Museum.

and ends of household goods, we may note that in the dictionaries of Christophe Plantin and Cornelis Kiliaan, the Netherlandish verb for plunder, that is, *plunder, plonder,* could refer to household objects of small value, even trash, while the noun *plonderij* signified "trash" and suchlike.[55]

Grauls concentrated almost exclusively on Griet and her companions, and with one exception he apparently assumed—and, I am inclined to believe, correctly—that the other details in Bruegel's painting function primarily as accessories—similar to what the ancients called *perergia* or *pererga* in painting—that create the infernal milieu and possess no further

symbolic meaning.[56] The exception singled out by Grauls is the monster
on the right in the picture (see Fig. 70) that ladles out from its egg-shaped
posterior coins that are caught by several housewives below.[57] Like the
distaff, the large spoon or ladle was a traditional attribute of the housewife and could even serve as a weapon in her struggle with the infernal
horde (see Fig. 76). But a devil wielding this domestic utensil is a dis-
tinct novelty. Grauls suggested that this figure was inspired by the expression "to ladle with a big spoon," signifying excessive liberality, waste,
and prodigality, an expression that he found in Satorius's *Adagorium Chi-
liades Tres* of 1561.[58] Taken together with the boat balanced on the monster's back, which he identified as the notorious *blauwe schuit*, or Blue Boat
filled with the good-for-nothings of this world, Grauls concluded that
this group alludes to drunkards, revelers, and their ilk who "ladle with
the big spoon," that is, waste their money in frivolous living. But how these
wastrels fit into Bruegel's apotheosis of shrewish women is unclear, and
Grauls's explanation becomes all the more doubtful when we realize that
the "big spoon" also has a long handle, which was proverbially recommended for dining with the Devil. Chaucer, for example, tells us, "'Therefore bihoveth hire a ful long spoon / That shal ete with a feend,' thus herde
I seye."[59] The reason for this caution is suggested in an English play of
1584: "He that eats with the deuil without a long spoone, his fare will be
ill."[60] However, this expression fits but uneasily with the general subject
of Bruegel's picture, and even if he was in fact inspired by some form of
the "long spoon" proverb, his monster with the ladle could simply be another example of *pererga*.

Bruegel may have painted the *Dulle Griet* for his own enjoyment, but
given its complexity, it was more likely done for a patron. What occasioned this particular commission, however, we shall never know. Perhaps
it was inspired by the unusual independence that Netherlandish women
seem to have enjoyed during Bruegel's lifetime. This freedom impressed
Lodovico Guicciardini. In his description of the Netherlands of 1567,
Guicciardini noted that women were much freer there than elsewhere to
conduct their own business affairs.[61] They are very sober and active, he

tells us, not only in managing their families but also in buying and sell-ing merchandise; after the death of their husbands, they often run the family businesses on their own. One such widow was Volcxken Diercx, who after the death of her husband Hieronymus Cock continued issu-ing prints under the sign of the Four Winds, possibly until her own death in 1600.[62] Others were Kenau Simonsdr. Hasselaer, the heroine of Haarlem, who in peacetime dealt in ship timber,[63] and Maeyken Verhulst (called Bessemers), widow of Pieter Bruegel's teacher Pieter Coecke van Aelst and later his mother-in-law. After Coecke's death in 1550, Van Man-der tells us, Maeyken Verhulst published his translation of Serlio's books on architecture; she may also have been a professional miniature painter.[64] But Guicciardini was not certain that this was all good, for he also com-plains that such independence, joined with "the natural avidity of women to dominate," makes them proud and imperious and often quarrel-some."[65] With Guicciardini's observations in mind, we may note that the translator of a Netherlandish edition of Brant's *Ship of Fools* (Antwerp, 1548) omitted the chapter on bad wives, perhaps in fear of alienating an important segment of his potential audience.[66]

But this must remain speculation. Aside from a reduced copy of the composition in pen and watercolor by an unknown artist (Düsseldorf, Kunstmuseum),[67] Bruegel's *Dulle Griet* does not seem to have enjoyed the popularity that so many of his other inventions did, especially those turned out in large numbers by Pieter Brueghel the Younger and his work-shop. The basic proverbs from which Bruegel developed his composition were still being depicted toward the middle of the seventeenth century by two Flemish painters, David Ryckaert III and David Teniers the Younger. In one picture, Ryckaert showed a wrathful old woman raid-ing Hell (Fig. 82); she vigorously brandishes a broom at a horde of terrified demons, her *plonder* spilling out of her apron. More discrimi-nating in taste than Bruegel's plundering harridan, she has confined her-self to looting jewels and plate. It cannot be determined with certainty if she represents Dulle Griet, although it is possible.[68] Another painting by Ryckaert, done about the same time, features a sword-wielding hag

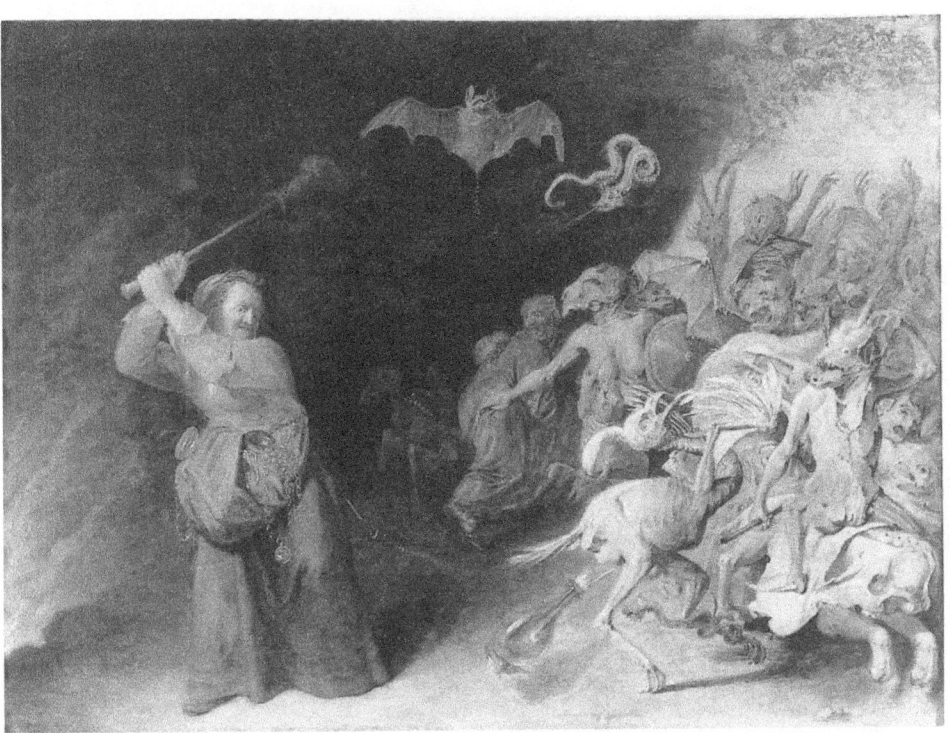

FIGURE 82. David Ryckaert III, *Old Woman Attacking Devils*. Vienna, Kunsthistorisches Museum.

who drives devils out of their fire-lit cave, jewels once more caught up in her apron, an illustration of the variant "She could go to Hell with sword in hand."[69] For his part, probably sometime in the mid-1630s David Teniers depicted an old woman binding a struggling dog-headed demon to a pillow, as his fellow devils flee her vicinity in panic (Fig. 83).[70] Whether she represents another Dulle Griet is unclear, but a proverb circulating in this period speaks of "the best Griet that one found, was the one who bound the Devil to a cushion," apparently a reference to the legend of St. Margaret and the Devil.[71] Nevertheless, Teniers's old woman can hardly be St. Margaret; rather, the artist apparently conceived her as a witch, for she kneels within a magic circle inscribed on the floor,

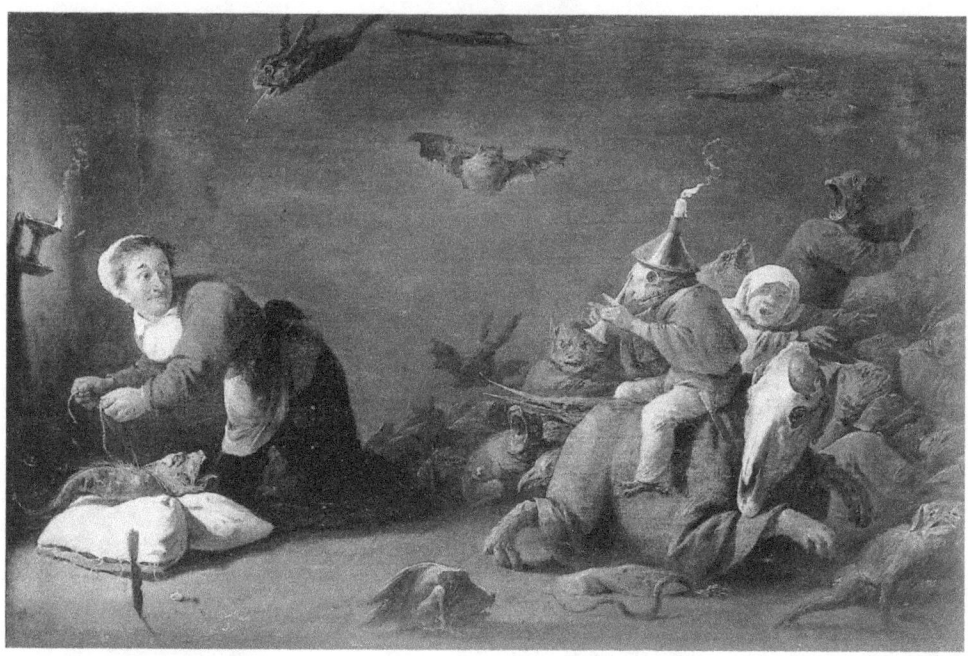

FIGURE 83. David Teniers the Younger, *Old Woman Binding a Devil to a Cushion*. Munich, Bayerische Staatsgemäldesammlungen, Alte Pinakothek.

whose rim is marked with characters impossible to decipher. But in both Teniers's and Ryckaert's pictures the infernal topography has been reduced to the barest indications,[72] and their old crones seem only mildly ill-tempered, in comparison with the demonic anger of Bruegel's Dulle Griet and her cohorts, as they seem to shake the very foundations of Hell in the violence of their fury. Out of old and slightly shopworn proverbs, jokes, and tales about nagging wives and rampaging old women did Bruegel thus forge one of his most comic creations.

EPILOGUE

TAKING LAUGHTER SERIOUSLY

You will marvel at how many jokes and laughter can accompany such
serious and weighty matters.

LEON BATTISTA ALBERTI, ca. 1443

Nothing is more fun than treating jokes seriously.

ERASMUS

It would probably be unwarranted to characterize the sixteenth century
as the Age of Laughter, but throughout western Europe Bruegel's contemporaries pursued laugher with an unprecedented vigor. They generally agreed with Aristotle and other ancient writers that man is a risible
animal—"laughter is man's special attribute [*rire est le propre de lhomme*]," as
Rabelais insisted in the introductory verses to his *Gargantua and Pantagruel*.
They also speculated endlessly on its causes, its physical and psycholog-
ical effects, and the objects and situations that incited it. The physician
Laurent Joubert examined laughter in detail in his *Traité de ris* of 1579, the
first treatise, as far as I know, devoted exclusively to that subject. Some
moralists still adhered to the prevailing medieval view that all laughter
was deplorable, the effects of original sin. More common, however, was
the belief that laughter helped preserve one's mental and physical well-
being, and it was recommended as a sovereign remedy in the treatment
of melancholy. Laughter was also discussed in the conduct books of Eras-

mus, Vives, and others, who distinguished between the proper and improper kinds of laughter, condemning the heartier varieties, especially the
guffaw, as vulgar, unfit for gentlefolk.

If laughter in its theoretical or social aspects was pondered by the more
serious-minded, its reality was enthusiastically embraced by people of all
kinds and conditions. There was, in fact, an international trade in laughter; jokes, humorous stories, and the plots of comic plays circulated from
one country to another, but nowhere, perhaps, was laughter more assid-
uously cultivated than in the Netherlands. Laughter was a major commodity supplied by the *rederijkers* in their farces and other *recreaties,* by the
professional fools, and by the jest books and songbooks of the day. Much
of this laughter, of course, was intended to do more than simply entertain. As Herman Pleij has usefully reminded us, "People were supposed
to absorb vital universal truths while laughing—a pedagogical technique
developed with great effectiveness by the mendicant orders."[1] Humor had
played an important role in medieval sermons and indeed in moral instruction in general, of which two outstanding examples, to note them
again, are Sebastian Brant's *Ship of Fools* and Erasmus's *Praise of Folly.* But
Pleij further contends that our own distinction between seriousness and
play was unknown in the early modern period,[2] and that even the most
farcical *kluchten* were no less edifying than the allegorical *sinnespelen,* in-
structing their audiences in proper religious and social behavior. This
claim would be difficult to sustain, if only because the distinction between
edification and entertainment, between *nut* and *vermaeck,* as Van Mander
would later put it, is made explicit in at least two collections of another
rederijker poetic form, the ever-popular *referein.* In his *Refereinbundel* of 1524,
the Antwerp publisher Jan van Doesborch places the *refereinen* "in the foolish mode [*in 't sot*]" after those "in the amorous or serious modes [*in 't
amoureus* and *in 't wijs*]," informing the reader they are intended to give pleasure and drive away melancholy.[3] Even more to the point is the *Testament
Rhetoricael,* a collection of *refereinen* assembled by the Bruges *rederijker* Eduard de Dene in 1561. De Dene distributed some thirty-five foolish *refereinen* at various places in the text, in order, he says, to provide relief from

the serious, often satirical or moralizing poems that constitute most of the volume, including an extensive group organized according to the seven deadly sins.[4] Finally, an ordinance of 1559 specifically distinguishes between allegorical plays or moralities and other things performed "in God's honor," and plays for the entertainment and honest *recreatie* of the people.[5]

Thus, we may doubt that such farces as the *Clucht van plaijerwater* were intended, as Pleij characterizes a fifteenth-century Netherlandish *boerd* with a comparable plot, to offer "contrasting propaganda for the world as God intended it: with order, harmony and true love in the family, and the priest as intermediary between earthly life and heaven,"[6] and it is even less likely that they were understood as such by contemporary audiences.[7] Similarly, the debate on the relative merits of bagpipe and lute in the *tafelspel Bot Verstant en Cloucken Geest* was surely intended simply *in 't sot*. And the same might be said about many other *tafelspelen* and *kluchten* that were performed on festive occasions, including the Twelfth Night *tafelspel* that, as we have seen, was written with the stated intention to banish "all heavy spirits," and the two *kluchten* that were received with such hilarity in the great square at Brussels in 1549, to the disapproval of the austere Dr. Kram. We must beware, it seems, of taking laughter too seriously.

To place Bruegel's art within the "laugh culture" of his time is not to reduce him to the status of the *Drolle Piet* or the "Peasant Bruegel" of earlier centuries. It cannot be denied that a significant number of Bruegel's works are *in 't wijs*, even if they do not exhibit the metaphysical profundity or abstruse symbolism so often and so enthusiastically attributed to them. Bruegel gave fresh and often moving interpretations of the old Christian themes in such works as the *Massacre of the Innocents*, *Christ Carrying the Cross*, and *Death of the Virgin*; the *Blind Leading the Blind* expands the parable into a tragic view of the human condition. Finally, the *Triumph of Death*, in which the dead swarm from their graves to snatch the living from their daily business and pastimes, presents an image of the end of time immeasurably more immediate and poignant than any Bosch had ever achieved.[8]

The same is true of many of the drawings that Bruegel made for the printmakers employed by Hieronymus Cock; they convey the same homely lessons that preachers and authors of moral tracts had long urged on their audiences and with an imagery, however original, whose import would have been easily grasped by a fairly wide spectrum of society. Bruegel's satires, moreover, chastise not so much "by a reprimand but by the enticement of a joke," as Erasmus had put it, and the object of Bruegel's satirical humor is "the vices of mortals" in general.[9] Greed and *eigenbaet* are ridiculed in the *Battle of Money Boxes*, *Big Fish Eat the Small*, and *Elck*, for example, and the follies of deceit and gullibility in the *Alchemist*. The last two prints, especially, are laced with a trenchant wit that skewers the artist's victims all the more deftly.

But much like the Flemish *rederijkers* of the period, Bruegel created at least some works in which *vermaeck* must have outweighed *nut*. This is very likely the case, for instance, of the *Seven Deadly Sins*. Despite their ostensible subject matter, they seem hardly more than a set of ingenious variations on the *droleries* that Bosch's followers had popularized in the generation or so before Bruegel, a display of visual wit on a par with the *Songes drolatiques de Pantagruel*, published by Richard Breton in 1565, and constituting a visual parallel to the verbal wit in the *refereinen in 't sot* of the *rederijkers*. In a similar vein, most likely, are his *Netherlandish Proverbs* of 1559 and the *Dulle Griet*. While the former comments on the folly of humanity in general and the latter on the folly of ill-tempered wives in particular, both pictures were painted mainly to provoke laughter at the absurdities involved in taking proverbs literally. But the two proverb pictures are quite different. In the *Netherlandish Proverbs*, Bruegel strings out a series of isolated proverbs unified only by their common setting of village and countryside; they would have been grasped by the beholder without too much difficulty. In the *Dulle Griet*, however, he confronts us with a nightmarish infernal landscape whose misshapen denizens retreat before a horde of infuriated housewives, and it must have taken some time before even the most quick-witted of Bruegel's contemporaries grasped the essence of his visual joke and could laugh at this ingenious fusion of several proverbial expressions ("to plunder in front of Hell and return unscathed" and "to tie the Devil to a cushion"). In this regard, the *Dulle Griet* surpasses even the *Elck* in its visual sophistication.

Another aspect of Bruegel's art of laughter was his gift for rendering the human face as expressing the motions of the mind, first evidenced in the *Alchemist*. The artist was not alone in his physiognomical interests. Beginning with Quentin Massys, Netherlandish artists exploited the humorous possibilities of expressive physiognomies offered by half-length scenes of tavern interiors and other low-life subjects. A group of physiognomical studies, or *tronies*, can be assigned to Bruegel, both original works, such as the *Peasant Woman* in Munich and, I am inclined to believe, the Brussels *Yawning Man*, and several paintings that have survived only in copies. Such exercises bore fruit in many of his serious subjects, including the *Christ Carrying the Cross, Massacre of the Innocents,* and especially the *Blind Leading the Blind*, but they also heighten the humor of his peasant subjects, as in the snoring reaper in the *Wheat Harvest* and the tipsy dancer in the Detroit *Wedding Dance*. But it is especially in the two late scenes of peasant revels in Vienna that Bruegel presents us with a gamut of human types of all ages and conditions: young and old, handsome and plain, demure or quarrelsome, sober or drunk, people animated by the breath of life itself.

The chief obstacle to our appreciation of these pictures for what they are lies, I suspect, in our failure to distinguish between the old peasant stereotypes and the actual peasants that Bruegel and his contemporaries must have encountered in real life. Peasants had long been caricatured in medieval *fabliaux* and *borden*, as well as in German carnival plays and *rederijker* farces. They are shown as boisterous, quarrelsome *boeren*, clodhoppers indulging their animal appetites; peasant men are also dull-witted, easily duped by their adulterous wives or henpecked by ill-tempered ones. Thus exhibiting the very opposite of what the upper classes considered proper behavior, these rustic stereotypes carouse in the rowdy kermises and wedding celebrations, frequently ending in drunken brawls, that were depicted in the prints of Barthel and Sebald Beham and other German artists of the period and, after about 1550, in the prints of Pieter van der

Borcht and other Antwerp artists. This development of peasant satire in
the visual arts of Germany and the Netherlands has been studied in depth
by Hans-Joachim Raupp, who correctly sees it as an autonomous artistic tradition that generally had little to do with what people might have
thought about actual peasants.[10]

But Raupp further insists that even if Bruegel actually mingled with
the peasants on their festive occasions, as Van Mander tells us he did, he
still could not have broken from the conventions of traditional peasant
satire.[11] This claim, however, does scant justice to Bruegel's repeatedly
demonstrated ability to transform the pictorial types developed by his
predecessors. He reinvigorated the Flemish world landscape tradition,
creating landscapes whose evocation of vast scale and even vaster distances
dwarf the creations of Joachim Patinir and Bles.[12] He brought to the "absurdities" of Bosch's followers a sparkling wit and inventiveness generally lacking in the works of Jan Mandijn and Pieter Huys. In the same
manner, Bruegel reworked the old and often hackneyed tradition of peasant celebrations to create a new and compelling vision of rustic life. This
transformation begins already in his designs for the *Hoboken Kermis* and
St. Joris Kermis. While he drew freely on the peasant celebrations of the
Beham brothers and their Netherlandish followers, these two kermises—
and despite the derogatory inscription added by the printmaker to the
Hoboken Kermis—are celebrated with noticeably greater restraint than
the raucous country festivals of Bruegel's predecessors.[13] And while in the
Detroit and Vienna paintings, he similarly turned to earlier artists for
inspiration, especially for figure poses, his peasants for the most part are
no longer stereotypes but robust individuals endowed with the same mon-
umental presence that other artists gave to the heroes of religious and
secular history.

In interpreting any phenomenon of the past, we must strive to put
aside our own values and prejudices. Nevertheless, I find it difficult to
believe that Bruegel's sturdy countryfolk were mere *zinnekens*, allegorical
puppets manipulated by their creator to warn us against gluttony, lust,
and the other unhappy manifestations of our fallen human nature. Nor

is it likely that viewers would have seen them that way. On the contrary, Bruegel's paintings show the peasants in a favorable, even idealized, light, a momentous transformation that in turn reflects a relationship between town and country that was entering a new phase during Bruegel's lifetime.

The meadows, woods, and villages lying just outside the city walls had long been an urban playground for the citizens of Antwerp. They strolled the country roads, they loitered in the local taverns, they attended the local festivals. The amenities they enjoyed were celebrated not only in the two sets of country views published by Hieronymus Cock in 1559 and 1560 but also in the many paintings of the period showing townspeople in attendance at rustic weddings and kermises. At the same time, the more affluent burghers of Antwerp increasingly sought to acquire country houses and even feudal estates, and it is from this social class that Bruegel most likely drew the patrons for his paintings.[14] For owners of feudal manors, their newly acquired titles must have been a source of immense pride, to judge from the frequent references to them in Guicciardini's description of the Netherlands. This also explains why Antoon van Straelen's portrait medal proclaims him as *heer* of Merksem and Dambrugge, while the rather unsavory fame of Hoboken did not discourage Balthazar Schetz from having the title Lord of Hoboken inscribed on his etched portait of 1561. In addition, both men formally took possession of their manors in miniature "joyous entries," in which the lord and his subjects solemnly affirmed their obligations to each other.

It is likely, therefore, that the very inhabitants of a feudal domain would have contributed much to the prestige and dignity of their landlord. In effect his subjects, they pledged their fidelity to him, and he in turn pledged to respect their rights and privileges; moreover, the villagers were often recipients of his good offices and material benevolence. Like Schetz, the owner of a feudal domain might preside at its local festivities, even inviting friends from the city for such occasions. Thus, pictures like Bruegel's *Wedding Dance* and the two Vienna panels, if owned by a lord of the manor, would have proclaimed the wealth and social standing of their owners and, equally important, their qualifications for a just and beneficent rule.

There is evidence that rustic festivities were employed in precisely this manner early in the following century by the rulers of the Spanish Netherlands, the archdukes Albert and Isabella. They endeared themselves to their subjects by attending their pastimes and celebrations, including those of the peasants.[15] They also commissioned from a son of Pieter Bruegel, Jan "Velvet" Brueghel, at least two pairs of paintings showing rustic celebrations, probably in the 1620s, each pair depicting a wedding procession and a wedding banquet graced by the presence of the archdukes themselves. One pair of pictures was displayed in the gallery of the archducal palace at Brussels, together with family portraits and scenes of their victorious battles. The other pair was dispatched to Philip IV in Spain. As Cordula Schumann has pointed out, writers of the period stressed that sovereigns should foster the loyalty and love of their subjects by taking part in popular festivities.[16] Their actual participation, however, tended to be limited, if we can take yet another painting by Jan as evidence. In *The Archdukes Albert and Isabella Attending a Peasant Wedding Feast* (Fig. 84), also in Madrid,[17] the two sovereigns preside in solemn state at the main table, and, surrounded as they are by courtiers and guards, they remain more aloof from the festivities than the landlord in Pieter Bruegel's *Wedding Banquet*, not to mention the city folk who amble through the village kermises and wedding feasts in the pictures by Lucas van Valckenborch, Maerten van Cleve, and their colleagues. Indeed, the bridal festivities seem hardly more than a show put on for the sovereigns. Nevertheless, as Schumann argues persuasively, the wedding ceremony itself could symbolize the marriage between the ruler and his realm. This was a major theme in the coronation ceremonies of Henri IV of France in 1594, while the joyous entry of the archdukes into Antwerp in 1599 included a symbolic wedding between "Antwerpia" and her new rulers.[18]

It is unlikely that the self-created seigneurs of Pieter Bruegel's time thought of their lordships in such exalted terms, but one more factor must be considered in our efforts to determine just how Bruegel's contemporaries might have viewed his peasant paintings. This is what we may call

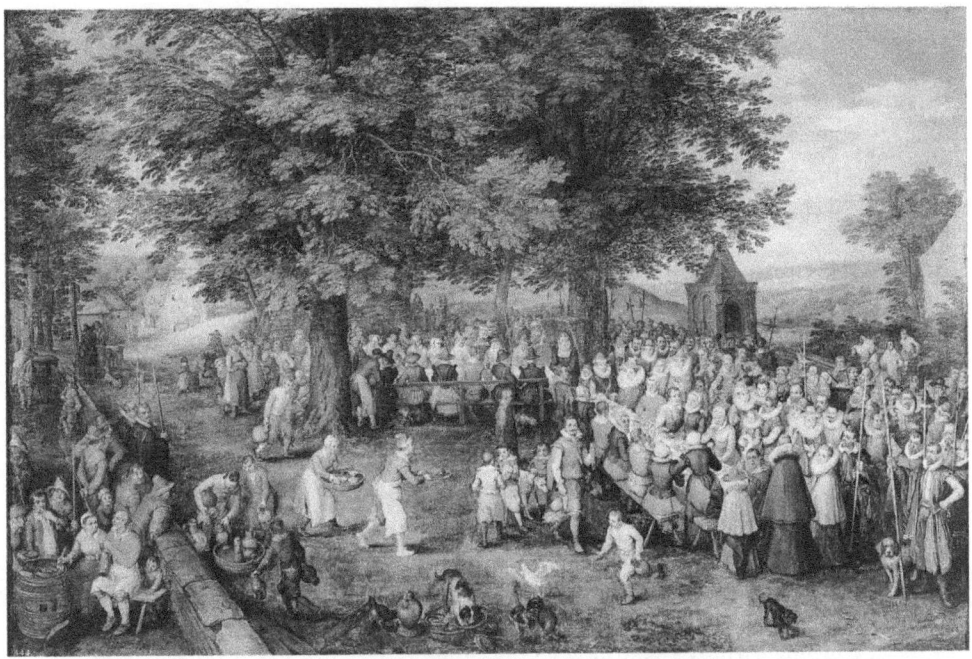

FIGURE 84. Jan Brueghel the Elder, *The Archdukes Albert and Isabella Attending a Peasant Wedding Feast*. Madrid, Museo del Prado.

the positive tradition of peasant imagery. All too often ignored in discussions of peasant festivals is the fact that such imagery stems ultimately from classical antiquity. Virgil and Horace, as we have seen, had exalted the virtuous life of agricultural workers and the countryside in general over the intrigues and corruption of court and city, and they were followed by a host of Renaissance writers in the same vein. Especially popular was the *Menosprecio de corte y alabanza de aldea* by Antonio de Guevara, a Spanish prelate and adviser to Charles V; first published in 1539, it was translated into many languages, including English (*A Dispraise of the Courtier's Life*), and read all over Europe. Guevara praised the life on the land, where people were healthier, the food better and more plentiful, and the amusements innocent and wholesome. Even Charles Estienne's more prosaic farming manual, *L'agriculture et maison rustique*, opens with an enthusiastic encomium of country existence, where the farmer, we are told in the English edition of 1600, leads a "life of libertie and inno-cencie."[19] Plantin, we may remember, dedicated the Netherlandish edi-tion of Estienne's manual to Antoon van Straelen. Suggestive, too, is the fact that at Crauwels, the country house of Michiel van der Heyden, its owner kept a volume of Virgil's *Opera* and French editions of Guevara's *Menosprecio de corte* and Estienne's manual, as well as a picture of a peasant wedding painted on linen.[20]

The Detroit *Wedding Dance* and the two peasant scenes in Vienna would thus have appealed to the landed gentry and to other owners of a *hof van plaisance*. And for those who, like Noirot, lacked country retreats of any type, these pictures, as Goldstein has suggested, might have offered an effective substitute. But a further ramification is suggested by the pres-ence of three of Bruegel's rustic revels in Noirot's dining room. It is very likely that the Netherlanders occasionally indulged in philosophical ban-quets and learned mealtime conversations, like those that Vives reported of Carolus Virulus, that followed the venerable tradition from Plato's *Sym-posium* onward, including some of the erudite feasts described in Eras-mus's *Colloquies*. But this was not the only way that Bruegel's countrymen comported themselves at the table: their propensity to make good cheer at such times was well known, if occasionally deplored. But mealtimes, in fact, had traditionally been times of relaxation and levity, and the guest who waxed too philosophical or moralizing, or who like Margery Kempe indulged in spiritual groans, might well have been ejected from the com-pany as a *vreuchtversmader*, or killjoy.[21]

In any case, Bruegel's peasant scenes would have contributed might-ily to mealtime socializing and relaxation. And thus, despite their many layers of social meaning, his peasant revels functioned ultimately, not *in 't wyze*, but *in 't sot*, but not as objects of mockery or moralizing. Indeed, a moralist would have found more to condemn in the pictures of carous-ing Olympians produced by Floris and his shop (see Fig. 60). Bruegel's country revels, I suspect, would more likely have elicited good-natured laughter as host and guests recalled their own pleasant experiences in the countryside. Such images of robust, uninhibited peasant celebrations would have formed a rustic but not inappropriate counterpoint to the presumably more sophisticated and refined festivities in an urban dining room.

And thus we return to the question once posed by Peter Burke: did the upper classes "associate popular culture with times and places of relaxation?"[22] This question, as I have suggested, can be answered in the affirmative. Further support for this claim comes from an unexpected source, a carnival entertainment presented in 1593 at the court of Philip II of Spain.[23] The king asked Jehan Lhermite, a native of Antwerp and a member of the royal household, to organize a masque in the "Flemish fashion." In response, Lhermite staged an upper-class wedding feast: first came the noble bridal pair and then the guests in order of rank, all wearing the fashions of Brabant and Holland; after them came the cook and his wife, he wielding a big spoon, she carrying a basket of warm carnival waffles. The banquet was interrupted by the appearance of a party of peasants, also dressed in the Flemish style, complete with bagpipes and flails. After several of the wedding guests had successfully pleaded for their admission to the banquet, the whole company danced, the peasants performing their native dances. The presence of these mock peasants, we are assured, contributed much to the hilarity of the occasion, and Philip is recorded as saying approvingly that it reminded him of the masked entertainments he himself had enjoyed in the Netherlands. Philip had sojourned in the Netherlands at various times between 1549 and 1558, some forty-five to fifty years before, that is, in Bruegel's lifetime. But while I am not aware of any Flemish court masques featuring peasants from the mid–sixteenth century, we cannot completely discount their existence in view of the peasant characters that appear in the farces and *tafelspelen* of the period. It is also possible that Philip had something quite different in mind, but even so, the Spanish entertainment of 1593 shows the peasants, not as objects of derision and social satire, but as honorable participants in a festive occasion. This is not likely to have been an invention on Lhermite's part, but reflects a practice begun much earlier.[24] To what extent rustic revels in the "Flemish fashion" permeated urban and courtly festivities of the seventeenth century is a subject requiring further study,[25] but there can be little doubt that Bruegel's paintings of country revels played a benign and even positive role in the festive urban culture of his day, and as such they were significant manifestations of his art of laughter.

NOTES

The book's epigraph is quoted from Rabelais-Cohen 1955, p. 36, dedicatory poem before book I.

PROLOGUE

Epigraph: Rabelais-Cohen 1955, p. 38 (author's prologue to *Gargantua*); I am indebted for this passage to Barolsky 1978, p. 194.

1. Van Mander-Miedema 1994–99, I: fol. 233 (pp. 190, 192). This statement follows Van Mander's observations on Bruegel's works in the style of Hieronymus Bosch, but that he would have included other works as well is clearly suggested by the episode of Aert Molckeman discussed below (see pp. 10–11).

2. A notable exception is Sullivan 1994, who titles her chapter 2: "Wit, humour, ingenuity (salus, ridiculo, ingenioisa)" (pp. 47–69), although any reader will quickly realize that her understanding of laughter differs markedly from the one presented in the following pages.

3. This phrase taken from the title of the volume published of the plays performed at the Antwerp *landjuweel* (dramatic competition) of the previous year: *Spelen van sinne, vol scoone moralisacien....* (Antwerp: Willem Silvius, 1562). In 1481 the magistrates of Aalst gave the Chamber of St. Katharina a subsidy, partly for their *scoone spelen van geestelike moralizatie* (beautiful plays of spiritual moralization); see Ramakers 1996, p. 104.

4. Müller 1999, p. 178, where Bruegel is called "learned painter as Christian painter." De Vries 2004 argues that Bruegel was known as a *pictor doctus* in his own day. For the concept of the *pictor doctus* in the Renaissance and later, see Lee 1967, pp. 41–48.

5.   Popham 1931; the full text also in Freedberg 1989, p. 65; Meadow 1996, p. 193; and Meadow 2002, pp. 109–110. For the original text, see Ortelius 1969, facsimile fols. 12v–13r; French translation, pp. 21–22. Müller-Hofstede 1979, p. 76 n. 2, suggests that the epitaph was composed over a period of time.

6.   Gibson 1977, p. 11; Melion 1991, p. 178; and the valuable discussions of Ortelius's epitaph in Muylle 1981; Meadow 1997, pp. 192–196; and Meadow 2002, pp. 108–117.

7.   Pliny 1968, p. 133 (35.96).

8.   For the passage in Pliny, see Pliny the Elder, *Natural History* 35.73 (Pliny 1968, pp. 116, 117). The scene is described in Euripides' play *Iphigeneia in Aulis*. Timanthes' depiction of Iphigeneia's sacrifice is also mentioned by, among others, Quintilian 1921–22, 1:294–295 (2.13.13); and Cicero, *Orator* 21.74; and later cited by Alberti (Alberti 1966, p. 78); and Franciscus Junius (Junius 1991, 1:215). For classical and Renaissance writers on the gesture of Iphigeneia's father, see Elizabeth McGrath, "The Painted Decoration of Rubens's House," *Journal of the Warburg and Courtauld Institutes* 41 (1978): 245–277, esp. 256–259.

9.   For the Cyclops, see Pliny, *Natural History* 35.73 (Pliny 1968, pp. 116, 117).

10.   Popham 1931, p. 187. For Bruegel's painting, see also pp. 47–48 below and 181nn. 58, 59.

11.   Cf. Melion 1991, p. 178, for similar comparisons between Bruegel's works and the pictures by Apelles and Timanthes described by Pliny.

12.   Van Mander-Miedema 1973, fol. 26r (pp. 170, 171): chap. 6, "Uytbeeldinghe der Affecten / passien / begeerlijckheden / en lijdens der Menschen," vv. 40–43.

13.   Van Mander 1969, fol. 70r.

14.   Van Mander-Miedema 1994–99, 1:362 (fol. 276r), where *heymlijcke verstanden* is translated as "concealed meanings." See the discussion of these passages in Muylle 1981, p. 330. For Ketel's iconography, see B. A. Heezen-Stoll, *"Cornelis Ketel, uytnemende schilder, van der Goude": een iconografische studie van zijn "historiën"* (Delft: Delftsche Uitgevers Maatschappij, 1967).

15.   De Tolnay 1935, pp. 332–333. However, De Tolnay had already reached a similar conclusion in his monograph on Bruegel's drawings of 1925, in which he claims, for example, that Bruegel's *Virtues* series ironically shows the reverse of each virtue depicted. See De Tolnay 1952, pp. 26–29.

16. Panofsky 1953, 1:141–142. It is doubtful that he intended to be as dogmatic and inclusive as this sounds; elsewhere in the same chapter, he insists that we have no way of knowing to what extent objects in a given picture may be symbolic and warned that the only answer to this problem was "the use of historical methods tempered, if possible, by common sense" (Panofsky 1953, 1:142.).

17. Otto Pächt, "Gestaltungsprinzipien der westlichen Malerei," *Kunstwissenschaftliche Forschungen* 2 (1933); the English translation is quoted from Wood 2000, p. 278.

18. Roger Fry, *Flemish Art: A Critical Survey* (New York: Brentano's, 1927), p. 35.

19. Ibid., pp. 18, 35 respectively.

20. Dirk Bax, *Ontcijfering van Jeroen Bosch* (The Hague: Martinus Nijhoff, 1949).

21. Pierre Vinken and Lucy Schlüter, "Pieter Bruegels *Nestrover* en de mens die de dood tegemoet treedt," in De Jong et al. 1996, pp. 54–79. For a summary and critique, see Walter S. Gibson, review of De Jong et al. 1996, in *Simiolus* 26 (1998): 120–129, esp. 120–121. The same subject is treated in Vinken and Schlüter, "Nogmaals Pieter Bruegels *Nestrover*," *Oud Holland* 113 (1999): 169–174. Both studies are based on an earlier article by Pierre Vinken, "De betekenis van Pieter Bruegel's Nestrover; een bijdrage tot de kennis van de verhouding tussen tekst en beeld in de zestiende eeuw," *Het Boek*, 3rd ser., 33 (1958–59): 106–115. For a more recent and more carefully nuanced reading of this picture, see Noll 1999.

22. Dreyer 1977.

23. Kenneth C. Lindsay, "Mystery in Bruegel's Proverbs," *Jahrbuch der Berliner Museen*, n.s., 38 (1996): 63–76; the quotation is from the abstract preceding the article.

24. Müller 1999, who tells us (p. 22) that in his study, "Franck's *Paradoxia* . . . is a decisive source for almost all interpretations of Bruegel's work." As Müller notes, De Tolnay had already linked some of Bruegel's drawings to the same text in his book on Bruegel's drawings of 1925; see De Tolnay 1952. Stridbeck 1956 also believes that Franck exercised a seminal influence on Bruegel's intellectual development and the symbolic content of his art.

25. Stein-Schneider 1985; idem, "Pieter Bruegel: peintre hérétique, illustrateur du message familiste," *Gazette des Beaux-Arts*, 6th per., 107 (February 1986): 71–74.

26.   Herbert L. Stein-Schneider, "Bruegel Revised," *Arts Magazine,* April 1972, 36–40. For a similar allegorical approach to Bruegel's landscape prints, see H. David Brumble III, "Peter Brueghel the Elder: The Allegory of Landscape," *Art Quarterly,* n.s., 2 (1979): 125–139.

27.   See, for example, George Hunston Williams, *The Radical Reformation,* 3rd ed., Sixteenth Century Essays & Studies XV (Kirksville, Mo.: Truman State University, 2002), pp. 724–729.

28.   Stein-Schneider 1985, p. 5.

29.   For Cock, see Riggs 1977. For the *schilderspand* and the location of Cock's shop, see Vermeylen 2003, pp. 50–61 and 50 respectively. Vermeylen also notes the significance of the close association of the new stock exchange and the artists' galleries (p. 169). Because of adverse economic conditions, the *schilderspand* was probably not in use until 1540–41.

30.   See Vermeylen 2003 for a valuable and comprehensive study of this topic, esp. chap. 5, "The Engines of Demand." In this context, Vermeylen rightly observes that Bruegel began his career as a "commercial artist" (p. 160).

31.   Gibson 1991, pp. 12–13.

32.   Ibid., p. 13. The eschatological reading of the *Wedding Feast* is offered by Weismann 1992.

33.   Stoett 1943, I: no. 621.

34.   Freedberg 1989, p. 57.

35.   De Tolnay 1935, I: introduction (unpaginated).

36.   The philosophical Bruegel also figures in Michael Frayn's novel *Headlong* (New York: Metropolitan Books, Henry Holt and Company, 1999), in which the protagonist attempts to authenticate a newly discovered Bruegel painting by searching for its hidden symbolism.

37.   For a fuller discussion of this composition, see pp. 41–43.

38.   On Bruegel's *Triumph of Death* and its iconographic sources, see Gibson 1991, pp. 53–86.

39.   Marijnissen, in Marijnissen and Seidel 1984, p. 24.

40.   This is well demonstrated in Silver 1997; and Kavaler 1999.

41.   Rotterdam–New York 2001, cat. nos. 64–77. The exception is the *Fortitudo,* in which Fortitude presides over a sort of psychomachia between human soldiers and Boschian monsters.

42.   In another painting by Bruegel, the *Conversion of Saul,* the dramatic mountain setting may allude to the passage through the Alps of the duke of Alva and his troops, dispatched by Philip II of Spain to subdue his Lowland provinces. Although Alva arrived only in 1567, the date of the painting, rumors of his expedition had circulated for several years. See Gibson 1989, p. 74.

43.   For the *rederijkers* and their relationship to Bruegel, see Gibson 1981, who cites earlier literature. See also Ramakers 1996; and Reinder P. Meijer, *Literature of the Low Countries: A Short History* (The Hague: Martinus Nijhoff, 1978), pp. 50–65, 73–77, 79–82, passim.

44.   For a brief but useful account of the Violieren chamber and its association with the painters' guild, see Vermeylen 2003, pp. 128–130; for Hans Franckaert, see p. 73 and 190–191n. 29 below.

45.   Gibson 1981, p. 428; C. Kruyskamp, ed., *Het antwerpse landjuweel van 1561: een keuze uit de vertoonde stukken,* Klassieke galerij, no. 146 (Antwerp: De Nederlandsche Boekhandel, 1962); and esp. Edward van Even, *Het landjuweel van Antwerpen in 1561* (Louvain: C.-J. Fonteyn, 1861).

46.   Gibson 1981, pp. 434 and 438–439 respectively.

47.   See, for example, Müller 1997; and Müller 1999, p. 18 and n. 1, who considers Van Mander's life of Bruegel as almost all rhetoric and suggests that even if Van Mander had precise information at hand that prejudiced his image of "Peasant Bruegel," he would have suppressed it. More balanced evaluations of Van Mander are offered by David Freedberg in Freedberg 1989, pp. 23–26; Muylle 1984; and Miedema 1998. Hessel Miedema and Jan Muylle convincingly demonstrate that Van Mander's characterization of Bruegel's art reflects a tradition going back to Bruegel's lifetime.

48.   From a series by Jan or Lucas van Doetecum after Hans Vredeman de Vries, *Scenographiae, sive perspective,* Hieronymus Cock, 1560, dedicated to Cardinal Granvelle. For the print, see Nalis 1998, 2: no. 178; original drawing in Vienna, Albertina, dated 1558; see Lemgo, Weserrenaissance-Museum Schloss Brake, and Antwerp, Koninklijk Museum voor Schone Kunsten, *Hans Vredeman de Vries und die Renaissance im Norden,* ed. Heiner Borggrefe et al. (Munich: Hirmer Verlag, 2002), p. 203, cat. no. 29h, ill. p. 208. For a surviving example of a mural of 1579 (Antwerp, house called Sint Jacob in Gallicie) showing two fictive arcades in perspective, see B. Terlinden, "Quelques ensembles de peinture murale au XVIième siècle

dans les édifices privés de Belgique," *Revue belge d'archéologie et d'histoire de l'art* 47 (1978): 57–75, esp. 70–71 and fig. 70.

49. Van Mander-Miedema 1994–99, 1: fols. 266r–v (pp. 322–325). The shirt is presumably befouled through the peasant's defecation. Van Mander says that the peasant had a *beseghelt* shirt; *beseghelt* (now spelled *bezegeld*), means "sealed," and modern Netherlandish translations of this passage generally leave the original word in quotation marks. However, a clue to the meaning of the word may be found in a woodcut by Pieter Flöttner of ca. 1535, in which an impoverished artisan raises a banner bearing the image of a large wine jar and a turd; in the accompanying poem, he tells us that the banner has been "sealed with a turd [*versigelt mit eym dreck*]"; see Geisberg-Strauss 1974, 3:793, G.828, for which I am greatly indebted to Alison Stewart. In a similar manner, perhaps, the shirt may be thought of as "sealed" or stained with the efforts of defecation, much as a piece of paper might be stained with drops of sealing wax, but this must remain conjecture.

50. Van Mander-Miedema 1994–99, 1: fol. 266v (pp. 324–325). Miedema tends to dismiss the story as one of Van Mander's own invention (5:55).

51. See Monballieu 1969.

52. For similar observations on Bruegel's art, see Muylle 1984; as B. A. M. Ramakers has aptly put it, there was room in Bruegel's art for the smile and the guffaw, as well as for serious thoughts (Ramakers 1997, p. 102).

CHAPTER 1

Epigraphs: Ozment 1986, p. 161; and Johan Huizinga, *The Waning of the Middle Ages: A Study of the Forms of Life, Thought and Art in France and the Netherlands in the XIVth and XVth Centuries* (New York: St. Martin's Press, n.d.), p. 206. This standard English edition was taken from an earlier German translation that had been approved by Huizinga. He expressed the same idea in a more diluted manner in his original Netherlandish text, which has been recently translated into English: Johan Huizinga, *The Autumn of the Middle Ages*, trans. Rodney J. Payton and Ulrich Mammitzsch (Chicago: University of Chicago Press, 1996), p. 268.

1. Miedema 1977, p. 211.

2. See Verberckmoes 1998, p. 41, who refutes the common notion that burghers did not laugh. It should be noted that Miedema 1981 qualified his remarks on laughter among the burghers; see esp. 208: "People did laugh, of course, but they nonetheless had to remain aware of the code

of manners that held that laughter had to be contained"; see also n. 68 below. However, at least one sixteenth-century writer would probably have agreed that Molckeman was no gentleman. In his commentary on Vitruvius concerning the proper subjects to paint in the rooms of private houses (*The Ten Books on Architecture*, 7:5), Gualtherus Rivius asks, "Who can receive pleasure from a picture of a truly drunken peasant, who shits and vomits behind a fence? Such repulsiveness gives pleasure to someone who is improper, has the sense of a peasant, and who can inappropriately be called human. To the shame of painting, there are so many nowadays who draw and paint such inhuman things that ought to horrify a reasonable person." See Gualtherus Hermanius Rivius [Walther Hermannus Ryff], *Vitruvius Teutsch* (Nuremberg, 1548), fol. ccxxxi (verso); I am greatly indebted for this quotation to a study in progress by Alison Stewart, and to Philips Salman for a photocopy of the original text. Similar complaints, I suspect, have been aired in every age; in his *De groote schilderboek* (1st ed., 1707), Gerard de Lairesse tells us that there is hardly a fine interior that is unadorned by "pictures of beggars, bordellos, taverns, . . . dirty children on their pots and other things more filthy and worse" (quoted in Gibson 2000, p. 148).

3.   Burke 1978, esp. pp. 271–272; Muchembled 1985; and Elias 2000.

4.   Elias 2000, pp. 61, 71, 110–111; cf. Burke 1978, p. 270, who tell us that "[i]n 1500 popular culture was everyone's culture, a second culture for the educated, and the only culture for everyone else. By 1800, however, in most parts of Europe, the clergy, the nobility, the merchants, the professional men—and their wives—had abandoned popular culture to the lower classes from whom they were now separated as never before."

5.   Aristotle, *De partibus animalium* 3.10 (Aristotle 1984, 1:1049). For the concepts of laughter from antiquity to the Renaissance, see Screech and Calder 1992; Bowen 1998, pp. 19–20; and Gilhus 1997, pp. 14–101. For Erasmus, who claimed that not laughter but speech was the unique property of man, see Screech and Calder 1992, p. 170.

6.   Screech and Calder 1992, p. 170.

7.   Quoted from his *Geschichtklitterung* (1575), in Bowen 1998, p. 21.

8.   Van Stipriaan 1996, pp. 22–23; Dekker 1997, pp. 15–17; and Verberckmoes 1998, pp. 250–254. Similarly, the "Letter of Lentulus," supposedly written during Christ's lifetime and popular in the later Middle Ages, asserts that although Christ wept at times, he never laughed; see Constable 1995, p. 235. Peter of Luxembourg claimed that while the Gospels tell us that Christ

wept, nowhere do they mention that he laughed; see Richard Kieckhe-fer, *Unquiet Souls: Fourteenth-Century Saints and Their Religious Milieu* (Chicago: University of Chicago Press, 1987), p. 39.

9.   See Curtius 1953, p. 420; and Lochrie 1991, p. 139.

10. Gilhus 1997, p. 63; and Morreall 1989, p. 245. Elsewhere, however, Chrysostom tells us that laughter had been "placed in our soul so that the soul may rest," quoted in Aron Gurevich, *Medieval Popular Culture: Problems of Belief and Perception*, trans. János M. Bak and Paul A. Hollingsworth (Cambridge: Cambridge University Press; Paris: Éditions de la Maison des Sciences de l'Homme, 1988), p. 251 n. 6. St. Gregory classified im-moderate laughter among the lighter sins that could be purged after death, "but only," he cautioned, "unless during his lifetime he deserved by his good works to receive such favor" (*Dialogues* 4.39); quoted in F. Homes Dudden, *Gregory the Great: His Place in History and Thought*, 2 vols. (London: Longmans, Green, 1905), 1:428. For other early writers who condemned laughter, see M. A. Screech, *Laughter at the Foot of the Cross* (Boulder, Colo.: Westview Press, 1999), pp. 132–134, 239.

11. Gilhus 1997, p. 79.

12. Quoted in Lochrie 1991, p. 140.

13. Kempe 1998, pp. 192–193 (chap. 54). For an excellent analysis of the significance of laughter in Margery's spiritual autobiography, see Lochrie 1991, pp. 135–166.

14. In her play *Comedy on the Passing of the King*; see Marguerite of Navarre 1992, p. 178, line 544.

15. In the play *Much, More, Little, Less*; Marguerite of Navarre 1992; pp. 117–153.

16. The story is told in W. Hüsken, "Preliminaries to the Study of the Comic Drama of the Rhetoricians," *Dutch Crossing* 22 (April 1984): 50–51. It ap-pears frequently in collections of *exempla* and other stories, including the *Gesta romanorum*; see the long list of sources in Tubach 1969, pp. 377–378, no. 4994, under "Trumpet of doom (Sword of Damocles)."

17. Jan Roelants, *Nyieu complexie boeck* (Antwerp, 1554 and 1564), cited in Ver-berckmoes 1998, pp. 40–41.

18. Luis Vives, *De anima et vita* (Basel, 1538), quoted in Machline 1998, p. 256. For Vives on laughter, see also Verberckmoes 1999, pp. 45–49. Cf. John Webster, *The White Devil*, act 3, scene 3: "What a strange creature is a laugh-

ing fool! / As if man were created to no use / But only to show his teeth";
see *Webster and Ford* 1954, p. 47. For contrasting views on laughter in Renaissance England, see Thomas 1977.

19. Lord Chesterfield, letter of 9 March 1748, quoted in Thomas 1977, p. 80.

20. Vives-Fantuzzi 2000, p. 125 (bk. 1, chap. 11). Even Pippa, the appren-
tice whore in one of Aretino's dialogues, is advised by her mother, Nanna,
never to laugh, "gaping your mouth and displaying everything you have
in your throat," but simply to smile; see Pietro Aretino, *Aretino's Dialogues*,
trans. Raymond Rosenthal (New York: Ballantine Books, 1971), p. 187
(part 2, dialogue 1). Similarly, an early-fourteenth-century Italian conduct book advises women not to laugh so much that they show their teeth;
see Perfetti 2003, pp. 69–70. See also Verberckmoes 2001, pp. 88–93.

21. Giovan Giorgio Trissino, *Epistola del Trissino de la vita, che dee tenere una donna
vedova* (Rome: Ludovico Vicentino and Lautizio Perugino, 1524); and
Giulio Cesare Cabei, *Ornamenti della donna gentil vedova* (Venice: Cristoforo
Zanetti, 1574); both cited in Bell 1999, pp. 269–270. For earlier advice
to women on avoiding laughter, including Christine de Pizan, see Perfetti 2003, pp. 1, 8, 10, passim.

22. Erasmus-McGregor 1985, pp. 275–276.

23. For Erasmus's manual and its successors, see H. de la Fontaine Verwey,
"Erasmus en zijn 'Boeckje aengaende de beleeftheidt der kinderlijcke ze-
den,'" in his *Uit de Wereld van het Boek I: Humanisten, Dwepers en rebellen in de
zestiende eeuw*, 2nd rev. ed. (Amsterdam: Nico Israel, 1976), pp. 41–50;
Franz Bierlaire, "Erasmus at School: The *De Civilitate Morum Puerilium
Libellus*," in DeMolen 1978, pp. 239–251; Jacques Revel, "The Uses of Ci-
vility," in *Passions of the Renaissance*, ed. Roger Chartier, trans. Arthur Gold-
hammer, vol. 3 of *A History of Private Life* (Cambridge, Mass.: Belknap Press
of Harvard University Press, 1989), pp. 168–190; and Elias 2000, pp.
42–47, reprinted in Norbert Elias, *On Civilization, Power, and Knowledge: Selected Writings*, ed. and intro. Stephen Mennell and Johan Goudsblom
(Chicago: University of Chicago Press, 1998), pp. 75–82.

24. Dekker 1997, p. 84. For similar comments, see also Dekker 1997, pp. 23,
52. A similar observation is made by Roger Chartier: "The determina-
tion to impose cultural models does not guarantee the way in which they
are received and used. Historians may describe at length the new standards to which people were supposed to adhere but they should not think
that these standards completely and generally shaped the behavior of the

popular class"; see Chartier, "Culture as Appropriation: Popular Cultural Uses in Early Modern France," in *Understanding Popular Culture: Europe from the Middle Ages to the Nineteenth Century*, ed. Steven L. Kaplan, New Babylon 40 (Berlin: Mouton Publishers, 1984), pp. 229–253, quotation at 235. While Rudolf Dekker speaks of seventeenth-century Holland and Chartier of the "popular class," their remarks would be equally true, perhaps more so, of sixteenth-century Brabant and Flanders, and probably include many members of the upper classes as well. Burke also cautions that we should not understand the "Elias thesis in too simple a manner," for this growing self-control "was gradual not sudden, it provoked resistance, and it was successful only to varying degrees and at different moments in different places, among different groups, or even in different kinds of situation"; see Peter Burke, "Frontiers of the Comic in Early Modern Italy, c. 1350–1750," in Bremmer and Roodenburg 1997, p. 71.

25. This expression appears in the play *Prochiaen, Coster en Wever*, published in 1565 (Hummelen 1968, no. 4 O 8), quoted in Pikhaus 1988–89, p. 321.

26. Castiglione 1959, pp. 144–145.

27. This section of *The Courtier* has not received much scholarly attention, but see JoAnn Cavallo, "Joking Matters: Politics and Dissimulation in Castiglione's *Book of the Courtier*," *Renaissance Quarterly* 53 (2000): 402–424. Barolsky 1978, pp. 6–17, provides a useful discussion of the various kinds of humor circulating in Renaissance Italy and the terms used to describe them.

28. Castiglione 1959, p. 182.

29. Burke 1995, p. 170, no. 149, and p. 163, no. 2; for the latter, see also pp. 105–106. Van Alkemade's goods were confiscated in 1568 after he had gone into exile. Castiglione's book, however, was not well received by everyone; about 1570 Jan Hanneman, *rentmeester*, or bailiff, of North Holland, tried to censor the text (ibid., p. 171, no. 163). Nevertheless, Karel van Mander referred to the text in his *Schilder-boeck* of 1604, fols. 124–125 (ibid., p. 173, no. 211). For recent evaluations of this book, see Baldesar Castiglione, *The Book of the Courtier: The Singleton Translation, an Authoritative Text Criticism*, ed. Daniel Javitch (New York: W. W. Norton and Company, 2002).

30. See Burke 1995, pp. 105 and 159–160, nos. 39, 69, both editions published by a certain Nuncio (Antwerp, 1544, 1561).

31. Quoted in Bowen 1998, p. 15; the same passage occurs in Barolsky 1978, on the title page. The *Nouvelles récréations* is a collection of stories that has been described as permeated by the spirit of Rabelais, from whom Des Périers took the injunction "Live well and rejoice." Toward the end of his life, Des Périers was discharged from the queen's service, not for his views on laughter, but because she was shocked by his openly expressed atheism. See *Dictionnaire de biographie française* (Paris: Librairie Letouze et Ané, 1932–), 10: cols. 1511–1512. For Castiglione's influence, see J. Woodrow Hassel Jr., "Des Périers' Indebtedness to Castiglione," *Studies in Philology* 50 (1953): 566–572. Hassel, incidentally, does not mention laughter in this connection.

32. Quoted in Burke 1978, p. 26, after C. R. Baskerville, *The Elizabethan Jig* (Chicago, 1929; reprint, New York, 1965), pp. 95ff.

33. Castligione 1959, p. 145. Mikhail Bakhtin's theories on popular laughter in the sixteenth century have been widely accepted, but also justly criticized. See Bakhtin 1968, and the trenchant critiques offered by Gábor Klaniczkay, "The Carnival Spirit: Bakhtin's Theory on the Culture of Popular Laughter," in Klaniczkay, *The Uses of Supernatural Power: The Transformation of Popular Religion in Medieval and Early-Modern Europe*, trans. Susan Singerman, ed. Karen Margolis (Princeton: Princeton University Press, 1990), pp. 10–27, esp. 21–22; Aaron Gurevich, "Bakhtin and His Theory of Carnival," in Bremmer and Roodenberg 1997, pp. 54–60; Yelena Mazour-Matusevich, "Writing Medieval History: An Interview with Aaron Gurevich," *The Journal of Medieval and Early Modern Studies* 35, no. 1 (Winter 2005): 121–157, esp. 135–138; Jody L. H. McQuillan, "Dangerous Dialogues: The *Sottie* as a Threat to Authority," in Farrell 1995, pp. 61–77; and, above all, Richard M. Berrong, *Rabelais and Bakhtin: Popular Culture in "Gargantua" and "Pantagruel"* (Lincoln: University of Nebraska Press, 1986). See also Verberckmoes 1999, pp. 108–121, in which he turns Bakhtin upside down, as he puts it.

34. Quoted in Verberckmoes 1998, p. 248. Puteanus delivered this opinion in a carnivalesque oration at the University of Louvain in 1611, but Verberckmoes notes his use of traditional arguments in his encomium of laughter and suggests that his oration was not as paradoxical as the occasion might indicate. For the oration and its context, see Verberckmoes 1998, pp. 249–250; and Verberckmoes 1999, pp. 172–173.

35. Quintilian, *De institutio oratoria*, bk. 6.3; see Quintilian 1921–22, 4:438–

501. See also Graf 1997, pp. 29–39. For Folly's remark, see Erasmus-Miller 1979, p. 82.

36. Cicero, *De oratore*, trans. E. W. Sutton and H. Rackham, Loeb Classical Library (London: William Heinemann; Cambridge, Mass.: Harvard University Press, 1942), 1:372–419 (2.58.235–71.290). For Castiglione's account, compare Cicero: "the essential nature of laughter, the way it is occasioned, where it is seated, and how it comes into being and bursts out so unexpectedly that, strive as we may, we cannot restrain it, and how at the same instant it takes possession of the lungs, voice, pulse, countenance and eyes—all this I leave to Democritus" (*De oratore* 2.58.235 [ibid., 1:373]. Castiglione's indebtedness to Cicero and Quintilian is also noted by Barolsky 1978, pp. 4, 6.

37. The influence of Cicero's *De oratore* on sixteenth-century discussions of laughter is emphasized in Bowen 1998, pp. 142–146.

38. Joubert-Rocher 1980, pp. 94–95. Joubert tells us that a translation of the first book had been published clandestinely more than twenty years previously, and it has been suggested that the last two books were written shortly before the 1578 publication (Machline 1998, p. 254). Like Vives and Erasmus, among others, Joubert counseled moderate laughter. For convenient summaries of Joubert's book, see Machline 1998; and Verberckmoes 1999, pp. 14–17. Useful, too, is Gregory de Rocher, *Rabelais' Laughters and Joubert's "Traité de ris"* (University: University of Alabama Press, 1979).

39. Bijns 1875, p. 43 (*Refereyn XIII*); printed in modern Netherlandish spelling in *'t Is al vrouwenwerk: Refreinen van Anna Bijns*, ed. Herman Pleij (Rotterdam: Em. Querido's Uitgeverij, 1994), p. 40.

40. Quoted in Van Stipriaan 1996, p. 36.

41. Nashe, in *Terrors of the Night*, quoted from Nashe, *The Unfortunate Traveller and Other Works*, ed. and intro. J. B. Steane (London: Penguin Books, 1985), p. 216. For Hildegard of Bingen, see Teresa Scott Soufas, *Melancholy and the Secular Mind in Spanish Golden Age Literature* (Columbia: University of Missouri Press, 1990), p. 37.

42. For a succinct but useful discussion of melancholia and its treatment, see Laurinda S. Dixon, *Perilous Chastity: Women and Illness in Pre-Enlightenment Art and Medicine* (Ithaca, N.Y.: Cornell University Press, 1995), pp. 197–207. See also Stanley W. Jackson, *Melancholia and Depression from Hippocratic Times*

to *Modern Times* (New Haven: Yale University Press, 1968); and esp. Schmitz 1972, pp. 116–156, who devotes considerable attention to the importance of laughter for melancholics.

43.   For Iambe (also called Baubo), see Gilhus 1997, pp. 33–34; *The Homeric Hymns to Demeter: Translation, Commentary, and Interpretative Essays*, trans. and ed. Helene Foley (Princeton: Princeton University Press, 1994), p. 12, commentary pp. 45–46. For another version of this story, see Apollodorus, *The Library*, trans. Sir James George Frazer, 2 vols., Loeb Classical Library (London: W. Heinemann; New York: G. P. Putnam's Sons, 1921), 1:37.

44.   Giovanni Marinello, *Delle medicine partenenti all' infermità delle donne* (Venice: Francesco de' Francheschi, 1563); and Girolamo Mercurio [Friar Scipione], *De gli errori popolari d'Italia* (Venice: Giovanni Ciotti, 1603), cited in Bell 1999, pp. 194 and 197 respectively. Martin Luther similarly advised against joking with pregnant women, for fear of "miscarriages, monsters, and various deformities"; see Karant-Nunn and Wiesner-Hanks 2003, p. 178.

45.   Quoted in Welsford 1968, p. 283.

46.   Pleij 1990; Verberckmoes 1998; Verberckmoes 1999; Dekker 1997; and Van Stipriaan 1996.

47.   Rabelais-Cohen 1955, p. 435, in the second version of the *Quart livre*, published in 1552; see Michael J. Heath, *Rabelais,* Medieval and Renaissance Texts and Studies, vol. 130 (Tempe: Medieval and Renaissance Texts and Studies, 1996), pp. 90–91.

48.   *Het volksboek van Ulenspiegel*, ed. Loek Geeraedts, Klassik galerij 42 (Kapellen: DNB / Uitgeverij Pelckmans; Amsterdam: Wereldbibliotheek, 1986), p. 93, "Die Prolooghe."

49.   *De pastoor van Kalenberg*, ed. Hinke van Kampen and Herman Pleij (Muiderberg: Dick Coutinho, 1981).

50.   See Bowen 1988.

51.   For a late-fifteenth-century French translation, frequently published in the next century, see *Les facecies de Poge,* trans. Guillaume Tardif, ed. Frédéric Duval and Sandrine Hériché-Pradeau (Geneva: Librairie Droz, 2003).

52.   See *Nyeuwe clucht boeck* 1983; also described in Verberckmoes 1999, pp. 27–28.

53.   Lambrecht 1945, p. 48, s.v., "Boerde oft cluchte": "quand on dit quelque chose par jeu et non point à bon esciënt." See also Verberckmoes 1999,

p. 28, who usefully reminds us that in the sixteenth century, a *cluchte* did not have to be comic, but "as a short anecdote in prose, it covers the plural meaning of joke, short comic play, trickery, disguise, lie, whim, simulation, riddle, delusion, etc." See also *Woordenboek* 1882–1998, s.v., "Klucht." The nearest word in English, *jest*, possessed a similar range of meanings; see the *Oxford English Dictionary*, s.v., "jest." An older form of the Netherlandish comic story, the *boerden*, like their French counterparts, the *fabliaux*, include many humorous stories similar in spirit to those in the *kluchtboeken*; for some examples, see Lodder 1996; Lodder 2003; and Brewer 2003; as well as Hogenelst 1997, 2: nos. 102, 113, 114, 120, several of which, in fact, were taken from French sources.

54. *Cluchtboeck, inhoudende vele recreative propoosten ende cluchten* (Antwerp: Heyndrick Heyndricsen [Hendrik Hendricksz], 1576); see Verberckmoes 1998, p. 196. Pleij, in *Nyeuwe clucht boeck* 1983, p. 16, notes a French translation of this work by Antoine Tyron, published by Heyndricsen in 1578.

55. Bowen 1988, p. 83.

56. Joubert-Rocher 1980, p. 20. For involuntary nudity as a source of amusement in the Middle Ages, see Curtius 1953, p. 433.

57. *Nyeuwe clucht boeck* 1983, p. 48.

58. Ibid., pp. 217–218, no. (246).

59. Verberckmoes 1999, p. 16.

60. *Nyeuwe clucht boeck* 1983, p. 183, no. 192 (1). Earlier appearances of this story are described in Bowen 1988, p. 3, no. 5: Petrarch, *Rerum memorandarum libri*, ca. 1343–45. For other sources and parallels, see Ernst Kris and Otto Kurz, *Legend, Myth, and Magic in the Image of the Artist: A Historical Experiment*, intro. E. H. Gombrich (New Haven: Yale University Press, 1979), pp. 115–116.

61. *Nyeuwe clucht boeck* 1983, pp. 219–220, no. (249). Summarized, with full particulars, in Verberckmoes 1999, pp. 30–31.

62. Burke 1997, p. 88, notes that some comic tales were moralized in later editions.

63. *The Scholar's Guide: A Translation of the Twelfth-Century "Disciplina Clericalis" of Pedro Alfonso*, trans. Joseph Ramon Jones and John Esten Keller (Toronto: Pontifical Institute of Mediaeval Studies, 1969), pp. 55–66. The translators draw the same conclusion that I do concerning this group of stories and speak of Alfonso's "tongue-in-cheek" seriousness in general (p. 13). Frederik Lodder arrives at similar conclusions concerning the medieval

boerden; see Lodder 1996, esp. pp. 147, 161. Cf. *Robrecht de Duyvel*, a Netherlandish prose romance published in 1516 after a French version. It can claim, perhaps, to be morally edifying, since it traces Robrecht's career from Devil's child to man of God, but the hero reaches his goal only after a series of less-than-edifying but highly entertaining adventures; see Rob Resoort, ed., *Robrecht de Duyvel* (Muiderberg: Dick Coutinho, 1980).

64.   See Lode Roose, *Anna Bijns: Een rederijker uit de hervormingstijd*, Koninklijke Academie voor Nederlandse Taal-en Letterkunde, VIe Reeks, Bekroonde werken, Nr. 93 (Ghent: Secretariaat van de Koninklijke Academie voor Nederlandse Taal-en Letterkunde, 1963), p. 342. For some erotic songs, with their many examples of wordplay of a sexual nature, in an Antwerp songbook of 1544, see Hermina Joldersma, "'Het Antwerps Liedboek': A Critical Edition," 2 vols. Ph.D. diss., Princeton University, 1983, I:XCV—XCVII.

65.   Brussels, Bibliothèque Royale, *La bibliothèque de Marguerite d'Autriche*. Exposition, 1940, p. 56, cat. no. 123.

66.   Pleij 1990, p. 96; Van Brouchoven possessed a copy of Johannes Pauli's *Schimpff und Ernst*; see Van der Feen 1918, p. 90, no. 130. For the presence of such literature in Dutch libraries, see Van Stipriaan 1996, pp. 82—84, among them Marnix's copies of the *Decameron* in Italian (p. 84).

67.   Quoted in Curtius 1953, p. 422: "Lo spirito allegro aquista più facilmente la perfezione christiana che non lo spirito malinconico." Apparently a great humorist himself, Neri identified his favorite jest book as one by the fifteenth-century priest and fool Piovano Arlotto; see Beatrice K. Otto, *Fools Are Everywhere: The Court Jester around the World* (Chicago: University of Chicago Press, 2001), pp. 169—170.

68.   On the earthy sense of humor of the upper classes in this period, see Bowen 1998, pp. 14, 82; and for the seventeenth-century Dutch middle class in particular, E. de Jongh, "Jan Steen, So Near and Yet So Far," in Washington-Amsterdam 1996, pp. 46—47.

69.   Burke 1978, p. 26.

70.   Welsford 1968, pp. 142—147.

71.   *Nyeuwe clucht boeck* 1983, pp. 67—68, nos. 22—24.

72.   Welsford 1968, pp. 144 and 283 respectively. For Tarleton, see also John Southworth, *Fools and Jesters at the English Court* (Phoenix Mill, U.K.: Sutton Publishing, 1995), pp. 108—109 and passim, esp. 114—117.

73. *Mary of Nemeghen*, in *Medieval Netherlandish Religious Literature*, trans. and
    intro. E. Colledge (Leiden: Sythoff; London: Heinemann; New York:
    London House and Maxwell, 1965), p. 211. This is how her priest-uncle,
    Marijken tells her demon lover, characterizes the *Play of Mascaron*, in which
    the Virgin intervenes to save humanity from God's harsh punishment. It
    has been suggested that the author of this play was a *rederijker*, perhaps
    Anna Bijns or someone in her literary circle (ibid., p. 15).

74. In the city accounts of Oudenaarde for 1553–54, the *Play of Naboth* is de-
    scribed as being *tot leeringhe, onderwijsinghe ende ghestichichede van alle menschen*;
    quoted in Ramakers 1996, p. 157.

75. Hummelen 1989, p. 24; similarly, in the Antwerp *landjuweel* of 1496, the
    highest prize for acting was destined for the funniest person in a play (ibid.,
    p. 41 n. 69). Cf. De Bloeiende Jeugd of Oudenaarde, probably a festive
    association of young men: their *charte* of 1538 for a carnival banquet in-
    vites similar groups to join in their festivities, especially those full of
    melancholy. In the same year, the Pax Vobis chamber of Oudenaarde was
    reimbursed by the city for expenses it had incurred *omme in ghenouchte te
    recreerne* (that is, for entertaining their audience). Both references from
    Ramakers 1996, p. 137.

76. See Coigneau 1994, pp. 116–117, for the great popularity of comic plays
    in the civic culture of the time.

77. For the *refereinen* (now spelled *refreinen*) in *het zotte*, see Coigneau 1980–83.

78. Concerning *esbattements*, Ramakers 1996, p. 154, notes that while many of
    them had religious subjects, by the sixteenth century they were generally
    comic plays. For an excellent survey of *tafelspelen*, see Pikhaus 1988–89;
    and for a useful brief discussion, Hüsken 1996, pp. 125–132. As for the
    term *klucht*, see below, n. 84.

79. The play *Tielebuijs* (1541) is described by one of the speakers as a *recreatie*;
    see Mak 1959, p. 350 (for two versions of the play, see Hummelen 1968,
    no. 1 OG 14, 2 O 5). A Mechelen record of 1593 notes that some children
    were paid for a *recreatie* during the choosing of the king on Twelfth Night;
    see Van Wagenberg-ten Hoeven 1997, p. 19. Similarly, in a play published
    in Rotterdam in 1621, one of the actors explains at its conclusion that the
    drama has been performed for the sake of *recreatien* (Hummelen 1968, no.
    3 S 4), quoted in Pikhaus 1988–89, 1:151.

80. Quoted in Van Wagenberg-ten Hoeven 1997, p. 56. Two more examples

are cited in Pikhaus 1988–89, p. 134: in one *tafelspel*, a player urges his audience to "maecht vreucht in desen recreatie!" that is, to take joy in this recreation, or play.

81.   Adapted from Horace 1991, pp. 6, 7 (*Satires* 1.1.24), or *Al lachende de waerheit seggen* in the Netherlandish of Bruegel's time; see Cornelis Kiliaan, *Dictionarium Teutonicolatinum*, 1574, quoted in Sullivan 1999, p. 245. For the relationship between instruction and delight in the sixteenth century and later, see Lee 1967, pp. 32–34; and, with some reservations, Pleij 1974–75.

82.   In his *Responsio* (Basel: Froben, 1529), a reply to Alberto Pio's condemnation of *The Praise of Folly*, quoted in Gilmore 1978, p. 114. In his defense of the same work in a letter to Martin Dorp (1514), Erasmus elaborates on this function of laughter with a quotation from Horace (*Satires* 1.1.24–25): "There is nothing to prevent you from telling the truth, as long as you do it with a smile," and he further alludes to Lucretius, who likens pleasure to the honey that doctors who are treating children smear on a cup of bitter medicine. See Sullivan 1994, pp. 47–69; and Erasmus-Miller 1979, p. 143. I owe the latter reference to Mark Meadow.

83.   Graf 1997, p. 29. Ramakers 2002, p. 35, observes that it is erroneous to believe that comedy functioned chiefly to criticize a particular social group. Cf. also Ramakers 1996, p. 134.

84.   The term *klucht* signified any entertaining story or incident; see n. 53 above; and Lambrecht 1945, p. 62, s.v., "Clute oft cluchte": "Farce, bourde *ou* gaberië." Hence we have both *kluchtboeken*, or jest books, and *kluchten*, or farces.

85.   For a succinct but useful definition of the farce, see Barbara Bowen, "Towards a Definition of the Farce as a Literary 'Genre,'" *Modern Language Review* 56 (1961): 558–660.

86.   For the original manuscript of the play, see Jan Van der Stock, ed., *La ville in Flandre: culture et société, 1477–1787* (Brussels: Credit Communal and Vlaamsche Gemeenschap, 1991), pp. 534–535, cat. no. 327.

87.   For the Baltens painting, and similar kermis scenes attributed to Pieter Bruegel the Younger, see Marlier 1969, pp. 294–305; Hummelen 1989, pp. 32–33; and Ramakers 2002, pp. 42–45.

88.   For the text of the play, see Hans van Dijk et al., "Plaijerwater. A Sixteenth-Century Farce, with an English Translation," *Dutch Crossing*, no. 24 (1984): 32–81. *Plaijerwater* as a variant of a popular medieval German story is discussed by Schmidt 1963, pp. 327–342. My translation of the play's title

is borrowed from Herman Pleij, *Dreaming of Cockaigne: Medieval Fantasies of the Perfect Life* (New York: Columbia University Press, 1997), p. 25. The motif of the supposedly therapeutic water appears again in a tale in the *Nyeuwe clucht boeck* 1983, pp. 141–142, no. 132, in which a husband feigns illness and orders his wife to fetch water from a fountain in the forest, where he has arranged for her to be murdered by a confederate.

89.   Hüsken 1996, p. 130, notes that the *kluchten* were usually presented after the allegorical plays. For their medieval forerunners, see Hüsken 1987, pp. 40–44, who aptly characterizes them as *delectatief*, or "pleasurable."

90.   Erasmus-Miller 1979, p. 9. Folly varies an old topos, found as early as classical antiquity, in which a speaker, finding his audience bored, interrupts his serious subject with a frivolous story, and upbraids his listeners for paying more attention to the story than to the serious matter; see William Hansen, *Ariadne's Thread: A Guide to International Tales Found in Classical Literature* (Ithaca, N.Y.: Cornell University Press, 2002), pp. 75–79, under "Catch-Tale: Demades the Orator."

91.   Theodor Distel, "Inhalt zweier, 1549 in Brüssel ausgeführter Theaterstücke," *Zeitschrift für vergleichende Litteraturgeschichte und Renaissance-Literatur* 4 (1891): 355–359. How often farces were performed on such occasions is not known, but see Ramakers 1996, p. 108, who notes that several *kluchten* were staged before the illuminated city hall of Oudenaarde during the triumphal entry of Margaret of Parma into the city in 1561. Kram's disparaging account of the audience is curious; presumably he had encountered similar reactions to the carnival plays of his native Germany.

92.   This condemnation occurs in the *afschieds spel* (farewell play) presented by the Violieren in the Antwerp *landjuweel* of 1561; see Coigneau 1994, pp. 117–118. In this regard, it is significant that while the chief prize in the *landjuweel* of 1561 went to a *spel van sinne*, in the dramatic competitions of 1496 and 1539, the top prize had been awarded to an *esbattement* (ibid.).

93.   For the *rederijker* fools and their activities, see Verberckmoes 1999, pp. 22–23; and esp. Hüsken 1996.

94.   For this event, see Hüsken 1996, pp. 122–125. The original text of the "proclamation" is published in R. J. Marijnissen, "De Eed van Meester Oom. Een Voorbeeld van Brabantse Jokkernij uit Bruegels Tijd," in Von Simson and Winner 1979, pp. 51–61. The part of the king was played by the Brussels painter Jan Colyns, alias Welravens, for whom see also

E. Roobaert, "Jan Walravens, alias Oomken, schilder en rederijker to Brus-
sel," *Bulletin, Musées Royaux des Beaux-Arts* 3−4 (1961): 83−100. For mock
orders, commands, and oaths in the late Middle Ages and Renaissance,
especially in the Netherlands, see Pleij 1979, pp. 86−108. For a related
German example, which implies a resemblance between the fool or fools
and the viewer, see Gregory Davies and Alison Stewart, "Head of a Jester,"
Print Quarterly 19 (2002): 170−174.

95.   Hüsken 1996, pp. 124−125. For the fool and his social function, see Verberckmoes 1999, pp. 20−23, who distinguishes between the moralizing
fool and the "fool for recreation." For a similar distinction in ancient Rome
between humor used for blame and censure and employed purely for fun,
see Graf 1997, pp. 36−37.

CHAPTER 2

Epigraphs: Aristotle, *Poetics* 5; quoted from Aristotle 1984, 2:2319 (1449a35−37);
and Joubert-Rocher 1980, p. 27 (bk. 1, chap. 4).

1.   Barolsky 1978. See, for example, his discussion of some paintings by Ti-
tian and his workshop, Bronzino's *Venus, Cupid, Folly, and Time* (London,
National Gallery) and Dosso Dossi's so-called *Bambocciata* (Florence,
Uffizi), pp. 90−91, 166−171, and 190−195 respectively.

2.   *The Enchiridion of Erasmus*, trans. and ed. Raymond Himelick (Bloomington: Indiana University Press, 1963), p. 90 (chap. 12). Erasmus refers to
Virgil, *Aeneid* 6:282−295. That devils could be a source of humor is evident in an incident mentioned by Muylle 1984, p. 140, concerning a painting over an altar dedicated to St. Anthony (possibly a *Temptation of St. Anthony*, perhaps by Pieter Huys, Jan Mandijn, or one of their followers; cf.
Fig. 9); in 1613 it was condemned by the ecclesiastical authorities as more
conducive to laughter than to devotion. Although, as Muylle reminds us,
this episode occurred in the wake of the Council of Trent with its stricter
definition of church art, it nevertheless suggests how such images might
have been received a generation or so earlier. As for Bosch, a *bort* (comic
subject) painted on canvas by Hieronymus Bosch is listed, along with a
Stone Operation (usually identified with the panel of this subject in the
Museo del Prado, Madrid), in the 1529 inventory of the estate of Philip
of Burgundy, bishop of Utrecht. See J. Sterck, *Philips van Bourgondie (1465−
1524), bisschop van Utrecht als protagonist van de Renaissance, zijn leven en maecenaat*
(Zutphen: De Walburg pers, 1980), pp. 225 and 248 respectively. For the

fortunes of Bosch's monstrous inventions, see Silver 1999. In some contexts, of course, such monsters were also employed for serious purposes; see Unverfehrt 1984; and Paul Vandenbroeck, "Zur Herkunft und Verwurzelung der 'Grillen.' Vom Volksmythos zum Kunst- und literaturtheoretischen Begriff, 15.–17. Jahrhundert," *De zeventiende eeuw* 3 (1987): 52–84.

3. See, for example, Jones 2002b, p. 155; and Michael Camille, *Image on the Edge: The Margins of Medieval Art* (Cambridge, Mass.: Harvard University Press, 1992), pp. 11–55. Camille stresses the playful element of marginal decoration in medieval manuscripts, often involving obscene puns and the like, and frequently inspired by the accompanying text. For a reading of marginalia as bearers of more weighty significance, see Andrew Taylor, "Playing on the Margins: Bakhtin and the Smithfield Decretals," in Farrell 1995, pp. 17–37.

4. See Gibson 1992c, with earlier literature; Jeanneret 1989; and Prescott 1998, pp. 147–161.

5. Horace 1991, p. 451, lines 1–5.

6. For grotesques in the Renaissance, see Dacos 1969.

7. For Ligorio, see ibid., 129–132; D. R. Coffin, "Pirro Ligorio and Decoration of the Late Sixteenth Century at Ferrara," *Art Bulletin* 37 (1955): 182.

8. De Barbaro, quoted in Dacos 1969, pp. 123–124.

9. Rabelais, in his prologue to *Gargantua*, writes, "Now a Silenus, in ancient days, was a little box, of the kind we see to-day in apothecaries' shops, painted on the outside with such gay, comical figures as harpies, satyrs, bridled geese, horned hares, saddled ducks, flying goats, harts in harness, and other devices of that sort, lightheartedly invented for the purpose of mirth" (Rabelais-Cohen 1955, p. 37). Although alluding to Plato, *Symposium* (Plato 1963, p. 566, sec. 215a–b), in which Alcibiades praises Socrates by comparing him to a Silenus figure that opens up to reveal a god, Rabelais clearly describes objects decorated with what we now call grotesques.

10. Cotgrave, *Dictionnairie*, 1611, quoted in David Evett, "Mammon's Grotto: Sixteenth-Century Visual Grotesquerie and Some Features of Spenser's *Faerie Queene*," *English Literary Renaissance* 12 (1982): 180–209, see esp. 194 n. 32. The *Songes drolatiques* was put to more serious use when it inspired four costumes designed by Inigo Jones in an English allegorical political drama of 1640 (Prescott 1998, pp. 157–159 and figs. 16–18).

11.   Joubert-Rocher 1980, pp. 20–23, cites various incongruities as objects of laughter.

12.   See Ruth Mortimer, *Harvard College, Department of Printing and Graphic Arts, Catalogue of Books and Manuscripts,* Part 1, *French 16th Century Books,* 2 vols. (Cambridge, Mass.: Harvard University Press, 1964), 2:612–613, no. 499, citing P. D. Plan, *Bibliographie rabelaisienne* (Paris, 1904).

13.   De Tolnay 1952, p. 19. For the series, see Rotterdam–New York 2001, pp. 144–160, cat. nos. 42–54.

14.   See Stoett 1943, 1:540, no. 1347. Cf. Pikhaus, 1988–89, 1:116, where the worthless *bolster* (cushion, pillow), filled with straw and thus symbolic of the worldly life of sin, appears in a Netherlandish *tafelspel* of the period as a gift that must be destroyed.

15.   A. J. J. Delen, *Oude Vlaamsche graphiek* (Antwerp: Het Kompas, 1943), p. 133. These items occur in a list of prints sent by Plantin to Martin le Jeune at Paris in 1558. The artists are unidentified, but Delen identifies a number of items as prints after Bruegel. There are two sets of *7 peches mortalz,* but as one is valued at 5 shillings (ibid., p. 132), the other at 2, it is uncertain if the same series is meant. The five-shilling set may have been hand-colored, but this is not indicated.

16.   For these two prints, see Rotterdam–New York 2001, pp. 137–139, cat. no. 37; and pp. 161–162, cat. no. 53 respectively.

17.   The demonic aspects of *drolerie* is noted by Serebrennikov 1993, p. 165. In sixteenth-century Netherlandish, the word *drol* was used to designate a type of demon or giant (cf. the English cognate *troll*); see *Woordenboek* 1882–1998, s.v., "drol." For the various meanings of *drolatiquiment, drolle,* and related terms in the sixteenth century, see Edmund Huguet, *Dictionnaire de la langue français du seizième siècle,* 7 vols. (Paris: Didier, etc., 1925–65), 3:279.

18.   Vasari 1878, 5:439; quoted in Serebrennikov 1993, pp. 164–165. See also Getscher 2003, p. 217.

19.   Dominicus Lampsonius, *Pictorum aliquot celebrium Germaniae inferioris effigies* (Antwerp, 1572); see Lampsonius-Puraye 1956, nos. 3 and 19. Van Mander characterizes Jan Mandijn's paintings in the manner of Bosch as "specters and drolleries *[ghespoock en drollerije]*" and elsewhere as "burlesques *[drollicheden]*"; see Van Mander-Miedema, 1994–99, 1: fols. 205r and 268v respectively (pp. 78–79, 332–333). See also Silver 1999, pp. 37, 44.

20.   Van Mander-Miedema 1994–99, 1: fol. 233 (p. 190). For a useful sur-

vey of opinions on Bruegel's art from Ortelius to Van Mander, see
Meadow 2002, pp. 104–107.

21.   For a similar gown, see Max von Boehn, *Modes and Manners*, trans. Joan
       Joshua, 4 vols. (Philadelphia: J. B. Lippincott, 1932–36), 2:169, after an
       engraving by Enea Vico.

22.   This phrase occurs in the subtitle of his book on the ancient, Italian, and
       German painters; see Van Mander 1969, unnumbered folio (fol. 58r). My
       thanks to Eddy de Jongh for this reference. This combination of in-
       struction and delight, *leering en vermaak* in modern Netherlandish, is per-
       ceptively analyzed by Eddy de Jongh in the introduction to his exhibition
       catalogue *Tot leering en vermaak: Betekenissen van Hollandse genrevoorstellingen uit
       de zeventiende eeuw* (Amsterdam: Rijksmuseum, 1976). For an English trans-
       lation, see De Jongh 2000, pp. 83–103. Other aspects of this subject are
       examined in Phillips Salman, "Instruction and Delight in Medieval and
       Renaissance Criticism," *Renaissance Quarterly* 32 (1979): 303–332.

23.   See Claude Bremond, Jacques Le Goff, and Jean-Claude Schmitt, *L'"Ex-
       emplum,"* Typologie des sources du Moyen Âge occidental, fasc. 40 (Turn-
       hout: Brepols, 1982). Cf. Erasmus, who in his *Praise of Folly* has Folly ob-
       serve that if the preacher explains his subject seriously, his congregation
       goes to sleep, but if he tells some old wives' tale, "it sits up and listens
       with open mouths" (Erasmus-Miller 1979, p. 71).

24.   Giovanni Boccaccio, *The Decameron*, trans. Frances Winwar (New York:
       Modern Library, 1935), p. 65. See also Perfetti 2003, pp. 67–68.

25.   Pleij 1974–75, pp. 119–120, who also notes the frequent objections in
       the Middle Ages to the use of comic anecdotes in sermons.

26.   These plays include the Netherlandish cycle of the *Seven Joys of Mary*; see
       Pleij 1988, p. 170.

27.   See W. M. H. Hummelen, *De sinnekens in het rederijkersdrama* (Groningen:
       J. B. Wolters, 1958), pp. 238–245, who describes the dialogues between
       evil *sinnekens* that are often very humorous; he observes that while such
       comic episodes served didactic ends, they must also have entertained con-
       temporary audiences. In contrast, devils are very seldom presented as
       comic (p. 374). A striking exception occurs in the fragmentary late-
       fifteenth-century *Maastrichtse Easter Play*: two devils try to save some souls
       from Christ by salting them like fish; see Herman Pleij, "Duivels in de
       Middelnederlandse literatuur," in *Duivelsbeelden: Een cultuurhistorische speur-*

tocht door de Lage Landen, ed. Gerard Rooijakkers, Léne Dresen-Coenders, and Margreet Geerdes (Baarn: Ambo, 1994), pp. 95–96.

28. When students of this period encountered passages in their reading that they wanted to remember, they recorded them in notebooks under various topics, often the Virtues and Vices (Meadow 2002, p. 74).

29. Stewart 1995, p. 360.

30. Gibson 1992a. For a different reading, see Paul Vandenbroeck, "Verbeeck's Peasant Weddings: A Study of Iconography and Social Function," *Simiolus* 14 (1984): 79–124.

31. Brant-Zeydel 1962, p. 18. There is no doubt that its lessons were taken seriously. In Strasbourg, Johannes Geiler von Kayserberg preached a series of sermons on the *Narrenschiff* just four years after its first publication; in the 1520 German edition of these sermons, Sebastian Brant's son Onophrius emphasized the moral teachings of the *Narrenschiff*. See Noll 1999, pp. 73–74.

32. Brant-Zeydel 1962, pp. 76–77, chap. 7, "Of Causing Discord."

33. See Verberckmoes 1999, p. 32, with further references.

34. *Nyeuwe clucht boeck* 1983, pp. 92–93, no. 57.

35. Some examples in Gibson 1981, pp. 438–439.

36. Andriessoon 2003, p. 29; the collection exists only in manuscript form. Andriessoon also copied plays by other *rederijkers* for use by his chamber.

37. Hüsken 1996, p. 113, who ascribes a somewhat different meaning to this expression. For more on this proverb, see pp. 115–116 below.

38. Brussels 1994, pp. 84–85, cat. no. 15 with ill. in color; and Hüsken 1996, p. 113 and fig. 9.

39. Grauls 1957, pp. 118–125.

40. Hüsken 1996, p. 113.

41. Rotterdam–New York 2001, pp. 140–144, cat. nos. 38–41.

42. Kavaler 1999, pp. 80–84, with earlier references.

43. For fuller discussions of this print, see Gibson 1992b, esp. p. 74; and esp. Kavaler 1999, pp. 77–93. The proverbs are restated in the verses in several languages added in the two editions of the first state; see Rotterdam–New York 2001, pp. 166–168, esp. n. 1, cat. nos. 58–59.

44. For a recent study of the *Elck* that emphasizes its playful elements, see

Bret Rothstein, "The Problem with Looking at Pieter Bruegel's *Elck,*" *Art History* 26 (2003): 143–173.

45. The latter figure is given by Grosshans 2003, p. 130, who also offers excellent color details of the painting.

46. Gibson 1977, pp. 71–76; Meadow 2002; and various essays in Mieder 2004, including Mori 2004. Meadow 2002, pp. 132–135, suggests that the word *abuisen* in the title inscription of Hogenberg's print does not mean "deceit," as commonly assumed, but "oddities," and if the word does refer to deceit, it cannot be applied to Bruegel's painting.

47. Alexander Barclay, *Ship of Fools,* fol. ccvvii^v, quoted in Robert C. Evans, "Forgotten Fools: Alexander Barclay's *Ship of Fools,*" in Davidson 1996, p. 64.

48. *Alchemy* and *Beggar Talk,* in Erasmus-Thompson 1965, pp. 238–245 and 248–254 respectively.

49. *Woordenboek* 1882–1998, s.v., "alchemist."

50. Getscher 2003, p. 216. See also Vasari 1878, 5:439: *stillandosi il cervello.*

51. This detail may have been inspired by the French satire *The Right Way to the Almshouse,* widely imitated during the sixteenth century, including a Netherlandish poem of about 1550; see *Veelderhande* 1971, pp. 126–141. Alchemists are not mentioned by name, but Bruegel's contemporaries would have numbered them among the feckless who make their way to the poorhouse.

52. An apparent variant of Bruegel's composition exists in a drawing attributed to Jan Verbeeck the Elder (Konstanz, Städtische Gemäldegalerie), including the bellows-wielding fool and several children climbing into an empty larder. The connection between the two drawings is unclear but deserves further investigation. Perhaps both artists were inspired by a common literary source that described the details shown in their works. See Malines 2003, p. 52, no. 14, with ill.

53. As noted in Rotterdam–New York 2001, pp. 170–173, cat. no. 60, these expressive physiognomies did not fare well in the translation of the drawing into a print executed possibly by Philips Galle and published by Hieronymus Cock.

54. Otto Benesch, *The Art of the Renaissance in Northern Europe: Its Relation to the Contemporary Spiritual and Intellectual Movements,* rev. ed. (London: Phaidon, 1965), pp. 108–110, the quote on 110; and Robert L. Delevoy, *Bruegel* ([Geneva]: Skira, 1959), p. 64. In an article of 1934, Hans Sedelmeyr com-

pared the eyes and mouths in Bruegel's faces to the "points" (presumably chunks of coal or suchlike) on a snowman; see Sedelmeyr, "Bruegel's Macchia (1934)," in Wood 2000, pp. 322–376, esp. 329.

55.   Joshua Reynolds, *Discourses on Art*, intro. Robert Lavine (New York: Collier Books, 1961), p. 72 (*Discourse Five*, 1772). Similarly, Charles Darwin observed that the great artists, painters and sculptors alike, are too preoccupied with physical beauty to represent the more intense human emotions. They avoid extreme emotion because the "strongly contracted facial muscles destroy beauty"; see Charles Darwin, *The Expression of the Emotions in Man and Animals* (1872; New York: Philosophical Library, 1955), introduction, p. 14.

56.   Bartolomeo Fazio, *De viris illustribus*, ca. 1453–57, quoted from *A Documentary History of Art*, vol. 1, *The Middle Ages and the Renaissance*, ed. Elizabeth Holt (Garden City, N.Y.: Doubleday Anchor Books, Doubleday and Co., 1957), p. 203.

57.   Van de Velde 1975, pp. 155–158, cat. no. 4. In later art, notable exceptions include the Old Testament paintings of Jan Steen and the mythological and biblical scenes of the young Rembrandt, a subject meriting further study.

58.   I owe this account of viewer expectations to several perceptive suggestions by Held 1996, pp. 178 and 186 n. 38.

59.   For a similar observation, see Zsuzsa [Susan] Urbach, "Notes on Bruegel's Archaism: His Relationship to Early Netherlandish Paintings and Other Sources," *Acta Historiae Artium* 25 (1978): 237–256, esp. 239.

60.   See ibid.; and Walter S. Melion, "'*Ego enim quasi obdormivi*': Salvation and Blessed Sleep in Philip Galle's *Death of the Virgin* after Pieter Bruegel," in De Jong et al. 1996, pp. 14–53. Henk van Os correctly stresses that in the later Middle Ages, "certain scenes that we today find abstract and hieratic originally functioned in an extremely emotional context"; see Henk van Os, "The Discovery of an Early Man of Sorrows on a Dominican Triptych," *Journal of the Warburg and Courtauld Institutes* 41 (1978): 65–75, quote on 73. See also Hans Belting, *The Image and Its Public: Form and Function of Early Paintings of the Passion*, trans. Mark Bartusis and Raymond Meyer (New Rochelle, N.Y.: Aristide D. Caratzas, 1990), p. 62.

61.   As in some devotional panels by Quentin Massys; see Friedländer 1967–76, 7: pls. 23–24.

62. For this subject, see Walter S. Gibson, "*Imitatio Christi*: The Passion Scenes of Hieronymus Bosch," *Simiolus* 6 (1972–73): 83–93, and esp. the illuminating study by James H. Marrow, *Passion Iconography in Northern Europe of the Late Middle Ages and Early Renaissance: A Study of the Transformation of Sacred Metaphor into Descriptive Narrative*, Ars Neerlandica, vol. 1 (Kortrijk: Van Gemmert, 1979).

63. Examples ill. in Friedländer 1967–76, 7: pls. 16–17 (Massys); 13: pl. 101, fig. 197 (Heemskerck).

64. Quoted in E. H. Gombrich, "The Grotesque Heads," in idem, *The Heritage of Apelles: Studies in the Art of the Renaissance* (Ithaca, N.Y.: Cornell University Press, 1976), p. 60.

65. For short discussions of these manuals, together with reproductions of some of their illustrations, see Grillot de Givry, *Witchcraft Magic and Alchemy*, trans. J. Courtenay Locke (New York: Dover Publications, 1971), pp. 256–261; and Kurt Seligmann, *Magic, Supernaturalism and Religion* (New York: Pantheon Books, n.d.), pp. 261–266. For Roelants, see Ilja M. Veldman, "Seasons, Planets and Temperaments in the Work of Maarten van Heemskerck: Cosmo-astrological Allegory in Sixteenth-Century Netherlandish Prints," *Simiolus* 11 (1980): 149–176, esp. 169 and n. 70; and Muylle 2001, pp. 180–181.

66. Sullivan 1994, pp. 79–83, suggests that Bruegel's depictions of peasant heads was influenced by these physiognomy manuals, but this is doubted by Muylle 2001, p. 180 n. 17.

67. Joubert-Rocher 1980, p. 6.

68. Paul Philippot, "L'integration de motifs de Raphaël et de Michel Ange dans l'oeuvre du monogrammiste de Brunswick," in *Relations artistiques entre les Pays-Bas et l'Italie à la Renaissance: Études dédiées à Suzanne Sulzberger*, Études d'Histoire de l'Art publiées par l'Institut Historique Belge de Rome, vol. V (Brussels: L'Institute Historique Belge de Rome, 1980), pp. 199–207. Indeed, we encounter much more expressive figures in the previous century, in a remarkable frontispiece miniature detached from a three-volume copy of Valerius Maximus's *Faits et dits mémorables des romains*. Executed by the Master of the Dresden Prayerbook in Bruges about 1475–80, the illuminations deftly contrast the sedate conduct of the temperate and the drunken debauchery of the intemperate at their respective tables. See Los Angeles, The J. Paul Getty Museum, *Illuminating the Renais-*

sance: The Triumph of Flemish Manuscript Painting in Europe, ed. Thomas Kren and Scot McKendrick, 2003, cat. no. 73, ill. p. 275.

69.   Cf. Carolus Scribanius, who, although he shared the common tendency to read emotions into the actors of a depicted scene, makes some acute observations concerning the expressive figures in the inner wings of Massys's St. John triptych (Antwerp, Koninklijk Museum voor Schone Kunsten), showing the martyrdom of John the Evangelist and the dance of Salome (Held 1996, p. 202).

70.   See Alison G. Stewart, *Unequal Lovers: A Study of Unequal Couples in Northern Art* (New York: Abaris Books, 1977); and Verberckmoes 2001, pp. 97–101.

71.   Hand and Wolff 1986, pp. 146–150, with a color ill.

72.   See Malines 2003, pp. 114–117, cat. no. 9, with a color ill., with a doubtful attribution to Jan Massys.

73.   See Buijnsters-Smets 1995, cat. nos. 8, 30–31, 36–37a, 46.

74.   Friendländer 1967–76, 12: pl. 95.

75.   Two examples in Malines 2003, pp. 114–123, cat. nos. 9–11.

76.   The probate inventory of Schetz's estate, made in 1579, lists *een tafereel van dronckeresse*; see Van Gelder 1972–73, no. 73; cited by Kavaler 1999, p. 134. For the painting by Jan Massys, see Buijnsters-Smets 1995, pp. 209–210, cat. no. 46.

77.   Houbraken 1943–53, 3:12; the translation quoted in Washington-Amsterdam 1996, p. 93. For similar observations on the relationship between genre subjects, comedy, and the depiction of the emotions, although in rather different contexts, see Hans-Joachim Raupp, "Ansätze zu einer Theorie der Genremalerei in den Niederlanden im 17. Jahrhundert," *Zeitschrift für Kunstgeschichte* 43 (1983): 401–418; and Barry Wind, "Pitture Ridicole: Some Late Cinquecento Comic Genre Paintings," *Storia dell'arte* 20 (1974): 25–35, esp. 29 and n. 29.

78.   Quoted in Van Stipriaan 1996, p. 265 n. 34; Netherlandish trans., p. 91. Ramakers 2002, pp. 31–33, discusses the connection between comedy and realism in ancient and sixteenth-century literary theory.

79.   This passage has been omitted in the translation in Washington-Amsterdam 1996, but see Houbraken 1943–53, 3:23–24. See also Mariët Westermann, *The Amusements of Jan Steen: Comic Painting in the Seventeenth Century*, Studies in Netherlandish Art and Cultural History, vol. I (Zwolle:

Waanders, 1997), pp. 24–25. Westermann's monograph presents an illuminating study of the comic element in Steen's art.

80.   But see Sluijter 1991; and De Jongh 2000, pp. 14–29.

81.   This anecdote is cited by Pier Paolo Vergerio, *The Character and Studies Befitting a Free-Born Youth* (ca. 1402–3); see Craig W. Kallendorf, ed. and trans., *Humanist Educational Treatises* (Cambridge, Mass.: Harvard University Press, 2002), p. 23.

82.   For Aristotle and Cato, see Verberckmoes 1998, p. 2; for St. Jerome, see Caroline Walker Bynum, *The Resurrection of the Body in Western Christianity, 200–1336* (New York: Columbia University Press, 1995), p. 87; for Bede (*Historia ecclasiastica, praef.*), see Constable 1995, p. 175. For other examples, see Gibson 2000, pp. 75–76; and particularly De Jongh 2000, pp. 100–102.

83.   Erika Rummel, *The Humanist-Scholastic Debate in the Renaissance and Reformation* (Cambridge, Mass.: Harvard University Press, 1995), pp. 42 and 73–74 respectively. Cf. Matthijs de Castelein, who in his *De Const van Rhetoriken* (Ghent: Jan Cauweel, 1555), defended the value of classical literature: "Tfy hemlien dan die de poëten versmaden, / Onder harte schale schuudt de zoete keerne" (roughly translated as: Scorn those who spurn the poets, beneath [whose] hard shell hides the sweet kernel), quoted in Ramakers 1996, p. 135.

84.   Prologue by Johannes Stigelius, quoted by Marvin Herrick, *Comic Theory in the Sixteenth Century* (Urbana: University of Illinois Press, 1950), p. 74. For other examples, see ibid., pp. 72–88; and Gibson 2000, pp. 75–76. Boccaccio asserts that a truly virtuous mind cannot be corrupted by obscene humor; St. Thomas Aquinas tells us that listening to ribald stories is not as bad as telling them (Perfetti 2003, pp. 25–26).

85.   Muylle 1984, p. 141, also doubts that such pictures were prized for their moral or didactic content. For similar objections, see Klaske Muizelaar and Derek Phillips, *Picturing Men and Women in the Dutch Golden Age: Paintings and People in Historical Perspective* (New Haven: Yale University Press, 2003), pp. 127–128. Cf. De Jongh 2000, p. 100, who aptly observes concerning seventeenth-century Dutch art and literature in general, "Sometimes the delight could completely overshadow the edifying or instructive aspect."

86.   See Andriessoon 2003, p. 139, no. 82.5, who comments, "That is: as some-

one leads so one follows him; if he does evil, one does evil too; if he does good, one also does good." But Aristotle was more neutral. In his *Problems* (bk. 7), he asks, "Why do men generally themselves yawn when they see others yawn?" (Aristotle 1984, 2:1369 [886a25–28]). Leonardo da Vinci prided himself on painting a yawning man so effectively that the viewer was compelled to yawn in response; see Bob Scribner, "Ways of Seeing in the Age of Dürer," in *Dürer and His Culture*, ed. Dagmar Eichberger and Charles Zika (Cambridge: Cambridge University Press, 1998), pp. 93–117, esp. 104. For the role of the yawn in traditional theories of the passions and the four humors, see Wolter Seuntjens, "Damp, walm en rook: Luchtige hartstochten in de literatuur van de zeventiende eeuw," *De zeventiende eeuw* 19, no. 2 (2003): 169–180. I owe this reference to Katharine Fremantle.

87.   E.g., Ertz 1988–2000, 2: 955–957; and Roberts-Jones 2002, p. 278.

88.   The *Head of a Lansquenet* is monogrammed "PB." For the *Head of an Old Man*, Bordeaux, Musée des Beaux-Arts, see Hughes and Bianconi 1967, p. 113, cat. no. 62, and ill. p. 92. On the basis of a recently discovered painting, *Head of a Peasant Man*, bearing the signature Pieter Brueghel the Younger and now in a German private collection, Klaus Ertz attributes these two pictures to Pieter Brueghel the Younger, as well as the *Yawning Man* (which he implausibly identifies as the head of a sick blind man). The form of the signature on the German *Peasant Man* leads him to date all these paintings after 1616, as he does a variant of the panel in Germany that appeared at auction in London in 1981 and a second peasant head (Switzerland, private collection). See Essen-Vienna-Antwerp 1997, pp. 364–372, cat. nos. 116–119; and Ertz 1988–2000, 2:953–962 and cat. nos. 1376–1381. However, differences in style and quality among the paintings in this group preclude their attribution to the same hand.

89.   Gaston van Camp, "Pierre Bruegel a-t-il peint une série des Sept Péchés Capitaux?" *Revue belge d'archéologie et d'histoire de l'art* 23 (1954): 217–223.

90.   De Vries 1989, p. 190, where he states that such *tronies* were not intended as allegorical figures but simply as studies in expression. Under the term *tronie*, he includes, correctly, I believe, some paintings by Brouwer that have been traditionally interpreted as personifications of the Vices, and several pictures by Rembrandt hitherto considered portraits. A *rederijker* document of 1618 mentions a *mascars tronie*, that is, a mask; see Pikhaus 1988–89, 1:96. For the use of the word *tronie* in the seventeenth century,

see Lydia de Pauw-de Veen, *Bijdrage tot de studie van de woordenschat in ver-band met de schilderkunst in de 17de eeuw*, Koninklijke Vlaamse Academie voor Taal-en Letterkunde, ser. VI, no. 79 (Ghent: Secretarie der Koninklijke Vlaamse Academie, 1957), pp. 19–20, who notes that the word could also refer to a portrait in our sense of the word.

91.   "Un Bâilleur du Vieux Breugel" is listed in the inventory of Rubens's paintings, and the Brussels picture was copied in reverse, with a change in format, in an etching by Lucas Vosterman, and inscribed "Pieter Brughel Pinxit" (Van Bastelaer-Gilchrist 1992, p. 334, no. 278). For this and other *tronies* in Rubens's possession, see Muller 1989, pp. 129–130, nos. 195–199. Ertz 1988–2000, 2:955–957, argues that the "Vieux Bruegel" cited in the Rubens inventory of 1640 refers, not to Pieter the Elder, but to either Jan Brueghel the Elder or Pieter the Younger (to distinguish him from his son Pieter III). He also suggests (p. 959) that the model for Vosterman's print was not the Brussels painting, but a variant that appeared in London in 1981.

92.   De Vries 1989, p. 191. For Floris's *tronies*, see the list in Van de Velde 1975, 1:554, s.v., "Studiekoppen." In the auction inventories of Jean Noirot (to be discussed below), the inventory of 30 August 1572 mentions "XI troyn-nien van Franciscus Floris op panneel . . . voer op de sale," while a second inventory lists sixteen, including one of Diana, one of Caritas, and two "antycxe tronnien, een mans ende een vrouwen" (two antique *tronies*, of a man and a woman). Their values range between four and thirty-six guilders, making them, as we shall see, among Noirot's less costly paintings (Smolderen 1995, p. 38). Among the studies of heads attributed to Floris, there is one of a woman whose crescent headdress possibly identifies her as Diana, and two bust portraits that may be of Roman emperors (Van de Velde 1975, cat. nos. 8, 42, and 53 respectively).

93.   Malines 2003, pp. 124–127, cat. no. 12, and pp. 132–135, cat. no. 14.

94.   Goldstein 2003, p. 205.

95.   Stappaerts 1987–88, inv. no. 216.14. Goldstein 2003, p. 252 n. 101, mentions that among the paintings owned by Joris Veselaer were "II onbol-lige tronien op paneelen." Assuming that *onbollige* is a misspelling of *oubol-lige* (crazy, foolish, silly), then we may translate this entry as "two silly *tronies* on panels."

96.   See Van Bastelaer-Gilchrist 1992, pp. 314–333, nos. 242–277; and Muylle

2001, pp. 176–178. For the third state, see also Muylle 2002, pp. 131–134, 140–147.

97. The first state is inscribed "P. Breugel Inventor" and "A. Brouwer in. et fec." See Van Bastelaer-Gilchrist 1992, pp. 312–333, nos. 230–241; and Muylle 2001, p. 178. These prints appeared four years after Brouwer's death. For both series, see also Nalis 1998, 2:148–168, cat. nos. 341–376.

98. The earlier reference occurs in the estate inventory of Jan Dircksz van Brouchoven of Leiden, dated 7 June 1588, in a section devoted to maps, which suggests that the "Verscheyden boeren troengen van bruegel gedaen" were also on paper; see Van der Feen 1918, p. 92, no. 38. For the later reference, see J. G. Hoogewerff and J. Q. Van Regteren Altena, eds., *Arnoldus Buchelius, "Res Pictoria: Aanteekeningen over Kunstenaars en Kunstwerken,"* Quellenstudien zur holländischen Kunstgeschichte 15 (The Hague: Martinus Nijhoff, 1928), pp. 56, 60. Buchelius saw these prints in the collection of a Leiden lawyer, who also had two *tronies* in watercolor or gouache (*waterverwe*). The owner thought they were by Lucas van Valckenborch, but Buchelius attributed them to Bruegel, and possibly they were hand-colored prints from the Doetecum series.

99. The attribution of the original designs to Bruegel is supported by Oberhuber 1979; Nalis 1998; and Muylle 2001 and 2002. Most earlier scholars, however, have rejected this attribution.

100. Van Mander-Miedema 1994–99, 1: fol. 233v (p. 193): "Then a *Massacre of the Innocents* in which many effective details can be seen, of which I have told elsewhere: how an entire family begs on behalf of a peasant child which one of the murderous soldiers has grabbed in order to kill; in which the grief and pallor of the mother and other effects are very well expressed." Van Mander cites a picture of the same subject in the chapter on emotion in *Den Grondt*, but here he describes a mother who beseeches the life of her child from a royal herald; the herald shows compassion but also displays the king's proclamation to her. Miedema notes that the herald displays no proclamation in any of the existing versions of the painting (Van Mander-Miedema 1973, 2:506). Another Netherlander, the Jesuit rector Carolus Scribanius, describes the same composition in similar terms, and while he was familiar with the *Schilder-boeck*, his description of this painting differs enough from that of Van Mander that Julius Held suggests that he personally knew either the original painting or a copy; see Held 1996, pp. 181–182 and n. 31, and p. 202.

101.   For the Hampton Court and Vienna versions, see Grossmann 1955, pls. 110–114 and p. 199.

102.   See Michael Francis Gibson, *The Mill on the Cross: Peter Bruegel's "Way to Calvary"* (Lausanne: Acatos, 2000), whose various observations about Bruegel's expressive physiognomies are aptly supported by the many detail illustrations.

103.   The connection between painting and poem is made in a perceptive article by Yoko Mori, "The Influence of German and Flemish Prints in the Work of Pieter Bruegel," *Bulletin of Tama Art School* 2 (1976): 17–60, esp. 53–55. For the original poem, see Bijns 1875, pp. 335–339 (*Refereyn* XXXIV) first published at Antwerp in 1567.

104.   Tony Torrilhon, "Brueghel était-il médecine?" *Connaissance des arts* 80 (October 1958): 68–77, esp. 71.

105.   For a number of examples by both artists, see the ills. in Marlier 1969, p. 115 passim.

106.   The iconographic unorthodoxy of this painting is stressed by Yona Pinson, "Bruegel's 1564 Adoration: Hidden Meaning of Evil in the Figure of the Old King," *Artibus et historiae* 30 (1994): 109–128.

CHAPTER 3

Epigraphs: *Al niet sonder gelt;* see *Proverbia Communia* 1947, pp. 47, 133, no. 91; a variant in pp. 43, 127, no. 67; and François Rabelais, *Gargantua and Pantagruel*, 2:16; see Rabelais-Cohen 1955, p. 222.

1.   Smolderen 1995. More details of Noirot's bankruptcy and the events leading to it are given in Goldstein 2003, who notes, pp. 257–258 and 270, that Noirot hid in the house of his brother-in-law at Antwerp, probably to avoid witnessing the sale of his possessions.

2.   Stappaerts 1987–88; for a summary of the collections, see p. 142.

3.   Smolderen 1995, p. 38; and Goldstein 2003, pp. 257–272.

4.   Goldstein 2000, p. 180, provides the same translation, although she does not discount the possibility (p. 192 n. 32) that the word *achter* simply meant that the dining room was toward the back of the house.

5.   Goldstein 2003, p. 263 and n. 133.

6.   Attributed to Bosch in old inventories are a *Wedding Banquet* owned by Rubens, and a *Flemish Dance* in the possession of Philip II of Spain; see

Gregory Martin and Mia Cinotti, *The Complete Paintings of Bosch* (New York: Harry N. Abrams, 1969), pp. 116–117, nos. 76, 121. They may well have been works by the Verbeeck family, for which see Paul Vandenbroeck, "Het schildergeschlacht Verbeeck: voorlopige werkkatalog," *Jaarboek Antwerpen*, 1981, 31–61; and Gibson 1992a, pp. 29–31.

7. Vermeylen 2003, p. 132: in 1575 the Antwerp artists' guild protested that art buyers were being cheated by illegal dealers who passed off copies as original paintings by "renowned and famous masters." See also ibid., Appendix 5, p. 199.

8. This observation is made by Smolderen 1995, p. 37.

9. Smolderen 1995 pp. 38, 39; the inventory lists a *boeren bruyloft op doeck* (peasant wedding on canvas) and a *bruyloften* (wedding), the latter most likely also a peasant wedding.

10. See Stappaerts 1987–88, p. 139. One of the earliest references to peasant subjects known to me is found in the probate inventory of 1568 for the estate of Vincent Laureysz, merchant at Middelburg. Among other pictures are a "little panel of a peasant dance" in the kitchen and a "panel of a bride and bridegroom in the wheelbarrow" (*corder wagen*, translated in Lambrecht 1945, p. 64, as *brouëtte*, or wheelbarrow) in the small kitchen (*cleyn kueken*); see Van Gelder 1972–73, p. 400, no. 79. Given the rustic nature of the conveyance, we may assume that the latter painting showed peasants as well. Martens and Peeters 2002, p. 880, note that in an analysis of inventories in the period 1532–46, pictures described simply as "a dance" could refer to genre scenes or to such biblical subjects as the dance around the golden calf or the dance of Salome.

11. Stappaerts 1987–88, p. 129; and Goldstein 2003, p. 251. Portraits by Joos van Cleve of Joris Veselaer and his wife, painted probably in 1518, are in the National Gallery of Art, Washington, D.C.; see Hand and Wolff 1986, pp. 57–62.

12. Sullivan 1994.

13. Ibid., p. 122.

14. Ibid., p. 69; see also pp. 128–129, where Pliny's praise of Timanthes' *ingenium* is understood as a reference to the intellectual side of his art.

15. Ibid., pp. 50–51, 59.

16. Ibid., p. 60.

17.   Ibid.

18.   Ibid., p. 93.

19.   Ibid.

20.   Ibid., pp. 94–95; quotation on p. 94.

21.   See esp. ibid., p. 69.

22.   Sullivan 1999, p. 256.

23.   This passage merits quotation in full: "In the context of Bruegel's own work, and the values of his audience, the dancers in the *Peasant Dance* [i.e., the Vienna *Kermis*], like the peasant dancers in his *Triumph of Time* [or *Triumph of Saturn*, a print perhaps after Bruegel's design; see Van Bastelaer-Gilchrist 1992, pp. 272–274, no. 204], a more obviously classical work, represent the careless, pagan life of people who are Christians in name only, the fools of the world about to be overtaken by death and time" (pp. 132–133).

24.   Ibid., pp. 100–105.

25.   But cf. the review of Sullivan's book by Nina Eugenia Serebrennikov in *Renaissance Quarterly* 49 (1996): 678–680. Other commentaries on Sullivan's thesis include Ramakers 1996, p. 95; and Ramakers 2002, pp. 24–25.

26.   Nor is this problem resolved by Sullivan's remark, 1994, p. 7: "We cannot know precisely what Bruegel 'intended' when he created the *Peasant Dance* and *Peasant Wedding Banquet*, but if we know what his friends and associates expected to find in these paintings, we are unlikely to misunderstand his art entirely."

27.   Quoted in Andriessoon 2003, p. 11.

28.   She tells us, for example, that Cardinal Granvelle may well have esteemed Bruegel's *Flight into Egypt* for its landscape, "but Bruegel's friends and associates were in a position to know that 'the flight into Egypt' had become a secret watchword, a warning to religious dissidents who were trying to escape the Cardinal's persecution" (Sullivan 1994, p. 137 n. 13). We can only hope that if Ortelius or his friends ever viewed this painting, they refrained from blurting out its "secret" meaning in the cardinal's presence.

29.   See Van Mander-Miedema 1994–99, 1: fol. 233a (pp. 190–191). Franckaert was recorded in the Antwerp painters' guild as "Hans Franckaert, Norenborger" and was received "in de Bloeme," that is, the Violieren. It

is generally assumed that Franckaert was a merchant from Nuremberg, but Adolph Monballieu has observed that persons listed "in de Bloeme" are identified by their occupations, not their place of origin, and suggests that Franckaert was a dealer in "Nuremberg wares," that is, knickknacks or small objects of iron. Monballieu, cited in Van Mander-Miedema 1994–99, 3:259, commentary for fol. 233r32. In a document of 1553 Cornelis Cock, a brother of the print publisher Hieronymus Cock, describes himself as a *coopman van norenborchswerken*, that is, a "merchant of Nuremberg wares"; see A. Monballieu, "P. Bruegels 'Schaatsenrijden bij de St.-Jorispoort te Antwerpen,' de betekenis van het jaartal 1553 en een archiefstuk," *Jaarboek Antwerpen*, 1981, 17–30, esp. 24.

30.   For Granvelle as patron of the arts, see Piquard 1947–48; and Van Durme 1953, pp. 247–249. For Bruegel's pictures in Granvelle's palace at Brussels, see Wauters 1914. In addition to the 1564 *Flight into Egypt* (London, Courtauld Gallery), other extant pictures by Bruegel have been identified as from Granvelle's collection, but such attempts remain speculative. While in Naples, Granvelle tried to recover an unspecified number of Bruegel paintings that had been plundered from his various palaces; see Wauters 1914, p. 89. In December 1572 Granvelle's vicar Maximilien Morillon wrote the cardinal that the Bruegel paintings looted from Granvelle's palace were available on the open market but would be very expensive to buy back. See also Claudia Banz, *Höfisches Mäzenatentum in Brüssel: Kardinal Antoine Perrenot de Granvelle (1517–1586) und die Erzherzöge Albrecht (1559–1621) und Isabella (1566–1633)*, Berliner Schriften zur Kunst 12 (Berlin: Gebrüder Mann, 2000), pp. 28–29.

31.   Smolderen 1996, p. 9.

32.   For the Bruegel paintings owned by Jonghelinck, see Van de Velde 1965, esp. p. 123, doc. II, listing the works given by Jonghelinck as a security for a debt of one Daniel de Bruyne. The original text reprinted in Denucé 1932, p. 5.

33.   For a similar observation, see Müller 1999, p. 20.

34.   For Bles and his workshop, see Gibson 1989, pp. 26–33; and Luc Serck, "Henri Bles et la peinture de paysage dans les Pay-Bas méridionaux avant Bruegel," 6 vols. (Ph.D. diss., Université Catholique de Louvain, 1990), who includes over one hundred items in his catalogue, some with many copies. For the commercialization of art in Antwerp during the sixteenth century, see Vermeylen 2003.

35.   The term *dozen* was a proverbial expression indicating anything of little significance, such as "friends by the dozen," and so forth. See *Woordenboek* 1882–1998, s.v., "Dozijn (1)." It is employed in this sense by Vermeylen 2003, p. 142. A contemporary of Bruegel, the poet Lucas D'Heere, uses *dosijn werck* to condemn the work of a painter he particularly disliked; see De Heere-Waterschoot 1969, p. 81, sonnet LXVI, line 39; and De Vries 2004, p. 45. For an English translation, see Meadow 1996, p. 182 and n. 12. It has been suggested that D'Heere's incompetent artist was none other than Bruegel, but this is doubted by Meadow (ibid.), while Lyckle de Vries plausibly argues that D'Heere could not have held Bruegel in such contempt (De Vries 2004, pp. 43–44).

36.   See Hughs and Bianconi 1967, pp. 89–90, no. 13; pp. 103–104, no. 39; p. 104, no. 40, respectively. However, Bruegel may have employed some assistants; at least Van Mander tells us that he often frightened his assistants (*knechten*) by making strange noises; Van Mander-Miedema 1994–99, 1: fol. 233v (p. 193).

37.   For the *Suicide of Saul* (Vienna, Kunsthistorisches Museum), see Grossmann 1955, pls. 46–47; for the *Labors of the Months*, see Gibson 1989, pp. 69–74, including the question of whether there were originally six or twelve paintings.

38.   A *Diana and Acteon* by Floris was in the collection of Charles de Croy, duke of Aarschot (1560–1612), last recorded in a Christie's sale in 1938 (present whereabouts unknown); see Van de Velde 1975, 1:303–304, cat. no. S164; 2: fig. 88.

39.   See Stappaerts 1987–88, p. 142. For the lesser value of paintings on canvas or cloth as compared with panel paintings, see Martens and Peeters 2002, p. 879.

40.   Peeter Stevens, a later art collector (see p. 96), informs us that Ortelius owned another Bruegel painting, a *Heyke*, presumably a heath landscape, that Stevens saw in the collection of Cornelis van der Gheest. J. Briels identifies it with a *Landscape with Peasants on the Way to Market* depicted in Willem van Haecht's picture of Van der Gheest's art gallery of 1628. See Briels 1980, pp. 199, 206, and figs. 2, 27. However, to judge from reproductions of Van Haecht's painting, the picture identified by Briels as Bruegel's *Heyke* recalls in both subject and composition some of the landscapes of his son Jan "Velvet" Brueghel, and may well be by him instead.

41. *Biog. Nat.* 1866–1932, 16: col. 315.

42. Van Mander tells us that Bruegel also did work for his friend Hans Franckaert, but we have no idea what it may have been; see Van Mander-Miedema 1994–99, 1: fol. 233r (pp. 190–191).

43. Piquard 1947–48, pp. 135–136.

44. Coenraerd Schetz, a member of the Schetz family discussed below (see pp. 80–81, 83–84), also had a number of books by classical authors in his library, among them Ovid and Virgil, as well as a Latin book by Petrarch and Augustine's *City of God*; see Van Gelder 1972–73, pp. 380–381.

45. Kavaler 1999, esp. pp. 29–56: chap. 1, "Commerce, Culture, Crisis."

46. See Riggs 1977 for prints and print series dedicated to Granvelle: list nos. 93 (*Moses and the Brazen Serpent* after Frans Floris), 174 (*Thermae Diocletiani*), 260 (antique vase in Granvelle's possession), 178 (*Disputa* after Raphael), 206 and 207 (two sets of architectural views after Hans Vredeman de Vries), among others; and list no. 78, for the *Labors of Hercules* series after Floris.

47. For Granvelle's connections with Plantin, see Van Durme 1953, pp. 254–257; and Leon Voet, "Plantin en de kring van Granvelle. Enkele nog onuitgegeven brieven en documenten," *De gulden passer* 37 (1959): 142–169.

48. Theodorus Pulmannus (or Poelman), for example, dedicated his 1564 edition of Virgil to Caspar Schetz, the first treasurer of Philip II, and his edition of Lucan, published the same year, to Nicolas Rockox, burgomaster of Antwerp; his 1574 edition of Suetonius's *Lives of the Twelve Caesars* is dedicated to Frederick Perronet, diplomat, warrior, and brother of Cardinal Granvelle (*Biog. Nat.* 1866–1932, 17: cols. 874–883). For Hooftman and Ortelius, see Kavaler 1999, p. 40; and esp. Zweite 1980, pp. 67–69.

49. See the abundant evidence on this point in Goldstein 2003.

CHAPTER 4

Epigraph: Johannes Agricola, *Drey hundert gemeyner Sprichwörter* (Erfurt: Conrad Treffer, 1529), p. 107. See Agricola 1971, pp. 190–191: *Burger und bawer / scheydet nichts denn die mawer*. A commentary to this proverb, added in the edition of 1534, explains that however much the burgher wants to be nobler than the peasant, it is only a wall that divides them.

1. See pp. 25–26.

2. See pp. 10–11.

3. *The Well-to-Do Beggars* (Erasmus-Thompson 1965, p. 209). For the "negative" and "positive" traditions of peasant imagery, see Gibson 1991, esp. pp. 17–26, with earlier literature. A recent and extended study of peasants in medieval thought and literature is Freedman 1999.

4. For the interaction between Antwerp and its surrounding countryside, see Gibson 1991, pp. 26–31; and Gibson 2000, pp. 14–20.

5. Abraham de Bruyn, *Omnium pene Europae, Asiae, Aphricae atque Americae gentium habitus* (Antwerp, 1577); see Kavaler 1999, p. 153 and fig. 74.

6. Van Kampen et al. 1980, p. 86, note to lines 59–62. Antwerp levied some taxes on the consumption of beer and wine, as well as grain (Baetens 1985, p. 176).

7. For these two series, see Gibson 2000, esp. pp. 1–10; and Nalis 1998, 1:94–135, nos. 118–161, here attributed to the Van Doetecum brothers. Alexandra Onuf is preparing a doctoral dissertation for Columbia University that discusses the *Small Landscapes* in detail, including their relationship to the taste for country life, treated below.

8. For summer places around Antwerp and their owners, see Monballieu 1974, pp. 153–160; Monballieu 1987, p. 190; and the extensive survey in Baetens 1985. Goldstein 2003, p. 14, notes that a number of country houses had been recently rebuilt to replace those destroyed by Marten van Rossem and his troops during their raids in the vicinity of Antwerp in July 1542.

9. Monballieu suggests that De Schott's country place is depicted in Jacob Grimmer's *A View of the Kiel near Antwerp* of 1578 (Antwerp, Koninklijk Museum voor Schone Kunsten); see Monballieu 1974, pp. 155 and 158–159, figs. 11–13. See also Gibson 1991, pp. 26–27, figs. 17, 18; and Gibson 2000, p. 17, figs. 26, 27. For Richard Clough, see Monballieu 1987, p. 190 and n. 17.

10. See Denucé 1932, p. 1, where Van der Heyden's country house is described as "speelhuys (genaempt Crauwels) buyten ende by Antwerpen gelegen" (*speelhuys* named Crauwels lying outside and near Antwerp). For Crauwels, see Baetens 1985, p. 188; and Goldstein 2003, pp. 143–158.

11. For this development, see Hugo Soly, *Urbanisme en kapitalisme te Antwerpen in de 16de eeuw: De stedebouwkundige en industriële ondernemingen van Gilbert van*

Schoonbeke, Historische Uitgeven Pro Civitate, Reeks in 8°, 47 (Brussels: Gemeentekrediet van België, 1977), pp. 186–191.

12.   For Jonghelinck's villa, see Van de Velde 1965, p. 117, and doc. I, pp. 122–123; and Smolderen 1996, p. 9.

13.   Granvelle's La Fontaine, also known as De Borre (*borre* or *bron*, i.e., "well" or "spring"), is discussed in Van Durme 1953, p. 216 and n. 36, pp. 340–341. For his residence at Cantecroix, see Piquard 1947–48, p. 137.

14.   Baetens 1985, p. 180; the number of villas near Antwerp is increased to 370 by Roland Baetens and Bruno Blondé, "Habiter la ville: la culture de l'habitat urbain," in *La ville en Flandre: culture et société, 1477–1787,* ed. Jan Van der Stock (Brussels: Crédit Communal, 1991), pp. 59–70, esp. 69.

15.   For Niclaes Jonghelinck's connections with the mint, see Smolderen 1996, p. 9; and Goldstein 2003, pp. 236–237. Noirot apparently owned no property other than a small house near Bruges, where his brother lived; even his city house was owned by the Antwerp mint (Goldstein 2003, p. 228). For Veselaer's country place, Het Lanteernhof, in Deurne just outside Antwerp, see ibid., pp. 254–256.

16.   See Lambrecht 1945, p. 109, s.v.,"Hof *oft* lochtingh: Iardin [jardin]." *Speelhuys* and *hof* (and the latter's variants) recur in the inventories listed in Stappaerts 1987–88; see, for example, p. 68, no. 29 (*speelhuys*), and p. 45, no. 106 (*hoff van plaisantien*). Other documents refer to *speelhoven* and *huysen van plaisanchien*; see Dierickx 1954, p. 333.

17.   For country estates as items of prestige, see Baetens 1985.

18.   For some of the purchasers of these seigneuries, see ibid. A similar phenomenon in the Dutch Republic in the seventeenth century is discussed in Gibson 2000, pp. 113–114.

19.   For Van Straelen's life, see *Biog. Nat.* 1866–1944, 24: cols. 131–143; the villages are mentioned in Guicciardini 1567, p. 150. Van Straelen's connections with the *rederijkers* are discussed in F. Mertens and K. L. Torfs, *Geschiedenis van Antwerpen sedert de stichting der stad tot onse tijden,* vol. 4 (Antwerp, 1848), pp. 275–277. For the medal, see Kavaler 1999, pp. 34–35 and fig. 13.

20.   *De Landwinninge ende Hoeve van M. Kaerle Stevens* [Charles Estienne], *Doctoor in de Medecijne* (Antwerp: Christophe Plantin, 1556), pp. 3–4. For this manual, see Gibson 1991, p. 21, with further references.

21.   For Hendrik's acquisition and development of Berchem, see Prims 1949, pp. 124–129, 141–144; and Baetens 1985, p. 179. But even before Hen-

drik's purchase of Berchem, it apparently contained other summer-
houses; see Prims 1949, pp. 293–315. For Cornelis van Dalem, see Kavaler
1999, p. 49.

22.   Kavaler 1999, p. 165. In addition to his country residences noted above,
        Granvelle also owned the seigneuries of Bosbeeck, Bouchout, and Sint-
        Laurent-ten-Hove, in the vicinity of Antwerp, all three named in a war-
        rent issued by Granvelle on 15 July 1563 to one Odet Viron to govern these
        properties. For the original document, see Antiquariaat Forum (Utrecht),
        *Short Title List with Recent Acquisitions and a Selection from Our Stock, 22nd Euro-
        pean Antiquarian Book and Print Fair at Amsterdam*, n.d.

23.   In "A Dialogue between a Noble, a Franciscan Monk, and a Lutheran";
        see Dirck Volckertsz Coornhert, *Weet of rust: Proza van Coornhert*, ed. Henk
        Bonger and Arie-Jan Gelderblom (Amsterdam: Em. Querido's Uitge-
        verij, 1993), pp. 45–46. As it happens, Baetens 1985, pp. 172–173, does
        not include these titles among the reasons why the wealthy classes so ea-
        gerly acquired feudal manors.

24.   Guicciardini 1567, p. 151, describes Caspar as "Baron de Wesemale, Seigneur
        de Grobbendonck, de Heist, & autres Seigneuries d'importance."

25.   Ibid., p. 150; see also *Biog. Nat.* 1866–1944, 8: cols. 314–324, s.v., "Grobben-
        donck," esp. cols. 315–317, 320. Few, if any, of the manor houses and other
        country residences discussed in these pages have survived war and ex-
        panding urbanization; the Jonghelinckshof, for example, was destroyed
        in 1584 on the eve of the siege of Antwerp by Spanish troops under
        Alexander Farnese (Smolderen 1996, p. 11). In his two series of the *Small
        Landscapes* of 1559 and 1561, Hieronymus Cock includes only three sub-
        stantial structures, two moated castles and a large residence, that might
        qualify as country estates (Van Bastelaer-Gilchrist 1992, cat. nos. 26, 38,
        39). However, some idea of the various forms they took can perhaps be
        gained from Antonius Sanderus's *Flandria illustrata*. Published some eighty
        years later, it contains many views of castles and country houses that could
        be seen in the county of Flanders in his time. See Antonius Sanderus,
        *Flandria illustrata sive Descriptio comitatus per totum terraru[m] orbem celeberrium
        III tomis absoluta*, 2 vols. (Cologne: Sumptibus Cornelii ab Egmondt et
        Sociorum, 1641), a copy in the Chapin Rare Book Library, Williams
        College.

26.   The complete inscription is "Die boeren verblyen hun in sulken feesten, /
        Te dansen springhen en dronkendrincknen als beesten / Sye moeten die

kermissen onderhouwen / Al souwen sy vasten en sterven van kauwen."
See Rotterdam–New York 2001, pp. 198–200, cat. no. 80. The last two
lines are generally translated as "They must hold their kermises / even
though they [must] fast and die from the cold." The meaning of the last
line is unclear, and it has been suggested that the word *kauwen*, generally
translated as "cold," may mean "chew." See Van Bastelaer-Gilchrist 1992,
p. 282 n. 250. For this print and its significance, as well as Hoboken as a
country resort, see Monballieu 1974; Monballieu 1987; and Gibson 1991,
p. 29, with further literature. Opinions differ as to whether Bruegel's design actually represents Hoboken. Dierckx 1954, pp. 68–70, concluded
that Bruegel's church was the same as that represented in a view of Hoboken depicted on a map of the Schelde River of 1468. This identification
was rejected for good reasons by Monballieu 1974, pp. 145–153, who nevertheless concluded that Bruegel referred specifically to Hoboken. Kavaler
1997, p. 317 n. 40, also believes that the print probably does not show
Hoboken and suggests that it was "published to meet an established market for such prints, and the name of the village may have been included
because of its local fame."

27.   Monballieu 1987, pp. 193–194, 205. The kermis (also spelled *kermisse*) was
       originally the annual mass celebrating the dedication of a church; it later
       came to include the festivities that followed. By Bruegel's time, it could
       signify any public festivity; hence the *Hoboken* print speaks of *kermissen*,
       even though the occasion depicted pertains to a guild and not a church
       anniversary. See Verdam ca. 1932, p. 288, s.v., "Kermisse." For the annual
       feast of the Hoboken Handbow Archers, see Dierickx 1954, pp. 122–123,
       who tells us that its concluding banquet often degenerated into a drunken
       carousal.

28.   It is unclear if the fool alludes specifically to the foolish behavior stressed
       in the inscription (as suggested, for example, in Rotterdam–New York
       2001, p. 199). He could be attached to the Handbow guild, or even to
       the household of the local seigneur. Antoon van Straelen, for example,
       had a private fool called Duffel, who headed the procession of the Vio-
       lieren in the 1561 *landjuweel* (Hüsken 1996, p. 113). Cardinal Granvelle kept
       at least one fool, a dwarf, in his household; for his portrait by Anthonius
       Mor, see Musée National du Louvre, *Catalogue raisonné des peintures du
       moyen-âge, de la Renaissance et des temps modernes. Peintures flamandes du XVe et du
       XVIe siècle*, cat. by Éduard Michel, 2 vols. (Paris: Éditions des Musées Na-
       tionaux, 1953), 1:222–224, and no. 2479; 2: pl. LV, fig. 132.

29. Monballieu 1987, p. 205; and Dierickx 1954, p. 75. See Monballieu 1974, pp. 157–169, for a group of kermis scenes that he believes, and I think correctly, do not depict Hoboken, as is sometimes assumed.

30. For the association of De Momper with the *schilderspand,* see Vermeylen 2003, pp. 54–61.

31. Monballieu 1974, p. 144; Van Kampen et al. 1980, p. 195, lines 75–76; and Gibson 1991, p. 29. Monballieu 1974, pp. 155–157, plausibly suggests that in Grimmer's *View of the Kiel near Antwerp* (see n. 9 above), the people on the road wending their way back to the city are returning from a festival in Hoboken.

32. See Dierickx 1954, pp. 333–349, for country houses in Hoboken in the sixteenth century and later.

33. Before acquiring his property in Hoboken, Guicciardini in 1564 bought two *hoven van plaisancien,* described in a contemporary document as "each with a stone house," which were situated near the house of Richard Clough and which he sold the following year (Monballieu 1987, p. 190 and nn. 17, 20; and Baetens 1985, p. 183). For Guicciardini's life and publications, see the essays in *Lodovico Guicciardini (1521–1589): Actes de colloque international des 28, 29 et 30 mars 1990,* Université Libre de Bruxelles, Travaux de l'Institut Interuniversitaire pour l'étude de la Renaissance et de l'Humanisme, X, ed. Pierre Jodogne (Louvain: Peeters Press, 1991).

34. Prims 1949, p. 141. Hoboken's popularity is reflected in the 1567 probate inventory of Fernando Bernuy, an Antwerp merchant who seems to have rented out properties in the village to tenants (Van Gelder 1972–73, pp. 388–391).

35. Inheriting Hoboken from his uncle, William in effect mortgaged the manor to raise money to pay the debts outstanding from his uncle's estate and later sold it to Melchior Schetz; see Dierickx 1954, pp. 32–34; and Monballieu 1974, pp. 141–142.

36. Dierickx 1954, p. 116. The original text of Balthazar's oath ends "Zo moet my God helpen ende all syn heylighen" (so must God help me and all his saints).

37. Van Mander-Miedema 1994–99, vol. 1: fol. 261v (p. 305): "In Middelburg with Mr. Wijntgis there is a beautiful, large piece in which the Messrs Schets, as lords of Hoboken, are very solemnly received by the peasants— full of details and figures." An oil painting on canvas depicting "la Dédi-

cation d'Hoboque" is listed in the estate inventory of Filips Willem van Oranje (Brussels, 1618), William of Orange's eldest son, who had been taken hostage by Philip II of Spain; see Monballieu 1974, pp. 140–141.

38. Van Haecht 1929–33, 1:11.

39. This is the only property mentioned by Guicciardini 1567, p. 151: "Balthasar, Seigneur de Hoboke[n]." For Sauvius's portrait, see Gibson 2000, p. 19, fig. 30.

40. See Dierickx 1954, p. 34, for an account of Balthazar's acquisitions of land, as well as his purchase of the rights to collect for himself the various taxes in Hoboken formerly collected by various individuals and religious institutions.

41. For the administrative organization of Hoboken, see Dierickx 1954, pp. 119–132.

42. Monballieu 1974, p. 142.

43. For these activities of the Schetz brothers in Hoboken, see ibid.

44. Katharine Fedden, *Manor Life in Old France from the Journal of the Sire de Gouberville for the Years 1549–1562* (New York: AMS Press, 1967), pp. 122–125; and Emmanuel Le Roy Ladurie, *The Territory of the Historian*, trans. Ben Reynolds and Siân Reynolds (Chicago: University of Chicago Press, 1979), pp. 156–160. On the close and often friendly relations that could exist between a landholder and his tenants, see also Pierre de Vaissière, *Gentilshommes campagnards de l'ancienne France: Étude sur la condition, l'état social et les moeurs de la noblesse de province du XVIe et XVIIe siècle* (Paris, 1903; Geneva: Slatkine Reprints, 1975), pp. 104–118.

45. H. A. Enno van Gelder, *Nederlandse dorpen in de 16e eeuw*, Verhandelingen der Koninklijke Nederlandse Akademie van Wetenschappen, afd. Letterkunde, N.S. 59, no. 2 (Amsterdam: Noord-Hollandsche Uitgevers Maatschappij, 1953), pp. 39–67, esp. 39–40.

46. Wilfrid Brulez, *De firma della Faille en de internationale handel van Vlaamse firma's in de 16de eeuw*, Verhandelingen der Koninklijke Vlaamse Akademie van Wetenschappen, Letteren, en Schone Kunsten van België, Klasse der Letteren, Verhandelingen, No. 35 (Brussels: Paleis der Academiën, 1959), p. 227. For other manors owned by the brothers Jacques and Jean della Faille, see *Biog. Nat.* 1866–1932, 32: cols. 192–196.

47. For Gillis Mostaert's collaboration with other painters, see Vermeylen 2003, p. 126, with further references.

200   NOTES TO PAGES 85–87

48.   Van Haecht 1929–33, 1:211; in the following year, there was talk of bring-
      ing Berchem and other villages within the city walls, then under en-
      largement; see ibid., 2:7.

49.   Jan van der Noot, *Lofsang van Braband, Hymne de Braband*, ed. C. A. Zaalberg
      (Zwolle: W. E. J. Teenk, 1958), p. 3, in his dedication to the lords of
      Brabant.

50.   Estienne 1600, pp. 27–28.

51.   Cited in Kavaler 1999, p. 196.

52.   Guicciardini 1567, p. 39.

53.   For the prohibitions against kermises, see Gibson 1991, p. 35, with fur-
      ther references.

54.   I owe this observation to Kavaler 1999, pp. 152–153, who also percep-
      tively notes that the country setting seems to offer the possibility of
      amorous adventure for all classes, but "hardly imply debauchery and dis-
      order" (p. 160); see also ibid., pp. 189–197, for a good discussion of city
      visitors at country celebrations.

55.   For several examples, see Heinrich Göbel, *Tapestries of the Lowlands*, trans.
      Robert West ([New York]: Hacker Art Books, 1974), figs. 236 and 241.
      It has been suggested, however, that in some cases at least, such scenes
      show aristocratic men and women dressed as shepherds and shep-
      herdesses (*La Noble Pastoral*); see Claudette Joannis, "Essai d'interpreta-
      tion ethnographique d'une tenture médiévale," *La Revue du Louvre et des
      Musées de France* 31 (1982): 335–341. Nevertheless, similar encounters be-
      tween courtiers and country girls occur in the earlier pastorals; see
      Cooper 1977, p. 57 and passim; and Freedman 1999, pp. 163–166. An-
      dreas Capellanus (twelfth century) devotes a whole chapter in his *Art of
      Courtly Love* to rustic romances, advising that if one should fall in love with
      a country girl, he should praise her extravagantly and, when it is conve-
      nient, take her by force; see Andreas Capellanus, *The Art of Courtly Love*,
      trans. and ed. John Jay Parry (New York: Frederick Ungar, 1959), pp.
      149–150. For a real-life instance (twelfth century), see Simons 2003, p.
      23. In general, it was assumed that country people were more open and
      casual about their lovemaking; see Vandenbroeck 1987, pp. 73–78. Jean-
      ice Brooks reproduces several French songs in which courtiers seduce and
      deflower country girls (Brooks 2000, pp. 339–340, 366–367).

56.   An exception occurs in a *Visit to the Wetnurse* by Maerten van Cleve of

1555–60 (Vienna, Kunsthistorisches Museum), in which the gentleman seated at the table at the left boldly thrusts his hand into the bodice of the serving girl, who modestly attempts to push it away; ill. in Leo van Puyvelde, *La peinture flamande au siècle de Bosch et Brueghel* (Paris: Elsevier, 1962), p. 147, fig. 63.

57. Grauls 1957, pp. 209–210. Cf. a fifteenth-century German carnival play, *Di Karg Baurnhochzeit* (The Meager Peasant Wedding), in which the cook complains that he cannot afford to buy rice and almonds (*von mandel und von reis*) to cook for the bridal feast; see Von Keller 1965–66, 2:784 (no. 104, line 34).

58. A *pottagie van rijs* is included in Vorselman-Cocks-Indestege 1971, p. 21, no. 22. Although the Netherlandish term *pottagie* is derived from the French word *potage*, it was not limited to soup, as is the modern French word, but referred to anything cooked in a pot, as opposed to foods that were roasted or baked; see *Woordenboek* 1882–1998, s.v., "Potage," art. I:3.

59. For the schoolmasters' feast, see Caroline B. Bourland, *The Guild of St. Ambrose, or Schoolmasters' Guild of Antwerp 1529–1579*, Smith College Studies in History, vol. XXXVI (Northampton, Mass.: Smith College, 1951), p. 20; for the use of saffron, see also *Een notabel boecxken van cokeryen*, ed. Ria Jansen-Sieben and Marleen van der Molen-Willebrands (Antwerp: Thomas van der Noot, ca. 1514; Amsterdam: De KAN, 1994), p. 41, no. 76. Then as now, saffron, incidentally, was very expensive (Delen 2002, p. 153).

60. For this picture, see Giorgio T. Faggin, "De genre-schilder Marten van Cleef," *Oud Holland* 80 (1965): 34–46, esp. 38; Kavaler 1999, p. 156 and n. 18; and Marlier 1969, pp. 341–350, who notes five other versions of this composition.

61. See London, Christie's, *Old Master Paintings*, 13 December 1985, lot 96, where it is identified as "A view of Hoboken(?) near Antwerp."

62. In 1559 the count of Hoorn sold the lordships of Burcht and Zwijndrecht, including the village of Ste.-Anneken, on the west shore of the Schelde, to the city of Antwerp, but the sale was annulled in 1562. See A. Monballieu, "De 'Twee aapjes' van P. Bruegel of de Singerie (singneurie) over de Schelde te Antwerpen in 1562," *Jaarboek Antwerpen*, 1983, 191–210, esp. 200 and n. 46.

63. See A. J. J. Delen, *Iconographie van Antwerpen* (Brussels: L. J. Kryn, 1930), cat. no. 11. Ste.-Anneken figures prominently in various views of Ant-

werp published in the 1550s and 1560s (ibid., cat. nos. 12, 27, 32, 36, with the accompanying plates), including a print by Melchisedek van Hoorn of 1550 (Gibson 2000, p. 16, fig. 25). Crowded ferryboats can often be seen making their way toward the village, presumably from Antwerp across the river.

64.   Rotterdam–New York 2001, pp. 196–197, cat. no. 79. For the possible political implications of this inscription, see Carroll 1987, pp. 295–302.

65.   For this group in Baltens's painting, see Ramakers 2002, pp. 44–47.

66.   Quoted from the "Burwell Lute Tutor" in Zecher 2000, p. 771. In Jost Amman's *Ständebuch* (Nuremberg, 1568), with verses by Hans Sachs, the harp and other stringed instruments are played by gentlemen in courtly dress; see Jost Amman and Hans Sachs, *The Book of Trades (Ständebuch)*, intro. Benjamin A. Rifkin (New York: Dover Publications, 1973), pp. 114–115.

67.   The bagpipe was a usual instrument for shepherds as well (Cooper 1977, p. 55).

68.   Rotterdam–New York 2001, pp. 225–227, cat. no. 98. Incidentally, precisely because the flute similarly distorted the face, Minerva, traditionally credited with its invention, cast it away after seeing her reflection in the water. Various versions of this anecdote are told by the ancient writers, including Ovid in his *Fasti* 6:697; see also Barolsky 1978, pp. 184–187.

69.   Munich 1999, p. 96; and Jones 2002b, pp. 269–270. But even the aristocratic lute had erotic connotations; its shape could evoke a woman's body (Zecher 2000, pp. 772–775).

70.   Brant-Zeydel 1962, chap. 54, pp. 186–187, "Of Impatience of Punishment." For this woodcut, see Munich 1999, pp. 95–96. Cf. Ramakers 1996, pp. 56–57 and fig. 3, who notes several processions in Oudenaarde, including the triumphal entry of Joanna of Castile in 1496, in which fools played bagpipes, among other instruments.

71.   Theodore de Bry, *Emblemata nobilitati et vulgo scitu digna* (Frankfurt, 1593); see Munich 1999, pp. 104–105, 196, cat. no. 39.

72.   *Bot Verstant en Cloucken Geest* (Hummelen 1968, no. 1 N 7); see Pikhaus 1988–89, pp. 216–217; and, for the complete text, Van Eeghem 1943, pp. 209–228. The play appears in a manuscript dated 1599, but Van Eeghem (p. 207) dates its origin to about 1560. For my translation of the two names, cf. Lambrecht 1945, p. 50, s.v., "Bot van verstand," and p. 62, s.v. "Clouck ofte clouckaert."

73. "Dus moetten de wyse met de botte haeren tyt passeeren," quoted in Van Eeghem 1943, p. 228, line 322.

74. Ibid., p. 228, lines 18–19. Formerly "nieces and nephews [*nichten en neuen*]" had a broader meaning than they generally do now and could designate even distant members of a family, as well as persons unrelated by blood with whom one was on friendly terms; see *Woordenboek* 1882–1998, s.v., "Neef" and "Nicht." "Nieces and nephews" is used in another sixteenth-century *tafelspel* to describe the followers of a personification of Folly; see Gibson 1992a, p. 36. In the play *Begheirlijcke Lust*, performed in Brussels in 1578, Sot Begrijp (Foolish Understanding) says that he prizes his *nichtkens*, or nieces (Hummelen 1968, no. 6 E 1; and printed in Houwaert 1579, see esp. p. 78).

75. Lucas D'Heere, "Een boerken van Buyten an een fraey steedsche Dochter," in De Heere-Waterschoot 1969, pp. 76–77, no. LXIV.

76. Kavaler 1999, p. 192, suggests that the lady "playfully dances" with the peasant, which is also possible.

77. Briels 1980, p. 220; and Kavaler 1999, pp. 193–195.

78. For the first two pictures, see Wied 1990, pp. 145–146, cat. nos. 31, 32, the later ill. in colorpl. 9. The third painting, formerly in the possession of Count Valamara, Vicenza, was offered by Rob Smeets, Milan, at the Maastricht Art Fair in 1996; I am greatly indebted to Dr. Alexander Wied for current information on these three pictures. Even before the appearance of the third, Wied had suggested that the date 1577 fit into the artist's stylistic development.

79. For the identification of the figures in this composition, see Alexander Wied, "Neues zu Lucas und Marten van Valckenborch," *Jahrbuch der Kunsthistorischen Sammlungen in Wien* 85–86 (1989–90): 9–23, esp. 9–14; Wied 1990, pp. 24–26; and Kavaler 1999, p. 194. A few years later, Ortelius published an account of this tour: *Itinerarium per nonnullas Galliae belgicae partes, Abraham Ortelius et Ionnaes Viviani* (Antwerp: Christophe Plantin, 1584).

80. Wied 1990, pp. 24–26. This identification is doubted by Kavaler 1999, p. 324 n. 14.

81. For examples, see Wied 1990, cat. nos. 18, 23, 28, 29, passim.

82. Van Mander, in his life of the Valckenborch brothers, notes that Marten and especially Lucas were accomplished players of the *Duytsche pijp*, a term that is rendered in Van Mander-Miedema 1994–99, 1: fol. 260r (p. 298)

as "German flute," but Wied 1990, p. 26, translates as *Dudelsack* or bagpipe. Another artist associated with the bagpipe is Hemessen, whom Carolus Scribanius identifies as the bagpiper in the latter's *Prodigal Son among
the Courtesans* (Brussels, Musées Royaux des Beaux-Arts; ill. in Held 1996,
p. 187, fig. 56). Julius Held suggests that Scribanius's identification
reflects an authentic tradition (pp. 188–190, 203). It might be noted that
the bagpipe enjoyed considerable popularity in the seventeenth century
among the French aristocracy, where it was known as a *musette*; see Washington, D.C., National Gallery of Art, *Anthony van Dyck*, cat. by Arthur K.
Wheelock Jr., Susan J. Barnes, Julius S. Held, et al., 1990–91, pp. 304–
306, cat. no. 81.

83.   Ramakers 1996, p. 101. The social interaction between city and country
       is also apparent in a *Village Kermis* perhaps by Maerten van Cleve (Zurich,
       Bührle Collection), in which one of the gentlemen is shown in conver-
       sation with several peasants; see Marlier 1969, p. 360, fig. 222.

84.   Tilman Susato, *Derde musyck boexcken* (Antwerp, 1551); see Wangermée
       1968, p. 166, who suggests that it was likely not an authentic transcrip-
       tion but was stylized to suit urban tastes. The dance has been recorded
       at least once on a compact disc, *Keeping the Watch*, performed by the
       Philadelphia Renaissance Wind Band on a Newport Classic label, NPD
       85527.

85.   Wangermée 1968, p. 323, defines a *branle* as "a dance of peasant origin
       very popular in the sixteenth century." Other peasant dances cultivated
       by the urbanites are listed in Vandenbroeck 1987, p. 92. For rustic music
       published in French song collections with new words, see François
       Lesure, "Élements populaires dans la chanson française au début du XVIe
       siècle," in *Musique et poésie au XVIe siècle*, Colloques internationaux du Cen-
       tre national de la Recherche scientifique, Sciences humaines, vol. V
       (Paris: CNRS, 1954), pp. 169–184, esp. 172. The *Hobokendans* may well
       have been a *branle* or *klompendans*.

86.   Claude Gauchet, *Plaisir des champs. Divisé en quatre parties selon les Quatres saisons
       de l'annee, . . . ou est traicté de la chasse, & de tout autre exercice recreatif, honneste &
       vertueux. . . .* (Paris: Nicolas Chesneau, 1583), pp. 57–72. For a description
       of Gauchet's book, see Brooks 2000, pp. 368–372. Burke 1978, p. 25, notes
       some manuscript collections of popular songs by members of the upper
       class in the sixteenth and seventeenth centuries. For the appeal of peasant
       songs and dances for the urban classes, see also Kavaler 1999, pp. 195–196.

87. Burke 1997, p. 130. Burke 1978, pp. 24–25, gives some examples of elite participation in popular festivals.

88. Cf. Ramakers 2002, pp. 38–39, for whom the festive culture of town and country had much in common. Even if there were differences, he tells us, the town also had kermises, annual markets, and other public and private celebrations. Stewart 1993 similarly stresses the interaction between town and country in the festive culture of Nuremberg.

89. Castiglione 1959, p. 101.

90. Montaigne-Frame 1948, p. 991.

91. See Gibson 1991, pp. 22–23. For a new edition, see Noël du Fail, *Propos rustiques*, trans. and ed. Gabriel-André Pérouse and Roger Dubuis, Centre lyonnais d'Étude de l'Humanisme U.R.A. C.N.R.S. D. 1348 (Geneva: Librairie Droz, 1994).

92. Fernand Braudel, *The Structures of Everyday Life*, trans. Siân Reynolds, vol. 1, *Civilization and Capitalism, 15th–18th Century* (New York: Harper & Row, 1981), pp. 274, 436–437.

93. See Ramakers 1996, pp. 94–102, who notes that both Bruegel and the *rederijkers* gathered their material from various cultural repertories.

94. Another good example of this is the manuscript proverb collection compiled by the Amsterdam *rederijker* Reyer Gheurtz; it includes both Erasmian *parabolae* (parallels) and popular sayings, confirming, as Meadow remarks, "the slippage between what we now term 'elite' and 'popular' cultures" (Meadow 2002, pp. 78–79).

95. Van Mander-Miedema 1994–99, 1: fol. 233 (p. 190). For doubts about this story, see, for example, Grossmann 1955, pp. 27–28, who suggests that Van Mander was inspired by Leonardo da Vinci's advice to artists to observe the conduct of people in real life, as well as the anecdote told by Giovanni Paolo Lomazzo (*Tratto dell'arte de la pittura*, 1584) of Leonardo's inviting peasants to a banquet so that he could study their expressions when they laughed at his jokes. Cf. also Müller 1999, p. 16; and Van Mander-Miedema 1994–99, 2:39–40. Miedema 1998, p. 321, suggests that the story of these "two not unlettered gentlemen" disporting themselves by studying the excesses of rustic celebrations may indeed have come from Bruegel himself to enhance the reputation of his peasant scenes, but that does not mean that he and Franckaert had actually done so.

96. See, with further references, Joseph Leo Koerner, "Albrecht Dürer's *Plea-*

sures of the World and the Limits of Festival," in *Das Fest,* Poetik und Hermeneutik 14 (Munich: Wilhelm Fink, 1989), pp. 180–216, esp. 182. Partly on the basis of these records, Koerner suggests that Van Mander's account may be correct (pp. 181–182).

97.   Ibid., with further references; and Simon 1998, p. 203.

98.   Samuel Kinser, "Presentation and Representation: Carnival at Nuremberg, 1450–1550," *Representations* 13 (Winter 1986): 1–41, esp. 10, 11. Samuel L. Sumberg suggests that the "predominant role given the peasant in the carnival celebration seems to be due not so much to the desire of the burgher to satirize the countryman as to the rustic origin of the spring festivities"; see Samuel L. Sumberg, *The Nuremberg Schembart Carnival* (1941; New York: AMS Press, 1966), p. 124.

99.   Thoinot Arbeau, *Orchesography*, trans. Mary Stewart Evans, with a new intro. and notes by Julia Sutton, and a new labanotation section by Mireille Backer and Julia Sutton (New York: Dover Books, 1967), p. 136.

100. Van Mander-Miedema 1994–99, 1: fol. 233r (pp. 190–191).

101. The map in question is from Lodovico Guicciardini, *Descrittione di tutti i Paesi Basi* (Antwerp: Christophe Plantin, 1582). I am very grateful to Adolph Monballieu for information he provided me on Kempen. For its geography, see *Winkler Prins Encyclopedie van Vlaanderen* (Brussels: Elsevier Sequoia, 1973), 3:475–476, s.v., "Kempen."

102. Kavaler 1999, pp. 174–175. Kavaler (pp. 161–163) notes the considerable interest of Breugel's contemporaries in the peasant costume of his day.

103. Cf. Muylle 2001, p. 182, who makes a similar observation.

104. Noted by Wolfgang Stechow, *Pieter Bruegel the Elder* (New York: Harry N. Abrams, 1955), p. 116.

105. The older peasant accompanying the distinguished guests in Valckenborch's *Village Fair* of 1577 wears a codpiece (see Fig. 55), but it is altogether more modest in size.

106. *Essays* 1:23: "Of custom, and not easily changing an accepted law"; quoted from Montaigne-Frame 1948, pp. 85–86. For the codpiece in general, see Grace Q. Vicary, "Visual Art as Social Data: The Renaissance Codpiece," *Cultural Anthropology* 4 (1989): 3–25, who suggests that its popularity was a response to the spread of syphilis and its treatment in this period. See also Ann-Sophie Lehmann, "Fluwelen fallussen," *Kunstschrift,*

no. 5 (1997): 30–38; and Persels 1997, two references I owe to Eddy de Jongh and Alison Stewart respectively.

107.   Rabelais-Cohen 1955, pp. 234–235 (bk. 2, chaps. 18–19). See Persels 1997.

108.   Rabelais-Cohen 1955, p. 55 (bk. 1, chap. 8). In this passage, Rabelais claims to have written a book, *On the Dignity of Codpieces*, undoubtedly fictitious.

109.   For the influence of Beham's *Months* on Bruegel's *Kermis*, see Goldstein 2003, p. 91. See also Yoko Mori, "The Influence of German and Flemish Prints on the Works of Pieter Bruegel," *Bulletin of Tama Art School* 2 (1976): 17–60, who notes Bruegel's indebtedness in his peasant scenes to Beham and Dürer.

110.   The young man has probably been drinking, but it is difficult to accept Sullivan's conclusion that he is "befuddled, foggy, and unsteady" and in a "drunken stupor" (Sullivan 1994, p. 56).

111.   See p. 72.

112.   Van Eeghem 1943, pp. 216, line 121, and 213, line 69, respectively.

113.   See p. 88.

114.   For Breugel's portrait, see Lampsonius-Puraye 1956, no. 19; a good illustration in Gibson 1991, p. 42, fig. 38. I am not so convinced as I was previously that it necessarily represents Bruegel himself (ibid., p. 41). For the portrait of Franckaert, see Kavaler 1999, p. 50 and fig. 23.

115.   For examples, see Raupp 1986, pp. 134–194, 245–257.

116.   See Van de Velde 1975, 1: cat. no. 116; for another example, ibid., 1: cat. no. S. 137; 2: fig. 71 (Stockholm, National Museum).

117.   The English translation in Meadow 1996, p. 193. A comparable sentiment appears in a sixteenth-century inscription attached to the reverse of Bruegel's *Cripples* (Paris, Musée du Louvre): "What is lacking in [our] nature, is lacking here in [our] art. So great is the talent given to this painter. Here is Nature expressed in painted figures, surprised to see that Bruegel is her equal, even seen in [the] cripples" (Muylle 1981, p. 335).

CHAPTER 5

Epigraphs: Goedthals 1568, p. 56; and Erasmus, *Auris Batavia*, in *Adages* IV 6 XXXVI, first included at the end of the 1508 edition, quoted in Erasmus-Phillips 1967, pp. 32–33.

1.   Goldstein 2003, pp. 262–263.

2.   Ibid., pp. 18–21.

3.   In the estate inventories in Stappaerts 1987–88, rooms are generally designated by their location in the house, very seldom by function. See also Martens and Peeters 2002, p. 878. The major exception is the kitchen.

4.   Iain Buchanan, "The Collection of Niclaes Jongelinck II: The 'Months' by Pieter Bruegel the Elder," *Burlington Magazine* 132 (1990): 541–550, esp. 549. For Beuckelaer, see Hans Buijs, "Voorstellingen van Christus in het huis van Martha en Maria in het zestiende-eeuwse keukenstuk," in *Pieter Aertsen. Nederlands Kunsthistorisch Jaarboek* 40 (1989): 93–128, esp. 111; for the panels: Ghent, Museum voor Schone Kunsten, *Joachim Beuckelar: het markt-en keukenstuk in de Nederlanden 1550–1650*, 1986, pp. 124–128, cat. nos. 8–11. Buijs notes that images of biblical banquets, such as the Marriage Feast at Cana, as well as Christ in the House of Mary and Martha, survive as decoration in several monastery refectories (pp. 110–111). As it happens, Noirot owned a large painting "named the kitchen of Martha," presumably a *Christ in the House of Mary and Martha*, but it apparently hung "in the room above the salon," use unknown, in company with the *Diana and Acteon* and a *Peasant Kermis* by Bruegel, among other pictures (Smolderen 1995, p. 38).

5.   These suggestions for the placement of Bruegel's *Months* and the market and kitchen scenes of Aertsen and Beuckelaer find a parallel in the series of erotic market scenes painted in 1580–81 for the dining room in the house of Hans Fugger, Schloss Kirchheim; see Barry Wind, "Vicenzo Campi and Hans Fugger: A Peep at Late Cinquecento Bawdy Humor," *Arte Lombarda*, n.s., 47–48 (1977): 108–114. I am grateful to Professor Wind for calling my attention to his article.

6.   Goldstein 2003, p. 52.

7.   Literally, "to finish off the stomach"; see the summary of courses in Vorselman-Cockx-Indestege 1971, pp. 264–265. Goldstein 2003, p. 269, suggests that banquets in Noirot's house ceased after 1567–68, due to his increasing financial problems.

8.   For the wines imported into the Netherlands in Bruegel's lifetime, see J. A. Goris, *Étude sur les colonies marchandes méridionales (Portugais, Espagnols, Italiens) à Anvers de 1488 à 1567. Contribution à l'histoire des débuts du capitalisme moderne*, 2 vols. in 1 (New York: Burt Franklin, n.d.), pp. 256–258. The household accounts of William of Orange for 1553–54 indicate the great variety of foreign wines then available (Delen 2002, pp. 149–150). See also Jervis Wegg, *Antwerp, 1477–1559: From the Battle of Nancy to the Treaty of Cateau Cambrésis* (London:

Methuen & Co., 1916), p. 286, where he notes that Spanish wine was first brought to the Netherlands in the middle of the reign of Charles V.

9.   Sullivan 1994, pp. 30–36, passim. For the two colloquies, *Convivium religiosum* (1522) and *Convivium poeticum* (1523), see Erasmus-Thompson 1965, pp. 46–78 and 158–176 respectively.

10. See Plato 1963, pp. 40–98 and 526–574 respectively.

11. For the dialogue as a subspecies of the *sermo* as defined by Cicero, see Gary Remer, *Humanism and the Rhetoric of Toleration* (University Park: Pennsylvania State University Press, 1996), pp. 26–27, 30–41.

12. Jean Bodin, *Colloquium heptaplomeres*; although completed in 1588, it was not published in full until 1857; for its contents, see Remer, *Humanism and the Rhetoric of Toleration*, pp. 211–230.

13. Quoted from *The Godly Feast*, in Erasmus-Thompson 1965, p. 56.

14. Juan Luis Vives, *On Education: A Translation of the "De Tradendis disciplinis,"* trans. and intro. Foster Wilson, foreword Francesco Cordasco (1913; Totowa, N.J.: Rowan and Littlefield, 1971), pp. 209–210 (bk. IV, chap. VI).

15. Hooftman had wanted Floris, but he was too expensive and worked too slowly; three of De Vos's paintings have survived. See Zweite 1980, pp. 67–84; and Kavaler 1999, pp. 43–44.

16. Sullivan 1994, pp. 99–100 and fig. 53, where it is called "attributed to Pieter Pourbus the Elder." However, it bears the signature of Frans Pourbus; see Koninklijke Musea voor Schone Kunsten van België, Departement Oude Kunst, *Inventariscatalogus van de oude schilderkunst* (Brussels, 1984), p. 230, Inv. 4435.

17. Sullivan 1994, p. 100; a similar observation in Kavaler 1999, p. 194.

18. See Van der Noot 1979, pp. 62–66.

19. See Laura Gelfand and Walter S. Gibson, "Surrogate Selves: The Devotional Portrait in the Late Middle Ages," *Simiolus* 29 (2002): 119–138.

20. For various meanings of *statelyc* and *statigh*, see *Woordenboek* 1882–1998, s.v., "statig," with a citation from Philips van Marnix van St. Aldegonde, who says that St. Peter "syne stemmicheyt ende graviteyt *statelick* gehouden heeft" (my italics), approximately translated as "retained his dignity and gravity in a stately manner." *Statelijc* is the word used for the costume prescribed for one character in a sixteenth-century *rederijker* play; see Pikhaus 1988–89, 1:102.

21.   See p. 1, and n. 1 above.

22.   Van Mander-Miedema 1994–99, 1: fol. 261v (pp. 304–305).

23.   For De Moucheron, see *Nieuw Ned. biog. woordenboek* 1911–37, 7: cols.
       890–891.

24.   In any study of portraiture, one might profitably consult the deportment
       recommended in the various "courtesy books" and other handbooks on
       manners.

25.   See Goldstein 2003, pp. 23–24, on the social significance of the dining
       table in the "Van Berchem" family portrait.

26.   For the symbolism in this picture, as well as the emblematic inscription
       on the original frame, see Van de Velde 1975, 1:290–292, cat. no. 150.

27.   See Erasmus-Miller 1979, p. 118, quoted from Horace, *Odes* 4.12 line 28;
       see Horace, *The Odes and Epodes*, trans. C. E. Bennett, Loeb Classic Library
       (Cambridge, Mass.: Harvard University Press; London: William Heine-
       mann, 1958), pp. 332–333, where it is rendered as "'Tis sweet at the fitting
       time to cast serious thoughts aside."

28.   For mealtimes seen as occasions for recreation, light conversation, jokes,
       even bawdy stories, see Jeanneret 1991, esp. pp. 91–97, passim.

29.   Kempe 1998, pp. 101–102 (chap. 27).

30.   See Jeanneret 1991, p. 96.

31.   Robert Burton, *The Anatomy of Melancholy*, ed. Floyd Dell and Paul Jordan-
       Smith (New York: Tudor Publishing Company, 1927), p. 485 (pt. 2,
       sec. 2, memb. 6, subs. 4).

32.   "Een vrolick hert en zoete praet, / Aen tafel dient, en oock wel staet." Jo-
       hannes de Brune, *Nieuwe Wyn in oude Leer-sacken: Bewijzende in Spreeckwoorden
       't vernuft der menschen ende 't gheluck van onze Nederlandsche Taele* (Middelburg:
       Z. Roman, 1636), p. 445. De Brune (p. 16) cites another proberb: "Wa-
       neer de Buyck is vol en soet / Een vrolick hooft steekt in de hoet" (roughly,
       When the stomach is full and sweet / a merry head is beneath the hat).
       For similar recommendations of mealtime jollity in the seventeenth cen-
       tury, see Verberckmoes 1998, pp. 79–81.

33.   Vorselman-Cockx-Indestege 1971, p. 104.

34.   Welsford 1968, p. 161. The fool's name is given in other sources as Paten-
       son and Pattenson.

35.   P. M. Zall, ed., *A Hundred Merry Tales and Other Jestbooks of the Fifteenth and Six-*

teenth Centuries (Lincoln: University of Nebraska Press, 1963), p. 8. Brewer suggests that the stories come from the circle of Thomas More (Brewer 1996, p. xxxiii).

36. The original painting is lost; for Holbein's drawing recording this picture and copies after it, see John Rowlands, *Holbein: The Paintings of Hans Holbein the Younger, Complete Edition* (Boston: David R. Godine, 1985), pp. 222–223, cat. no. L. 10, and figs. 188–190.

37. Erasmus-Thompson 1965, p. 382. I thank Claudia Goldstein for calling this text to my attention.

38. In his commentary on the proverb "Ollas ostenare" (to make a show of pots; *Adages* 2.2.11); see Erasmus-Phillips and Mynors 1989–92, 33:94.

39. Erasmus-McGregor 1985, p. 280. Elsewhere Erasmus counsels that "it is bad manners to be sad at a banquet or to sadden anyone else . . . nor should one's personal sorrows be unburdened on another on such an occasion" (pp. 281, 285).

40. See *The Godly Feast, The Poetic Feast, The Fabulous Feast, The Sober Feast,* and *The Profane Feast,* in Erasmus-Thompson 1965, pp. 46–78, 158–176, 254–266, 454–457, and 591–614 respectively.

41. Sullivan 1994, pp. 100–101.

42. Guicciardini 1567, pp. 39–40. I have used "entertainments" to translate *esbatements* in the original text.

43. Rekers 1972, p. 20; in a less critical mood, Montano later says that the carnivals and the table manners of the Flemings remind him of the ancient Greeks (p. 32).

44. See the epigraph to this chapter. Cf. Albrecht Dürer, who in the journal of his trip through the Netherlands in 1520–21 notes that at a banquet presented by the Antwerp painters' guild, they "spent a long and merry time together till late in the night." See Albrecht Dürer, *Diary of His Journey to the Netherlands 1520, 1521,* intro. J.-A. Goris and G. Marlier (Greenwich, Conn.: New York Graphic Society, 1971), pp. 57–58, entry for St. Oswald's day [5 August] 1520.

45. Carolus Scribanius, *Antwerpia* (Antwerp: ex. off. Plantin, 1610), p. 60; cited from Verberckmoes 1998, p. 98.

46. For this expression, with its connotations of revelry, especially at mealtime or in the alehouse, see *Woordenboek* 1882–98, s.v., "Sier." The ex-

pression occurs several times in the *Nyeuwe clucht boeck* (ed. 1983, nos. 1, 44 (1), 65, and 147). Guicciardini 1567, p. 39, also reports that the Belgians like "faire grand chere ensemble" (make good cheer together). For the English equivalent, "to make (do, give) good cheer," see *Oxford English Dictionary*, s.v., "Cheer," pars. 5, 6.

47.   Andriessoon 2003, no. 42.3.

48.   Guicciardini 1567, p. 32. Montano also criticizes the Flemish for their heavy drinking (Rekers 1972, p. 20). On such excesses, see also Sullivan 1994, pp. 100–105, who distinguishes such behavior from the presumably more temperate behavior of Ortelius and his circle.

49.   Tacitus, *Germania* 21–230; see *The Complete Works of Tacitus*, trans. Alfred John Church and William Jackson Brodribb, ed. Moses Hadas (New York: Modern Library, 1942), pp. 719–720.

50.   Erasmus, *Auris Batavia*; see Erasmus-Phillips 1967, p. 32. Alison Stewart reminds me (personal communication) that the Germans were similarly accused, a subject she addresses in a forthcoming book.

51.   Goldstein 2003, pp. 104–106.

52.   See pp. 93–94. These comic banquet plays are surveyed by Pikhaus 1988–89; see 1:100, for their humor.

53.   Pikhaus 1988–89, 1:80–85, nos. 27 and 68 respectively. For some fools' plays, see ibid., nos. 17, 18, and 39, the last titled *A Fool Invited to a Wedding*.

54.   Ibid., 1:145–146.

55.   In the *De civilitate*, Erasmus says that at meals, "continuous eating should be interrupted now and again with stories"; see Erasmus-McGregor 1985, p. 284.

56.   Leon Battista Alberti, *Dinner Pieces: A Translation of the "Intercenales,"* trans. David Marsh, Medieval & Renaissance Texts & Studies, vol. 45; The Renaissance Society of America, Renaissance Texts Series, vol. 9 (Binghamton, N.Y.: Medieval & Renaissance Texts & Studies in conjunction with the Renaissance Society of America, 1987), p. 5.

57.   Jeanneret 1991, p. 96.

58.   Quoted in Bowen 1988, p. 84. See also *Heinrich Bebels Facetien. Drei Bücher*, ed. Gustav Bebermeyer (Leipzig: Karl W. Hirschmann, 1931), p. 105. Similarly, both the French *fabliau* and the Dutch *boerd* were very likely primarily an "after-dinner" genre, as Charles Muscatine characterizes the former,

"told for amusement, in a mood of relaxation and confidence, and, despite their frequently bawdy subject matter, recited in mixed company"; see Charles Muscatine, "The Fablieux," in *A New History of French Literature*, ed. Denis Hollier (Cambridge, Mass.: Harvard University Press, 1989), p. 70; and Lodder 1996, pp. 120–122.

59.   *Nyeuwe clucht boeck* 1983, pp. 48 and 44 respectively; see p. 44 for Wickram's further assurance that his collection is suitable for use on ship voyages and in bathhouses, and for commercial travelers.

60.   *The Fabulous Feast* (1524); Erasmus-Thompson 1965, pp. 254–266, esp. 265–266: in a jocular discussion concerning the most honorable part of the body, one guest maintains that it is the mouth, the other insists that it is "the part which we sit on . . . because priority in seating is allowed to belong to the highest rank." At their next meeting, the first guest breaks wind in the other's face, on the grounds that he is greeting him with the most honorable part. This was perhaps not the most prudent story to include in a book intended to teach Latin to schoolboys (the 1524 edition of the *Colloquies* was dedicated to the son of Johannes Froben, at that time eight years old). However, in both *De civilitate* and the *Colloquies*, Erasmus counsels his young readers to feign ignorance of any bawdy stories told in their presence; see Wesseling 2002, p. 128. For a discussion of the *Colloquies* as pedagogy, see Elias 2000, pp. 143–148. For scatology and obscenity elsewhere in Erasmus's writings, see Wesseling 2002, pp. 126–128; and, more generally, Barbara C. Bowen, "The 'Honorable Art of Farting' in Continental Renaissance Literature," in Persels and Ganim 2004, pp. 1–13.

61.   Amsterdam, Rijksmuseum, *Mirror of Everyday Life: Genreprints in the Netherlands, 1550–1700*, catalogue by Eddy de Jongh and Ger Luijten, trans. by Michael Hoyle, 1997, pp. 71–74, cat. no. 7. Cf. Rabelais, who has Panurge say that Nature made the sun to light our daily labors, but takes it away at night, so that we may stop working, eat, and relax. See Rabelais-Cohen 1955, pp. 328–329 (bk. 3, chap. 15).

62.   Starter 1974, fol. A1v; also quoted in Van Stipriaan 1996, pp. 25 and 24, fig. 3. The Dutch proverb is found as early as 1550; see *Kamper spreekwoorden* 1959, p. 52, no. 15: "Hy laet den Geck wt der mouwe kijcken," with a variant in no. 16: "Hy en can den Geck in der mouwen niet holden" (He cannot keep the fool in the sleeve). This proverb is also alluded to in the play *Bot Verstant en Cloucken Geest* (Van Eeghem 1943, p. 227, line 308),

in which Cloucken Geest says of his companion, "Tis waer maer ghij laet den sot te ser vt de mou cijken" (It's true that you let the sot peek too often from the sleeve).

63. See p. 41 above. Cf. Horace, *Odes* 4.12.28.

64. "Elck dingh heeft synen tyd: 't is prijslick dat een man / Is Wijs in syn beroep en Vrolyck by de kan"; Starter 1974, p. 7.

65. See Raupp 1986, pp. 99–103, who (p. 103) stresses the purely decorative function of this kind of peasant imagery.

66. Goldstein 2003, pp. 85–93.

67. See p. 100 above.

68. For the *tafelspelen* with peasants, see Pikhaus 1988–89, 1:80–85, nos. 17 and 86 respectively. In five other *tafelspelen*, five characters are named Boer (peasant); see Pikhaus (2:545–547). Further research might show that other personages in these plays had rustic associations.

69. See Jan [Jean] Denucé, *Oud-Nederlandse kaartmakers in betrekking met Plantijn*, 2 vols., Maatschappij der Antwerpsche Bibliophilen, Uitgave nos. 27–28 (Antwerp: De Nederlandsche Boekhandel; The Hague: Martinus Nijhoff, 1912–13), 2:160.

70. Johannes Sturm, *Adagia classica: Schola Argentinensibus digesta* (Strasbourg: Ribelius, 1573); quoted in Meadow 2002, p. 55; and Andriessoon 2003, pp. 14–15.

71. For this and related expressions, see *Woordenboek* 1882–1998, s.v., "Kermis (I)" "'t Is een arm (of slecht) dorp (of: land) waar het niet eenmael ('s jaars), of waar het nooit kermis is." It was a popular expression, appearing as early as the *Proverbia Communia* (Deventer: Jacob van Breda, ca. 1480); see *Proverbia Communia* 1947, p. 263, no. 626. Thereafter, various versions of the proverb appear in Goedthals 1568, p. 34; and *Kamper spreekwoorden*, 1959, p. 26, no. 10, as well as in numerous German proverb collections.

72. See Stoett 1943, 2:412–413, no. 2391; and Goedthals 1568, p. 34, who cites the Netherlandish proverb together with its French equivalent: "Tousjours ne sont pas nopses" (It is not always a wedding).

73. *Kamper spreekwoorden* 1959, p. 32, no. 25: "Men late den Edeluyde[n] haer wildtbraet / den Buyren haer kermisse / den Honden haer hochtyt / so blijft men ongeropt." See also Carroll 1987, p. 307 n. 47, on the same proverb in Johannes Agricola's *Drey hundert Gemeyner Sprichtwörter*, 1st ed., 1529.

74. Goedthals 1568, p. 36: "In bruloften ende kinderbedden / onderhoudt men
vrientschappe." Cf. the French proverb, "Aux nopces et aux funerailles,
Cognois amis et parentailles" (At weddings and funerals, one gets to know
friends and relatives); see Lambrecht 1945, p. 229, s.v., "Wtvaert." I would
like to thank Charity Cannon Willard for her help in translating this
proverb.

75. "Liever bijder wijncanne dan bijder bruyt te sitten" is paired with "Goulard
ayme beaucoup mieux les nopses, qui l'espouse"; see Goedthals 1568,
p. 117. The French proverb occurs in a late-fifteenth-century French manuscript; see *Proverbes en Rimes: Text and Illustrations of the Fifteenth Century from
a French Manuscript in the Walters Art Gallery, Baltimore*, ed. Grace Frank and
Dorothy Miner (Baltimore: Johns Hopkins University Press, 1937), pl.
LXXXV, poem on p. 5.

76. See Gibson 1965, p. 201, although I no longer believe that Bruegel intended a specifically perjorative connotation. Closer to Bruegel's bride
in time and appearance is her counterpart in a *Marriage Feast at Cana* engraved by Jan Wierix for Benito Arias Montano's *Humanae salutis monumenta*
(Antwerp: Plantin, 1571), fol. G1r, ill. in Karen L. Bowen and Dirk Imhof,
"Reputation and Wage: The Case of Engravers Who Worked for the
Plantin-Moretus Press," *Simiolus* 30 (2003): 161–195, esp. 168, fig. 7.

77. Or Bruegel may have been familiar with the hungry bagpiper in Erhard
Schoen's *Peasant Wedding Celebration*, a woodcut of 1527; see Gibson 1991,
p. 14, fig. 4, and pp. 37–39.

78. *Kamper spreekwoorden* 1959, p. 48, no. 26.

79. For the first saying, see ibid., p. 48, no. 23, with references to Agricola and
Servilius. A variant appears in Rabelais's *Gargantua and Pantagruel*, "a bagpipe will not play unless its belly is full"; see Rabelais-Cohen 1955, p. 198
(bk. 2, chap. 9). The other saying is inscribed on a drawing by Van Mander depicting a bagpiper and two drinking peasants; for the inscription,
see Otto Benesch, ed., *Die Zeichnungen der niederländischen Schulen des XV. und
XVI. Jahrhunderts*, Beschreibender Katalog der Handzeichnungen in der
Graphische Sammlung Albertina, vol. 2 (Vienna: Anton Schroll, 1928),
p. 36, no. 362 (Inv. 8012), pl. 94; *Karel van Mander*, comp. Marjolen Lees-
berg, ed. Huigen Leeflang and Christiaan Schuckman, *The New Hollstein.
Dutch and Flemish Etchings, Engravings and Woodcuts, 1450–1700* (Rotterdam:
Sound & Vision Publishers in cooperation with the Rijksmuseum, Am-
sterdam, 1999), cat. no. 97, no. 3, text on p. lxxv.

80.   In a document of 1588 four people who had attended the wedding of the
      artist Peeter Baltens, some years earlier, testified that his bride had worn
      a wreath on her head, because in Antwerp, this symbolized her virginity.
      See Stephen J. Kostyshyn, "'Door tsoecken men vindt': A Reintroduc-
      tion to the Life and Work of Peeter Baltens Alias Custodius of Antwerp
      (1527–1584)," 3 vols. (Ph.D. diss., Case Western Reserve University, 1994),
      1:92–93, 400–401, doc. 81.

81.   Such demeanor, of course, was a traditional sign of virginal modesty in
      general. An example occurs in Van der Noot's previously mentioned poem
      commemorating a wedding of 1563, in which the young lady receives her
      future husband's offer of marriage with "her eyes cast down [heur ooghen
      nederwaert]"; see Van der Noot 1979, p. 59, line 98.

82.   For the Netherlandish locution, see Verwijs and Verdam 1885–, 1:1469,
      s.v., "Bruut (Bruyt)." For the German expression, see Röhrich 1974, 1:151,
      s.v., "Brautsar"; this entry is appropriately accompanied by an illustration
      of Bruegel's bride, although I have not encountered precisely this locu-
      tion in Netherlandish. For later references to similar bridal demeanor,
      see Thomas Firminger Thiselton-Dyer, Folklore of Woman: As Illustrated by
      Legendary and Traditionary Tales, Folk-Rhymes, Proverbial Sayings, Superstitions, etc.
      (London: Elliot Stock, 1905; Detroit: Omnigraphics, 1992), p. 208, who
      refers to a well-known saying, "She simpers like a bride on her wedding
      day," alluding "to the brides of old times who were bound, in courtesy,
      to smile on all who approached them."

83.   See Woordenboek 1882–1998, s.v., "Bruid (I)." The term vuile bruid appar-
      ently is derived from vuile ei, or "dirty egg," said of fertilized eggs. In an
      anecdote current in Bruegel's time, a man boasts that he has eaten an
      egg with a chicken in it while paying only for the egg: but "he had eaten
      a dirty egg!" we are told (Nyeuwe clucht boeck 1983, p. 216, no. 245). For
      the vuile bruid as a traditional carnival figure, see Coigneau 1980–83,
      2:302–303; and Paul Vandenbroeck, Jheronimus Bosch: tussen volksleven en stad-
      scultuur (Berchem: EPO, 1987), pp. 333–335. The vuile bruid and her male
      consort appear in Bruegel's Carnival and Lent painting of 1559 (Grossmann
      1955, pl. 12) and in his only woodcut block, the Wedding of Mopsus and Nisa,
      whose design was later published as an engraving by Hieronymus Cock
      (Rotterdam–New York 2001, pp. 246–248, cat. nos. 111–112). See also
      Coigneau 1980–83, 2:310–311, for a poem describing a nun character-

ized as a *vuile bruydt* who violently lets wind because she has eaten a *raap* (turnip), here used as a euphemism for the phallus.

84.   Erasmus-Phillips and Mynors 1989–92, 32:69–70, no. 6 (I vii 6).

85.   Rotterdam–New York 2001, pp. 248–251, cat. no. 113. The address Aux quatre vents at the bottom of the sheet indicates that it was issued sometime after Cock's death in 1570. Nadine Orenstein suggests that the print possibly was not derived from an original composition by Bruegel but was adapted from the Detroit picture by someone in Cock's atelier.

86.   John Webster, *The White Devil*, 4.3; in *Webster and Ford* 1954, p. 63.

87.   *Ovid in Six Volumes*, vol. 5, *Fasti*, trans. James George Frazer, Loeb Classical Library (Cambridge, Mass.: Harvard University Press; London: William Heinemann, 1976), pp. 159, 161 (*Fasti* 3, lines 523–542). Ovid describes, apparently without disapprobation, the feast of Anna Perenna, held every March. "The common folk come, and scattered here and there over the green grass they drink, every lad reclining beside his lass. Some camp under the open sky; . . . But they grow warm with sun and wine, and . . . they sing the ditties they picked up in the theatres, beating time to the words with nimble hands; they set the bowl down, and trip in dances lubberly, while the spruce sweetheart skips about with streaming hair. On the way home they reel, a spectacle for vulgar eyes, and the crowd that meets them calls them 'blest.' I met the procession lately; I thought it notable; a drunk old woman lugged a drunk old man." Whether the reveling man and woman in Bruegel's *Gloomy Day* are similarly drunk is uncertain (see Fig. 3), but drunken peasants supported by their womenfolk are often encountered in the kermis scenes of his followers. That sixteenth-century observers could view their own country festivals, and depictions of them, in classical terms is suggested by Carolus Scribanius, who wrote that Peeter Baltens, "following the example of Callimachus, portrayed, not Spartan women dancing, but rather a rustic throng, warmed by beer, so true to rural customs that you would not find Bacchus lacking—nor seductive pipes." See Carolus Scribanius, *Antwerpia* (Antwerp, 1610), quoted from Held 1996, p. 203. Scribanius alludes to the bronze group of dancing Spartan girls described in Pliny, *Natural History* 34.92 (Pliny 1968, p. 79). While neither text is cited in Sullivan 1994, I suspect that the investigation of these and similar passages from antiquity might shed light on the iconography of these peasant scenes.

CHAPTER 6

Epigraph: Prologue to *The Ship of Fools*, 1494, quoted from Brant-Zeydel 1962, p. 61.

1.   Roberts-Jones 2002, p. 96.

2.   Van Mander-Miedema 1994–99, 1: fol. 233v (pp. 192–193). The translation is my own. An inventory taken in 1647–48 of the paintings in the Hradschin, the royal *burcht* in Prague, includes "[e]in Daffel mit Feuerstbrunst, dorbey die Furia mit unterschidlichen Monstern" (a panel with fire and with it a Furia [i.e., Dulle Griet] and various monsters), which has been taken as a reference to Bruegel's *Dulle Griet*. See Grauls 1957, p. 47, for this entry and the putative later history of the painting. However, De Coo 1978, p. 33, stresses that there is absolutely no proof that Bruegel's painting was the one described in the inventory of 1647–48. Indeed, it could have been a more contemporary painting, perhaps a work by Ryckaert or Teniers discussed at the end of this chapter (see Figs. 82, 83), which show that the proverb "to plunder in front of Hell" was not unknown in the seventeenth century.

3.   Grauls 1957, pp. 6–76.

4.   Ibid., p. 28. Griet is derived from the name Margaret, sometimes spelled *Margriete* in Netherlandish (ibid., p. 11), and Grauls assumes that its use to designate ill-tempered women was inspired by the legends of St. Margaret, who successfully struggled with the Devil several times. Other connotations of the name Griet are discussed in W. S. Heckscher, "Is Griet's Name Really so Bad?" *Manitoba Arts Review* 4, no. 3 (1945): 26–32.

5.   Goedthals 1568, p. 139: "Daer twee Grieten in een huys zijn; en behoeft gheenen bassenden hont."

6.   Griet Suermuyl (Griet Sourmouth) appears in a *factie* (a comic dramatic performance) given by the Lier chamber of *rederijkers* at the Antwerp *Haechspel* of 1561, while Schele Griet (Cross-eyed Griet) is a character in a Haarlem play of about 1600 (Hummelen 1968, 3 C 57 and 1 OK 5 respectively). Griet Snatertans (precise meaning unclear, but denoting one who babbles or cackles; see Lambrecht 1945, p. 180, s.v., "Snateren" and "Snatere") figures in another farce of about 1600 (Hummelen 1968, 1 OG 11). For several later examples of Griet in Dutch drama, see Hummelen 1968, 1 OA 10, 4 36. In Erasmus's colloquy *The Poetic Feast*, the surly maid is appropriately named Margaret; see Erasmus-Thompson 1965, pp. 158–176, who notes that this lady is based on Erasmus's real-life servant of the same

name, whom he referred to as "my Xanthippe," after the shrewish wife of Socrates (ibid., pp. 159–160).

7. Grauls 1957, p. 39, who notes later cannons bearing similar names.

8. *Kamper spreekwoorden* 1959, p. 52, no. 21; Goedthals 1568, p. 54. In De Laet 1962, p. 24, no. 399, it is given as the Flemish equivalent of a French proverb; see p. 139 below. See also Grauls 1957, p. 44.

9. Lambrecht 1945, p. 165, s.v., "Roof."

10. Grauls's identification of the main figure was anticipated by several perceptive observations of Leo van Puyvelde, *Pieter Bruegel: The Dulle Griet*, trans. Robin Fedden, Gallery Books (London: P. Lund Humphries, 1946), pp. 3–4. Just why the plundering takes place *before* Hell, rather than *within* it, is unclear, unless it was because no one who entered Hell ever escaped. Cf., for example, a song of the Netherlandish nobles rebelling against Spain, in which the men pledge to follow their leader "to the suburb of Hell. / There profit and freedom are to be gained [*Tot dat in de voorstad van de hel. / Daer winst en vryheid is to halen]*"; see Grauls 1957, p. 44. Nevertheless, in several folk tales, as we shall see, the Devil does take a woman to his domain but quickly is all too eager to restore her to earth.

11. For summaries of earlier scholarly opinion on the *Dulle Griet*, see Grauls 1957, p. 49 and passim; De Coo 1978, pp. 33–40, with an excellent bibliography; and Hughes and Bianconi 1967, pp. 96–97, cat. no. 27. In addition to Serebrennikov 1993, more recent interpretations of the painting include Thierry Boucquey, "Bruegel, intertexte fou de la farce: choréographie de *La Fete [sic] des Fous* et *Dulle Griet*," *Word and Image* 5 (1989): 227–259; Gibson 1979; René Graziani, "Pieter Bruegel's 'Dulle Griet' and Dante," *Burlington Magazine* 115 (1973): 209–219; Panse and Schmidt 1967; Yona Pinson, "Folly and Vanity in Bruegel's *Dulle Griet*: Proverbial Metaphors and Their Relationship to Bosch's Imagery," *Studies in Iconography* 20 (1991): 185–213; Margaret A. Sullivan, "Madness and Folly: Peter Bruegel the Elder's *Dulle Griet*," *Art Bulletin* 59 (1977): 55–66; and Irving C. Zupnick, "Bruegel and the Revolt of the Netherlands," *Art Journal* 23 (1964): 283–289.

12. In the *factie* of the Lischbloemen chamber; see E. van Autenboer, *Volksfeesten en rederijkers te Mechelen (1400–1600)* (Ghent: Koninklijke Vlaamse Academie voor Taal-en Letterkunde, 1962), p. 248.

13. *Kamper spreekwoorden* 1959, nos. 17–20 and 29. Grauls offers no comment

on the context in which the proverb "She could plunder in front of Hell . . ." appears in the *Kamper spreekwoorden*. The proverb about the blind man receives an extensive commentary in Agricola 1971, 1:554, no. 748.

14. See respectively Brant-Zeydel 1962, chap. 64, pp. 212–215 (the quotation on p. 214); *Dichten en spelen van Jan van den Berghe*, ed. C. Kruyskamp, Uitgave van de Vereeniging der Antwerpsche Bibliofielen, 2nd ser., no. 4 (The Hague: Martinus Nijhoff, 1950), p. 28, lines 645–655; and Thomas Nashe, *The Anatomie of Absurdities*, quoted in De Bruyn 1979, p. 130.

15. *Three Days Lord*, in *Netherlandic Secular Plays from the Middle Ages: The "Abele Spelen" and the Farces from the Hulthem Manuscript*, trans. and ed. Theresia de Vroom, Carleton Renaissance Plays in Translation 29 (Ottawa: Dovehouse Editions, 1997), p. 235, lines 69–70.

16. Modern literature on the shrewish wife is extensive, but see Gibson 1979, with further references; and more recently Van Engeldorp-Gastelaers 1984; and Kusue Kurokawa, "Noah's Wife as a Virago: A Folkloric Figure in English Mystery Plays," *The Profane Arts of the Middle Ages / Les arts profanes du moyen-âge* 5, no. 2 (Fall 1996): 218–235.

17. Goedthals 1568, pp. 39–40: "En jaarmarkt sonder dief / En schoone maeght sonder lief / En schure met coren sonder musen / En oudt man sonder lusen / En oudt wijf sonder schelden / Dese vijf dinghen vindt men selden" (An annual market without a thief / A beautiful girl without love / A grain harvest without mice / An old man without lice [or fleas] / An old wife without scolding / These five things one finds seldom). A variant of this verse can be found in *Veelderhande* 1971, p. 2.

18. Described in F. Muller, *De Nederlandsche geschiedenis in platen: Beredeneerde beschrijving van Nederlandsche historieplaten, zinneprenten en historische kaarten*, 4 vols. (Amsterdam: F. Muller, 1863–82), 1: no. 418 Ae II. The impression illustrated is a fairly late reissue, for it is inscribed "Hugo Allardt excudit," the address of a publisher active in Amsterdam until his death in 1684. Jones 2002a, p. 220, no. 9, notes that it is a later state of a print published by Cornelisz Visscher, who died in 1558 (no. 8).

19. In the inscription accompanying this print, we learn that the Bigorne symbolizes the grave that frees men from the mistreatment of their wives. For later variants of this composition, and some related English prints, see Jones 2002a, pp. 220–221, nos. 7–10, and 212–213, figs. 1, 2 respectively.

20. Chaucer-Benson 1987, p. 152, line 1188. See the note to these lines for

further references to these two monsters, as well as Taylor 1980; Jones 2002a; and Jones 2002b, pp. 246–247. Several English misericords show Bigorne swallowing a patient husband; see Christa Grössinger, *Picturing Women in Late Medieval Art* (Manchester: Manchester University Press, 1997), p. 119, fig. 52, and p. 121.

21.   Taylor 1980, p. 104.

22.   *Mariken van Nieumeghen*; Hummelen 1968, 4 03, vv. 118–119; quoted in Grauls 1957, p. 32: "Ick stae quaet ghenoch om den duven te snoeren, / Oft om op een cussen te binden al waer hi kintsch."

23.   Grauls 1957, pp. 23–24, quoted from *Gheneuglijck Tafel-speelken van een droncken man / ende zijn wijf / hoe hem 'twijf dwinght de Lantaren te dragen* (Hummelen 1968, 3 H 1, 5 A 2): "Al waert een van die seven wijven / Die den duyvel opt kussen deden blijven." See *Veelderhande* 1971, p. 7. A somewhat different connotation is given this expression in the *Evangelien van de Spinrocke*, in which six old women discuss various aspects of marriage; they are characterized as being so clever and wise in their time that they could "conjure up the blue devil or bind him to a cushion"; see *Die evangelien vanden spinrocke* (Antwerp: Michiel Hillen van Hoochstraeten, ca. 1520; reprinted with an endnote by G. J. Boekenoogen, The Hague, Martinus Nijhoff, 1910), p. 2; quoted in Grauls 1957, p. 23.

24.   See A. Hind, *Early Italian Engraving* (London: B. Quaritch for M. Knoedler, New York, 1938–48), 1:64–65, cat. no. A.II.6, who suggests that it was copied after a lost work by the Master of the Banderoles. The three inscriptions are as follows: over the Devil on the gallows, "O mala chonpagnia" the woman with the whip calls out, "Aspetta upqho un poco" (or "Aspetta un poco"), and her quarry replies, "Oime, oime" ("Ohime, ohime" in modern Italian).

25.   For women binding the Devil to a cushion, see Elaine C. Block, "Iconography of Choir Stalls in Barcelona," *The Profane Arts of the Middle Ages / Les arts profanes du moyen-âge* 6 (1997): 240–257, esp. 248 and fig. 11; idem, "Liturgical and Anti-Liturgical Iconography on Medieval Choir Stalls," in *Objects, Images, and the Word: Art in the Service of the Liturgy*, ed. Colum Hourihane, Index of Christian Art Occasional Papers VI (Princeton: Index of Christian Art in Association with Princeton University Press, 2003), pp. 161–179, esp. 175 and fig. 16; and Herman A. van Duinen, *De Koorbanken van de Grote- of Onze Lieve Vrouwekerk te Dordrecht* (Leiden: Primavera Pers, 1997), p. 123, fig. 212.

26.   In the *Vitae Adae et Evae* and other medieval apocryphal accounts of the
      lives of our First Parents after the Fall, the Devil deceives Eve a second
      time when, disguised as an angel, he persuades her to abandon her
      penance of fasting while standing in the River Tigris for a number of days;
      see Brian Murdoch and J. A. Tasioulas, eds., *The Apocryphal Lives of Adam
      and Eve, Edited from the Auchinleck Manuscript and from Trinity College, Oxford, MS
      57* (Exeter, U.K.: University of Exeter Press, 2002), pp. 8–9, 45–46, lines
      242–276, and 70–71, lines 181–216.

27.   In the *Towneley Plays*; see De Bruyn 1979, pp. 133–134. In the early-four-
      teenth-century Queen Mary Psalter (London, British Library, MA Royal
      2B.vii), one miniature (fol. 6), shows the Devil tempting Noah's wife into
      working against her husband; see Anne Rudolff Stanton, *The Queen Mary
      Psalter: A Study of Affect and Audience,* Transactions of the American Philo-
      sophical Society 91, part 6 (Philadelphia: American Philosophical Soci-
      ety, 2001), pp. 88–90 and fig. 25. This episode occurs in a fragmentary
      fifteenth-century mystery play written at Newcastle upon Tyne; see *The
      Non-Cycle Mystery Plays...*, ed. Osborne Waterhouse, EETS, extra series
      104 (London: Early English Text Society, 1909), pp. xxxvi–xxxviii, 22–25.

28.   See Franco Mormando, *The Preacher's Demons: Bernardino of Siena and the So-
      cial Underworld of Early Renaissance Italy* (Chicago: University of Chicago
      Press, 1999), pp. 58–59.

29.   For the Devil's mother *(mater inferni)* and grandmother in medieval liter-
      ature and drama, see Wright 2002, p. 163 n. 16; Jacob Grimm, *Deutsche
      Mythologie*, 3 vols., 4th ed. (Berlin: Ferd. Dümmler, 1875–78), 2:841–843,
      3:297. Thompson 1955–58, 3:333–334, lists a number of folktales dealing
      with the women in the Devil's family. See also A. Barb, "Centaura: The
      Mermaid and the Devil's Grandmother," *Journal of the Warburg and Cour-
      tauld Institutes* 29 (1966): 1–23, esp. 10–12. For proverbs involving the
      Devil's mother and grandmother in German-speaking lands, see Isabel
      Chamberlain, "The Devil's Grandmother," *Journal of American Folk-Lore* 13
      (1900): 278–280; see 279 for medieval proverbs. For the Devil's dam in
      Shakespeare, see Barb, p. 11. The comic possibilities offered by the Devil's
      family did not go unexploited. In one late medieval German play, *Ludus
      Mariae Magdalenae in gaudio*, the Devil bars the entrance of Hell to several
      infamous womanizers for fear they might seduce his grandmother; see
      Hellmut Rosenfeld, "Die Entwicklung der Ständesatire im Mittelalter,"
      Zeitschrift für deutsche Philologie 71 (1952): 196–207, esp. 202. In 1534 Philip

of Hesse sent two cannons for the siege of Münster, one called the Devil, the other the Devil's Dam; see Anthony Arthur, *The Tailor-King: The Rise and Fall of the Anabaptist Kingdom of Münster* (New York: St. Martin's Press, 1999), p. 45.

30. Both proverbs occur in Andriessoon 2003, nos. 21.5 and 96.5 respectively.

31. Max Lehrs, *Late Gothic Engravings of Germany and the Netherlands*, ed. A. Hyatt Mayor (New York: Dover Publications, 1969), fig. 669.

32. The English translation quoted from ibid., p. 349, note for fig. 669.

33. She may be none other than Lilith, who, according to Talmudic legend, was Adam's first wife. Refusing to submit to his authority, she ran off and consorted with devils. See Louis Ginsberg, *The Legends of the Jews*, 7 vols. (Baltimore: Johns Hopkins University Press, 1998), 1:65, 2:233. For Lilith as a siren in pagan and Jewish antiquity, see Jacqueline Leclercq-Marx, *La Sirène dans la pensée et dans l'art de l'Antiquité et du Moyen Âge: Du mythe païen au symbole chrétien* (Brussels: Académie royal de Belgique, Classe des Beaux-Arts, 1997), pp. 18, 42. Closer to the spirit of Van Meckenem's print is the play *Fraw Jutta*, written by the priest Dietrich Schernberg about 1480–85 but not published until 1565. Based on the old story of Pope Joan, the play's first scene shows the Devil summoning his council, which includes his grandmother, here named Lillis, a variant of Lilith. See *Medieval German Drama. Four Plays in Translation: The Innsbruck (Thuringian) Easter Play, the Innsbruck (Thuringian) Corpus Christi Play, the Mülhausen Play of St. Catherine, the Play of Lady Jutta*, ed. and trans. Stephen K. Wright, with a note on the music by Wright and Keith Glaeske, Early European Drama Translation Series 4 (Fairview, N.C.: Pegasus Press, 2002), pp. 161–219, esp. 163–164. For a description of the play, see ibid., pp. 15–18.

34. The virago's traditional antagonism toward the Devil may have had an honorable origin in Eden, where God told the serpent, "I will put enmities between thee and the woman, and thy seed and her seed; she shall crush thy head . . ." (Gen. 3:15, Douay-Rheims version). But it is more likely an expression of her own ill temper, for according to an old proverb, "he must act terrible who would frighten the Devil"; see *Proverbia Communia* 1947, pp. 74–75, no. 403, and commentary, pp. 210–211.

35. Goedthals 1568, p. 68. In the play *Begheirlijcke Lust*, performed before William of Orange at Brussels in 1578 (Hummelen 1968, 6 E 1), Sot Begrijp (Foolish Understanding) says that he would rather come against

ten devils than two bad women, because the latter are much worse; see
Houwaert 1579, p. 70.

36. *Das Jad von Wirtemberg,* in Adelbert von Keller, ed., *Erzählungen aus alt-
     deutschen Handschriften,* Bibliothek des Litterarischen Vereins in Stuttgart
     35 (Stuttgart: Litterarischer Verein, 1855), pp. 80–92, esp. 90 for the ad-
     vice on robbing Hell; for the poem, see Franz Brietzmann, *Die böse Frau
     in der deutschen Literatur des Mittelalters* (Berlin: Mayer and Müller, 1912),
     pp. 193–194.

37. For the woodcut with its accompanying text, see Eugen Diederichs,
     Deutsches Leben der Vergangenheit in Bildern, intro. H. Kienzle (Jena: Eugen
     Diederichs, 1908), p. 140, fig. 462; and Keith Moxey, *Peasants, Warriors,
     and Wives: Popular Imagery in the Reformation* (Chicago: University of Chicago
     Press, 1989), pp. 105 and 107, fig. 5.8.

38. Von Keller 1965–66, 1:483–495, no. 56.

39. *Nyeuwe clucht boeck* 1983, pp. 73–74, no. 31.

40. De Bruyn 1979, p. 132, translates *helleveeg* as "hellsweep," alluding to that
     wifely instrument, the broom. However, Verwijs and Verdam 1885–, 3:
     col. 303, note that *helleveeg* is derived not from *vegen,* "to sweep," but from
     veeg, meaning "damned" or "cursed," hence "the damned out of Hell." In
     modern Netherlandish dictionaries, *helleveeg* is translated as "shrew" or
     "hellcat."

41. Von Keller and Goetze 1870–1908, 9:35–46.

42. Ibid., 9:284–287; summarized in De Bruyn 1979, pp. 143–144. The ba-
     sic plot is old with many variations. One appears in Niccolò Machiavelli's
     tale *Belphagor,* written probably shortly after 1515. The devil Belphagor is
     dispatched by Pluto to the Upperworld to ascertain if women are as evil
     as commonly reputed. Belphagor marries a Florentine woman who
     makes his life so miserable that he escapes, and after several adventures,
     the prospect of his wife catching up with him sends him fleeing back to
     Hell. See Niccolò Machiavelli, *Belphagor,* illus. Danuta Laskowska (Em-
     maus, Pa.: Rodale Press, 1954).

43. Translation quoted in De Bruyn 1979, p. 145 n. 78; the text in Von Keller
     and Goetze 1870–1908, 14:47–59. See also Sachs's poem, *Der teufel nam
     ein alts weib zu der eh* (1557), in ibid., 9:284–287. For Sachs's carnival plays
     dealing with old women and the Devil, cf. the sixteenth-century Ger-
     man chronicler Simon Gronau, who reports a carnival prank in Thorn,

West Prussia, about 1443, in which men dressed as devils and hunted up old women and supposedly carried them off to Hell; see R. W. Scribner, *Popular Culture and Popular Movements in Reformation Germany* (London: Hambledon Press, 1987), p. 88. Further research might determine if this incident was isolated or reflects a common carnival custom.

44. Variants of this tale appear in a number of medieval *exempla* collections (Tubach 1969, p. 405, no. 5361), and it inspired plays for several centuries after Sachs (Schmidt 1963, pp. 70–78). For further examples in art, see also Jones 2002b, pp. 189–190.

45. Karant-Nunn and Wiesner-Hanks 2003, pp. 124, 135.

46. Geisberg-Strauss 1974, 1:140 (Geisberg, no. 161). I am very grateful to Professor Gisela Luther for a translation of this poem. The poem may be by Hans Sachs; see Nuremberg, Stadtgeschichtliche Museen, *Die Welt des Hans Sachs: 400 Holzschnitte des 16. Jahrhunderts*, 1976, p. 101, cat. no. 121.

47. Hollstein [1949]–, 4:59, no. 117, there erroneously described as "The Witch and the Devil."

48. Christine de Pizan, *Treasure of the City of Ladies, or the Book of the Three Virtues*, trans. and intro. Sarah Lawson (Harmondsworth: Penguin Books, 1985), p. 129.

49. My illustration is of a damaged impression in the Rijksprentenkabinet, Amsterdam, attributed to Remigius Hogenberg. For this and other images of Kenau Hasselaer published during the later sixteenth and seventeenth centuries, see Peacock 1999, pp. 18 and passim and pp. 26–28, figs. 15–17. Cf. some contemporary images of the triumphant Judith in Margarita Stocker, *Judith, Sexual Warrior: Women and Power in Western Culture* (New Haven: Yale University Press, 1998), figs. 1, 2, 13, 15, 17. For Hasselaer's life, see Kurtz 1956, esp. pp. 16–41, on her heroic role in the siege of Haarlem. Trijnje van Leemput and her companions performed similar martial deeds in the defense of Utrecht (Peacock 1999, pp. 18, 29, fig. 18).

50. For a similar contrast between Kenau Hasselaer and Dulle Griet, see Simon Schama, *The Embarrassment of Riches: An Interpretation of Dutch Culture in the Golden Age* (New York: Alfred A. Knopf, 1987), p. 418.

51. See Gibson 1979, p. 11, for the theme of the Fight for the Breeches. In a woodcut picture series of about 1700 from East Flanders, the wife donning the trousers is labeled Quaey Griet or "Bad Griet" (Röhrich 1974, 1:440).

52. Gibson 1979, p. 11.

53. See pp. 112–113 above.

54. Goedthals 1568, p. 54: "Eenen roof voor d'helle halen / Il yroit a l'enfer l'espee au poing"; Lambrecht 1945, p. 165, s.v., "Roof": "hy zou eenen Roof voor de helle halen: Il iroit en enfer l'espee au point." In Hans de Laet's proverb collection (Antwerp, 1549), the French proverb is given first, followed by a Flemish translation and then the Flemish equivalent: "Il yoit en enfer lespee au poing. Hy soude inde helle gaen met sweerd inde handt / Ofte aldus [Or thus] / Hy soude eenen roof voor de helle / ende comen ongescheynt weder." See De Laet 1962, p. 24, no. 399. Cf. Luther, who insisted that scolding wives carried a sword in their mouths (Karant-Nunn and Wiesner-Hanks 2003, p. 95).

55. *Woordenboek* 1882–1998, s.v., "Plunder"; see also s.v., "Plundermaerckt," defined as jumble sale and as *Forum scrutarium*, or trash market.

56. For the term *pererga*, derived from the Elder Pliny's account of Protogenes, see E. H. Gombrich, *Norm and Form: Studies in the Art of the Renaissance*, 2nd ed. (London: Phaidon, 1971), pp. 113–114.

57. This monster may be compared with several carvings showing little male figures defecating coins, which Christa Grössinger sees as an allusion to the old German proverb "money does not fall out of my backside"; see Christa Grössinger, *Humour and Folly in Secular and Profane Prints of Northern Europe, 1430–1540* (London: Harvey Miller, 2002), pp. 1–2 and fig. 2, p. 3; and Jones 2002b, pp. 284–285.

58. Grauls 1957, p. 51; see also *Woordenboek* 1882–1998, s.v., "pollepel" and "opscheppen." Philips van Marnix van St. Aldegonde speaks of the Roman clergy dishing up the wealth of the church with the big ladle ("met de groote Pollepel opscheppen"); see Philips van Marnix van St. Aldegonde, *De bijenkorf der H. Roomsche kercke*, selections ed. W. A. Ornée and L. Strengholt (Zutphen: B. V. W. J. Thieme & Cie., [c. 1974]), p. 148. Magdalena Paumgartner employed the expression in a related sense when she wrote her husband in July 1584 that she had "dined with a great spoon," that is, dined sumptuously, at the home of a nearby count. See Ozment 1986, p. 113.

59. Geoffrey Chaucer, *Canterbury Tales, The Squire's Tale*; see Chaucer-Benson 1987, p. 176, lines 602–603.

60. Quoted in Bartlett Jere Whiting, *Proverbs in the Earlier English Drama*, Harvard Studies in Comparative Literature, vol. XIV (1938; New York: Octagon Books, 1969), p. 272. For other examples of this, see Walter W. Skeat, *Early English Proverbs, Chiefly of the Thirteenth and Fourteenth Centuries, with Illustrative Quotations* (Oxford: Clarendon Press, 1910), p. 119, no. 282; and R. W. Dent, *Proverbial Language in English Drama Exclusive of Shakespeare, 1495–1616: An Index* (Berkeley and Los Angeles: University of California Press, 1984), p. 645. In Groningen, the pawnbroker was called a *lange lepel*, because he counted out the money and gave it to his customers in a long ladle; see Stoett 1943, p. 394, no. 1019, n. 3. I have not been able to ascertain if this expression was prevalent in Bruegel's day.

61. Guicciardini 1567, p. 38. Women enjoyed a similar economic independence in earlier centuries; see Simons 2003, p. 10.

62. Lydia Pauw de Veen, "Archivialische gegevens over Volcxken Diercx, weduwe van Hieronymus Cock," in *Bijdragen tot de geschiedenis van de grafische kunst opgedragen aan Prof. Dr. Louis Lebeer ter gelegenheid van zijn tachtigste verjaardag / Contributions à l'histoire de l'art graphique dédiées à la occasion de son quatrevingtième anniversaire* (Antwerp: Vereeniging van de Antwerpsche Bibliophielen, 1975), pp. 215–247. Diercx married again, to Lambert Bottin, but he died sometime before 1582. Artists' wives occasionally sold their husbands' works, and the widows of art dealers often continued their husbands' enterprises; see Vermeylen 2003, pp. 69–70.

63. Kurtz 1956; and Kurtz 1973, p. 69.

64. Van Mander-Miedema 1994–99, 1: fol. 218v (pp. 132–133), 3:78. For Verhulst's activity as a publisher, see Marlier 1966, pp. 30–31. Van Mander says that she taught the art of painting miniatures to her grandson Jan "Velvet" Brueghel (Van Mander-Miedema 1994–99, 1: fol. 234r (pp. 194–195). Guicciardini 1567, p. 134 (sec. I), includes her among the living women painters but says nothing about the nature of her art. For Verhulst's life in general, see also A. Monballieu, "De kunstenaars familie Verhulst Bessemeers," *Handelingen van de Koninklijke Kring voor Oudheidkunde, Letteren en Kunst van Mechelen* 78 (1974): 105–121, esp. 109, 116.

65. Guicciardini 1567, p. 38. Bruegel's mother-in-law may have been one of these strong-minded women: according to Van Mander, she consented to his marriage to her daughter only if he would agree to move to Brussels, where she lived, and abandon Antwerp and a mistress he kept there; see Van Mander-Miedema 1994–99, 1: fols. 233r–v (pp. 190–193).

66.   Six editions of the Netherlandish version were published between 1500 and 1635; see Sebastian Brant, *Der sottenschip oft dat narrenschip, Antwerpen 1548*, ed. Loek Geeraerdts (Middelburg: Uitgeverij Merlijn, 1981). For the absence in this Netherlandish edition of the chapter on evil women (chap. 64 in Brant-Zeydel 1962), see ibid., p. 23.

67.   See Berlin, Preussischer Kulturbesitz, Staatliche Museen, Kupferstich-kabinett, *Pieter Bruegel d. Ä. als Zeichner: Herkunft und Nachfolge*, 1975, pp. 76–77, cat. no. 88 and fig. 118. See also Panse and Schmidt 1967, p. 6, fig. 1, with details; p. 42, fig. 12, passim. For the various attributions of this painting, most often to Pieter Brueghel the Younger, see De Coo 1978, pp. 36–37.

68.   See Bernadette van Haute, *David III Ryckaert: A Seventeenth-Century Flemish Painter of Peasant Scenes* (Turnhout: Brepols, 1999), p. 145, cat. no. A145. Van Haute identifies the subject as Dulle Griet; dating it to the 1650s, she suggests that it was intended as a pendant for a *Temptation of St. Anthony* (cat. no. A147), which is the same size. The proverb "to plunder in front of Hell," incidentally, appears in W. A. Winschooten, *Seeman* (Leiden, 1681), p. 214, "hij sou' een roof voor de hel van daan haalen"; quoted in Grauls 1957, p. 44.

69.   Location unknown. Van Haute, *David III Ryckaert*, pp. 145–146, pl. 146, identifies the protagonist as a witch.

70.   Jane P. Davidson, *David Teniers the Younger* (Boulder, Colo.: Westview Press, 1979), p. 22 and colorpl. 4. Davidson suggests that the woman is a witch who has conjured up the devils, binding one of them to a pillow as part of her ritual, and looks around in alarm at the hellish horde behind her. However, her expression is more baleful than fearful and the general movement of the devils is distinctly away from her.

71.   Examples occur in Roemer Visscher's *Brabbeling* (Amsterdam, 1614) and the *Klucht van Oene*, a farce by Jan Vos (Amsterdam, 1646). In the latter, one character explicitly refers to this saying as a proverb. See Grauls 1957, pp. 24–25.

72.   A painting in which "Dulle Griet den rooff uut die hel haelt" (Dulle Griet takes booty out of Hell) is listed in the death inventory of one Herman Neyt, an otherwise unknown Antwerp artist who died in 1642 (Denucé 1932, p. 98; and De Coo 1978, p. 34). It may have been one of the paintings just discussed by Teniers or Ryckaert or a work from Neyt's own hand, but we can only speculate.

EPILOGUE

Epigraphs: Leon Battista Alberti, *Momus*, trans. Sarah Knight, Latin text ed. Virginia Brown and Sarah Knight, The I Tatti Renaissance Library, no. 8 (Cambridge, Mass.: Harvard University Press, 2003), p. 199 (bk. 3); Erasmus, *The Fabulous Feast*, in Erasmus-Thompson 1965, p. 266.

1.   Pleij 1995, p. 6.

2.   Pleij 1974–75, pp. 116–117.

3.   Coigneau 1980–83, 1:14; see Van Doesborch-Kruyskamp 1940, 2:228: *Refereynen int sot / om ghenoucht te verwecken / ende swaricheyt en menlancholie te verdriven.*

4.   Coigneau 1980–83, 1:15; see also pp. 74–82 for a description of this manuscript.

5.   *Woordenboek* 1882–1998, s.v., "recreatie."

6.   Pleij 1995, p. 6. This anecdote concerns a man who, finding his wife with the local priest, is convinced by the couple that he is dead. After laying him out for burial with a sheet over him, they continue their lovemaking, while the "corpse" complains that if he were not dead, he would put an end to their affair. For this story, titled "Lacarise den keitijf" (Lazarus the Wretch), see Karel Eykman and Fred Lodder, eds., *Van de man die graag dronk en andere Middlenederlandse komische verhalen* (Amsterdam: Prometheus / Bert Bakker, 2002), pp. 142–147. The story ends with an "elaborate moral," as Pleij puts it, warning against unfaithful wives, but as Lodder convincingly argues, such moralizing served chiefly to heighten the comic effect (Lodder 1996, pp. 152, 166, 167, with specific reference to "Lacarise"). Cf. Régine Reynolds-Cornell, who in discussing medieval farces observes, "laughter took precedent over the moral message, if there was one at all"; see Marguerite of Navarre 1992, p. 19.

7.   Cf. Morreall 1989, p. 256, who pertinently observes on this point: "Think of Shakespeare's Falstaff in *Henry IV*. We do not leave the theater saying to ourselves, 'I must be careful never to act like Falstaff!'"

8.   For the last-named picture, see p. 160, n. 38.

9.   Erasmus, in his defense of *The Praise of Folly* against Alberto Pio, 1529; quotations from Gilmore 1978, p. 114.

10. See Raupp 1986; and for the Flemish prints of peasant celebrations, also Gibson 1991, p. 32, with further references. Both Carroll 1987 and Stew-

art 1993 argue that the German peasant scenes were not as negative as generally assumed. In this context, see also Stewart 1995, esp. p. 360.

11.   Raupp 1986, p. 298, sec. d. For a somewhat earlier controversy over Bruegel's peasant scenes, see Alpers 1972–73; Miedema 1977; and Alpers 1978–79.

12.   Gibson 1989, pp. 60–75.

13.   Cf. Stewart 2004, p. 129, who notes that in Bruegel's *Hoboken Kermis* some of the peasants adopt poses that "suggest bodily acts without specifically depicting them."

14.   Further research into the Antwerp archives, along the lines of Stappaerts 1987–88 and Goldstein 2003, might give us additional information concerning the owners of peasant scenes in sixteenth-century Netherlands. However, such future endeavors are complicated by the Eighty Years' War, in which wealthy Protestants went into exile or lost their fortunes and even their lives. Antoon van Straelen, for example, was condemned to death by the Council of Blood for his activities on behalf of the Lutherans, and the contents of his Antwerp residence confiscated (*Biog. Nat.* 1866–1944, 24: col. 141). Other magnates suffered from the decline of commerce at this time, among them Niclaes Jonghelinck, whose art collection was sold off after his death in 1570 to pay his debts (Van de Velde 1965; Smolderen 1996, p. 9).

15.   De Maeyer 1955, p. 155, who cites a panegyric written at Albert's death, *Le soleil eclipsé ou discours sur la vie et la mort du sérénissime archduc Albert* (Brussels, 1622).

16.   Schumann 1998.

17.   See Klaus Ertz, *Jan Brueghel der Ältere (1568–1625): Die Gemälde mit kritischem Oeuvrekatalog* (Cologne: Dumont, 1979), p. 364, cat. no. 246; color ill. p. 227, fig. 291, here dated ca. 1621–23.

18.   Ibid., p. 155.

19.   Estienne 1600, in the introduction, "A Caveat or lession of instruction to the Reader by F. Anth. Langvier, C. C. Doctor of Divinitie of Ries." Cf. Marguerite of Navarre's play *Most, Much, Little, Less*, in which Much (a great secular ruler) asks the two peasants Little and Less: "But must you not work with your hands?" The reply is: "Yes, but our minds are at ease"; see Marguerite of Navarre 1992, p. 144, lines 697–698.

20.   Gibson 1991, p. 43; and Goldstein 2003, p. 212, who cites Guevara's volume as well as a copy of *De agricultura* by Constantine Caesar.

21.   See Mak, 1959, pp. 510–511, with a citation of this word from the mid–sixteenth century.

22.   Burke 1997, p. 130.

23.   For an account of this entertainment, see Verberckmoes 2002, pp. 53–56.

24.   This question is addressed in my article, "Festive Peasants before Bruegel: Three Case Studies and Their Implications," forthcoming in *Simiolus*.

25.   In this connection can be mentioned a "large table [presumably a panel painting] of the maner of banquetting in Flaunders" that is found in an English inventory of 1590; see Lionel Cust, "The Lumley Inventories," *The Sixth Volume of the Walpole Society 1917–1918*, pp. 15–35, esp. 27.

SELECT BIBLIOGRAPHY

BOOKS AND ARTICLES

Agricola 1971. Agricola, Johannes. *Die Sprichtwörter Sammlungen,* edited by Sander L. Gilman. Berlin: Walter de Gruyter.

Alberti 1966. Alberti, Leon Battista. *On Painting,* translated by John Spencer. Rev. ed. New Haven: Yale University Press.

Alpers 1972–73. Alpers, Svetlana. "Bruegel's Festive Peasants." *Simiolus* 6:163–176.

———. 1978–79. "Taking Pictures Seriously: A Reply to Hessel Miedema." *Simiolus* 10:46–50.

Andriessoon 2003. Adriessoon, Symon. *Duytsche Adagia ofte spreecwoorden,* edited by Mark A. Meadow and Anneke C. G. Fleurkens, introductions by S. A. C. Dudok van Heel and Herman Roodenburg. Antwerp: Alssens, 1550. Hilversum: Verloren.

Aristotle 1984. *The Complete Works of Aristotle,* edited by Jonathan Barnes. 2 vols. Bollingen Series LXXI, 2. Princeton: Princeton University Press.

Baetens 1985. Baetens, Roland. "La 'villa rustica,' phénomène italien dans le paysage brabançon au 16ème siècle," pp. 171–191. In *Aspetti della vita economica medieval. Atti del Convegno di Studie nel X Anniversario della morte di Federigo Melis, Firenze-Pisa-Prato, 10–14 marzo 1984.* Florence: Istituto di storia economica, Università degli studi Firenze.

Bakhtin 1968. Bakhtin, Mikhail. *Rabelais and His World,* translated by Helene Iswolsky. Cambridge, Mass.: MIT Press.

Barolsky 1978. Barolsky, Paul. *Infinite Jest: Wit and Humor in Italian Renaissance Art.* Columbia: University of Missouri Press.

Van Bastelaer-Gilchrist 1992. Van Bastelaer, René. *The Prints of Pieter Bruegel the Elder. Catalogue Raisonné. New Edition,* translated and revised by Susan Fargo Gilchrist. San Francisco: Alan Wolfsky Fine Arts. First published as *Les estampes de Pierre l'ancien.* Brussels: G. Van Oost & Co., 1908.

Bell 1999. Bell, Rudolph M. *How to Do It: Guides to Good Living for Renaissance Italians.* Chicago: University of Chicago Press.

Bijns 1875. *Refereinen van Anna Bijns,* edited by W. L. van Helten. Rotterdam: J. H. Dunk.

Biog. Nat. 1866–1944. *Biographie National, publiée par l'Academie Royale des Sciences, des Lettres et des Beaux-Arts de Belgique.* 28 vols. Brussels: H. Thiry-van Buggenhout et al.

Bowen 1988. Bowen, Barbara C., ed. *One Hundred Renaissance Jokes: An Anthology.* Birmingham, Ala.: Summa Publications.

———. 1998. *Enter Rabelais, Laughing.* Nashville: Vanderbilt University Press.

Braet et al. 2003. Braet, Herman, Guido Latré, and Werner Verbeke, eds. *Risus medievalis: Laughter in Medieval Literature and Art,* Medievalia Lovaniensia, Series I, Studia XXX. Louvain: Leuven University Press, 2003.

Brant-Zeydel 1962. Brant, Sebastian. *The Ship of Fools,* translated by Edwin H. Zeydel. New York: Dover Publications.

Bremmer and Roodenburg 1997. Bremmer, Jan, and Herman Roodenburg, eds. *A Cultural History of Humor: From Antiquity to the Present Day.* Cambridge: Polity Press; Malden, Mass.: Blackwell Publishers.

Brewer, 1996. Brewer, Derek, ed., *Medieval Comic Tales.* 2nd ed. Cambridge: D. S. Brewer.

———. 2003. "The Comedy of Corpses in Medieval Comic Tales." In Braet et al. 2003, pp. 11–29.

Briels 1980. Briels, J. "Amator Pictoriae Artis: De Antwerpse kunstverzamelaar Peeter Stevens (1590–1668) en zijn Constkamer." *Jaarboek Antwerpen,* 137–226.

Brooks 2000. Brooks, Jeanice. *Courtly Song in Late Sixteenth-Century France.* Chicago: University of Chicago Press.

De Bruyn 1979. De Bruyn, Lucy. *Woman and the Devil in Sixteenth-Century Literature.* Tisbury, Wiltshire: Compton Press.

Buijnsters-Smets 1995. Buijnsters-Smets, Leontine. *Jan Massys: Een Antwerps schilder uit de zestiende eeuw.* Zwolle: Waanders Uitgevers.

Burke 1978. Burke, Peter. *Popular Culture in Early Modern Europe.* New York: Harper & Row.

———. 1995. *The Fortunes of the "Courtier": The European Reception of Castiglione's "Cortegiano."* Cambridge: Polity Press in association with Blackwell Publishers.

———. 1997. *Varieties of Cultural History.* Ithaca, N.Y.: Cornell University Press.

Carroll 1987. Carroll, Margaret D. "Peasant Festivity and Political Identity in the Sixteenth Century." *Art History* 10:289–314.

Castiglione 1959. Castiglione, Baldesar. *The Book of the Courtier,* translated by Charles S. Singleton. Garden City, N.Y.: Anchor Books, Doubleday & Company.

Chaucer-Benson 1987. *The Riverside Chaucer*, 3rd ed., edited by Larry D. Benson. Boston: Houghton Mifflin Company.

Coigneau 1980–83. Coigneau, Dirk. *Refereinen in het zotte bij de rederijkers*. 3 vols. Verhandeling van de Koninklijke Academie voor Nederlandse Taal-en Letterkunde, VIe Reeks, Nr. III. Ghent: Secretariaat van de Koninklijke Academie voor Nederlandse Taal-en Letterkunde.

———. 1994. "'Maer de steden apaert': Over het rederijkerslandjuweel en het haagspel van 1561." In *Volkscultuur in Brabant*, edited by Fernand Vanhemelryck, pp. 115–141. Brussels: Katholieke Universiteit, Centrum Brabantse Geschiedenis.

Constable 1995. Constable, Giles. *Three Studies in Medieval Religious and Social Thought*. Cambridge: Cambridge University Press.

De Coo 1978. De Coo, J. *Museum van den Bergh, Catalogus I*. Antwerp.

Cooper 1977. Cooper, Helen. *Pastoral: Mediaeval into Renaissance*. Ipswich, U.K.: D. S. Brewer; Totowa, N.J.: Rowman & Littlefield.

Curtius 1953. Curtius, Ernst Robert. *European Literature and the Latin Middle Ages*, translated by Willard R. Trask. New York: Harper Torchbooks, Harper & Row.

Dacos 1969. Dacos, Nicole. *La découverte de la Domus Aurea et la formation des grotesques à la Renaissance*. London: Warburg Institute, University of London; Leiden: E. J. Brill.

Davidson 1996. Davidson, Clifford, ed. *Fools and Folly*. Early Drama, Art, and Music Monograph Series 22. Kalamazoo: Medieval Institute Publications, Western Michigan University.

Dekker 1997. Dekker, Rudolf. *Lachen in de Gouden Eeuw: Een geschiedenis van der Nederlandse humor*. Amsterdam: Wereldbibliotheek.

Delen 2002. Delen, Marie-Ange. *Het hof van Willem van Oranje*. Amsterdam: Wereldbibliotheek.

DeMolen 1978. DeMolen, Richard L., ed. *Essays on the Works of Erasmus*. New Haven: Yale University Press.

Denucé 1932. Denucé, Jean. *De Antwerpsche "Konstkamers": Inventarissen van kunstverzamelingen te Antwerpen in de 16e en 17e eeuwen*. Bronnen tot de geschiedenis van de Vlaamsche kunst, vol. 2. The Hague: Martinus Nijhoff.

Dierickx 1954. Dierickx, Hendrik. *Geschiedenis van Hoboken: evolutie van plattegemeente tot industrieel centrum (1100–1950)*. Antwerp: De Sikkel.

Van Doesborch-Kruyskamp 1940. *De refereinenbundel van Jan van Doesborch*, edited by C. Kruyskamp. 2 vols. Leidsche drukken en herdrukken uitgegeven vanwege de Maatschappij der Nederlandsche Letterkunde te Leiden, Kleine Reeks II. Leiden: E. J. Brill.

Dreyer 1977. Dreyer, Peter. "Bruegels Alchemist von 1558: Versuch einer Deutung ad Sensum Mysticum." *Jahrbuch der Berliner Museen* 19:69–113.

Van Durme 1953. Van Durme, Maurice. *Antoon Perronet, Bisschop van Atrecht, Kardinaal van Granvelle, Minister van Karel V en Filips II (1517–1586)*. Verhandelingen van de Koninklijke Vlaamse Academie voor Wetenschappen, Letteren en Schone Kunsten van België, Klasse der Letteren, jaargang xv, nr. 18. Brussels: Palais der Academiën.

Van Eeghem 1943. Van Eeghem, W. "Doedelzak contra luit." In *Prosper Verheyden gehuldigd ter gelegenehid van zijn zeventigste verjaardag, 23 October 1943*, pp. 205–234. Antwerp.

Elias 2000. Elias, Norbert. *The Civilizing Process: Sociogenetic and Psychogenetic Investigations,* translated by Edmund Jephett. Revised ed., edited by Eric Dunning, Johan Goudsblom, and Stephen Mennell. Oxford: Blackwell Publishers.

Van Engeldorp-Gastelaers 1984. Van Engeldorp-Gastelaers, Wilma. *Ic sal u smiten op uwen tant: Geweld tussen man en vrouw in laatmiddeleeuwse kluchten*. Doctoralscriptie, oktober 1983. Korenbloem 1. Amsterdam: Vakgroep Historische Letterkunde, Instituut voor Neerlandistiek, Universiteit van Amsterdam.

Erasmus-McGregor 1985. Erasmus, Desiderius. *On Good Manners for Boys. De civilitate morum puerilium,* translated and annotated by Brian McGregor. In *Collected Works of Erasmus,* vol. 25, *Literary and Educational Writings* 3, *De conscribendis epistolis, Formula, De civilitate,* edited by J. K. Sowards, pp. 277–289. Toronto: University of Toronto Press.

Erasmus-Miller 1979. Erasmus, Desiderius. *The Praise of Folly,* translated and edited by Clarence H. Miller. New Haven: Yale University Press.

Erasmus-Phillips 1967. Phillips, Margaret Mann. *Erasmus on His Times: A Shortened Version of the "Adages" of Erasmus.* Cambridge: Cambridge University Press.

Erasmus-Phillips and Mynors 1989–92. Erasmus, Desiderius. *Adages,* vols. 1–4, translated by Margaret Mann Phillips and R. A. B. Mynors, annotated by R. A. B. Mynors. In *Collected Works of Erasmus,* vols. 31–34. Toronto: University of Toronto Press, 1989–92.

Erasmus-Thompson 1965. Erasmus, Desiderius. *The Colloquies of Erasmus,* translated by Craig R. Thompson. Chicago: University of Chicago Press.

Ertz 1988–2000. Ertz, Klaus. *Pieter Brueghel der Jüngere (1564–1637/38): Die Gemälde mit kritischem Oeuvrekatalog.* 2 vols. Lingen: Luca Verlag.

Estienne 1600. Estienne, Charles. *Maison Rustique, or The Countrie Farme. Compiled in the French Tongue by Charles Stevens and Iohn Liebault, Doctors of Physicke. And translated into English by Richard Surflet.* London: Edm. Bollifant for Bonham Norton.

Farrell 1995. Farrell, Thomas J., ed. *Bakhtin and Medieval Voices*. Gainesville: University Press of Florida.

Van der Feen 1918. Van der Feen, G. B. C. "Noord-Nederlandsche Boekerijen in de 16de eeuw" (part 1). *Het Boek* 7 (1918): 6–92.

Freedberg 1989. Freedberg, David, ed. *The Prints of Pieter Bruegel the Elder*. Exh. cat. Tokyo: Tokyo Shimbun.

Freedman 1999. Freedman, Paul. *Images of the Medieval Peasant*. Stanford, Calif.: Stanford University Press.

Friedländer 1967–76. Friedländer, Max J. *Early Netherlandish Painting*. 14 vols. Leiden: A. W. Sijthoff; Brussels: La Connaissance.

Geisberg-Strauss 1974. Geisberg, Max. *The German Single-Leaf Woodcut: 1500–1550*. Revised and edited by Walter L. Strauss. 4 vols. New York: Hacker Art Books.

Van Gelder 1972–73. Van Gelder, H. A. Enno, ed. *Gegevens betreffende roerend en onroerend bezit in de Nederlanden in de 16de eeuw*. 2 vols. Rijks Geschiedkundige Publicatiën, Grote Serie 140–141. The Hague: Martinus Nijhoff.

Getscher 2003. Getscher, Robert H. *An Annotated and Illustrated Version of Giorgio Vasari's History of Italian and Northern Prints from His "Lives of the Artists" (1550 and 1568)*. 2 vols. Lewiston, N.Y.: Edwin Mellen Press.

Gibson 1965. Gibson, Walter S. "Some Notes on Pieter Bruegel the Elder's Peasant Wedding Feast." *Art Quarterly* 28:194–208.

———. 1977. *Bruegel*. London: Thames and Hudson; New York: Oxford University Press. Reprint, New York, 1988, 2002.

———. 1979. "Pieter Bruegel, *Dulle Griet* and Sexist Politics in the Sixteenth Century." In *Pieter Bruegel und seine Welt*, edited by Otto von Simson and Matthias Winner, pp. 9–15. Berlin: Gebrüder Mann Verlag.

———. 1981. "Artists and *Rederijkers* in the Age of Bruegel." *Art Bulletin* 63:426–446.

———. 1989. *"Mirror of the Earth": The World Landscape in Sixteenth-Century Flemish Painting*. Princeton: Princeton University Press.

———. 1991. *Peter Bruegel the Elder: Two Studies*. Franklin D. Murphy Lectures XI, Spencer Museum of Art. Lawrence: University of Kansas Press.

———. 1992a. "Verbeeck's Grotesque Wedding Feasts: Some Reconsiderations." *Simiolus* 21:29–39.

———. 1992b. "Speaking Deeds: Some Proverb Drawings by Pieter Bruegel and His Contemporaries." *Drawing* 14:73–77.

———. 1992c. "Bosch's Dreams: A Response to Bosch's Imagery in the Sixteenth Century." *Art Bulletin* 74 (1992): 205–218.

———. 2000. *Pleasant Places: The Rustic Landscape in Dutch Painting from Bruegel to Ruisdael*. Berkeley and Los Angeles: University of California Press.

———. 2003. *The Art of Laughter in the Age of Bosch and Bruegel.* Twelfth Gerson Lecture, Rijksuniversiteit Groningen, 20 November 2003. Groningen: The Gerson Lectures Foundation.

Gilhus 1997. Gilhus, Ingvild Saelid. *Laughing Gods, Weeping Virgins: Laughter in the History of Religion.* London: Routledge.

Gilmore 1978. Gilmore, Myron P. "*Apologiae*: Erasmus's Defenses of Folly." In DeMolen 1978, pp. 111–123.

Goedthals 1568. Goedthals, François. *Les proverbs anciens flamengs et françois.* Antwerp: Christophe Plantin.

Goldstein 2000. Goldstein, Claudia Edith. "Artifacts of Domestic Life: Bruegel's Paintings in the Flemish Home." *Wooncultuur in de Nederlanden / The Art of Home in Netherlands, 1500–1800,* edited by Jan de Jong, Bart Ramakers, Herman Roodenburg, Frits Scholten, and Mariët Westermann. *Nederlands Kunsthistorisch Jaarboek* 51:173–193.

———. 2003. "Keeping Up Appearances: The Social Significance of Domestic Decoration in Antwerp, 1542–1600." Ph.D. diss., Columbia University.

Graf 1997. Graf, Fritz. "Cicero, Plautus and Roman Laughter." In Bremmer and Roodenburg 1997, pp. 29–39.

Grauls 1957. Grauls, Jan. *Volkstaal en volksleven in het werk van Pieter Bruegel.* Antwerp: N. V. Standaard Boekhandel.

Grosshans 2003. Grosshans, Rainald. *Pieter Bruegel d. Ä: Die niederländischen Sprichwörter.* Berlin: Gemäldegalerie, Staatliche Museen zu Berlin, Preussischer Kulturbesitz.

Grossmann 1955. Grossmann, F. *Bruegel: The Paintings, Complete Edition.* London: Phaidon Press.

Guicciardini 1567. Guicciardini, Lodovico. *Description de tout de le Païs-Bas.* Antwerp: Guillaume Silvius.

Van Haecht 1929–33. *De Kroniek van Godevaert van Haecht over de troubelen van 1565 to 1574 te Antwerpen en elders,* edited by Rob. Van Roosbroeck. 2 vols. Antwerp: De Sikkel.

Hand and Wolff 1986. Hand, John Oliver, and Martha Wolff. *Early Netherlandish Painting. The Collection of the National Gallery of Art: Systematic Catalogue.* Washington, D.C.: National Gallery of Art.

De Heere [D'Heere]-Waterschoot 1969. D'Heere, Lucas. *Den Hof en Boomgaerd der Poësen,* edited by W. Waterschoot. Zwolse drukken en herdrukken voor de Maatschappij der Nederlandse Letterkunde te Leiden, no. 65. Ghent: Ghileyn Manilius, 1565. Zwolle: W. E. J. Tjeenk Willink.

Held 1996. Held, Julius S. "Carolus Scribanius's Observations on Art in Antwerp." *Journal of the Warburg and Courtauld Institutes* 59:174–204.

Hogenelst 1997. Hogenelst, Dini. *Sproken en sprekers: Inleiding op en repertorium van de Middelnederlandse sproke.* 2 vols. Nederlandse literatuur en cultuur in de Middeleeuwen, XVI. Amsterdam: Prometheus.

Hollstein [1949]–. Hollstein, F. W. H. *Dutch and Flemish Etchings, Engravings and Woodcuts, ca. 1450–1700.* Amsterdam: Menno Hertzberger et al.

Horace 1991. Horace. *Satires, Epistles and Ars Poetica,* translated by H. R. Fairclough. Loeb Classical Library. Cambridge, Mass.: Harvard University Press.

Houbraken 1943–53. Houbraken, Arnold. *De groote schouburgh der Nederlantsche Kunstschilders en schilderessen,* edited by P. T. A. Swillens. 3 vols. Maastricht: Leiter-Nypels.

Houwaert 1579. Houwaert, Jean Baptista. *Declaratie van die triumphante Jncompst vande Doorluchtighen ende Hoogheboren Prince van Oraingnien, binnen die Princelijcke Stadt van Brussele, geschiet t'iaer ons Heeren Duysent, vijfhondert, achtentseventich, den acchthiensten Septembris.* Antwerp: Christophe Plantin.

Hughs and Bianconi 1967. Hughes, Robert, and Piero Bianconi. *The Complete Paintings of Bruegel.* New York: Harry N. Abrams.

Hummelen 1968. Hummelen, W. M. H. *Repertorium van het rederijkersdrama 1500–ca. 1620.* Assen: Van Gorcum & Comp. N.V.–Dr. H. J. Prakke and H. M. G. Prakke.

———. 1989. "Toneel op de kermis, van Bruegel tot Bredero." *Oud Holland* 103 (1989): 1–45.

Hüsken 1987. Hüsken, W. N. M. *Noyt Meerder Vreucht: Compositie en structuur van het komische toneel in de Nederlanden voor de Renaissance.* Deventer Studiën 3. Deventer: Sub Rosa.

———. 1996. "The Fool as Social Critic: The Case of Dutch Rhetoricians' Drama." In Davidson 1996, pp. 112–145.

Jeanneret 1989. *Les songes drolatiques de Pantagruel.* Facsimile with introduction by Michel Jeanneret. La Chaux-de-Fonds: Editions (vwa). New edition with an afterword by Frédéric Elsig. Geneva: Librairie Droz, 2004.

———. 1991. *A Feast of Words: Banquets and Table Talk in the Renaissance,* translated by Jeremy Whiteley and Emma Hughes. Chicago: University of Chicago Press.

Jones 2002a. Jones, Malcolm. "Monsters of Misogyny: Bigorne and Chicheface—suite et fin?" In *Marvels, Monsters and Miracles: Studies in the Medieval and Early Imaginations,* edited by Timothy Jones and David A. Sprunger, pp. 203–221. Studies in Medieval Culture XLII, Medieval Institute Publications. Kalamazoo: Western Michigan University.

———. 2002b. *The Secret Middle Ages: Discovering the Real Medieval World.* Foreword by Marina Warner. Phoenix Mill, U.K.: Sutton.

De Jong et al. 1996. De Jong, Jan, Mark Meadow, Herman Roodenburg, and Frits Scholten, eds. *Pieter Bruegel. Nederlands Kunsthistorisch Jaarboek 47.*

De Jong et al. 2002. *Het exotische verbeeld 1550–1950: Boeren en verre volken in de Nederlandse kunst / Picturing the Exotic, 1550–1950: Peasants and Outlandish People in Netherlandish Art,* edited by Jan de Jong et al. *Nederlands kunsthistorisch Jaarboek 53.*

De Jongh 2000. De Jongh, Eddy. "To Instruct and Delight." In *Questions of Meaning: Theme and Motif in Dutch Seventeenth-Century Painting,* translated and edited by Michael Hoyle, pp. 83–103. Leiden: Primavera Press.

Joubert-Rocher 1980. Joubert, Laurent. *Treatise on "Laughter,"* translated and annotated by Gregory David de Rocher. University: University of Alabama Press. Translation of *Traité des causes du ris et tous ses accidents.* 1st complete ed. Paris, 1579.

Junius 1991. Junius, Franciscus. *The Painting of the Ancients. De pictura veterum,* edited by Keith Aldrich, Philipp Fehl, and Raina Fehl. 2 vols. Berkeley and Los Angeles: University of California Press.

Van Kampen et al. 1980. Van Kampen, Hinke, Herman Pleij, Bob Stumpel, Annebel Venmans, and Paul Vriesema, eds. *Het zal koud zijn in 't water als 't vriest: Zestiende-eeuwse parodieën op gedrukte jaarvoorspellingen.* The Hague: Martinus Nijhoff.

Kamper spreekwoorden 1959. *Kamper spreekwoorden naar de uitgave van Warnersen. Anno 1550,* edited by G. G. Kloeke. Assen: Van Gorcum & Comp.–Dr. H. J. Prakke and H. Makke. 1st ed., *Gemeene duytsche spreekwoorden: Adagia oft Proverbia ghenoemt.* Kampen: Warnersen, 1550.

Karant-Nunn and Wiesner-Hanks 2003. Karant-Nunn, Susan C., and Merry E. Wiesner-Hanks, eds. and trans. *Luther on Women: A Sourcebook.* Cambridge: Cambridge University Press.

Kavaler 1999. Kavaler, Ethan Matt. *Pieter Bruegel: Parables of Order and Enterprise.* Cambridge: Cambridge University Press.

Von Keller 1965–66. Von Keller, Adelbert, ed. *Fastnachtspiele aus dem Fünfzehnten Jahrhundert.* 3 vols. and *Nachlese.* 1st ed., 1853, 1858. Darmstadt: Wissenschaftliche Buchgesellschaft.

Von Keller and Goetze 1870–1908. Von Keller, Adelbert, and Edmund Goetze, eds. *Hans Sachs.* 26 vols. Tübingen: Literarischer Verein.

Kempe 1998. *The Book of Margery Kempe,* translated and introduced by John Skinner. New York: Image Books, Doubleday.

Kurtz 1956. Kurtz, Gerda H. *Kenu Symons Dochter van Haerlem.* Assen: Van Gorcum & Comp.–G. A. Hakke and Dr. J. J. Prakke.

———. 1973. "Kenau." In Haarlem, Vleeshal, Vishal, and Hoofdwacht, *Men sagh Haarlem bestormen . . . Uitgegeven ter gelegeneheid van de herdenking van het Beleg van Haarlem 1573–1973,* pp. 65–75. Haarlem: Schuyt & Company.

De Laet 1962. De Laet, Hans. *"Seer schoone spreeckwoorden oft proverbia" (In Franse and Vlaamse taal) in 1549 te Antwerpen verschenen,* edited by G. G. Kloeke. Assen: Van Gorcum & Comp.–Dr. H. J. Prakke and H. M. Prakke.

Lambrecht 1945. Lambrecht, Joos. *Het Naembouck van 1562. Tweede druk van het Nederlands-Frans Woordenboek van Joos Lambrecht,* edited by R. Verdeyen. Bibliothèque de la Faculté de Philosophie et Lettres de l'Université de Liège, fascicule XCVIII. Liège: Faculté de Philosophie et Lettres; Paris: Librairie E. Droz.

Lampsonius-Puraye 1956. Lampson, Dominique [Dominicus Lampsonius]. *Les effigies des peintres célèbres des Pays-Bas,* edited by Jean Puraye. Liège: Éditions Desclée De Brouwer.

Lee 1967. Lee, Rensselaer W. *Ut pictura poesis: The Humanistic Theory of Painting.* New York: W. W. Norton & Co.

Lochrie 1991. Lochrie, Karma. *Margery Kempe and Translations of the Flesh.* Philadelphia: University of Pennsylvania Press.

Lodder 1996. Lodder, Frederik Joris. *Lachen om list en lust: Studies over de middelnederlandse komische versvertellingen.* Ph.D. diss., Rijksuniversiteit te Leiden, 1997. Ridderkerk: Boekhandel "De Ridderhof."

———. 2003. "Of Wives and Men: Middle Dutch Fabliaux on a Hot Urban Issue." In Braet et al. 2003, pp. 181–194.

Machline 1998. Machline, Vera Cecília. "The Contribution of Laurent Joubert's *Traité du ris* to Sixteenth-Century Physiology of Laughter." In *Reading the Book of Nature: The Other Side of the Scientific Revolution,* edited by Allen G. Debus and Michael T. Walten, pp. 251–264. Sixteenth Century Essays & Studies, vol. 41. Kirksville, Mo.: Sixteenth Century Journal Publishers.

De Maeyer 1955. De Maeyer, Marcel. *Albrecht en Isabella in de schilderkunst.* Verhandelingen van de Koninklijke Vlaamse Academie voor Wetenschappen, Letteren en Schone Kunsten, Verhandeling, Nr. 9. Brussels.

Mak 1959. Mak, J. J., *Rhetoricaal glossarium.* Taalkundige bijdragen van Naord en Zuid, vol. XII. Assen: Van Gorcum and Comp.–Dr. H. J. Prakke and H.M.G. Prakke, 1959.

Van Mander 1969. Van Mander, Karel. *Het Schilder-Boeck.* Haarlem: Paschier van Wesbusch, 1604. Utrecht: Davco Publishers.

Van Mander-Miedema 1973. Van Mander, Karel. *Den grondt der edel vry schilder-const,* translated and edited by Hessel Miedema. 2 vols. Utrecht: Haentjens Dekker & Gumbert.

———. 1994–99. *The Lives of the Illustrious Netherlandish and German Painters, from the First Edition of the "Schilder-boeck" (1603–1604),* translated and edited by Hessel Miedema. 6 vols. Doornspijk: Davaco.

Marguerite of Navarre 1992. Marguerite of Angoulême, Duchess of Alençon and of Berri, Queen of Navarre. *Théâtre profane*, translated and edited by Régine Reynolds-Cornell. Ottawa: Dovehouse Editions.

Marijnissen and Seidel 1984. Marijnissen, Roger H., and Max Seidel. *Bruegel*. New York: Harrison House.

Marlier 1966. Marlier, Georges. *La Renaissance flamande: Pierre Coeck d'Alost*. Brussels: Éditions Robert Finck.

———. 1969. *Pierre Brueghel le Jeune*. Brussels: Éditions Robert Finck.

Martens and Peeters 2002. Martens, Maxiliaan P. J., and Natasje Peeters. "Antwerp Painting before Iconoclasm: Considerations on the Quantification of Taste." In *Economia e arte secc. XIII–XVIII. Atti della "trentatreesima Settimana di Studi," 30 aprile–4 maggio 2001*, edited by Simonetta Cavachiocchi, pp. 875–895. Istituto Internazionale di Storia Economica "F. Datini," Prato, Serie II, Atti delle "Settimana di Studi" e altri Convegni 33. Florence: Le Monnier.

Meadow 1996. Meadow, Mark. "Bruegel's *Procession to Calvary*, Aemulatio and the Space of Vernacular Style." In De Jong et al. 1996, pp. 180–205.

———. 2002. *Pieter Bruegel the Elder's "Netherlandish Proverbs" and the Practice of Rhetoric*. Zwolle: Waanders.

Melion 1991. Melion, Walter S. *Shaping the Netherlandish Canon: Carel van Mander's "Schilder-Boeck."* Chicago: University of Chicago Press.

Miedema 1977. Miedema, Hessel. "Realism and the Comic Mode: The Peasant." *Simiolus* 9, no. 4: 205–219.

———. 1981. "Feestende boeren—lachende dorpers. Bij twee aanwinsten van het Rijksprentenkabinet." *Bulletin van het Rijksmuseum* 29 (1981): 191–213; English summary, pp. 243–45.

———. 1998. "Pieter Bruegel weer; en de geloofwaardigheid van Karel van Mander." *Jaarboek Antwerpen*, 309–327.

Mieder 2004. Mieder, Wolfgang, ed. *The Netherlandish Proverbs: An International Symposium on the Pieter Brueg[h]els. Proverbium*, Supplement series, vol. 16. Burlington, Vt.: University of Vermont.

Monballieu 1969. Monballieu, A. "Een werk van P. Bruegel en H. Vredeman de Vries voor de tresorier Aert Molckman." *Jaarboek Antwerpen*, 113–135.

———. 1974. "De 'Kermis van Hoboken' bij P. Brueghel, J. Grimmer en G. Mostaert." *Jaarboek Antwerpen*, 139–169.

———. 1987. "Nog eens Hoboken bij Bruegel en tijdgenoten." *Jaarboek Antwerpen*, 185–206.

Montaigne-Frame 1948. Montaigne, Michel de. *The Complete Works of Mon-*

taigne, translated by Donald M. Frame. Stanford, Calif.: Stanford University Press.

Mori 2004. Mori, Yoko. "'She Hangs the Blue Cloak over Her Husband': The World of Human Follies in Proverbial Art." In Mieder 2004, pp. 71–101.

Morreall 1989. Morreall, John. "The Rejection of Humor in Western Thought." *Philosophy East and West* 39, no. 3: 243–265.

Muchembled 1985. Muchembled, Robert. *Popular Culture and Elite Culture in France, 1400–1750,* translated by Lydia Cochrane. Baton Rouge: Louisiana State University Press.

Muller 1989. Muller, Jeffrey M. *Rubens: The Artist as Collector.* Princeton: Princeton University Press.

Müller 1997. Müller, Jürgen. "'Pieter der Drollige' order der Mythos vom Bauern Bruegel." In Essen-Vienna-Antwerp 1997, pp. 42–53.

———. 1999. *Das Paradox als Bildform: Studien zur Ikonologie Pieter Bruegels d. Ä.* Munich: Wilhelm Fink.

Müller-Hofstede 1979. Müller-Hofstede, Justus. "Zur Interpretation von Pieter Bruegels Landschaft: Äesthetischer Landschaftsbegriff und Stoische Weltbetrachtung." In Von Simson and Winner 1979, pp. 73–142.

Muylle 1981. Muylle, Jan. "Pieter Bruegel en Abraham Ortelius: Bijdrage tot de literaire receptie van Pieter Bruegels werk." In *Archivum artis lovaniense: Bijdragen tot de geschiedenis van de kunst der Nederlanden opgedragen aan Prof. Em. J. K. Steppe,* edited by M. Smeyers, pp. 319–337. Louvain: Peeters.

———. 1984. "'Pier den Drol'—Karel van Mander en Pieter Bruegel. Bijdrage tot de literaire receptie van Pieter Bruegels werk ca. 1600." In Vekeman and Müller-Hofstede 1984, pp. 137–144.

———. 2001. "Tronies toegeschreven aan Pieter Bruegel: Fysiognomie en expressie (1)." *De zeventiende eeuw* 17, no. 2:174–204.

———. 2002. "Tronies toegeschreven aan Pieter Bruegel: Fysiognomie en expressie (2)." *De zeventiende eeuw* 17, no. 2:115–148.

Nalis 1998. Nalis, Henk, comp. *The Van Doetecum Brothers,* edited by Ger Luijten and Christiaan Schuckman. 4 vols. *The New Hollstein. Dutch and Flemish Etchings, Engravings and Woodcuts, 1450–1700.* Rotterdam: Sound & Vision Publishers in cooperation with the Rijksmusem, Amsterdam.

Nieuw Ned. biog. woordenboek 1911–37. *Nieuw Nederlandsch biographisch Woordenboek.* 10 vols. Leiden: A. W. Sijthoff.

Noll 1999. Noll, Thomas. "Pieter Bruegel d. Ä.: Der Bauer, der Vogeldieb und die Imker." *Münchner Jahrbuch der bildenden Kunst,* 3rd ser. 50:65–106.

Van der Noot 1979. Van der Noot, Jan. *Het Bosken en Het Theatre*, edited by W. A. P. Smit. Utrecht: HES Publishers.

Nyeuwe clucht boeck 1983. *Een nyeuwe clucht boeck*, edited by Herman Pleij et al. Populaire Literatuur, no. 4. Muiderberg: Dick Coutinho.

Oberhuber 1979. Oberhuber, Conrad. "Pieter Bruegel und die Radierungsserie der Bauernköpfe." In Von Simson and Winner 1979, pp. 143–147.

Ortelius 1969. Ortelius, Abraham. *Album amicorum Abraham Ortelius*. Reproduced in facsimile and edited by Jean Puraye with Marie Delcourt et al. Amsterdam: A. L. Van Gent & Co.

Ozment 1986. Ozment, Steven. *Magdalena and Balthasar: An Intimate Portrait of Life in 16th-Century Europe Revealed in the Letters of a Nuremberg Husband and Wife*. New York: Simon and Schuster.

Panofsky 1953. Panofsky, Erwin. *Early Netherlandish Painting: Its Origins and Character*. 2 vols. Cambridge, Mass.: Harvard University Press.

Panse and Schmidt 1967. Panse, Fr., and H. J. Schmidt. *Pieter Bruegels Dulle Griet: Bildnis einer psychisch Kranken*. Leverkusen: Bayer Leverkusen.

Peacock 1999. Peacock, Martha Moffitt. "Proverbial Reframing—Rebuking and Revering Women in Trousers." *Journal of the Walters Art Gallery* 57:13–34.

Perfetti 2003. Perfetti, Lisa. *Women and Laughter in Medieval Comic Literature*. Ann Arbor: University of Michigan Press.

Persels 1997. Persels, Jeffrey C., "Bragueta Humanística, or Humanism's Codpiece." *Sixteenth Century Journal* 23:79–99.

Persels and Ganim 2004. Persels, Jeffrey C., and Russell Ganim, eds. *Fecal Matters in Early Modern Literature and Art: Studies in Scatology*. Studies in European Cultural Transition, vol. 21. London: Ashgate.

Pikhaus 1988–89. Pikhaus, P. *Het tafelspel bij de rederijkers*. 2 vols. Koninklijke Vlaamse Academie voor Taal- en Letterkunde, Reeks VI. Ghent: Secretariaat van de Koninklijke Academie voor Nederlandse Taal- en Letterkunde.

Piquard 1947–48. Piquard, Maurice. "Le Cardinal de Granvelle, les artistes et les écrivains." *Revue belge d'archéologie et d'histoire de l'art* 17:133–147.

Plato 1963. *The Collected Dialogues of Plato, Including the Letters*, edited by Edith Hamilton and Huntington Cairns. Bollingen Series LXXI. Princeton: Princeton University Press.

Pleij 1974–75. Pleij, Herman. "De sociale funktie van humor en trivialiteit op het rederijkerstoneel." *Spectator* 6:108–127.

———. 1979. *Het gilde van de Blauwe Schuit: Literatuur, volksfeesten en burgermoraal in de late middeleeuwen*. Amsterdam: Muelenhof.

———. 1988. *De Sneeuwpoppen van 1511: Literatuur en stadscultuur tussen middeleeuwen en moderne tijd.* Amsterdam: Muelenhof; Louvain: Kritak.

———. 1990. "Literatuur als medicijn in de late middeleeuwen." In idem, *Nederlandse literatuur van de latemiddeleeuwen,* pp. 79–100. Utrecht: HES.

———. 1995. "With a View to Reality: The Rise of Bourgeois Ideals in the Late Middle Ages." In *Flanders in a European Perspective: Manuscript Illumination around 1400 in Flanders and Abroad; Proceedings of the International Colloquium Leuven, 7–10 September 1993,* edited by Maurits Smeyers and Bert Cardon, pp. 3–24. Corpus van verluchte handschriften / of Illuminated Manuscripts, vol. 8, Low Countries Series 4. Louvain: Peters.

Pliny 1968. Pliny the Elder. *The Elder Pliny's Chapters on the History of Art,* translated by E. Jex-Blake, with commentary and introduction by E. Sellers. London: Macmillan, 1896; Chicago: Argonaut, 1968.

Popham 1931. Popham, A. E. "Pieter Bruegel and Abraham Ortelius." *Burlington Magazine* 59:184–188.

Prescott 1998. Prescott, Anne Lake. *Imagining Rabelais in Renaissance England.* New Haven: Yale University Press.

Prims 1949. Prims, Floris. *Geschiedenis van Berchem tot bij de aanvang der XXste eeuw.* Berchem: Gemeentebestuur van Berchem.

Proverbia Communia 1947. *Proverbia Communia: A Fifteenth Century Collection of Dutch Proverbs Together with the Low German Version,* edited by Richard Jente. Indiana University Publications, Folklore Series, No. 4. Bloomington: Indiana University.

Quintilian 1921–22. *The Institutio Oratoria of Quintilian,* translated by H. E. Butler. 4 vols. Loeb Classical Library. London: William Heinemann; New York: G. P. Putnam's Sons.

Rabelais-Cohen 1955. Rabelais, François. *The Histories of Gargantua and Pantagruel,* translated and with an introduction by J. M. Cohen. Harmondsworth: Penguin Books.

Ramakers 1996. Ramakers, B. A. M. *Spelen en figuren: toneel en processiecultuur in Oudenaarde tussen Middeleeuwen en Moderne Tijd.* Amsterdam: Amsterdam University Press.

———. 1996. "Bruegel en de rederijkers: schilderkunst en literatuur in de zestiende eeuw." In De Jong et al. 1996, pp. 81–105.

———. 2002. "Kinderen van Saturnus: Afstand en nabijheid van boeren in de beeldende kunst en het toneel van de zestiende eeuw." In De Jong et al. 2002, pp. 13–51.

Raupp 1986. Raupp, Hans-Joachim. *Bauernsatiren: Entstehung und Entwicklung des bäuerlichen Genres in der deutschen und niederländischen Kunst ca. 1470–1570*. Niederzier: Lukassen Verlag.

Rekers 1972. Rekers, B. *Benito Arias Montano (1527–1598)*. London: Warburg Institute, University of London; Leiden: E. J. Brill.

Riggs 1977. Riggs, Timothy A. *Hieronymus Cock (1510–1570): Printmaker and Publisher at the Sign of the Four Winds*. New York: Garland Publishing, 1977.

Roberts-Jones 2002. Roberts-Jones, Philippe, and Françoise Roberts-Jones. *Pieter Bruegel*. New York: Harry N. Abrams.

Röhrich 1974. Röhrich, Lutz. *Lexikon der sprichtwörtlichen Redensarten*. 2 vols. 3rd ed. Freiburg: Herder.

Schmidt 1963. Schmidt, Leopold. *Die Volkserzählung: Märchen. Sage. Legende. Schwank*. Berlin: Erich Schmidt.

Schmitz 1972. Schmitz, Heinz-Günther. *Physiologie des Scherzes. Bedeutung und Rechtfertigung der Ars Iocandi im 16. Jahrhundert*. Deutsche Volksbücher in Faksimiledrucken, Reihe B. Untersuchungen zu dem deutschen Volksbüchern, vol. 2. Hildesheim: Georg Olms.

Schumann 1998. Schumann, Cordula. "Court, City and Countryside: Jan Brueghel's Peasant Weddings as Images of Social Unity under Archducal Sovereignty." In *Albert and Isabella, 1598–1621: Essays*, edited by Werner Thomas and Luc Duerloo, pp. 151–160. Turnhout: Brepols.

Screech and Calder 1992. Screech, M. A., and Ruth Calder. "Some Renaissance Attitudes to Laughter." In Screech, *Some Renaissance Studies: Selected Articles, 1951–1991, with a Bibliography*, edited by Michael J. Heath, pp. 166–178. Travaux d'Humanisme et Renaissance, no. CCLXII. Geneva: Librairie Droz. First published in *Humanism in France*, edited by A. H. T. Levi, pp. 216–228. Manchester: Manchester University Press, 1970.

Serebrennikov 1993. Serebrennikov, Nina. "On the Surface of *Dulle Griet*: Pieter Bruegel in the Context of Rabelais." In *Rabelais in Context: Proceedings of the 1991 Vanderbilt Conference*, edited by Barbara C. Bowen, pp. 158–178. Birmingham, Ala.: Summa Publications.

Silver 1996. Silver, Larry. "Pieter Bruegel in the Capital of Capitalism." In De Jong et al. 1996, pp. 125–153.

———. 1999. "Second Bosch: Family Resemblance and the Marketing of Art." In *Kunst voor de markt / Art for the Market, 1500–1700*, edited by Reindert Falkenburg et al. *Nederlands Kunsthistorisch Jaarboek* 50:31–56.

Simon 1998. Simon, Eckehard. "Carnival Obscenities in German Towns." In *Obscenity: Social Control and Artistic Creation in the European Middle Ages*, edited by Jan M. Ziolkowski, pp. 193–213. Cultures, Beliefs and Traditions, vol. 4. Leiden: Brill.

Simons 2003. Simons, Walter. *Cities of Ladies: Beguine Communities in the Medieval Low Countries, 1200–1565.* Philadelphia: University of Pennsylvania Press.

Von Simson and Winner 1979. Von Simson, Otto, and Matthias Winner, eds. *Pieter Bruegel und seine Welt.* Berlin: Gebrüder Mann.

Sluijter 1991. Sluijter, Eric J. "Didactic and Disguised Meanings? Several Seventeenth-Century Texts on Painting and the Iconological Approach to Northern Dutch Painting of This Period." In *Art in History. History in Art. Studies in Seventeenth-Century Dutch Culture: Issues and Debates,* edited by David Freedberg and Jan de Vries, pp. 175–208. Santa Monica, Calif.: Getty Center for the History of Art and the Humanities. Reprinted with revisions in *Looking at Seventeenth-Century Dutch Art: Realism Reconsidered,* edited by Wayne Franits, pp. 78–87. Cambridge: Cambridge University Press, 1997.

Smolderen 1995. Smolderen, Luc. "Tableaux de Jérôme Bosch, de Pieter Bruegel l'Ancien et de Frans Floris dispersés en vente publique à la Monnaie d'Anvers." *Revue belge d'archéologie et d'histoire de l'art* 64:33–41.

———. 1996. *Jacques Jonghelinck: sculpteur, médailleur et graveur de sceaux (1530–1606).* Publications d'histoire de l'art et d'archéologie de l'Université catholique de Louvain, 90; Numismatica Lovaniensa, 15. Louvain-la-Neuve: Dép. d'Archéologie et d'Histoire de Séminaire de numismatique Marcel Hoc.

Stappaerts 1987–88. Stappaerts, Greet. "Bijdrage to de studie van schilderijen in privé-bezit te Antwerpen in de zestiende eeuw." Licentiaat, Vrije Universiteit Brussels.

Starter 1974. Starter, Jan Jansz. *Friesch Lust-Hof.* Amsterdam: Paulus van Ravesteyn, 1621. Amsterdam: N. V. Buijten & Schipperheijn, 1974.

Stein-Schneider 1985. Stein-Schneider, Herbert L. "Les Familistes: Une secte néo-cathare du 16e siècle et leur peintre Pieter Bruegel l'Ancien." *Cahiers d'études cathares* 36th year, 2nd ser., no. 105:3–44.

Stewart 1993. Stewart, Alison. "Paper Festivals and Popular Entertainment: The Kermis Woodcuts of Sebald Beham in Reformation Nuremberg." *Sixteenth Century Journal* 24:301–350.

———. 1995. "Large Noses and Changing Meanings in Sixteenth-Century German Prints." *Print Quarterly* 12:343–360.

———. 2004. "Expelling from Top and Bottom: The Changing Role of Scatology in Images of Peasant Festivals from Albrecht Dürer to Pieter Bruegel." In Persels and Ganim 2004, pp. 118–137.

Van Stipriaan 1996. Van Stipriaan, René. *Leugens en vermaak. Boccaccio's novellen in de kluchtkultuur van de Nederlandse renaissance.* Amsterdam: Amsterdam University Press.

Stoett 1943. Stoett, F. A. *Nederlandsche spreekwoorden, spreekwijzen, uitdrukkingen en gezeg-den.* 5th ed. Zutphen: W. J. Thieme & Cie.

Stridbeck 1956. Stridbeck, Carl Gustaf. *Bruegelstudien: Untersuchungen zu den ikonol-ogischen Problemen bei Pieter Bruegel d. Ä. sowie dessen Beziehungen zum niederländischen Romanismus.* Stockholm: Almqvist & Wiksell.

Sullivan 1994. Sullivan, Margaret A. *Bruegel's Peasants: Art and Audience in the North-ern Renaissance.* Cambridge: Cambridge University Press.

———. 1999. "Aertsen's Kitchen and Market Scenes: Audience and Innovation in Northern Art." *Art Bulletin* 81:236–266.

Taylor 1980. Taylor, Steven M. "Monsters of Misogyny: The Medieval French 'Dit de Chincheface' and 'Dit de Bigorne.'" *Allegorica* 5:98–113.

Thomas 1977. Thomas, Keith. "The Place of Laughter in Tudor and Stuart En-gland." *Times Literary Supplement,* January 21, 1977, pp. 77–81.

Thompson 1955–58. Thompson, Stith. *Motif-Index of Folk-Literature.* Rev. and enl. ed. 6 vols. Bloomington: Indiana University Press.

De Tolnay 1935. De Tolnay, Charles. *Pierre Bruegel l'Ancien.* 2 vols. Brussels: Nou-velle Société d'Éditions.

———. 1952. *Die Zeichnungen Pieter Bruegels.* 1925. Zurich: Rascher Verlag.

Tubach 1969. Tubach, Frederic C. *Index Exemplorum: A Handbook of Medieval Religious Tales.* FF Communications, No. 204. Helsinki: Suomalainen Tiedakatemia / Akademia Scientiarum Fennica.

Unverfehrt 1984. Unverfehrt, Gerd. "Christliches Exempel und profane Alle-gorie. Zum Verhältnis von Wort und Bild in der Graphik der Boschnachfolge." In Vekeman and Müller-Hofstede 1984, pp. 221–241.

Vandenbroeck 1987. Vandenbroeck, Paul. *Beeld van de andere, vertoog over het zelf: over wilden en narren, boeren en bedelaars.* Antwerp: Ministerie van de Vlaamse Gemeen-schap; Koninklijk Museum voor Schone Kunsten, Antwerp.

Vasari 1878. Vasari, Giorgio. *Le opere,* edited by G. Milanese. 9 vols. Florence: Sansoni.

Veelderhande 1971. *Veelderhande geneuchlijcke dichten, tafelspelen ende refereynen.* Antwerp: Jan van Ghelen, 1600. Reprint. Leiden: E. J. Brill, 1899. Utrecht: Hes.

Vekeman and Müller-Hofstede 1984. Vekeman, Herman, and Justus Müller-Hofstede, eds. *Wort und Bild in der niederländischen Kunst und Literatur des 16. und 17. Jahrhunderts.* Erftstadt: Lukassen Verlag.

Van de Velde 1965. Van de Velde, Carel. "The Labours of Hercules, a Lost Se-ries of Paintings by Frans Floris." *Burlington Magazine* 107:114–123.

———. 1975. *Frans Floris (1519/20–1570): Leven en werken.* 2 vols. Verhandelingen van de Koninklijke Academie voor Wetenschappen, Letteren en Schone Kunsten van België, Klasse der Schone Kunsten, Jaargang XXXVII, Nr. 30. Brussels: Paleis der Academiën.

Verberckmoes 1998. Verberckmoes, Johan. *Schertsen, schimpen en schateren: Geschiedenis van het lachen in de Zuidelijken Nederlanden, zestiende en zeventiende eeuw*. Nijmegen: SUN.

———. 1999. *Laughter, Jestbooks and Society in the Spanish Netherlands*. Houndmills, Basingstoke: Macmillan Press; New York: St. Martin's Press.

———. 2001. "Het geslacht van het lachende lichaam in de zestiende en de zeventiende eeuw." In *Het lichaam (m/v)*, edited by Kaat Wils, pp. 89–101, 279–281. Louvain: Universitaire Pers Leuven.

———. 2002. "Parading Hilarious Exotics in the Spanish Netherlands." In De Jong et al. 2002, pp. 53–69.

Verdam ca. 1932. Verdam, J., ed. *Middelnederlandsche handwoordenboek*, reprinted with the entry for "sterne" revised by C. H. Ebbinge Wubben. The Hague: Martinus Nijhoff.

Vermeylen 2003. Vermeylen, Filip. *Painting for the Market: Commercialization of Art in Antwerp's Golden Age*. Studies in European Urban History (1100–1800), no. 2. Turnhout: Brepols.

Verwijs and Verdam 1885–. Verwijs, Eelco, and Johann Verdam. *Middelnederlandsch woordenboek*. 11 vols. The Hague: Martinus Nijhoff.

Vives-Fantazzi 2000. Vives, Juan Luis. *The Education of a Christian Woman: A Sixteenth-Century Manual*, edited and translated by Charles Fantazzi. Chicago: University of Chicago Press.

Vorselman-Cockx-Indestege 1971. *Eenen Nyeuwen Coock Boeck: Kookboek samengesteld door Gheeraert Vorselman en gedrukt te Antwerpen in 1560*, edited by Elly Cockx-Indestege. Wiesbaden: Guido Pressler.

De Vries 1989. De Vries, Lyckle. "Tronies and Other Single Figures in Netherlandish Painting." *Leids Kunsthistorisch Jaarboek* 8:185–202.

———. 2004. "With a Coarse Brush: Pieter Bruegel's 'Brooding Artist.'" *Source: Notes in the History of Art* 24, no. 4:38–48.

Van Wagenberg-ter Hoeven 1997. Van Wagenberg-ter Hoeven, Anke A. *Het Driekoningenfeest: De uitbeelding van een populair thema in de beeldende kunst van de zeventiende eeuw*. Publicaties van het P. J. Meertens-Instituut, Deel 29. Amsterdam: P. J. Meertens-Instituut.

Wangermée 1968. Wangermée, Robert. *Flemish Music and Society in the Fifteenth and Sixteenth Centuries*, translated by Robert Erich Wolf. New York: Frederick A. Praeger.

Wauters 1914. Wauters, A.-J. "Pierre Bruegel et Cardinal Granvelle." *Académie Royale de Belgique, Bulletins de la Classe des Lettres et des Sciences morales et politiques de la Classe des Beaux-Arts,* 87–90.

Webster and Ford 1954. *Webster and Ford: Selected Plays,* edited by G. B. Harrison. 1933. London: J. M. Dent & Sons; New York: R. P. Dutton.

Weismann 1992. Weismann, Anabella. "Was hört und sieht der Dudelsackpfeifer auf der Baurenhochzeit? Bemerkungen über ein allzu bekanntes Gemälde von Pieter Bruegel." In *Schweigen: Unterbrechung und Grenze der menschlichen Wirklichkeit,* pp. 225–245. Reihe Historische Anthropologie, Band 18. Berlin: Dietrich Reimer Verlag.

Welsford 1968. Welsford, Enid. *The Fool: His Social and Literary History.* 1935. London: Faber and Faber.

Wesseling 2002. Wesseling, Ari. "Dutch Proverbs and Expressions in Erasmus' Adages, Colloquies, and Letters." *Renaissance Quarterly* 55:81–147.

Wied 1990. Wied, Alexander. *Lucas und Marten van Valckenborch (1535–1597 und 1534–1612): Das Gesamtwerk mit kritischem Oeuvrekatalog.* Freren: Luca Verlag.

Wood 2000. Wood, Christopher S., ed. *The Vienna School Reader: Politics and Art Historical Method in the 1930s.* New York: Zone Books.

Woordenboek 1882–1998. *Woordenboek der Nederlandsche taal.* 29 vols. The Hague: Martinus Nijhoff et al. See also *Het Woordenboek der Nederlandsche Taal op CD-Rom.* Rotterdam: AND Publishers, c. 2000.

Zecher 2000. Zecher, Carla. "The Gendering of the Lute in Sixteenth-Century French Love Poetry." *Renaissance Quarterly* 5:769–791.

Zweite 1980. Zweite, Armin. *Marten de Vos als Maler: Ein Beitrag zur Geschichte der Antwerpener Malerei in der zweiten Hälfte des 16. Jahrhunderts.* Berlin: Gebrüder Mann.

EXHIBITION CATALOGUES

Brussels 1994. Brussels, Koninklijke Bibliotheek Albert I. *Uyt Ionsten Versaemt: Het Landjuweel van 1561 te Antwerpen.* Catalogue by Dirk Coigneau et al.

Essen-Vienna-Antwerp 1997. Essen, Kulturstiftung Ruhr, Villa Hügel; Vienna, Kunsthistorisches Museum; and Antwerp, Koninklijk Museum voor Schone Kunsten. *Pieter Brueghel der Jüngere—Jan Brueghel der Ältere: Flämische Malerei um 1600. Tradition und Fortschritt.*

Malines 2003. Malines, Centrum voor Oude Kunst, 't Vliegend Peert. *De zotte schilders: Moraal ridders van het penseel rond Bosch, Bruegel en Brouwer,* edited by Eric De Bruyn and Jan Op de Beeck. Ghent: Uitgeverij Snoeck.

Munich 1999. Munich, Neue Pinakothek. *O Musica du edle Kunst: Musik und Tanz im 16. Jahrhundert / Music for a While: Music and Dance in 16th-Century Prints.* Catalogue by Thea Vignau-Wilberg. Munich: Staatliche Graphische Sammlung München.

Rotterdam–New York 2001. Rotterdam, Museum Boijmans Van Beuningen; and New York, The Metropolitan Museum of Art. *Pieter Bruegel the Elder: Drawings and Prints*, edited by Nadine M. Orenstein, with contributions by Orenstein et al. New York: Metropolitan Museum of Art; New Haven: Yale University Press.

Washington-Amsterdam 1996. Washington, D.C., National Gallery of Art; and Amsterdam, Rijksmuseum. *Jan Steen: Painter and Storyteller*. Catalogue by H. Perry Chapman et al. New Haven: Yale University Press.

INDEX

264

INDEX

EDITOR
Stephanie Fay

ASSISTANT ACQUISITIONS EDITOR
Sigi Nacson

COPYEDITOR
Fronia Simpson

INDEXER
Andrew Joron

DESIGNER
Jessica Grunwald

PRODUCTION COORDINATOR
John Cronin

TEXT
10.5/15 Requiem Text

DISPLAY
Requiem Small Caps

COMPOSITOR
Integrated Composition Systems

www.ingramcontent.com/pod-product-compliance
Lightning Source LLC
La Vergne TN
LVHW091826210925
821611LV00006B/8/J